The New Philosophy of Criminal Law

The New Philosophy of Criminal Law

Edited by Chad Flanders
and Zachary Hoskins

ROWMAN &
LITTLEFIELD
INTERNATIONAL
London • New York

Published by Rowman & Littlefield International, Ltd.
Unit A, Whitacre Mews, 26-34 Stannary Street, London SE11 4AB
www.rowmaninternational.com

Rowman & Littlefield International, Ltd. is an affiliate of Rowman & Littlefield
4501 Forbes Boulevard, Suite 200, Lanham, Maryland 20706, USA
With additional offices in Boulder, New York, Toronto (Canada), and London (UK)
www.rowman.com

British Library Cataloguing in Publication Information Available
A catalogue record for this book is available from the British Library

ISBN: HB 978-1-78348-413-3
ISBN: PB 978-1-78348-414-0

Library of Congress Cataloging-in-Publication Data

The new philosophy of criminal law / Edited by Chad Flanders and Zachary Hoskins.
pages cm
Includes bibliographical references and index.
ISBN 978-1-78348-413-3 (cloth : alk. paper) — ISBN 978-1-78348-414-0 (pbk.) — ISBN 978-1-78348-415-7 (electronic)
1. Criminal law—Philosophy I. Flanders, Chad, editor. II. Hoskins, Zachary, 1973– editor.
K5018.N49 2016
345.001—dc23
2015033054

∞™ The paper used in this publication meets the minimum requirements of American National Standard for Information Sciences Permanence of Paper for Printed Library Materials, ANSI/NISO Z39.48-1992.

Printed in the United States of America

Contents

Introduction

Chad Flanders and Zachary Hoskins

It is always risky to say that one is doing anything "new" in philosophy, a discipline that has been characterized as nothing more than a series of footnotes to Plato. But it is precisely the ambition of this volume to stimulate new thinking about the philosophy of criminal law. The realities of crime and criminal justice in the Western world are changing, and it is appropriate for theories trying to explain and assess these realities to change with them.

There is a genuine sense today that the criminal law and criminal justice system are broken. To take only two of the more obvious examples, concerns are now routinely raised (especially, though not solely, in the United States) about the phenomena of "overcriminalization" and "mass incarceration." For the philosophy of criminal law, this means that theorizing about traditional questions of "what makes a criminal law just?" and "what justifies punishment?" is being done in the shadow of overcrowded prisons, frequently abusive police tactics, and an ever-expanding net of criminal laws. It is a system in which most defendants "plead out" rather than go to trial, and where convicted offenders are subject to substantial legal restrictions well after they have completed their sentences. What should our criminal law theories say when the reality they purport to address has changed so dramatically, and varies wildly from its own stated aims? How should the philosophy of criminal law adjust?

If the problems that the philosophy of criminal law has traditionally dealt with are changing, then the philosophy of criminal law should change with them. And we can see this beginning to happen, in three broad ways. The philosophy of criminal law is becoming more *holistic*, more *critical*, and more *interdisciplinary*. Let us briefly describe what we mean by these terms.[1]

By "holism," we mean that the philosophy of criminal law should no longer treat the various parts of the criminal justice system solely in isolation from one another. Instead, we must look at the system as a whole, and how the parts of it interact. In a way, this is obvious. The legitimacy of a system of punishment depends not only on whether punishment itself is justified but also on whether the laws people are punished for breaking are just, and whether the procedures used to convict them are fair. Conversely, we cannot fully determine whether our criminal laws are just without considering the costs of breaking them. But if this is true, then it follows we cannot look at the parts of the criminal justice system separately. We can't determine whether punishment is justified simply by looking at the various traditional rationales for punishment, nor can we look at criminal laws by themselves to see if they are just: we must consider whether the entire system of criminal justice can be justified. This is not to say that there is no value in focusing on particular questions; it is just to say that we must not lose sight of the forest for the trees. Focusing too closely only on the various parts of the system oversimplifies, and distorts, the criminal law theorist's task.

By saying that the criminal law has become more "critical," we mean of course that it is critical of existing arrangements, but we also mean something broader. In law schools, the study of criminal law can be strictly doctrinal: for example, going through the "elements" of the most common crimes and the most common excusing or justifying conditions (self-defense, duress, etc.). Sometimes philosophy follows the teaching of criminal law in just this way, by trying to provide an analysis and a justification for the traditional concepts of the criminal law. This way of approaching the topic of criminal law tends to be conservative. It assumes that the categories the various legal systems of the world (or, usually, the U.S. and English legal systems) have given us are roughly correct, and that the challenge is to explain them, to show how they fit together, and to offer a sensible interpretation of them.

A more critical take on the criminal law asks not what the best interpretation is of our current practices or categories, but why we have these practices and categories in the first place. It is "radical" in the sense of getting to the root of things—to the deep foundations of the criminal law. What results from these investigations is not necessarily a validation of the status quo. It may be a wholesale rethinking of the concepts of "crime" or of "punishment." It may result in a diminished respect for the line that divides the civil and the criminal, for example. Or it may, instead, result in a renewed respect for the distinction, but for reasons of which we were previously unaware, or only dimly aware—so that we no longer treat these categories as we did in the past. Being "critical" in this sense fits well with being holistic, because being critical means abstracting from narrow doctrinal categories and taking a more comprehensive view of what the criminal justice system is, and how it is justified.

Finally (and related to the previous two points), the philosophy of criminal law is more avowedly "interdisciplinary." Traditional boundaries between the various areas of philosophy—moral, political, and legal theory—are giving way. For example, criminal law theorists examining punishment's justification are recognizing that this is not merely a question of legal or even moral philosophy, but of political philosophy as well. Legal punishment, after all, is the paradigmatic exercise of a state's power over its citizens, and determining whether this exercise is legitimate requires engagement with political as well as moral concepts. Similarly, philosophers of criminal law are increasingly recognizing that the tools and resources of other disciplines (history, sociology, the hard sciences, etc.) can be of use in exploring traditional questions about punishment, criminal responsibility, and other concepts.[2]

These three themes represent what we see coming together in a "new" philosophy of criminal law: it is more holistic, aggressively critical, and increasingly interdisciplinary. Accordingly, the remainder of this introduction does two things. First, it offers a more expansive discussion of the changing landscape of criminal law theory by focusing on three major, current problems facing criminal justice systems and society more generally. An understanding of these problems is important in its own right, but the problems themselves also challenge us to rethink how we engage in criminal law theory.

The second thing this introduction does, of course, is to introduce the chapters in this volume. We think each of the chapters, in different ways, represents the new thinking about the criminal law that we've described here: as being, in various respects, holistic, critical, or interdisciplinary. They also, in their various ways, come to grips with the new landscape of crime and criminal justice described in the first part of this introduction. The chapters in this volume show the philosophy of criminal law as it is being pursued today as open and flexible, responsive to the current crises in our practices of criminal justice, and looking beyond these crises to a time when our criminal law will be fair, just, and effective. The contributors do not all agree, but rather show the health and vigor of the state of debate in the philosophy of criminal law.

I. THE NEW CHALLENGES OF THE CRIMINAL LAW

Traditionally, a major puzzle of the philosophy of criminal law has been whether (and how) punishment is justified. Today's criminal law theorists continue to grapple with punishment, to be sure—and with good reason, given the modern phenomena of mass incarceration, increasingly harsh punishments, and racial disparities in how we punish. But, as we have said, theorists today are recognizing and engaging with a broader range of relevant questions, realizing that the justification of punishment is related to a host of other normative issues underlying the criminal law. What's more, those writing about punishment's justification increasingly are looking for new accounts that will break the logjam of the traditional consequentialist-retributivist dichotomy.

Similarly, the traditional question of "what behaviors should be made criminal?" can no longer be addressed in the same way as it has been in the past: namely, as primarily a question of whether private and consensual activities could or should be criminalized. We have, today, a huge criminal justice apparatus that criminalizes so many things that it is becoming increasingly difficult for an ordinary person to go through the day without committing an offense.[3] The issue is no longer simply about whether this or that criminal law is moral or not; it is really about *over*criminalization.

Old problems can look different given a new social reality, and they may sometimes become different problems altogether. The sheer quantity of people being punished and the sheer quantity of criminal laws present new challenges of justification and rationalization. In this section, we briefly describe some relatively new problems of crime and criminal justice, and how these problems give rise to new philosophical puzzles. We focus on three especially prominent examples, although of course there are many others.

A. Overcriminalization

The problem of what sorts of behavior should be criminalized is a classic one, but also one that gets subtly but importantly changed when the issue becomes one of having *too many* criminal laws. What is meant by "overcriminalization"? One meaning we could give it, certainly, would be to say that we have many criminal laws that are not justified, or have the wrong kind of justification. Those who see the criminal law as an expression of the community's morality may say that we have many existing laws that criminalize things that are actually not immoral. Alternatively, some may object that many of our criminal laws do not protect against any genuine harm, or that other means besides criminalization would be better suited to accomplishing this goal. Or, to take a perspective from political philosophy, an objection might be made that many of our criminal laws lack the right kind of pedigree: they no longer have the support of the majority of the people, or they were passed based on biased or mistaken information. All of these reasons would support removing or at least reforming many criminal laws.

But overcriminalization might be a problem even if each law, taken separately, could be justified. There might be something wrong with having too many criminal laws, in and of itself: it may be bad that we are put at such a risk of violating the laws, and a vast tapestry of laws may be giving the state too much power to regulate us. This type of objection would also be from political philosophy, but it would not be about particular laws, taken one by one. It would not say, that is, that any particular law is unjustified. Rather, it would be making the larger claim that simply having *too many* laws is something we might be worried about in its own right, that the sheer quantity of laws (and the scope of behaviors they cover) can affect the quality of political and social life.

More concretely, more laws give police officers more reasons to suspect people of breaking the law, and so a greater ability to stop people to confirm or dispel those suspicions. More laws give prosecutors more leeway in threatening charges—and so a stronger hand in plea bargaining negotiations. If there are so many criminal laws that it is nearly inevitable that we are breaking one or another of them, then this means it is in the end simply up to the state to decide who gets punished, and for what. This is something we might find independently troubling—again, even if taken one by one, most or even all of those laws can be justified. Our relationship to the state on this picture becomes one of constant dread that we might at any moment be prosecuted for something merely because someone wants to prosecute us. This might seem to be an exaggeration, but it is less so for some groups of people than for others (indeed, the racial disparities throughout the criminal justice system only exacerbate these concerns). At any rate, something like this may be at the bottom of many worries about overcriminalization—and it has to do not, or not only, with the fact that there are many *unjust* laws but with the fact that there simply may be too many laws.

B. Mass Incarceration

Related to overcriminalization is the phenomenon of "mass incarceration." If there are more laws to break, then there will be more chances for people to be put under the control of the state, with the paradigmatic and most coercive example being imprisonment. But there are two ways to look at the problem: One way is to say that people are being sent to prison unjustly—or if they are justly imprisoned, then perhaps they are being held for too long. If these are the main, or only, problems with incarceration today, then we may be best suited to keep our focus on the traditional questions of the justification of punishment. We condemn the unjust cases as obviously unjust, and focus on justifying the sentences that are truly deserved. But, as with "overcriminalization," calling our current situation one of "mass incarceration" or "mass imprisonment" suggests that there is something wrong with the sheer quantity of people being punished, not just the fact that the wrong people are being punished. Of course, the two may be related: perhaps, for example, people imprisoned for nonviolent drug crimes shouldn't be there, or they shouldn't be there for as long. This might be one way to solve the problem of mass incarceration, or at least reduce it.

But it won't go all the way, because the fact that such a large percentage of a nation's population is under the control of the state has ramifications even if many of those under the state's control deserve to be there. Mass incarceration can devastate entire communities, when a substantial number of adult males are in prison rather than at home or at work.[4] Moreover, when we incarcerate large numbers of people, we have to address on a much greater scale the issue of easing the transition of prisoners back into "normal" life. In a way, the problems become not only larger but also different problems. It is not just the problem that one person is locked up when he or she shouldn't be. It is the problem of living in a system where large numbers of certain groups are routinely imprisoned and cycle through the criminal justice system on a regular basis.

At the limit, when prisons—and not some other means, such as education or welfare or job training—are used to control and manage people, this may put into question the legitimacy of the state that uses such means. This all becomes even more salient given the range of restrictive legal measures the state imposes on these prisoners during and, frequently, long after their actual prison terms. So we again find that the new problems of criminal law cannot be dealt with solely as problems of moral philosophy but are matters of political philosophy as well.

C. Plea Bargaining

Another key part of the engine of the modern criminal justice system, at least in the United States, is the process of plea bargaining, whereby criminal suspects agree to a lesser sentence in exchange for giving up their right to a trial. It has been frequently (and correctly) observed that without plea bargaining, the U.S. criminal justice system would come to a halt: the system simply couldn't handle so many trials. Many have condemned this state of affairs and for a variety of reasons, from the possibility of coerced or pressured pleas, to the mass giving up of a right (the right to a trial by a jury of one's peers) guaranteed by the U.S. Constitution. But these criticisms face the objection that in many individual cases, it is the rational thing to do for the suspect to plead to a lesser charge rather than face the risk of a longer sentence after trial. And again, doing away with plea bargaining leaves the practical challenge of accommodating so many defendants in possibly drawn-out (and expensive) trials. For these reasons, plea bargaining ends up being the linchpin of the criminal justice system—connecting the criminal law to the prison industrial complex. The vast panoply of criminal laws gets people into the system, plea bargaining expeditiously processes them, and the result is mass incarceration.

In the United States, more than 90 percent of federal defendants plead out instead of going to trial, and as a result the trial is no longer—as it is frequently portrayed in philosophy and popular culture—the centerpiece of the criminal justice system.[5] It is a rarity, and in many cases a luxury, when people can afford adequate representation to give them a shot at effectively testing the state's case against them. But the fact of plea bargaining frequently gets overlooked in the philosophy of criminal law. If plea bargaining is itself a system that is unjust, or less than just, then this certainly must affect how we look at the number of people in prison—people who have been put there not as the consequence of a trial, but as the consequence of a plea. It also should change how we look at overcriminalization. If fewer behaviors were criminalized, fewer people would be pulled into the system, and so we would not need a mechanism that could process them in such a short amount of time with limited resources.

In a classic essay and book, Herbert Packer describes two models of criminal justice, the due process model and the crime control model.[6] Plea bargaining is the apotheosis of the crime control model—where procedural protections are slimmed down or eliminated in an effort to keep dangerous people off the streets. But it may be too generous to call plea bargaining—or for that matter overcriminalization or mass incarceration—part of any "model," as if these were parts of a well-thought-out system, rather than measures that were taken at different times for different reasons, but that still interact and have effects on one another. There is undoubtedly a historical story as to how we got where we are with overcriminalization, mass incarceration, and plea bargaining, and in a certain way the three things do fit together. But it would be quite charitable to say that they are part of a rational whole. It is here that we need theory, both to show the failings in the current system and to show us a better way.

II. THE NEW PHILOSOPHY OF CRIMINAL LAW

The three problems of the contemporary criminal justice system just described shouldn't be seen as setting a strict agenda for the contributions in this volume. They do not. Some of the chapters in the volume explicitly address the problems described above—as with Richard Lippke's chapter on the plea bargaining process, and how it might be reformed. Other chapters are implicitly shaped by them, whereas others still focus on distinct (albeit related) challenges. Our point is that the new philosophy of criminal law works in the shadow of the modern penal state, and must respond to its problems and pathologies. Normative analyses and proposals for reform can do no less, if they demand to be taken seriously.

Each of the five parts of the book represents an area about which, we believe, new thinking in the criminal law is warranted, and supplies examples of that new thinking. The order of the parts is meant to reflect a rough chronology of the phases of the criminal justice system. Roughly, the parts cover the following ground. Part 1 investigates how we should think about crimes and the function of criminal law. Part 2 examines the basis of the state's (or international community's) authority to implement and enforce the criminal law. Part 3 focuses on two of the most basic players in the criminal justice system: the offender and the victim. Part 4 looks at how we process suspects through the system, and how our attitude toward them should—or shouldn't—change as they progress through the system. Finally, part 5 examines the sanctions that follow from a conviction: what could justify them, when—if ever—we should show mercy rather than punish, and how we should think about so-called collateral restrictions.

A. Crime and the Function of the Criminal Law

One of the foundational questions of criminal law theory is what the proper boundaries of the criminal law are. But it is also one that is too routinely given banal or deflationary answers. Some answers to the question of what things are properly called "crimes" are explicitly positivist: they say that crimes are simply whatever the statutes in a given jurisdiction say are crimes. Other answers are only slightly more illuminating: a "crime" is something that inspires the disapproval or disgust or even outrage of the community.[7] But which community, and how much outrage? Couldn't we be mistaken in the objects of our outrage?

Vincent Chiao and Joshua Kleinfeld, in their starkly opposed chapters, open this volume with novel accounts of the foundations of the criminal law. Chiao takes as his target what he terms the "private law" conception, which sees the criminal law as a more or less straightforward application of moral philosophy to the law. For the private law conception, "crime" and "punishment" are stand-ins, on the societal level, for "wrongs" and "discipline." But this, Chiao contends, is a mistake. Crimes, he argues, are just those things to which we believe society needs to respond with hard treatment. And the substance of these crimes is a matter for each jurisdiction to figure out: there is no necessity to make some things crimes and others not. Overall, Chiao's view is that we have overmoralized the criminal: we take it too much as a vehicle for asserting our highest moral norms, rather than just another tool that governments use to help order and organize society. Thus for him, there is no intrinsic need for crimes to be punished with hard treatment. Rather, hard treatment is just one strategy that we employ to reduce the occurrence of crimes. We might spend more money on punishment, Chiao reasons, but we might equally decide to spend more money on education or on preventive policing.

In sharp contrast to Chiao's account, Joshua Kleinfeld contends that the criminal law is an expression of a community's culture and norms—and punishment is necessary, not optional, as a way of symbolically reaffirming its norms. Kleinfeld would accordingly resist Chiao's collapsing of the distinction between the criminal and the civil, and between punishment and other forms of treatment. Kleinfeld is especially reluctant to dismiss punishment as just another tool to promote public safety and order; rather, punishment serves a valuable expressive function in its own right. But Kleinfeld is cognizant of the ways in which norms of the criminal law can go wrong, precisely by becoming detached from the communal norms they purport to represent. Society is an organic whole for Kleinfeld, but the criminal law can become alienated from that whole; when it does so—as it has done today—we may need to pare down the criminal law.

Stuart Green provides more applied analysis of the criminal law, or more precisely, of a particular class of criminal laws: the sexual offenses. Green's aim is to sort out what a "sexual offense" is, what its contours are; in short, what is and is not properly called a sexual crime. By engaging in conceptual analysis, Green challenges us to rethink whether—and, if so, why—sex offenses are in fact a unified class of crimes. His exploration of the topic is timely. In the past several decades, legislatures and courts have repeatedly engaged with, and defined and redefined, the sexual offenses—from rape to sexual assault to sodomy to indecency. Here is an area where legal concepts have changed repeatedly, and so we need to subject these concepts to deeper theoretical scrutiny. What should the class of sexual offenses comprise, and what makes them distinctive? Green attempts to sort through these questions, which places him at the cutting edge in many current debates about reforming our laws about sex.

B. Authority and Legitimacy

Despite its preoccupation with the justification of punishment, the philosophy of criminal law has been relatively silent about the state's legitimacy and its authority to punish. Political philosophy, by contrast, has devoted attention to questions of state authority and legitimacy but, for the most part, not to questions of punishment. John Rawls, for example, the dominant figure in political philosophy in the past several decades, gives only scant attention to punishment in his books *A Theory of Justice* and *Political Liberalism*. These traditional disciplinary walls are beginning to come down, however. A number of philosophers have in recent years begun to regard questions of punishment and criminal justice as fundamentally matters of political philosophy.

Alice Ristroph's chapter exemplifies the holistic approach to criminal law theorizing. Ristroph contends that theorists have too often focused on abstract or in-principle defenses of punishment without properly attending to the often massively unjust conditions that prevail before, during, and after punishment. Punishment could serve all sorts of ostensibly good ends in the abstract: it could deter, rehabilitate, express condemnation, or mete out deserved suffering. But if the means we have for determining guilt are flawed, or if the state itself is illegitimate, then none of these valuable ends suffices to justify punishing someone. Thus Ristroph outlines a range of conditions that must be met for impositions of punishment to be legitimate. Indeed, if these conditions are not met, it may be open for the accused to resist his punishment.[8]

Douglas Husak's chapter, like Ristroph's, engages with questions of state authority to punish. Husak focuses on why the *state* has the authority—indeed, the sole authority—to punish. His answer? The state doesn't have a monopoly on punishment. He contends that there is no deep distinction between when the state punishes and when teachers punish students in school, say, or when parents punish children. Moreover, he argues that the justification for punishment will be essentially the same across these contexts. In this he appears to disagree with Chiao, who sees something different taking place when the state punishes and when we punish in other contexts.

Husak notes, however, that even if state punishment is not particularly distinctive, we still need an account of what state interests are substantial enough to justify punishment. He distances himself from those legal moralists who hold that we have a prima facie duty to punish every wrong. And he accepts that in the real world, punishment costs money—and so there are resource constraints on even the most well-thought-out and justified criminal justice system.[9]

Next, Jovana Davidovic addresses the question of authority to punish but from an international perspective. She asks: What gives the international community the authority to punish some crimes? On one prominent view, some crimes (genocide, torture) are so heinous that the international community, so long as its procedures are fair, is justified in prosecuting them. Another view contends that heinousness alone is not enough to justify international prosecution; what's needed is an account of why the international community, in particular, has standing to hold the perpetrators to account. Davidovic raises concerns about both of these views and then defends her own account. On her view, the heinousness of the crimes is relevant, but what makes these crimes the business of the international community is that the community in fact recognizes certain norms against especially heinous crimes. If the international community fails to prosecute and punish those who perpetrate these crimes, this impunity undermines the rule of law, and thereby hinders the maintenance of peace and the protection of human rights.

C. Offenders and Victims

Part 3 focuses on two central players in the criminal justice process: offenders and victims. One chapter challenges traditional legal-philosophical conceptions of criminal responsibility, while the other offers a provocative call for greater attention to victims in the criminal justice process: not primarily, as we might expect, greater attention to victims' rights, but rather a greater emphasis on victims' duties in the aftermath of crime.

Arlie Loughnan's chapter is an excellent example of the value of an interdisciplinary perspective on criminal law issues, and in particular the relevance of sociology and history to the philosophy of criminal law. Loughnan points out that notions of responsibility, whether in the criminal law or in other contexts, are socially and historically situated, and a socio-historical approach to responsibility can provide insights that those working solely in the legal-philosophical tradition may miss. Nevertheless, the socio-historical approach has been somewhat marginalized in philosophical discussions of criminal responsibility. Loughnan considers various reasons why this has been so, and she offers the beginnings of an account of how the socio-historical approach might inform debates in the philosophy of criminal law. In particular, she suggests that these debates might benefit from considering broader, extra-legal notions of responsibility. She concludes by discussing the intriguing case of how society thinks about responsibility for defendants who are also veterans.

Sandra Marshall's chapter, as with others in this volume, shines a light on a neglected facet of the criminal law: the role and responsibilities of the victim. Discussions of criminal law tend to present victims as essentially *passive* characters—they are the objects of the crime. But victims are also agents. More than this, they are often citizens. As such, they may have civic duties to act that go beyond simply being the starting point of a criminal investigation and prosecution. Victims may have the responsibility to report that they have been victims, to offer cooperation to the relevant authorities, and so on. Marshall's chapter thus raises questions about the status of those who, for various reasons, choose not to report crimes, or who refuse to press charges. Critics may object that thrusting obligations on victims, and then holding them accountable for failing to meet these obligations, only multiplies their suffering. But even as victims, Marshall contends, they are nonetheless members of the political community, and as such they have obligations to ensure that other members of the community are held accountable.

D. Criminal Procedure

Of all facets of the criminal law, philosophers seem to write least about criminal procedure. Perhaps this is due to the fact that criminal procedure can be a relatively local affair—with rules about evidence, or about the restrictions on the police, or about proper trial practices, differing widely from jurisdiction to jurisdiction. It may be hard to make generalizations about what criminal procedure is, or even what it should be. Here the contrast between countries that have an adversarial criminal procedure, as opposed to an inquisitorial or nonadversarial one, may loom large. Still, there is plenty of room for theorizing about things such as the moral constraints on police investigations, or about the rights of the accused prior to and during trial. We might be able to make larger observations about how the criminal justice system should work, in the crucial stages between the commission of the crime and the punishment of the perpetrator. The two chapters in part 4 bring this critical scrutiny to two under-theorized elements of criminal procedure: plea bargaining and the presumption of innocence.

First, Richard Lippke builds on the important work he has done previously in the area of plea bargaining. In the U.S. criminal justice system, plea bargaining has replaced the trial as the main point where the rights of the accused get asserted, and claims to innocence are aired and tested. But many have contended that plea bargaining is no substitute for a trial—hence the growing calls to abolish plea bargaining. Lippke doesn't go this far, but he does argue that plea bargaining should be made more rigorous, and that judges should play a more active role in the process.

Lippke's chapter also invites further thinking about the real and the ideal in the philosophy of the criminal law. Maybe the ideal is that every defendant should exercise his or her right to have a full-dress trial. Maybe we should *encourage* defendants to do this, even in cases where they could easily plead out, with the idea that this would "crash the system" and force people to reform the system. But Lippke believes this is unrealistic, and that it is not a bad thing to modify some of our ambitions in light of what is possible—to be attentive to the limits that the real puts on how critical we can be of the status quo.[10]

R. A. (Antony) Duff examines a fundamental concept of criminal procedure, the "presumption of innocence," but he considers it holistically. The presumption is usually thought to be especially (perhaps only) salient at the trial. The prosecution has to prove guilt beyond a reasonable doubt, because the accused has a strong presumption of innocence. But Duff asks whether the presumption of innocence exists before and after the trial: How should a presumption of innocence affect decisions about setting bail? Is the presumption relevant at sentencing? Can "aggravating factors" that have not been proven beyond a reasonable doubt be considered as a basis for adding months or years to the sentence? How does the presumption of innocence function during an appeal? What about after a person has completed his term of punishment? Ultimately, Duff suggests that we should think of many "presumptions of innocence," such that what can be presumed, of whom, and by whom, may differ somewhat in different contexts.

E. Sanctions

In our final section, we turn to consider how a state responds to those it convicts of crime. The most obvious response to crime, as we have discussed, is punishment. And although we have suggested that the philosophy of criminal law benefits from expanding its horizons to consider a broader array of questions, it remains the case that punishment is the most vivid example of a state's exercise of power over its citizens. The chapters in this section are not traditional accounts of the justification of punishment, however. Each of them, in various ways, challenges traditional approaches to thinking about punishment.

Christopher Bennett provides a restatement and defense of a provocative account of punishment's justification that he first articulated in his 2008 book *The Apology Ritual.*[11] Bennett urges us to attend to the insights we get from considering the interpersonal practices of blame and apology. On his account, punishment can be justified as a way of making an offender engage in the sort of apologetic behavior in which he would choose to engage if he were genuinely sorry for what he did. Thus punishment draws its justification in part from the deeper social meanings that attach to the practices of apology and blame. But an offender need not sincerely apologize (this is the ritualistic piece); it is enough that the state require him to do what he would do if he were genuinely sorry and intended to make amends. This is, for the state, a way of dissociating itself from the offender's actions—and this dissociation, Bennett contends, is linked to the state's legitimate interest in setting limits on how citizens treat each other. Thus although this apology ritual account is perhaps most comfortably situated as a version of retributivism, it defies easy classification in the traditional retributivist or consequentialist camps.

Mary Sigler's chapter examines mercy in criminal justice. One might think that mercy is needed in a world with increasingly "harsh justice," to use James Whitman's term.[12] Sigler suggests that we don't need mercy, but her reasons for this conclusion are nuanced. Calls for mercy, she argues, are often confused. People say we need mercy when what they really mean is that we need *equity*. The difference is important. Mercy means reducing the amount of just, deserved punishment someone receives. Equity means making sure a person gets the punishment she deserves—so if we opt for equity, we don't have to compromise on justice. Sigler especially worries about giving individual institutional actors too much discretion to reduce sentences as they see fit. How do we know such actors will make the right decisions, and what mechanisms do we have to hold them accountable if they make the wrong ones? Sigler's chapter, then, is a plea for focus on the *kinds* of reforms we should be making. If we want to change sentences, it is better to do so at the wholesale level, and not just bit by bit at the retail level.

Zachary Hoskins's chapter closes out our collection, but it is—like many of the other chapters in the volume—an invitation to further investigate a relatively unscrutinized area of criminal law. Hoskins focuses not on formal punishment itself, but on another class of legal restrictions that face those with criminal records. Offenders are subject to legal restrictions on employment, housing, the vote, and many other goods. These restrictions have not traditionally been regarded as part of an offender's punishment. Rather, they have been treated as civil measures, as "collateral" restrictions. Hoskins examines whether these so-called collateral restrictions are really just additional forms of punishment. He critiques both the traditional legal view, on which all collateral restrictions are treated as civil measures rather than criminal sanctions, and the competing view that all of these restrictions are in fact forms of punishment. Instead, he offers a more nuanced conceptual account that classifies particular measures as civil measures or punishment depending on their underlying intentions, purposes, and social meaning.

The authors in this volume do not all agree—far from it. Sometimes their differences are stark and profound, ranging from the method with which they approach problems in the criminal justice system to their suggestions as to how to reform the system. Nonetheless, we suggest that what unites them is a commitment to thinking differently about the criminal law and its problems: a commitment to looking beyond the traditional categories and puzzles of the criminal law. It is hard, sometimes, with the pathologies that cripple the administration of criminal justice systems around the world to be hopeful about whether anything can change. But if things can change, it will not be by trying to defend the status quo, or by rehashing debates in the same traditional terms. It will be by approaching things in new ways, in practice and also in theory.

* * *

We had a lot of help in completing this volume. In addition to the authors, we would like to thank especially Joseph Welling, a third-year law student at Saint Louis University Law School, who did heroic work in proofreading and compiling an index in a timely and efficient manner. Michelle Dempsey, Jae Lee, Ian Loader, and an anonymous referee offered us valuable comments on the structure and presentation of the book as a whole. Finally, Vincent Chiao, Antony Duff, and Kim Ferzan gave us extremely useful feedback on the introduction.

NOTES

1. For further developments of these themes, see Chad Flanders, *Can Retributivism Be Saved?* 2014 BYU L. REV. 309 (2014) (on holism), and Chad Flanders, *Retribution and Re-*

form, 70 MD. L. REV. 87 (2010) (on the need for a critical attitude in philosophy of criminal law).

2. Although the perspectives of the hard sciences are not represented in this book, they are nevertheless relevant. For example, they may affect our sense that we are responsible, and thus rightly punished, for wrongdoing. *See, e.g.*, Joshua Greene & Jonathan Cohen, *For the Law, Neuroscience Changes Nothing and Everything*, 359 PHIL. TRANSACTIONS ROYAL SOC'Y LOND. B 1775–85 (2004).

3. Glenn Harlan Reynolds, *Ham Sandwich Nation: Due Process When Everything Is a Crime*, 113 COLUM. L. REV. SIDEBAR 102 (2013), http://www.columbialawreview.org/ham-sandwich-nation_Reynolds ("the proliferation of federal criminal statutes and regulations has reached the point where virtually every citizen, knowingly or not (usually not) is potentially at risk for prosecution").

4. *See, e.g.*, Dorothy E. Roberts, *The Social and Moral Cost of Mass Incarceration in African American Communities*, 56 STAN. L. REV. 1271, 1281 (2004).

5. "[C]riminal justice today is for the most part a system of pleas, not a system of trials. Ninety-seven percent of federal convictions and ninety-four percent of state convictions are the result of guilty pleas." Lafler v. Cooper, 132 S. Ct. 1376, 1388 (2012).

6. HERBERT L. PACKER, THE LIMITS OF THE CRIMINAL SANCTION 150–73 (1968); Herbert L. Packer, *Two Models of the Criminal Process*, 113 U. PA. L. REV. 1, 2–68 (1964).

7. Henry A. Hart, *The Aims of the Criminal Law*, 23 LAW & CONTEMP. PROBS. 422 (1958).

8. *See* Alice Ristroph, *The Incomplete Legitimacy of Punishment*, *in* HOBBES TODAY: INSIGHTS FOR THE 21ST CENTURY (Sharon Lloyd ed., 2014).

9. *See also* Douglas Husak, *Holistic Retribution*, 88 CAL. L. REV. 991 (2000).

10. See also Lippke's discussion of plea-bargaining in a "non-ideal world" in his book, THE ETHICS OF PLEA BARGAINING 90–96 (2011).

11. CHRISTOPHER BENNETT, THE APOLOGY RITUAL: A PHILOSOPHICAL THEORY OF PUNISHMENT (2008).

12. JAMES Q. WHITMAN, HARSH JUSTICE: CRIMINAL PUNISHMENT AND THE WIDENING DIVIDE BETWEEN AMERICA AND EUROPE (2003).

Part I

Crime and the Function of Criminal Law

Chapter One

Two Conceptions of the Criminal Law

Vincent Chiao[1]

In commenting on H. L. A. Hart's *Punishment and Responsibility*, John Gardner poses the following rhetorical question: "Doesn't the criminal justice system attempt, in its inevitably clumsy way, to institutionalize certain moral practices, including the practice of punishment with its familiar relationships to wrongdoing and guilt, that already exist quite apart from the law and its institutions?"[2] The idea that Gardner here so succinctly expresses is a prevalent—one might even say predominant—idea about what the criminal law and its associated institutions are for. This is the idea that the way in which institutions matter for the criminal law is that they serve to give force to, and to make more precise, moral relationships between people that exist anyway. Call this the "private right" conception of the criminal law. The aim of this chapter is to contrast the private right conception with a sharply contrasting conception, one that I, borrowing a term from Malcolm Thorburn, refer to as the "public law" conception. On the public law conception, the criminal law serves to contribute to securing the viability of the rule of law as an ongoing project, and hence serves to make possible moral relationships—such as that of free and equal citizens—that would not otherwise be possible. The rule of law depends on stable and broadly shared expectations of mutual compliance, and the criminal law is a means—one among many—for securing those expectations.

To be clear, my sympathies are squarely with the public law conception. That said, my aim in this chapter is not to defend the public law conception, nor is it to critique the private right conception. My aim is to sketch in a perspicuous—and hence inevitably somewhat exaggerated—form what I take to be the core of the contrast between the private right and public law conceptions. The private right and public law conceptions as I will present them are ideal types, rather than characterizations of any particular theorist's views. The utility of the contrast between a private right and public law conception lies in how well (or how poorly) it serves to illuminate and synthesize a range of more particular substantive and methodological disagreements in the philosophy of criminal law.

In parts I and II of the chapter, I sketch the outlines of the private right and public law conceptions, and in part III, I consider some implications of this stylized contrast for the substantive agenda and methodology of the philosophy of criminal law. I seek to make the contrast vivid in part IV, by considering the case of preventive policing as an alternative mode of response to crime from punishment administered *ex post*. I argue that a private right conception is committed to viewing preventive policing as a fundamentally different type of endeavor—one subject to entirely different principles of justification—from punishment. In contrast, from a public law point of view, *ex post* punishment is functionally continuous with attempts to manage the social risk of criminal victimization through prevention and other forms of regulation.

I.

I start by identifying two central features of the private right conception.

(PR1) The criminal law is an institution that serves to enforce people's independent moral rights. A right is "independent" insofar as its existence does not depend on it being granted or otherwise protected by a system of positive law, and a right is a "moral" right insofar as it is a right each person has in virtue of being a person, and not, for instance, as a result of a private agreement he or she has entered into.

(PR2) What is distinctive about the criminal law, and the criminal justice system more generally, is that it seeks to vindicate private rights through the means of punishment. Punishment is not simply hard treatment; rather, it is hard treatment that is motivated, in part, by the belief that an unwarranted violation of another's independent moral rights creates a *pro tanto* reason in favor of some form of negative reaction toward the rights violator.

The link between (PR1) and (PR2) stems from the thought that crimes, as moral wrongs, call out not just for deterrence or prevention, but punishment in particular. The criminal justice system is for this reason set apart from society's other basic allocative institutions. Punishment is a distinctive kind of good that is subject to a distinctive standard of allocation. To ignore that standard of allocation is to ignore that what one is allocating is *punishment*, not health care, or security, or spots in classrooms.[3]

Putting (PR1) and (PR2) together yields the result that the criminal law is the institutional representation of a familiar moral practice from everyday life, which is that on occasion people transgress moral norms, and when they do, other people react negatively by gossiping about them, shunning or ostracizing them, or punishing them in other ways. The state, through its criminal justice system, simply does on a bigger scale what we all do in our everyday lives. Hence, even when a private right theorist emphasizes the role of the state in punishment, it is from a curiously apolitical point of view: it is simply a matter of responding to wrongs on a bigger scale, and there is no *further* question of the political legitimacy of punishment specific to the operation of large, public, and highly coercive institutions. On a private right conception, the authority that the state claims it has to punish is "no more in need of explication than the authority to punish in other kinds of cases in which wrongs are committed against whomever inflicts a punitive sanction."[4] In short, a private right conception, as Corey Brettschneider puts it, is focused on "the question of what is deserved by the criminal *qua* person rather than the question of what punishment the state can rightfully mete out."[5]

Given the strong association between retribution and moral deservingness, there is a natural consilience between retributive theories of punishment and a private right conception, but the relation is not one of mutual implication. After all, the reason created by rights-violating conduct is only *pro tanto*, and it may be that anything approximating an institutionalized practice of punishment would require supplementation by instrumental reasons of various sorts. Conversely, one could defend a retributive theory of punishment that describes the wrongs requiring retribution in terms of politically generated, rather than purely moral, obligations.[6]

It follows from (PR1) and (PR2) that the criminal law is a body of law that hangs together in a particular way: it is about punishing violations of independent moral rights. In other words, the private right view conceives of the criminal law as a body of law that is identified by the union of a specific subject matter—the vindication of independent moral rights—and a specific means of regulating it—punishment. Thus:

(PR3) Only conduct that either is, or can in some way be plausibly connected to, the violation of independent moral rights should be criminalized. A distinction at least roughly corresponding to the traditional distinction between *mala in se* and *mala prohibita* is therefore of central importance to the philosophy of criminal law.

(PR4) The justification of punishment is a—perhaps *the*—central question for the philosophy of criminal law. Punishment is here understood in the sense of (PR2), rather than as merely an instance of state coercion generally.

Other bodies of law may serve to protect independent moral rights (for instance, by allocating municipalities with the authority to provide public lighting, or to search bags on public transportation); and other bodies of law may also impose costs on people (for instance, through administrative sanctions, or preventive detention), but only the criminal law protects independent moral rights by means of punishment. There can be, of course, a wide range of responses to rights-violating conduct, but only hard treatment motivated by an intention to respond to the wrongness of the accused's conduct constitutes punishment. When the state punishes, it engages in intentional infliction of harm, and this makes it particularly difficult to justify.[7]

The private right conception of the criminal law is thus bound up with—it is hard to say whether it supports or is supported by—an understanding of the criminal law as a distinct legal institution subsystem, one that stands apart from other superficially parallel state institutions. Other state institutions sometimes inflict harm, and sometimes knowingly inflict harm. But what is distinctive about the criminal law is that it inflicts harm intentionally. Indeed, from a private right point of view, this feature of the criminal law marks a fundamental divide between the criminal law and the other institutions comprising modern welfare states. While it may be that punishing people has the effect of enhancing security or welfare, what the criminal law is for is fundamentally the vindication of independent moral rights through punishment (i.e., the intentional infliction of hard treatment). While the vindication of those rights might not be sufficient on its own to justify creating a criminal justice system, it nevertheless remains an important feature of that system, and is moreover a feature that other parts of the welfare state do not share.[8]

The private right conception might as well be labeled the traditional conception, for two reasons. First, the view is traditional in the sense that for many it resonates with an intuitive, everyday understanding of the meaning of crime and punishment; of what it means to describe a person or conduct as "criminal"; of the significance of seeking public prosecution for murderers, rapists, drug dealers, and so forth. It is also traditional in a more polemical sense, in that it reflects an implicit understanding of the legal universe as separated into conceptually and functionally autonomous fiefdoms, one of which is the vindication of private right. The growth of the administrative state is, from this point of view, a distraction from the proper functioning of the criminal law. This understanding of the legal universe is most at home in the context of minimal government, since it is more likely that there could be truly distinct legal subsystems when the state is simply not in the business—either by choice or by necessity—of providing many services to begin with. When the government is not regulating food safety, traffic, financial markets, pollution, animal welfare, public transportation, health care, alcohol and narcotics, education, public utilities, intellectual property, and on and on, then there is of course no need to enforce those regulations through the threat of criminal sanctions. *Mala prohibita* offenses can be—as indeed they are in most contemporary criminal law scholarship—sidelined as extrinsic to the "core" of the criminal law. However, when so-called *mala prohibita* offenses come to vastly outnumber the relatively tiny number of "core" *mala in se* offenses because of the expansive reach of the administrative state, and when the state is in the position to manage *ex ante* the risk that people will in the future engage in rights violating conduct—rather than simply respond to particular occurrences *ex post*—it becomes correspondingly more difficult to view the criminal law, and the institutions that administer it, as simply devoted to the vindication of private right.[9] Of course, this is no criticism of the private right conception, since a private right theorist can simply insist that the use of nonpunitive means to prevent crime *ex ante*, as well as the use of *ex post* sanctions as a means of response to a wide range of socially managed problems beyond "true crimes" shows how defective modern criminal justice systems are by her lights. My claim is only that the descriptive adequacy of the private right conception of criminal law is diminished in the age of the administrative state.

II.

A public law conception takes a contrasting view on both the subject matter of the criminal law and the nature of the means it uses to regulate that subject matter.[10]

(PL1) The criminal law provides an enforcement mechanism for a jurisdiction's legal rules, regardless of the substantive content of those rules—and, hence, regardless of the particular justification given in favor of having those rules in the first place.

(PL2) What is distinctive about the criminal law is that it enforces legal rules through the imposition of unusually harsh or invasive sanctions on violations, rather than the spirit in which the sanction is imposed or its social meaning.

Underlying the public law conception is a more or less orthodox account of the value of the rule of law. The rule of law solves a series of otherwise endemic and intractable collective action problems. The resolution of social problems is often, as Scott Shapiro has recently put it, complex, contentious, or arbitrary.[11] In the context of large, heterogeneous populations, disagreement about the terms of shared social life is the norm, not the exception. The problems of disagreement, free riding, and social coordination are, moreover, significantly more pressing as the range of publicly provided goods and services increases, from simple protection of person and property to regulation of complex financial markets, public health, education, and the regulation of trades and professions, to name but a few examples. In the context of anything approaching the modern administrative state, it is extremely important that the state have means of coordinating the activities of a great number of people for it to be possible for them to act collectively in a reasonably coherent and consistent manner. The threat of sanctions—in some cases, ultra-harsh ones—is one such means for encouraging compliance, though hardly the only one, and in many cases not even a particularly effective one.

On a public law conception, the central function of the criminal law is not to vindicate independently existing moral relationships but to contribute to making the rule of law possible. The criminal law does not "institutionalize" preexisting moral relationships, as Gardner suggests, but rather contributes to establishing the institutional and political preconditions for developing and sustaining novel moral relationships—most notably, those of free and equal citizenship. From this point of view, the criminal law is valuable only insofar as the rule of law—that is, coordinated public action rather than private dispute resolution—is itself valuable. The degree to which it *is* valuable in any given instance is a function of, among other things, the content of the laws enforced and the grimness of the alternatives.

For a great many decisions, it is more important that people coalesce around a particular rule of conduct than it is that they choose the "right" one. This is, again, a condition that one should expect to obtain with increasing frequency as collectivities seek to coordinate greater and greater areas of life: in a world where the only roads are dirt paths and the only vehicles are burros and pushcarts, perhaps it is not so important to decide which side of the road to travel on. Rather than relying on each person's view of the merits of some disputed question, or on spontaneous ordering, law establishes dedicated institutions and procedures for arriving at decisions and coordinating conduct. By deferring to those decisions, individuals and officials under the law's jurisdiction are able to coordinate their conduct because they will be able to form stable expectations about what others will do. Moreover, they are empowered to coordinate their conduct even as they remain in private disagreement with each other. In no small measure, the function of legal ordering is to enable people to coordinate action regardless of each person's private view on the merits, or indeed, regardless of whether they even have a private view on the merits. By doing so, a system of law substitutes what are hopefully easier questions (What is the position of the appropriate legal authority?) for harder or more controversial questions, such as: Is the death penalty immoral? Should the state provide universal health care? Is abortion on demand permissible? These are evidently different questions, but for purposes of coordinating social conduct, private agreement on such matters is not required. What is required is only that a person be able to identify what the relevant legal authority has determined, and to use that determination as a guide to his or her own conduct.

It is not enough for the rules to be explicit; often, they must be enforceable as well. Compliance with rules requiring some level of shared sacrifice is often individually rational only in the presence of the credible threat of sanctions, even when everyone involved shares a common goal. Naturally, this is not to insist that threatening to impose costs on people is the primary means for ensuring compliance with law. Probably for most people, most of the time, compliance is fostered by some combination of habit, conformity to social norms and attitudes of reciprocity. Moreover, it is hard to see how a decent level of compliance could be otherwise achieved, at least in anything short of a police state. That said, the threat of coercively imposed sanctions remains valuable to provide a back-up sanction, and to provide reassurance that those who conform to the rules will not be taken advantage of by those who are tempted to circumvent them. These sanctions thereby render expectations of mutual compliance individually rational.

As with the private right conception, two corollaries can be derived:

(PL3) The image of "core" and "periphery" in the definition of crimes is misleading, at least if it is meant to suggest anything more than a distinction between more and less novel crimes; crimes may differ in the importance of the interests they invade, but so long as they are valid law, they are not more or less "crimes" for that reason.

(PL4) The justification of punishment (in the sense of proposition [PL2]—for example, as a form of rights vindication) is irrelevant to a normative defense of the criminal law. The relevant normative question centers on the public use of coercion as a means of promoting compliance: the conditions under which it is legitimate, its scope and the aims to which it should be put.

As these corollaries are simply the inverse of (PR3) and (PR4), my remarks here are fairly cursory. As to (PL3), from a public law perspective, murder is on par with driving without a license insofar as they are both legal offenses backed by criminal sanctions. They are, of course, vastly different in terms of the seriousness of the conduct and the seriousness of the resulting sanction. But the former has no greater claim to being a conceptually "purer" instance of the legal category of crime than the latter. There are different reasons to criminalize one rather than the other, and the interests they protect differ in their urgency. But, as far as the criminal law is concerned, they are both instances of conduct hedged in by the threat of ultra-harsh sanctions, and hence are equally "central" cases of criminal law.[12]

As to (PL4), from a public law perspective, what is unique about the criminal law is simply the severity of its sanctions. *That* is what is hard to justify about the criminal law, and it is hard to justify regardless of whether or not those sanctions are *also* the vindication of independent moral rights through a moralized conception of punishment.[13]

Endorsing (PL4) does not commit the public law conception to the view that criminal sanctions do not, often, come laden with expressive or condemnatory meaning. What it is committed to is, rather, that what makes the use of such sanctions so difficult to justify is not its condemnatory message per se but rather the degree of coercion with which those messages are conveyed. Whether citizens or officials regard those sanctions as moralistic condemnation, or simply a price meant to force people to internalize some of the costs of their conduct, is not particularly important for understanding the legitimacy of those sanctions. What is more important is that the sanctions be consistent with an encompassing view of the legitimacy conditions for coercive state action generally.

It might be thought that a public law conception is authoritarian, in that rather than portraying the criminal law as the embodiment of righteous moral indignation, it instead portrays the criminal law merely as a way of fostering compliance with positive law by imposing costs on noncompliance. A more conciliatory way of framing the public law conception would be this: The rule of law rests on the willingness of citizens to comply with legal rules, and given that defection from those rules will often be privately rewarding (although publicly disastrous), a scheme for sanctioning defection may serve to stabilize what Rawls refers to as a shared sense of justice, a willingness to cooperate contingent on a similar willingness on the part of others. However it is framed, the claim is that criminal law is justified only if state coercion is justified; and how state coercion is justified is, of course, a central question of political philosophy, not interpersonal morality. But note that the claim is qualified in a crucial way: the criminal law is undoubtedly a heavy-handed way of stabilizing pro-social norms of cooperation. When more sophisticated and less heavy-handed means of achieving this end are readily available—as they are in the age of the administrative stage—the fact that state coercion is justifiable will not suffice to explain why criminal law is justifiable.[14]

III.

Having sketched the contours of the private right and public law models, I now turn to consider the implications of adopting one or the other model for the agenda and method of the philosophy of criminal law. I focus on two substantive implications for the agenda of the philosophy of criminal law, and one implication for its methodology.[15]

First, a private right conception suggests that the evaluation of criminal justice institutions and policies is to be conducted solely by reference to the independently existing moral rights of individuals. From this point of view, criminal justice is an instance of a nonpatterned theory of justice in Robert Nozick's sense. A society's criminal justice system is just insofar as it permits each person to respect the independent moral rights of the others with whom she interacts, and prohibits only the violation of those rights. Criminal justice is not intended to make any contribution to other social goals—such as a fair distribution of opportunities or resources in society—and should accordingly not be assessed in those terms. Just as, for Nozick, distributive justice can be analyzed completely in terms of (a) an initial distribution consistent with the Lockean proviso, and (b) compliance with consensual transfer thereafter, for a private rights theorist, criminal justice can be analyzed completely in terms of (a') an initial state in which each person possesses certain independent moral rights, and (b') compliance with moral rules (enacted as law) that specify what counts as an unwarranted violation of those rights.

In contrast, construing the criminal law as essentially a primitive yet high-salience enforcement mechanism, as the public law model suggests, is to turn this picture on its head. Insofar as the criminal law is a rule-enforcing mechanism, how we should feel about that mechanism obviously depends on how we feel about the rules it is called upon to enforce. It is worth emphasizing at this point that these rules are not simply the rules against murder and rape. The threat of criminal sanctions, at least in the United States and Canada, is regularly used as a last-resort enforcement tool for a myriad of state activities: collecting taxes, enforcing immigration regulations, protecting decorum in the courtroom, turnstile jumping on the subway, environmental protection, the regulation of socially dangerous substances, and so on. Whether the use of the criminal law to enforce these laws is justifiable depends, in part, on whether or not the laws themselves are justifiable. But the evaluation of, for instance, the use of criminal sanctions to backstop a legal scheme devised for the protection of depleted fisheries is not furthered by considering whether people might have a pre-legal right to fish. It is, rather, a question about the appropriate terms of social cooperation, both among those currently existing and with future generations.[16]

What this means is that from a public law perspective there is no philosophically interesting distinction between criminal justice (or "theories of punishment") and distributive justice (or "theories of equality"). Criminal justice institutions serve to enforce the allocation of social benefits and burdens—prerogatives, opportunities, duties, resources, welfare, and so on—that a society's public institutions have settled on. By doing so they enable people to expect that some of their interests will be protected, and do so by imposing serious costs on those who would invade them, with predictable consequences for both protected and targeted individuals, families, and communities. From a public law perspective, the first step in evaluating the operation of criminal justice institutions is, therefore, to evaluate the degree to which the allocations they enforce are consistent with an appropriate theory of social justice—not, as a private right conception would have it, with the evaluation of the moral quality of individual transactions and relationships.[17]

The second substantive implication for the agenda of the philosophy of criminal law concerns what Rawls referred to as the fact of reasonable pluralism. To illustrate: the U.S. Supreme Court recently decided that the federal Defense of Marriage Act is unconstitutional insofar as it denies benefits to same-sex partners of federal employees, benefits that opposite-sex partners are entitled to claim. Immediately after the opinion was released, Representative Michele Bachmann, an elected member of the House of Representatives, issued a statement condemning it. "No man, not even a Supreme Court, can undo what a holy God has instituted," she stated. "For thousands of years of recorded human history, no society has defended the legal standard of marriage as anything other than between man and woman."[18]

Whether or not same-sex couples are entitled to legal recognition is, as Bachmann's statement reminds us, a question that remains intensely controversial in much of the world. However, many people believe that the answer to this question is obvious, and it may be hard for these people to conceive how there could be a genuine dispute about it among reasonable and morally sensitive people. Unfortunately, the people who feel this way do not agree among themselves as to what that allegedly obvious answer is. It is worth bearing in mind here that while Bachmann's views on same-sex marriage are rapidly losing ground in the United States, they are by no means idiosyncratic. Currently, thirty-one American states have constitutional bans on same-sex marriage, all of them enacted within the last fifteen years, and frequently with overwhelming popular support.[19]

The Bachmann problem—the problem of reasonable pluralism—is the problem of finding a way to nevertheless live together in the face of intractable disagreement about matters of fundamental importance.[20] A private right conception of the criminal law does not view reasonable pluralism as a real problem; from this point of view, there is a fact of the matter about which independent moral rights people have, and it is the theorist's role to help us identify these moral truths and show how they should guide criminal law and policy. Taking the problem of reasonable pluralism seriously, however, is taking seriously the concern that people who are motivated to reason together about how to organize a common life will not necessarily converge under, as it were, the gravitational pull of the objective moral truth. The inability to come to consensus is endemic, and cannot always be chalked up to bad faith or stupidity. Taking the problem of reasonable pluralism seriously, in other words, is taking seriously the thought that the appropriate scope and use of the criminal law is a *political* rather than a *moral* problem. It is a question for a theory of politics, not a quasi-religious debate among adherents of different comprehensive doctrines.

Naturally, the fact that reasonable people disagree about the answer to a given question does not show that there isn't a right answer to it. However, what is objectionable about Bachmann's views is not that they are morally dubious and even retrograde, although they are; it is that she provides no publicly available reasons for accepting them, reasons that those who disagree with her can at least view *as* reasons. As Chad Flanders has put the point, from a public law point of view, "We will not say, 'this should be criminalized because the best moral theory says it's wrong.' We will say, 'we can justify this use of the state's coercive power in terms we can all endorse.' Public reason will be our standard, not first-order moral philosophy."[21] Unless and until there is a mutually acceptable and epistemically respectable way of convincing those on the other side of any given issue that it is in fact *your* side that has correctly discerned the true state of the moral world, the existence of an objective fact of the matter is more or less irrelevant.[22] Liberals may point out that these bans deny gays and lesbians equal protection under the law. But since conservatives deny that gays and lesbians are entitled to such protection in the first place, this observation is not likely to move them. Pervasive and genuine disagreement on this proposition means that it too, no less than the conclusion it is meant to support, is unavailable as a shared premise for collective decision-making. Meanwhile, there is a pressing practical problem about how Americans—gay and straight, religious and secular, liberal and conservative—are supposed to devise terms of social cooperation that all can be expected to abide by.[23]

To be sure, the question of marriage equality does not bear directly on the criminal law. However, I have dwelt on this example because it illustrates, in a particularly vivid form, the persistent and genuine disagreement that is characteristic of a great deal of public policy—including criminal justice. The same point applies even in the context of traditionally "core" areas of criminal justice. Reasonable people have widely divergent views about the legal construction of consent in sexual assault, the right to "stand your ground," capital punishment, the use of mandatory minimums, the so-called war on drugs, racial profiling, preventive detention, and so on. Reasonable people disagree about the importance of defending their "honor," of giving people what they pre-justicially deserve, of how much punishment is proportionate for a given offense, about the significance of "victimless" crimes, of the moral salience of bad character as opposed to bad acts, and so on. Persistent disagreement among people motivated to cooperate with each other is, in all likelihood, endemic in large, diverse populations, including on very basic questions of criminal law.

In contrast to a private right conception, a public law conception cannot afford to ignore the impact of reasonable pluralism on criminal justice. This is because the criminal law, on this view, is a means for effectuating the rule of law. In the paradigmatic case, it stabilizes expectations of compliance by rendering compliance individually rational; the rule of law is itself of value because of its contribution to resolving social problems whose solutions require coordination on matters that are complex, contentious, or arbitrary. But precisely because the rule of law is of greatest value when spontaneous consensus and coordination is unavailing, the use of harsh criminal sanctions to encourage compliance among a population presents a profound problem of political legitimacy. Corey Brettschneider, writing in the context of contractualist political theory, puts the point crisply:

> Contractualism aspires to be a theory of legitimate coercion. Never is the state more coercive than when it punishes. Therefore, if punishment is a paradigmatic example of coercion, and contractualism hopes to justify coercion, it must explain how punishment can be justified within the contractualist framework. If it cannot, this speaks ill of contractualism's core ambition.[24]

The choice between a private right and public law conception of the criminal law thus bears on the degree to which the question of political legitimacy is on the agenda of the philosophy of the criminal law. Legitimacy goes beyond simply asking whether public coercion would be an effective means for protecting people's basic interests, though it includes that too. It is, additionally, a matter of determining how to make collective decisions in the face of persistent and *bona fide* disagreement about the rights that people have, and what ought to be done about their violation. This is a very different type of question than the specification of independent moral rights.

Finally, these substantive differences between the private right and public law models have a methodological corollary. A good deal of recent theorizing about the criminal law has adopted what could be described as the desert island approach. On this approach, the central theoretical question is, in effect, this: Supposing we are transported to an otherwise uninhabited and remote desert island, what would it be wrong for me to do to you, and what could you do to resist me while remaining within your rights? The preferred way of answering such a question is through a liberal priming of the intuition pump, particularly through the use of hypotheticals involving private interactions between a small number of individuals—rather than the operation of public institutions affecting large numbers of people with diverse interests and differing opinions about how those interests are to be harmonized. To be clear, the salient aspect of the desert island approach is not so much the appeal to intuition—that appeal is more or less inevitable in this area, at least as a starting point—but rather the idea that the resolution of hypothetical one-off disputes between particular individuals is a reliable guide for the design of large social institutions under conditions of pervasive moral and factual uncertainty.

A public law conception of the criminal law casts serious doubt on the desert island approach. First, on a public law conception, the criminal law is primarily a matter of using coercive sanctions to stabilize the rule of law, and the kind of freedom that the rule of law in turn makes possible. It is not a matter of determining which rights people would have even in the absence of legal institutions. Second, intuitions do not provide impartial reasons that all can be expected to acknowledge. This is particularly true for those who do not share them—and who may in fact have opposing intuitions—but with whom one wishes nevertheless to form stable cooperative arrangements. Third, as a stabilizer of institutions, the criminal law must be sensitive at a very basic level to concerns about institutional design—the alignment of incentives, the scope of discretion among institutional actors, trade-offs between efficiency and fairness, and so forth. These concerns are not adequately addressed by a desert island approach.

IV.

I have drawn a stylized contrast between a private right conception of the criminal law, which, like Gardner, sees the criminal law as "institutionalizing" preexisting moral relationships between people, and a public law conception, which approaches the criminal law as a means of stabilizing the rule of law. On the private right conception, the philosophy of criminal law is fundamentally an exercise in applied moral philosophy, whereas on a public law conception, its questions are political in form and content: in content, because they are questions about the fair allocation of the benefits and burdens of social cooperation (e.g., the risk of victimization and the risk of incarceration), and in form, because the answers proffered must satisfy a test of public justification.

My aim in this chapter is not to argue for the superiority of one conception over the other. However, it is worth pausing here to note a perhaps surprising implication of the private right conception, which is that because it is exclusively focused on the vindicating rights-violations *ex post* through punishment, it provides no guidance on how to weigh the value of *ex post* vindication as against *ex ante* forms of risk management. From the point of view of a public law conception, threatening to impose sanctions on rule violations is simply *one* means—and a destructive and none too effective means at that—for promoting pro-social conduct. Insofar as ensuring that people's rights are less likely to be invaded in the first place is a more effective, and less destructive, means for promoting compliance, there is a strong reason to favor it over, or at least in addition to, *ex post* punishment. From a public law point of view, in other words, *ex post* punishment is simply a primitive form of regulating criminal conduct, one that can freely be substituted for with more sophisticated, less destructive forms of regulation—rather than, as on a private right conception, an intrinsically apt response to crime, conceived of purely in terms of *ex post* rights violations.

Consider the rise of preventive policing in Britain and the United States. Intuitive as it may be, the idea that policing is an "inherently" public function is in fact relatively novel. In the American context, it appears to have arisen in the second half of the nineteenth century, in part in reaction to the Pinkerton agency's role in fighting labor unions.[25] This is not surprising, as the history of organized policing as a publicly provided service of any kind itself scarcely extends past the nineteenth century, at least in Britain and the United States. The first public police force in Britain—Peel's Metropolitan Police—was only instituted in 1829, with versions in American and Canadian cities following in subsequent decades.[26] While the idea that the physical safety of its citizens, as well as the security of their property, is in some sense the state's responsibility no doubt has a longer lineage, the idea that it might be specifically the state's role to protect those interests through preventive policing is relatively novel.

Regardless of its specific institutional form, the preventive function of policing is a clear departure from the criminal law's typical approach to crime as a fire that needs to be put out, instead amounting to an approach to crime as a risk that needs to be managed *ex ante*. However desirable it might be to prevent people's rights from being violated in the first place, this preventive goal is completely distinct from the goal of the criminal law for the simple reason that if no right has been violated, then there is no right subsequently to vindicate through trial, conviction, and punishment. This suggests that, somewhat surprisingly, on a private right conception, prosecutors, criminal courts, and prisons are engaged in a fundamentally different enterprise than the police, at least insofar as the police spend their time preventing crime *ex ante* rather than investigating it *ex post*.

It is in this respect that the institutional conservatism of the private law conception emerges most clearly. After all, under what conditions does it make sense to adopt an exclusively *ex post* perspective on crime? Perhaps the answer is: under conditions where the state is institutionally ill equipped to take meaningful measures to prevent crime other than through threatening those who are adjudicated guilty of committing crimes.[27] This arguably describes the state of Britain and the United States in the early part of the nineteenth century; without organized police forces at their disposal, the detection and prevention of crime was an inevitably disorganized and *ad hoc* affair, and largely in the hands of the victim rather than shouldered by the state.

It is worth remembering that criminal cases were typically *privately* prosecuted until the nineteenth century. In England, the idea that the gathering of evidence and the presentation of a case against the accused was the Crown's responsibility is, it turns out, not much older than the idea that preventive policing could be an acceptable manner of crime control. Prior to public prosecutions, it had been common for wealthy men to form private associations designed to provide their members with what we would now think of as public prosecutorial services.[28] Moreover, the development of preventive policing could be thought of as presenting an *alternative* to criminal punishment as an *ex post* response to crime. Clive Emsley has suggested that an important motivation behind the establishment of the Metropolitan Police was meliorating the harshness of Britain's "Bloody Code" by raising the likelihood of conviction and punishment through an organized effort at policing.[29] Eric Monkkonen makes a similar observation:

> The creators of the new police introduced a new concept in social control: the prevention of crime. . . . Taking an argument of the Italian criminal law reformer, Beccaria, they claimed that regular patrolling, predictable detection of offenses, and rational punishment would deter potential offenders. They even extended Beccaria's argument, claiming that the sight of the police uniform itself would deter potential offenders.[30]

As Monkkonen notes, this new form of social control implies a shift from an *ex post* response to crime to an attempt to "explain and predict criminal behaviour" *ex ante*. By this telling, the history of modern policing in the English-speaking world is bound up with popular acceptance of the idea that crime is not just a problem of case-by-case adjudication of independent rights violations, but rather a problem of social policy whose resolution required the development of controversial and powerful new institutions.[31]

From a public law perspective, the development of preventive policing over the course of the nineteenth century represents the development of a further means for fostering compliance with legal rules, one that does not depend entirely on the threat of harsh sanctions for those found violating them. The threat of receiving a serious sanction contingent upon commission of a crime is but one mechanism among others for encouraging pro-social conduct, and is functionally continuous with a wide range of noncriminal means for encouraging compliance. Some of these alternatives include investing in locks, fences, lights, and cameras; changing social norms via public awareness campaigns; regulating access to alcohol; increasing employment rates among young men; subsidizing early childhood education and nutrition; random inspections of regulated facilities; and adopting technology that renders certain forms of crime essentially obsolete. What these have in common is that they are all ways of trying to prevent crimes from occurring in the first place rather than ways of dealing with crimes only once they have occurred. While preventive policing no doubt relies on the threat of punishment as well, the use it makes of it is to encourage compliance by raising its salience *ex ante*, rather than relying on *ad hoc* applications of ultra-harsh sanctions *ex post*. Preventive policing is, in this respect, arguably a less primitive form of regulation than the exemplary application of harsh sanctions—though of course, as the law of criminal procedure continually reminds us, it is a form of regulation that comes with its own attendant dangers.[32]

V.

The contrast between the private right and public law conceptions is no doubt overdrawn in various respects. However, they are not intended as a representation of the claims of particular theorists, but should rather be treated as an attempt to make explicit the assumptions that stand in the background of a range of both doctrinal and philosophical arguments about the content and function of the criminal law. These assumptions concern the reasons for having a distinct procedural and institutional regime for "criminal" matters; the relation between "retributive" and "distributive" justice; and, perhaps most broadly, the value served by the rule of law—or, perhaps more accurately, the rule of legally constituted public institutions. The contrast between the private right and public law conceptions will have served its purpose if it sheds light on how differing views on these typically unarticulated background assumptions contribute to shaping both the agenda and methodological orientation of the philosophy of the criminal law.

NOTES

1. My thanks to Chad Flanders, Alon Harel, Zach Hoskins and Malcolm Thorburn, who all provided detailed written comments on an earlier draft.
2. John Gardner, *Introduction* to H.L.A. HART, PUNISHMENT AND RESPONSIBILITY: ESSAYS IN THE PHILOSOPHY OF LAW, at xlix (2d ed. 2008).
3. As Michael Walzer puts it, "If we distributed punishment differently, it would not be punishment at all . . . We might vote for the people we punish, as the ancient Athenians did when they chose citizens for ostracism; or we might look for the most qualified candidates, as contemporary advocates of preventive detention would have us do. Both of these are eminently practical arrangements; but insofar as they distribute dishonor, they do so, I think, tyrannically." MICHAEL WALZER, SPHERES OF JUSTICE: A DEFENSE OF PLURALISM AND EQUALITY 270 (1983).
4. Douglas Husak, *Does the State Have a Monopoly to Punish Crime? in* THE NEW PHILOSOPHY OF CRIMINAL LAW 104 (Chad Flanders & Zachary Hoskins, eds., 2015).
5. Corey Brettschneider, *The Rights of the Guilty: Punishment and Political Legitimacy*, 35 POL. THEORY 183 (2007).
6. For a prominent instance, see ALAN BRUDNER, PUNISHMENT AND FREEDOM (2009). In contrast, Victor Tadros has recently defended an account of punishment that is in this respect the inverse of Brudner's. On the one hand, Tadros has no use for punishment as an inherently condemnatory or retributive practice. On the other hand, Tadros bases his account on a pre-political account of each person's independent moral rights. *See* VICTOR TADROS, THE ENDS OF HARM (2011).
7. As a result of (PR3), the private right conception can only view *mala prohibita* offenses as a puzzle, or a derogation from the true morality-tracking function of the criminal law—

whereas on a public law conception, *mala prohibita*, insofar as that is a useful category at all, comes close to embodying the *general* form of crime.

8. *See* Sam Scheffler, *Justice and Desert in Liberal Theory*, 88 CAL. L. REV. 965, 965–90 (2000).

9. If, indeed, the criminal law ever had this character, at least in common law jurisdictions. For an influential discussion, see Douglas Hay, *Property, Authority and the Criminal Law*, *in* DOUGLAS HAY, PETER LINEBAUGH, JOHN G. RULE, E.P. THOMPSON & CAL WINSLOW, ALBION'S FATAL TREE: CRIME AND SOCIETY IN EIGHTEENTH-CENTURY ENGLAND 17–63 (1957).

10. Perhaps the most prominent defender of a public law conception of the criminal law is Malcolm Thorburn; *see, e.g*, Malcolm Thorburn, *Criminal Law as Public Law*, *in* PHILOSOPHICAL FOUNDATIONS OF CRIMINAL LAW (R.A. Duff & Stuart Green, eds., 2011); Malcolm Thorburn, *Justifications, Powers and Authority*, 117 YALE L. J. 1070 (2008).

11. SCOTT J. SHAPIRO, LEGALITY, 133–4 (2011).

12. Consider the view that while *mala prohibita* do not describe things that would be morally wrong to do on a desert island, they do describe things that become morally wrong once we have a set of public institutions. This view undermines the point of distinguishing between *mala in se* and *mala prohibita*; for, by this account, any valid legal rule hedged by criminal sanctions will for that very reason describe a moral wrong. If both independent moral wrongs and institutionally defined moral wrongs are equally worth vindicating through the means of the criminal law, it is hard to see what the point of distinguishing between them in the first place is meant to be. For a recent discussion of the role of *mala prohibita* offenses within the framework of what I would consider to be a public law conception, see Chad Flanders, *Public Wrongs and Public Reason*, DIALOGUE (forthcoming 2015).

13. A private right conception thus faces a puzzle that does not arise on a public law conception, which is why vindicating independent moral rights, even assuming that is of such overriding importance, must take the form of *punishment*, rather than, say, simply calling someone to account through expressive disavowal. See Thorburn's critique of Antony Duff on this point, Malcolm Thorburn, *Constitutionalism and the Limits of the Criminal Law*, *in* THE STRUCTURES OF THE CRIMINAL LAW 96 (R.A. Duff et al., eds., 2011).

14. I thank Malcolm Thorburn for urging me to address this point, as with many others.

15. To be clear, I should note that the contrast between the private right and public law conceptions is meant to provide an axis along which theories of the criminal law can be arrayed. I am not claiming that every theory of, say, punishment belongs to one camp or the other, but rather that they can be usefully compared in terms of how near or far they are from a paradigmatic statement of the private right or public law conception.

16. *See* R. v. Pierce Fisheries Ltd., [1971] S.C.R. 5 (Can.); *Re* B.C. Motor Vehicle Act, [1985] 2 S.C.R. 486 (Can).

17. It is beyond the scope of this chapter to suggest what such a theory might be. I articulate and defend such an approach in CRIMINAL LAW IN THE AGE OF THE ADMINISTRATIVE STATE, forthcoming with Oxford University Press.

18. *Live Analysis of the Supreme Court Decisions on Gay Marriage: Boehner Waits to Respond; Bachmann Jumps In*, N.Y. TIMES (June 26, 2013, 10:21 AM), http://projects.nytimes.com/live-dashboard/2013-06-26-supreme-court-gay-marriage -sha=062eb6686.

19. Since this chapter was drafted, the Supreme Court has held that gays and lesbians have a constitutionally protected right to marry. Obergefell v. Hodges, 135 S. Ct. 2584, 2607 (2015).

20. It is not entirely clear that Bachmann's views would qualify as a reasonable comprehensive doctrine, but the underlying point should be clear.

21. Flanders, *supra* note 12, at 3.

22. *See* JEREMY WALDRON, LAW AND DISAGREEMENT 180–87 (1999).

23. Waldron has put the point like this: Law has authority not because "there are lawmakers who know better than we do (nor even that there are officials who have more power or access to more lethal weapons than any of us). The authority of law rests on the fact that there is a recognizable need for us to act in concert on various issues or to co-ordinate our behavior in various areas with reference to a common framework, and that this need is not obviated by the fact that we disagree among ourselves as to what our common course of action or our common framework ought to be." *Id.* at 7.

24. Corey Brettschneider, *The Rights of the Guilty: Punishment and Political Legitimacy*, 35 POL. THEORY 175, 182 (2007). (I note that I would replace the references to "punishment" in the quoted text with the more neutral term "sanctions.")

25. *See* David A. Sklansky, *The Private Police*, 46 UCLA L. REV. 1165, 1210–15 (1999). The popularity of the idea that policing might be an inherently public function also appears to track the growth in the capacity and professionalism of public police forces during this formative period. *See id.* at 1219.

26. *See* ERIC H. MONKKONEN, POLICE IN URBAN AMERICA: 1860–1920, 30–64 (2004).

27. I am here—as elsewhere—indebted to Dan Priel for many discussions about the development of the administrative state, and its significance for legal theory.

28. *See* J.M. BEATTIE, CRIME AND THE COURTS IN ENGLAND, 1660–1800, 48–50 (1986). Notably, Crown responsibility for prosecuting regulatory crimes appears to predate Crown responsibility for prosecuting ordinary felonies, largely because of growth in the institutions—e.g. the Mint, the Treasury, the Bank of England, the Post Office—that sought to enforce the laws that lay within their institutional mandate. *See* JOHN H. LANGBEIN, RENÉE LETTOW LERNER & BRUCE P. SMITH, HISTORY OF THE COMMON LAW: THE DEVELOPMENT OF ANGLO-AMERICAN LEGAL INSTITUTIONS 686–87 (2009).

29. *See* CLIVE EMSLEY, POLICING IN ITS CONTEXT, 1750–1870, 59 (1983). Emsley cites a contemporary reformer's observation that while Britain had 223 capital offenses, France—which had a public police force—had only six.

30. MONKONNEN, *supra* note 26, at 40–41.

31. One might thus argue that by clinging to an exclusively *ex post* conception of the criminal law as rights vindication, a private right conception is to that extent clinging *literally* to a night watchman state—that is, a state in which police simply respond to crimes, rather than seek actively to prevent crime in the first place. Tapio Lappi-Seppälä has noted that use of incarceration among poor countries appears to increase with GDP for a while, plateaus, and then decreases afterward. This finding is consistent with the claim suggested above—namely, that criminal sanctions are essentially a primitive form of social regulation, and one whose utility may be superseded as legal, social, political, and economic institutions become denser and more comprehensive in scope. Tapio Lappi-Seppälä, *Trust, Welfare and Political Culture: Explaining Differences in National Penal Policies*, 37 CRIME & JUST. 313, 344 (2008). As Lappi-Seppälä notes, "There is an inverse relation between commitment to welfare (the generosity of welfare provisions) and the scale of imprisonment." *Id.* at 356.

32. The argument may be over-determined, in that a strictly moralistic view of crime might also have been more politically appropriate in early modern states characterized by smaller populations and a lesser degree of ethnic and religious diversity than is the case in, for instance, the contemporary United States or Canada. My thanks to Chad Flanders for pointing this out.

Chapter Two

Embodied Ethical Life and the Criminal Law

Joshua Kleinfeld

INTRODUCTION[1]

Some intellectual traditions consist in a body of ideas held in common and passed down over time within a group of people who are conscious of one another and of building something shared. The theory of justice in the wake of John Rawls is an intellectual tradition of this kind. What I will call the "Reconstructive tradition of criminal theory" is an intellectual tradition of another sort, in which multiple people address the same thing in their own ways, some influenced by one another, some not, but all producing similar or complementary ideas because they are driven by a common object of interest. Theories of interpretation—from legal theory to literary theory to philosophy of language to Biblical hermeneutics and beyond—are an example. The theorists in such cases constitute a tradition only in the sense that those who follow them can assemble the ideas they severally produced into a unitary body of thought. The reason to do this is because the ideas in question are stronger together than apart, and because seeing the points of intersection may in some cases, as here, bring to light a sort of Ur argument whose steps are at the foundation of all thought of the type.

The reconstructive tradition of criminal theory is an offshoot of a broader theoretical tradition, handed down from Hegel to philosophical sociologists like Weber and Durkheim to contemporary sociological philosophers like Axel Honneth, Michael Walzer, and Charles Taylor.[2] The central theme of this line of thought is that our social practices and institutions are constituted as they are in part because of values that are implicit, embodied, instantiated, or (best) *immanent* in them—that there is some organic link between, say, the practice of voting and the value of equality, the practice of jazz improvisation and the values of spontaneity and individuality, the practice of modern science and the values associated with evidence-based reason. A society's form of life (the whole of which those practices and institutions are the parts) thus becomes an *embodied ethical life*, or what Hegel termed *Sittlichkeit*, and in turn an important object of normative philosophy comes to be bringing the immanent values that make up this embodied ethical life to light, rendering them explicit. That is, the role of philosophy is not chiefly to define and defend some set of abstract or a priori ethical ideals, which are then applied to the world to dictate how it should be ordered, but to rationally reconstruct the normative order already at work in the world in order to see that normative order more clearly and critique it from an internal point of view (or at least to critique it only after understanding it from an internal point of view). The philosopher thus stands in an interpretive rather than a concept-application relationship to the social world.

It happens that several of the most prominent figures in the *Sittlichkeitian* tradition, particularly Hegel and Durkheim, wrote at length about criminal law, and on the other side it happens that a number of important criminal theorists have written about criminal law in ways that (unconsciously in most cases) echo *Sittlichkeitian* themes. It is not obvious why this should be so: the idea of embodied ethical life is not in any direct way an idea about crime and punishment. What, then, is the link?

This chapter's purpose is to uncover that link. My view in essence is that, once one focuses on and valorizes *Sittlichkeit*, as Hegel and Durkheim did, one begins to understand it as a fragile social good which wrongdoing threatens, which punishment protects and reinforces, and which thereby implies a special place in the world for criminal law. Separately—now approaching the matter from the opposite direction—when one theorizes crime and punishment along certain lines (as, for example, expressing social norms, as an outgrowth of a people's culture), one is led to the idea of a normatively laden social fabric worth protecting and reinforcing—that is, to the idea of a *Sittlichkeit*. In other words, *the function of criminal law has everything to do with embodied ethical life*, and a diverse array of scholars and lawyers working on different questions with different methodologies have seen the connection. From Hegel to James Fitzjames Stephen to Nietzsche to Durkheim to Devlin to Foucault to Henry Hart to contemporaries such as Jean Hampton, Jeffrie Murphy, David Garland, Antony Duff, Dan Kahan, Paul Robinson, Nicola Lacey, and Günther Jakobs, they have seen it—and of those, I would argue, Hegel, Durkheim, Hampton, and Duff have seen it best.[3] But these scholars and lawyers have not been systematically aware of one another or aware that they collectively constitute a tradition and therefore have not seen their way to the bottom of the connection. At the bottom of the connection is this idea: criminal law's distinctive social function is to reconstruct ethical life in the wake of an attack on ethical life—that is, criminal law is an instrument of normative reconstruction, and the theoretical perspective that so views it may be termed reconstructivism.

Thus in the pages that follow I attempt to assemble this fragmented tradition in criminal theory.

I. THE POINT OF DEPARTURE

The belief that the justification of punishment is the beginning and organizing question of criminal theory has become, it is not too much to say, a convention. George Fletcher's classic, *Rethinking Criminal Law*, for example, opens with the words: "Criminal law is a species of political and moral philosophy. Its central question is justifying the use of the state's coercive power against free and autonomous persons."[4] The casebooks used to teach law students begin the same way. This point of departure gives criminal theory a libertarian cast, as it makes state power the field's foremost concern; the question is like a slot into which Mill's harm principle or something like it might slide. The focus on punishment's justification also gives criminal theory an almost wholly normative orientation: the purpose of the enterprise is not in the first place to *understand* punishment as a social phenomenon (nor to understand crime, nor criminal law), but firstly and mainly to identify reasons on the basis of which to *support* or *oppose* punishment.[5] And the question lends criminal theory a certain Enlightenment-humanist emotional flavor, for its spiritual root is revulsion at suffering—all suffering, even that of offenders, or perhaps especially that of offenders, as their suffering is inflicted by deliberate social choice. Bentham so hated suffering that he saw even deserved punishment as a defeasible evil—indeed, so hated suffering that he thought morality itself had no purpose but to reduce it.[6] Beccaria's rationalistic arguments against the death penalty were (one can sense) posterior to his revulsion at its violence.[7] There are other ways of thinking about moral life than this; no ancient ever did or ever would have felt pain to be of such overwhelming moral importance. But the spirit of the field is Bentham's and Beccaria's: criminal theory is filled with their longing for a gentler social world and their spirit of activist rationalism in trying to create such a world. Punishment is naturally the central issue if one begins from that longing and spirit, because to punish is deliberately to inflict suffering.[8]

But the reconstructive tradition begins, not with the justification of punishment, but with the nature of wrongdoing. What is a wrong—that is, how are we to understand wrongdoing itself? And how are we to live in a world in which others wrong us—that is, how are we rationally to cope with, come to terms with, and above all respond to wrongdoing? If one thinks of crime and punishment as an ordered sequence (which of course it is), the reconstructive tradition starts its work at an earlier point in the sequence than punishment theory. The analytic structure is this: as crime is ordinarily a species or special case of wrongdoing,[9] the question of how to understand crime is one part of a larger question about how to understand wrongdoing in general. To understand wrongdoing is to learn something about the response wrongdoing calls for, which in turn implies a position as to what punishment is and what it is for. Every one of the theorists making up the reconstructive tradition works within this structure.

In Hegel's case, the point of departure is quite clear, for the bulk of secondary work adumbrating his "theory of punishment" comes from a single chapter of *The Philosophy of Right* that is explicitly about wrongdoing; the chapter's very title is "Wrong."[10] Its central idea is related to the central idea animating all of *The Philosophy of Right* (indeed all of Hegel's mature work): that moral concepts take shape in a fully specified way and are equipped to play their part in advancing individuals' agential dignity and flourishing only when actualized in social life, and therefore the proper focus of moral and political philosophy is not finally abstract concepts at all but instantiated concepts—concepts as realized in forms of life.[11] Hegel's views of wrong, right, crime, and punishment, which I will explicate at more length, play out against this backdrop. Suffice it to say here that, as actualization is central to his concerns, he takes wrong and right to be linked along an axis of *de-actualization* and *re-actualization*: wrongdoing's key feature is that it renders that which is right "a semblance,"[12] making the right, not conceptually false, but false as a description of social reality. For example, the norm requiring that people respect one another's physical security is de-actualized when one person assaults another: though no less valid as an abstract, conceptual matter, the norm no longer holds as a description of actual social arrangements. Punishment, in turn, re-actualizes the right, making it something "fixed and valid,"[13] in the wake of a wrong. (Hegel also thinks, more radically, that the right is established in the first place by the negation of wrongdoing.) The point for now is not to understand these claims to the bottom but simply to see that, by their very architecture, they make the nature of wrongdoing and crime conceptually prior to the theory of punishment—prior, that is, not only rhetorically, as a matter of how the argument unfolds (though they are that too), but also analytically. One cannot understand punishment as re-actualizing a norm unless one first understands crime as de-actualizing the norm.

Durkheim did not write one tract about criminal law laying out his views with finality; he developed his views in a variety of places and always in the context of some other or larger project, which must be understood if the criminal theory is to be understood. Yet the basic structure of his theory never wavered: it begins from the tremendous value Durkheim attached to social solidarity. That we feel bonded to one another and that we substantially share views of right, wrong, good, and bad is necessary if a collection of individuals are to form as a society, he thought, and a functioning society is a moral achievement of profound importance to human welfare. *The Division of Labor in Society*, for example, probably the work in which Durkheim sets forth his views on crime and punishment most completely, opens with three ideas: that the division of labor is *the* fundamental sociological fact of modernity; that the division of labor not only makes us more economically productive but also tends to stitch society together in ways that create social solidarity; and that law, as the external manifestation of social solidarity, offers clues into how society's solidaristic processes work. The question for any particular department of law, then, is how it reflects or advances the project of social solidarity. It is in this context that Durkheim takes up crime and punishment. His opening question is "what in essence . . . crime consists of."[14] His argument, in brief (I return to it next), is that crime in some way threatens, challenges, or undermines social solidarity—both the bondedness to one another and the shared norms. The usual metaphor here is of a social fabric: crime is a tearing of the social fabric, and punishment is a re-stitching of that torn social fabric. As with Hegel, this view of punishment does not make sense without a certain understanding of crime.

Jean Hampton also develops her views in successive works, but the most important is her book-length dialogue with Jeffrie Murphy, *Forgiveness and Mercy*.[15] Her project at the relevant point in the book is to explain, *contra* Murphy, how one can forgive without thereby minimizing the magnitude of the wrong one is forgiving. In the course of working out an answer, she arrives at a simple question that becomes the leitmotif of everything else she would say in the discourse and much else she would say in the remainder of her career: "What is it that really bothers us about being wronged?"[16] Her answer, as I will show, has to do with the ways in which wrongs degrade, but for now the point is the question; it is the question that shows us her point of departure. When in later work she set herself expressly the task of developing a theory of punishment, she circled back to this question, now taken up outside the mercy/forgiveness context. If we are to understand punishment, she argues, we must "link . . . punishment to that which makes the wrongful action wrong. . . . What we need . . . is a good theory of the wrongfulness of punishable conduct."[17] That is, we need to answer the question: "What is a wrong?"[18]

Normative unstitching/re-stitching is thus the architectonic along which every member of the reconstructive tradition works in his or her own way. They start with wrongdoing. That is not to say—a drastic overstatement—that non-reconstructive criminal theory is altogether silent as to wrongdoing: contemporary, non-reconstructive criminal theorists do address the nature of wrongdoing to some extent, generally under the rubric of what should be criminalized. Michael Moore, for example, has recognized the tripartite linkage from wrongdoing to criminalization to punishment,[19] as has Douglas Husak.[20] There has indeed been a recent flurry of interest in criminalization, pushed forward, interestingly, by perhaps the most reconstructive criminal theorist alive today: Antony Duff.[21] But what is striking here is how late this interest comes in the maturation of the field and how small it is relative to the massive attention given to punishment. As Husak wrote in 2008, "I find the lack of scholarly interest in the topic of criminalization to be baffling. . . . *[N]o* contemporary theorist in the United States or Great Britain is closely associated with a theory of criminalization."[22] That might have been too strong even in 2008: the harm principle is a theory of criminalization, which Joel Feinberg, among others, has examined in exquisite detail.[23] But Husak's broad point is right: the theory of criminal wrongdoing is a pinprick relative to the theory of punishment.

This disproportion is important, not just because it leaves a stone unturned, but because it shows that the field has generally treated criminalization and punishment as conceptually separate. The idea of a "crime," until the recent flurry of interest, has usually served as a placeholder in debates about punishment (which is how the debate about criminalization can be so much smaller and younger than the debate about punishment). To a reconstructivist, this is like heart surgery without cardiovascular theory, for it is reconstructivism's contention that the nature of crime and the grounds of punishment are conceptually connected. In fact, the claim is stronger still (and this is where reconstructivism departs even from Moore and Husak): a theory of crime is conceptually *prior* to a theory of punishment, because it is only by understanding the nature of crime that we can see why and how we should punish. There cannot be a normative re-stitching without a normative unstitching.

The focus in mainstream criminal theory on how to justify punishment, absent a starting point in the theory of wrongdoing, is a consequential one. It has, by ignoring or minimizing the question of what crime and wrongdoing are, deprived itself of the resources by which to answer its own question—for if the reconstructive tradition is right, understanding punishment depends on understanding wrongdoing. It has made the issue of state power loom excessively large. It has lost track of what makes crime and punishment so culturally riveting—the magnetism of the subject, its hold on the public imagination from the *Oresteia* through *Law and Order*, does not arise from proto-libertarian concerns about state power. It has made the theory of punishment normative without a foundation in understanding the phenomenon being judged, without, that is, good philosophical description—and normative theory of that sort tends to be shallow and error-prone. But most of all, the focus on punishment alone has made criminal theory unduly insular, concerned with a question which even in philosophy constitutes a relatively discrete and isolated subfield: the theory of punishment. The question of what wrongdoing is and the rationally justified response to wrongdoing, by contrast, should be of interest to anyone who wants to understand how communities function, for (again) if the reconstructive tradition is right, it is impossible to understand social organization and impossible to understand embodied ethical life without this wrongdoing-redress apparatus. Reconstructivism thus reconnects criminal theory to the main part of political philosophy—as Hegel and Durkheim connected criminal theory to the main part of their political philosophies.

II. WHAT IS THE NATURE OF CRIME AND WRONGDOING?

The "expressive theory of punishment" is well-known. It turns on noticing that punishment has expressive characteristics—that it is a kind of symbolic communication. Reconstructivism is a sub-type of expressivism, a distinctive member of the category in part because it insists not only that punishment is expressive but also that wrongdoing is expressive. Wrongdoing is *communication*, and understanding what it communicates is key to understanding what it is that punishment must express in response. In other words, the reconstructive tradition sees crime and punishment as an *exchange of meanings*. We begin here with the crime side of that exchange. Hegel, Durkheim, and Hampton were not perfectly aligned with regard to what crime expresses, and each of them, in my view, makes theoretical missteps. But they were roughly aligned, and their separate accounts can be combined into something greater than any of them had by themselves.

Durkheim argued that the concept of harm is inadequate to any sociologically realistic account of crime. Societies criminalize conduct that is not tangibly harmful all the time: "The act of touching an object that is taboo, or an animal or man who is impure or consecrated, of letting the sacred fire die out, of eating certain kinds of meat, of not offering the traditional sacrifice on one's parents' grave, of not pronouncing the precise ritual formula, or of not celebrating certain feasts, etc."[24] And even when a criminalized act does cause harm, it is not harm that drives its punishment: "In the penal law of most civilized peoples murder is universally regarded as the greatest of crimes. Yet an economic crisis, a crash on the stock market, even a bankruptcy, can disorganize the body social much more seriously than the isolated case of homicide."[25] As Durkheim well knew, of course, none of this rebuts the normative contention that criminal law *should* be restricted to harm, but that is why it is significant to develop an account of criminal theory that is meant to explain in the first place and critique in the second. There is something in certain acts that alarms societies, that leads societies to make the acts criminal. What is that something? That was Durkheim's question. If his examples are correct—and they seem correct to me—the answer is not "harm." Harm may or may not mark out the normative limits of criminalization, but it cannot explain crime's nature; social life is operating according to something other than the harm principle.

One might think crime has no unifying characteristic, no nature at all, unless it is expediency; crime is just the grab-bag of what societies have addressed, where pragmatic considerations warranted, by means of the instrument most likely to spur compliance.[26] Durkheim denied this view, too, though in a subtle way. He did not claim, and in fact denied, that we will find the same things prohibited in every society, "[f]or . . . if there are acts that have been universally regarded as criminal, these constitute a tiny minority."[27] Further, the concerns or purposes motivating criminalization "have varied infinitely, and can vary again. Nowadays it is altruistic sentiments that manifest this characteristic most markedly. But at one time, not at all distant, religious or domestic sentiments, and a host of other traditional sentiments, had precisely the same effect."[28] Nonetheless, amidst the variety of prohibitions and purposes, the "species of crime have something in common . . . some common basis."[29]

That common basis, Durkheim argued, was that crime breaks the bonds of social solidarity by violating the norms on which social solidarity rests. Crime is offense to embodied ethical life: "The totality of beliefs and sentiments common to the average members of a society forms a determinate system with a life of its own. It can be termed the collective or common consciousness. . . . [A]n act is criminal when it offends the strong, well-defined states of the collective consciousness."[30] Durkheim is often at pains to emphasize that crime "disturbs those feelings that in any one type of society are to be found in every healthy consciousness"[31] and that crime is "condemned by the members of each society,"[32] and he sometimes appears to argue that these responses define crime itself: crime is whatever happens to disturb the feelings of and spur condemnation by ordinarily socialized members of a community. But the whole picture is something more like this: ordinarily socialized members of a community find that which threatens solidaristic bonds disturbing and respond with condemnation and punishment, for they understand at some level that they depend for their welfare and identity on their membership in a group and that the crime tears at the bonds on which the group is based. The mark or evidence of such a thing is that it disturbs feelings and spurs condemnation, but disturbance and condemnation don't define crime so much as enable us to detect it, just as physicists detect a particle by measuring the effects it has on the system around it. We know that an act offends the ideas on which a community's social organization is based because well-socialized members of that community react to the act with revulsion, anger, and condemnation. But the nature of the act is that it attacks the ideals on which social organization is based.

Durkheim emphasizes the ways in which crime *offends* embodied ethical life; he generally does not argue that crime might also threaten—genuinely threaten—social organization, that it might put a society's embodied ethical life in jeopardy. In fact, he sometimes suggests the opposite, as though crime to a strongly constituted society is, like a fly to an elephant, the kind of minor irritation that never could be an existential threat.[33] In my view, this is a significant flaw. He corrects it to some extent in his posthumous *Moral Education*, which is, though superficially an account of classroom discipline, in fact (and as David Garland has emphasized[34]) one of Durkheim's major works on crime and punishment:

> With the child as with the adult, moral authority is a creature of opinion and draws all its force from opinion. Consequently, what lends authority to the rule in school is the feeling that the children have for it, the way in which they view it as a sacred and inviolable thing quite beyond their control; and everything that might attenuate this feeling, everything that might induce children to believe that it is not really inviolable can scarcely fail to strike discipline at its very source. To the extent that the rule is violated it ceases to appear as inviolable.[35]

Coupling this argument with the one in *Division of Labor*, we may say this: crime not only offends the norms on which social solidarity is based but also, by showing that those norms can be violated, saps them of authority. A crime declares, "The norm against what I have just done is for fools and suckers. It does not hold." An assault says, "The right to physical security does not hold"; a theft says, "The right to property does not hold"; a murder says, "The right to life does not hold"; and so on. What effect that message has on the capacity of society to maintain itself will depend on particular conditions—how many people violate the norm, how tempting it is to violate the norm, what attitudes accompany the norm's violation, how likely punishment is, and the like—but the message itself is inherently a threat to the social organization. I would indeed go further. Society's normative structures are fragile; crime really does threaten them. If students start cheating on their exams and see that teachers, who could do something about it, turn a blind eye, the norm against cheating will dissolve and dissolve quickly. If providing information to the police is punished by the community, a norm against "snitching" will quickly form. Norms change by action; the jeopardy is real. Seeing that jeopardy is part of motivating the reconstructive perspective.

What is missing in all of Durkheim's work on the nature of crime is an understanding of what crime expresses about its victim (tabling for the moment the issue of victimless crimes). He was so oriented to society as a collective that he did not see the individual victim's position as one of special significance; that aspect of meaning was lost upon him. But it is exactly here that Murphy and Hampton—themselves blind to many of the social dimensions of wrongdoing on which Durkheim is focused—make their distinctive contribution. They, like Durkheim, begin by emphasizing the inadequacy of the concept of harm: "The trouble with wrongdoing is not simply that wrongdoings threaten or produce physical or psychological damage, or damage to our careers, interests or families. However much we may sorrow over our bad fortune, when the same damage is threatened or produced by natural forces or by accidents, we do not experience that special anger that comes from having been insulted."[36] But at that point they swerve, bringing to light a second dimension of expressive meaning in wrongdoing—namely, what wrongdoing communicates about the individual victim of the wrong. Per Murphy: "One reason we so deeply resent moral injuries done to us is not simply that they hurt us in some tangible or sensible way; it is because such injuries are also messages—symbolic communications. They are ways a wrongdoer has of saying to us, 'I count but you do not,' 'I can use you for my purposes,' or 'I am here up high but you are there down below.' Intentional wrongdoing insults us and attempts (sometimes successfully) to degrade us—and thus it involves a kind of injury that is not merely tangible and sensible. It is moral injury, and we care about such injuries."[37] As Hampton puts the point, "When someone wrongs another, she does not regard her victim as the sort of person who is valuable enough to require better treatment."[38] To wrong someone is to make a statement about her worth, to devalue her, and we resent that statement potentially as much or more than we do the harm.

In Murphy's and Hampton's hands, this point is largely one about individual psychology, about what wrongdoers believe or impliedly believe when they act and how victims feel when they are acted upon. It seems to me that neither Hampton nor Murphy ever saw the sociological side of their claims. To Hampton's mind, if the victim resists the communication, although she is "demeaned in the sense that she has been forced to endure treatment that is too low for her," she suffers "no literal degradation as a result of the wrongdoing."[39] To Murphy, the social significance of the degradation is that it hurts our self-respect: "Most of us tend to care about what others (at least some others) think about us—how much they think we matter. Our self-respect is social in at least this sense, and it is simply part of the human condition that we are weak and vulnerable in these ways."[40] The problem with these views is that they fail to see the respects in which ill treatment really does degrade, no matter how strong the individual victim's psychology is, because the issue is not just self-respect but social status, and social status is not a matter of individual psychology; it is intersubjective. A distinction is useful here between *self-respect*, as a psychological state; *human dignity*, that quasi-mystical core of worth that human beings are thought to have just in virtue of being human; and *social status*, the social phenomenon of having a position within a social hierarchy—a rank, a way of being regarded and valued by one's fellows. Self-respect depends finally on one's own psychology; human dignity depends, let us say, on one's humanity, but social status is a socially given thing. When the first white man in the Jim Crow South took to calling black men "boy," and went echoed and uncorrected by his fellows, a social hierarchy was *accomplished*, however much the degradation left (as it could not but leave) black men's true dignity untouched, and even if it had left black men's sense of self-worth untouched. At the time that one is made a victim, a proposal is made: "You are of lowered social status." The proposal is presented not just to the victim but also to society in the form of a question: "Will this lowering be affirmed or disaffirmed?" One is in a liminal space. Society will decide by its response how that proposal will be answered.

Putting the Durkheim and Murphy/Hampton threads together, we might say this: wrongdoing challenges two parts of the social fabric of moral life. It says of the abstract norm, "This norm does not hold," and of the victim, "You—and those like you—are degraded." The moral order that sustains social life consists in equal measure of a system of abstract norms or rights and a social hierarchy; societies must protect the one no less than the other. Wrongdoing offends and puts into jeopardy both parts of that moral order.

It is Hegel who sees all parts of this equation most clearly, though also (characteristically) Hegel who expresses it most opaquely. Wrongdoing is, in the first place, he says, "negation of the right." That sounds on the level of abstract norms, rather than victims. But, as he also says, "a wrong committed against [the right] is a force directed against the existence . . . of *my freedom*," which undercuts "the universal and infinite element in the predicate 'mine'—i.e., in *my capacity for rights*."[41] That is to say, wrongdoing is at once a claim to the effect that "the right does not hold here" and a claim to the effect that "this person, the victim, is not a free person entitled to have his or her rights respected."

If crime is communication, who or what determines the content of what is communicated? Is it the intentions of the criminal (the crime means whatever he or she means by it)? I think this idea is more plausible than it might initially sound. Consider an argument in the street that escalates into a fight and then a beating. The person administering that beating might be acting so thoughtlessly that his mind carries no expressive content at all, but I'd guess that in many or even most instances the offender takes himself to be "telling" the victim and others who is in charge, means to express his hatred or condescension, and most of all means to let the world know that he is not cowed by the victim, by the prospect of a fight, or by the law. A lot of behavior carries deliberate expressive content—such as one person refusing to shake another's hand—and crime is no different. Having said this, however, I think it would be a mistake to focus too much on "authorial intent" in determining the communicative content of a crime. Meaning in general is intersubjective;

if one person refuses to shake another's hand for idiosyncratic reasons (maybe fear of germs), the act still carries the public meaning a culturally literate member of the community would assign it. As Hampton, who develops a Gricean account of crime's behavioral meaning, puts it, "[C]ertain behaviors have fixed conventional meanings, so that, for example, blowing a raspberry will be taken to convey disrespect in this society, even if one intended it as a compliment."[42]

Hegel has a distinctive contribution to make in this vein: he argues that crime's expressive character and the content of what it is expressing follow inexorably as soon as there exists a legal order. This feature of his thought is not to be found in his early chapter on criminal law, titled "Wrong." *The Philosophy of Right* is a book in three large parts, the first of which is about moral concepts in the abstract and the last of which is about embodied ethical life. The chapter on which most Hegel interpreters have focused, "Wrong," is in part I, which is problematic, because part I is not supposed to be anything more than conceptual analysis, and Hegel insists that philosophy must be more than conceptual analysis. It is important, then, to build into our understanding of Hegel's theory the material on crime and punishment in part III, which has a great deal to say about how actual legal systems function. Hegel's part III argument on crime and punishment is this: "Since property and personality have legal recognition and validity in civil society, *crime* is no longer an injury merely to a subjective infinite [that is, to an individual person],[43] but to the *universal* cause. . . . [T]he injury now affects the attitudes and consciousness of civil society, and not just the existence of the immediately injured party."[44] What is crucial here is the word "since": a society under a legal order effectively makes, Hegel thinks, certain claims to all. "There is a right to property here," it claims. "There is a right to physical security here." "There is a right to sexual autonomy here." To commit a theft is therefore necessarily to negate the claim, "There is a right to property here." To commit a rape is necessarily to negate the claim, "There is a right to sexual autonomy here." The expressive content of crime is therefore not a contingent matter—certainly not a matter of the criminal's (contingent) intentions, nor even a matter of society's (contingent) conventions—but necessarily fixed by the existence of the legal order. Perhaps in a state of nature, the meaning of a crime would be more open-ended, but in a legal order, the meaning of a crime is fixed by the existence of the law itself.

One advantage of reconstructivism's account of the nature of crime is that it provides a highly specified account of why crime does harm to society, rather than to the individual victim alone. Criminal theory relies on the idea that crime is a collective problem because criminal theory needs that claim to make sense of why criminal law is public law, but the idea is more often invoked than explained; the *reason* crimes harm society is hard to discern. The explanation most often given is that the risk of crime to future victims justifies a social response, but that rationale is problematic in two ways. First, it does not distinguish crimes from torts (more on that in a moment). Second, it does not treat society as a true collective (a collective unity) at all: society on this picture is just a set of individuals consisting of the actual victim and possible future victims. But if crimes harm *Sittlichkeit*, they harm a true collective good, for *Sittlichkeit* is both a common resource and a common product.

The contrast between crime and tort is useful here. Crimes are a matter of public law and torts are a matter of private law, and the reason cannot be (a) that torts are nonharmful (they are more reliably harmful than crimes because harm is an element of all torts); (b) that torts are nonwrongful (in a system that is generally negligence-based, which is to say fault-based, torts are civil wrongs); or (c) that torts are not a fit target for deterrence (deterrence is a major factor in tort law, even in defining negligence itself on the Hand formula). But most torts are negligent accidents, and what do negligent accidents *express*? Typically that "the author of this harm behaved stupidly," rather than "the author of this harm denies the claims of our moral culture." Merely negligent accidents do not greatly offend or threaten *Sittlichkeit*.[45] Crimes do. The one is concerned with a true collective good, while the other is not. It thus makes sense that criminal law should be public and tort law private.

III. WHAT PUNISHMENT IS FOR

I earlier argued that the expressive theory of punishment, though right about punishment's communicative function, is incomplete because it leaves *crime's* communicative character out of the equation. Turning now to punishment, the problem with expressivism is that the theory is on its terms wide open with respect to what punishment expresses. The reconstructive tradition, while agreeing with the expressive insight, is more specific; it insists that punishment does or should have a *particular* meaning. (The entailment relation is this: a punishment expressivist need not be a criminal law reconstructivist, but a criminal law reconstructivist must be a punishment expressivist.) The essential idea follows naturally from understanding what a crime is: if a crime says of the norm or right it violates, "This norm or right is insecure," and of the person it violates, "This person or this kind of person is not one whose rights need to be respected," and if in doing so the crime potentially puts both society's system of norms and its status hierarchy in jeopardy, what punishment must do is decisively reaffirm the violated norm and elevate the violated victim. Punishment is the communicative negation of the message of the crime. In a certain sense, punishment *falsifies* the claims made by the crime—not only declaring the crime to be morally wrongful but also making it, as a matter of social realities, descriptively untrue.

Hegel, for example, characteristically refers to punishment as "the cancellation of the crime" or "the nullity of this nullity" and holds that to thus cancel the crime, to punish, is "a restoration of right," a way of moving "through punishment . . . to affirmation, i.e., to morality."[46] That is, *contra* Bentham, punishment is not an evil that we accept to reduce the total stock of evil in the world over time. "The theory of punishment is one of the topics which have come off worst in the positive jurisprudence of recent times," for

> [i]f the crime and its cancellation . . . are regarded only as *evils* in general, one may well consider it unreasonable to will an evil merely *because another evil is already present*. This superficial character of an evil is the primary assumption in the various theories of punishment as prevention, as a deterrent, a threat, a corrective, etc.[47]

Punishment on any such theory is just violence in a good cause: "To justify punishment in this way is like raising one's stick at a dog; it means treating a human being like a dog instead of respecting his honor and freedom."[48] But to punish as an affirmation of morality is respectful of all, including the offender, and renders punishment not a *prima facie* evil but, where used appropriately to secure the right, simply the language in which one expresses a commitment to what is moral.

For Hegel, the normative logic of punishment—"the nullity of this nullity"—is abstract, a matter of conceptual entailment, and there is something off-putting in that: the context calls for theoretical sociology, not abstract logic.[49] But Durkheim fills this gap. For Durkheim, the normative logic of punishment is not conceptual but sociological and what punishment accomplishes is not necessarily a world in which the right prevails over the wrong (that could only happen in any case in societies that happen to have good values) but social solidarity: the "real function" of punishment, he says, "is to maintain inviolate the cohesion of society by sustaining the common consciousness in all its vigor," and "[t]he sole means of doing so is to give voice to the unanimous aversion that the crime continues to evoke, and this by an official act, which can only mean suffering inflicted upon the wrongdoer."[50] Punishment is therefore not "cruelty" but "a sign indicating that the sentiments of the collectivity are still unchanged."[51] Durkheim does not deny in the radical way that Hegel does that punishment might also and quite properly "intimidate possible imitators through threats,"[52] but deterrence "is neither the unique nor even the chief reason for punishment. For if it [punishment] had no other object, the functions it performs would be of altogether secondary importance, and one might well ask whether they are worth the quite considerable disadvantages."[53] Nor does Durkheim wholly deny that punishment might also "atone for the infraction,"[54] in the spirit of some forms of retributivism, by making the offender "expiate his crime through suffering,"[55] But though Durkheim finds something in this view "to hold onto," he thinks its functional inertness, its insistence that to punish is to do justice without regard to any end that punishment might serve, is ultimately mysticism. Punishment's chief function is "to buttress those consciences which violations of a rule can and must necessarily disturb in their faith—even though they themselves aren't aware of it; to show them that this faith continues to be justified."[56] Again, to appreciate this view, one must see that the threat infractions pose to a functioning morality is real: "[I]t is not punishment that gives discipline its authority; but it is punishment that prevents discipline from losing this authority, which infractions, if they went unpunished, would progressively erode."[57]

Hampton went through two phases in her understanding of what punishment is for, although both, I think, were tied to her instinct for the restoration of a violated normative order. In her early work on punishment as moral education, she argues that punishment not only sets up certain barriers but also "conveys a larger message to beings who are able to reflect on the reasons for these barriers' existence."[58] Human beings are reason-givers, and to effectively prevent wrongs in a community of reason-givers requires not just making wrongs costly but persuading people freely to reject them. Punishment is a "speech act":[59] it conveys to the wrongdoer that his or her action was "morally wrong and should not be done for that reason"[60] (*that* reason and not simply fear of the costs) and further, because the lesson is public, "it conveys an educative message not only to the convicted criminal but also to anyone else in the society who might be tempted to do what he did."[61] This is of course altogether consistent with the Durkheim of *On Moral Education* (though Hampton appears throughout her oeuvre to be unaware of Durkheim). Later in her career, however, after writing *Forgiveness and Mercy*, Hampton added to this picture what she came to call "an expressive theory of retribution."[62] "[H]uman behavior can carry meaning with regard to human values," she argues.[63] Where the meaning of that behavior constitutes "an affront to the victim's value or dignity,"[64] it warrants a response the nature of which is "to vindicate the value of the victim denied by the wrongdoer's action through the construction of an event that not only repudiates the action's message of superiority over the victim but does so in a way that confirms them as equal by virtue of their humanity."[65] Hampton at this point in her career understood this as a kind of retributive theory, separate from (though, she thought, not inconsistent with) the moral education theory she had previously expounded. But in fact, however labeled, they are part and parcel of the same essential ideas. Crime and punishment are on both theories an exchange of behaviorally encoded meanings concerning the value of persons and the moral authority of certain norms. Whether she knew it or not, both phases of her thought were reconstructive.

Reconstructivism's account of punishment, like its account of crime, fits organically into criminal law's character as public law. To the extent crime is harm-doing, punishment cannot undo the harm; it is a commonplace that punishing the murderer does not bring a loved one back to life. At most criminal law might reduce the incidences of harm in the future. But to the extent crime is a claim that the norm it violates is defunct, punishment can quite literally undo it; punishment makes that claim untrue. Likewise, to the extent crime is a claim that the person it violates is of lowered social status, punishment can literally undo it, because status is socially given and punishment is the social performance of the conviction that the victim merits better treatment. In other words, since the message of a crime is a social one—a proposal submitted to the community that can only become true if the community approves it—punishment, provided it is collective, genuinely undoes the crime. To be clear, while punishment cannot literally reverse the *individual harm* done by the crime, it can reverse the crime's *message*, because the message is a proposal about rights and victims that punishment proves false. This is why a mature system of criminal law must be public law. Private vengeance, even if just (and vengeance might be just), cannot by its nature accomplish this nullification. As Hegel puts it, the *content* of revenge "is just so far as it constitutes retribution. But in its *form* it is the action of a *subjective* will."[66] Public punishment is different, not because the emotions accompanying it are different (the emotions motivating the community and its officials are not at issue) but because it is public, because "[i]nstead of the injured party, the injured universal now makes its appearance, and it has its distinctive actuality in the court of law."[67] Insofar as punishment is filtered through public institutions discharging a public duty, the punishment does not just satiate private anger but affirms public right.

CONCLUSION

I began this chapter by suggesting a connection between *Sittlichkeit* and criminal theory, a connection that explains why theorists interested in the former end up writing about the latter and vice versa. The connection is this: the nature of criminal wrongdoing is that it violates and threatens *Sittlichkeit*, and the nature of criminal punishment is that it restores and protects *Sittlichkeit* in the wake of the crime. Punishment does so for the sake of social solidarity and because respect for the society's normative order and the worth of all persons, including both offender and victim, demands it.

NOTES

1. This chapter is an excerpt from a longer piece, the full version of which can be found in Joshua Kleinfeld, *Embodied Ethical Life and Criminal Law*, 129 HARV. L. REV. (forthcoming 2015).

2. For a fuller accounting of this rich tradition, see AXEL HONNETH, FREEDOM'S RIGHT: THE SOCIAL FOUNDATIONS OF DEMOCRATIC LIFE 1–11 (Joseph Ganahl, trans., 2014).

3. My focus below is on the two world-historic members of the tradition, Hegel and Durkheim, and, because she fills in an essential piece of the picture that might otherwise be missed, on Hampton—but not, in this piece, on Duff. Duff is a distinctive member of the reconstructive family in part because it is his mission to make reconstructive ideas about criminal law compatible with political liberalism. I both admire this project and have misgivings about it, but in either case, it means that his work requires an independent, article-length treatment, and that Hegel, Durkheim, and Hampton are more useful for getting at the basic structure of reconstructivism; Duff comes in at a later point in the theory-building.

4. GEORGE P. FLETCHER, RETHINKING CRIMINAL LAW, at xix (1978).

5. There are exceptions of course; to say that it is conventional to focus normatively on justifying punishment is not to say it is universal. *See, e.g.,* Nicola Lacey, *Normative Reconstruction in Socio-Legal Theory*, 5 SOC. & LEGAL STUD. 131 (1996) (endorsing a reconstructive rather than purely normative approach).

6. Utilitarianism can usefully be regarded as moral philosophy for people who think suffering is the most important feature of the moral world. JEREMY BENTHAM, AN INTRODUCTION TO THE PRINCIPLES OF MORALS AND LEGISLATION, at I.1, XV.2 (1780) ("Nature has placed mankind under the governance of two sovereign masters, *pain* and *pleasure.* It is for them alone to point out what we ought to do. . . . [A]ll punishment is mischief: all punishment in itself is evil. Upon the principle of utility, if it ought at all to be admitted, it ought only to be admitted in as far as it promises to exclude some greater evil").

7. CESARE BECCARIA, ON CRIMES AND PUNISHMENTS, at chap. 28 (1764) ("The punishment of death is pernicious to society, from the example of barbarity it affords").

8. Rehabilitative punishment might be thought of along different lines, but most criminal theorists agree that "hard treatment" is a component of punishment as such. *See, e.g.,* DOUGLAS HUSAK, OVERCRIMINALIZATION: THE LIMITS OF THE CRIMINAL LAW 57 (2008).

9. I say "ordinarily" because criminal law also encompasses *malum prohibitum* offenses, which are not special cases of wrongdoing.

10. *See* G.W.F. HEGEL, ELEMENTS OF THE PHILOSOPHY OF RIGHT, at I.3 (Allen W. Wood ed., H.B. Nisbet trans., 1991) (1820). Focusing exclusively on the "Wrong" chapter can lead Hegelian criminal theory in the wrong direction, as he touches again on criminal law (in a different way) later in the *Philosophy of Right*, III.2.B–C, as well as at other points in his career.

11. *See* HEGEL, ELEMENTS, *supra* note 10, at 25, § I ("Philosophy has to do with Ideas and therefore not with what are commonly described as *mere concepts*," where a "mere concept" is a noumenal thing and an "Idea" is a "concept . . . and its actualization").

12. *Id.* § 83.

13. *Id.* § 82.

14. EMILE DURKHEIM, THE DIVISION OF LABOR IN SOCIETY 31 (W.D. Halls, trans., 1984) (1893).

15. JEFFRIE G. MURPHY & JEAN HAMPTON, FORGIVENESS AND MERCY (1988).

16. *Id.* at 43.

17. Jean Hampton, *Correcting Harms Versus Righting Wrongs: The Goal of Retribution*, 39 UCLA L. REV. 1659, 1661 (1992).

18. *Id.*

19. *See, e.g.,* Michael S. Moore, *Liberty's Constraints on What Should Be Made Criminal*, *in* CRIMINALIZATION: THE POLITICAL MORALITY OF THE CRIMINAL LAW 182, 191 (R.A. Duff et al. eds., 2014).

20. *See, e.g.,* HUSAK, *supra* note 8.

21. Over the last five years, Duff has sponsored four volumes of work (his own and others) on criminalization: THE BOUNDARIES OF THE CRIMINAL LAW (R.A. Duff et al. eds., 2010), THE STRUCTURES OF THE CRIMINAL LAW (R.A. Duff et al. eds., 2011), THE CONSTITUTION OF THE

CRIMINAL LAW (R.A. Duff et al. eds., 2013), and CRIMINALIZATION: THE POLITICAL MORALITY OF THE CRIMINAL LAW (R.A. Duff et al. eds., 2014).

22. *See* HUSAK, *supra* note 8, at 58, 60.

23. JOEL FEINBERG, THE MORAL LIMITS OF THE CRIMINAL LAW, vol. I–IV (1986, 1988, 1989, 1990).

24. DURKHEIM, *supra* note 14, at 32–33.

25. *Id.* at 33.

26. *See, e.g.*, William J. Stuntz, *The Pathological Politics of Criminal Law*, 100 MICH. L. REV. 505, 508 (2001) ("American criminal law's historical development has borne no relation to any plausible normative theory—unless 'more' counts as a normative theory").

27. DURKHEIM, *supra* note 14, at 34.

28. *Id.* at 34.

29. *Id.* at 32.

30. *Id.* at 38–39.

31. *Id.* at 34.

32. *Id.* at 33.

33. Emile Durkheim, *Two Laws of Penal Evolution, in* DURKHEIM AND THE LAW (Steven Lukes & Andrew Scull eds., 1986) (1901).

34. DAVID GARLAND, PUNISHMENT AND MODERN SOCIETY: A STUDY IN SOCIAL THEORY 28, 60 (1990).

35. EMILE DURKHEIM, MORAL EDUCATION 165 (Everett K. Wilson ed., 1961) (1902–03).

36. MURPHY & HAMPTON, *supra* note 15, at 43–44.

37. *Id.* at 25.

38. *Id.* at 44.

39. *Id.*

40. *Id.* at 25

41. *See* HEGEL, ELEMENTS, *supra* note 10, at 10, § 95 (emphasis added).

42. Hampton, *supra* note 17, at 1676; *see also id.* at 1670 ("The analogies between the meaningfulness of language and the meaningfulness of behavior are striking enough that one can use the Gricean theory of linguistic meaning to distinguish different ways in which human conduct can be meaningful; and in what follows, I will employ Gricean categories in the course of explaining how wrongful conduct is meaningful").

43. Hegel uses this term, "subjective infinite," when he seeks to emphasize that individuals are dignity-bearing subjects. HEGEL, ELEMENTS, *supra* note 10.

44. *Id.* at 250, § 218.

45. Two notes are in order here. First, many torts—particularly intentional torts—overlap crimes. They are just the civil actions undertaken, separately from a criminal trial, to provide compensation to crime victims for any monetary loss caused by the crime. Second, although there are crimes based on negligence just as there are torts based on negligence, the two departments of law do not use the same definition of negligence. Tortious negligence involves merely deviating from a reasonable person standard of care; criminal negligence typically involves gross disregard for the well-being of others. Where a tort is committed that involves criminal levels of negligence, it might well overlap with a crime.

46. *Id.* at 124, 132, §§ 99, 218.

47. *Id.* at 124, § 99.

48. *Id.* at 125, § 99.

49. In fairness to Hegel, I emphasize again that at this point in *The Philosophy of Right* he only means to engage in conceptual analysis; the sociology comes later.

50. DURKHEIM, *supra* note 14, at 63.

51. *Id.*

52. DURKHEIM, *supra* note 35, at 167.

53. *Id.* at 161.

54. *Id.* at 164.

55. *Id.* at 167.

56. *Id.*

57. *Id.*

58. Jean Hampton, *The Moral Education Theory of Punishment*, 13 PHIL. & PUB. AFFAIRS 208, 212 (1984).
59. *Id.* at 215.
60. *Id.* at 212.
61. *Id.*
62. Hampton, *supra* note 17, at 1659.
63. *Id.* at 1670.
64. *Id.* at 1666.
65. *Id.* at 1686.
66. HEGEL, ELEMENTS, *supra* note 10, at 130, § 102 (emphasis added).
67. *Id.* at 252, § 220.

Chapter Three

What Are the Sexual Offenses?

Stuart P. Green[1]

INTRODUCTION

Our law criminalizes a broad array of sexual, and sex-related, conduct. Among the offenses that do this (or did until recently) are rape, sexual assault, coercion, human sex trafficking, female genital mutilation, forced marriage, sexual humiliation, voyeurism, public nudity and public indecency, sexual transmission of disease, selling and buying sexual services (prostitution), pimping and pandering, statutory rape and child molestation, abuse of position of trust, child grooming, creating and possessing child pornography, revenge porn, failure to register as a sex offender, fornication, sodomy, adultery, assault by sadomasochism, adult and child incest, bigamy, polygamy, miscegenation, bestiality, necrophilia, and sale of sex toys.

While many of these offenses, taken separately, have generated a significant body of analysis, there have been relatively few attempts to look at the category of sexual offenses systematically, across the board. In this chapter, I intend to take a first step in considering the sexual offenses as a whole by seeking to define the category itself. Specifically, I will address two basic issues.

First, given the wide range of conduct that is covered, what exactly is to be gained by looking at the sexual offenses as a whole? I will argue, among other things, that many of these offenses, whether consensual, nonconsensual, or aconsensual, make use of, or rely on, the same set of basic concepts (including "sexual conduct," "consent," and "autonomy") and ultimately reflect an interlocking set of common legal interests, rights, duties, harms, and wrongs. Looking at how the concepts are used in one context may yield insights about their application in a different, related context.

Second, what, if anything, distinguishes the sexual offenses from other kinds of criminal offenses? I will argue that there is no one set of necessary and sufficient conditions that defines the category and thereby distinguishes sex crimes from other kinds of crime. Rather, we need to look to several overlapping forms of prohibitions: on one or more kinds of socially disfavored sexual acts; on conduct that is presumed to be preparatory of, or conducive to, future (illicit) sexual acts; and on conduct that, though it does not involve sex as such, nevertheless infringes on some aspect of another's right to sexual autonomy. Part of the challenge here will be to say what it means for conduct to be "sexual" and what distinguishes sexual autonomy from other forms of autonomy.

I. WHY CONSIDER THE RANGE OF SEXUAL OFFENSES AS A WHOLE?

The offenses listed earlier involve an extraordinarily wide range of conduct. What can legal theory hope to gain by looking at the sexual offenses as a whole? Let me suggest three reasons for doing so: To begin with, the category has real doctrinal significance. There are extensive collections of criminal statutes in Anglo-American law labeled as "sexual offenses," as well as provisions that subject a wide range of "sex offenders" to registration and notice requirements, under which those convicted of offenses as diverse as rape, incest, bestiality, voyeurism, and indecent exposure are all subject to the same regulatory regime.[2] Determining what these offenses have in common is thus essential to determining whether such regimes make sense.

A second reason for this comprehensive approach is that, from a historical perspective, the sexual offenses can be said to have "grown up together." The offenses were, and to some extent still are, largely complementary; they work in combination to define the limits of permissible sexual conduct. For example, in an era in which the only kind of sex officially valued by society was consensual, marital, vaginal intercourse, it may well have made sense that the only sort of act treated as rape was forced, nonmarital, vaginal intercourse, and that almost everything else was treated as criminal—typically, as fornication or sodomy—whether or not it was consensual.[3] What constituted rape was also dependent on what constituted seduction; what constituted statutory rape was dependent on what constituted incest; and what constituted prostitution was dependent on what constituted sodomy (and vice versa). Today, as society's sense of what kinds of sexual activity constitute a "legitimate" and "acceptable" means of expressing one's sexuality has evolved and broadened, to include not just marital intercourse but a wide range of other forms of sexual activity as well, it is not surprising that the definition of what constitutes rape or sexual assault, as well as incest and prostitution, would continue to broaden and evolve as well. Nor is it surprising that offenses like fornication, sodomy, and adultery would have virtually disappeared from the scene.

Finally, and perhaps most fundamentally, the offenses that make up this category of crime share a common set of conceptual building blocks, which ultimately reflect an interlocking set of legal interests that cut across the consensual and nonconsensual offenses. For example, we need to have a coherent conception of *sexual conduct* in order to define both presumptively nonconsensual offenses like abuse of position and child incest as well as presumptively consensual offenses like adult incest and prostitution. Similarly, we need to know what *sexual autonomy* is and how it can be infringed in order to understand both why rape is a crime and why fornication and sodomy, and perhaps sadomasochism, no longer should be. And we need to understand the nature of *consent* to explain the criminalization not just of rape, but also of statutory rape and bestiality. More generally, consideration of the sexual offenses can help us understand why certain kinds of sexual interests and behaviors are highly valued, and worthy of legal protection, while others continue to be reviled and even feared, and are arguably worthy of legal condemnation.

II. DEFINING THE SEXUAL OFFENSES

To determine what should count as a "sexual offense," we will certainly want to consider how the issue is addressed in positive law. But it would be a mistake simply to survey the existing statutes, list the sex offenses, and consider the question answered. We need to know what the sexual offenses have in common, and how they differ from nonsexual offenses. We need an approach that will give us a basis for evaluating schemes across different jurisdictions. We need some external criteria for deciding whether the classification of sexual offenses in a given system is overinclusive or underinclusive.[4] Are there offenses that should be regarded as sexual offenses that are not generally included on the list? Are there offenses that are regularly included on the list that should be excluded?

Although I will rely on existing sexual offense provisions as a starting point for analysis, that is no more than a start. It will be necessary to draw out certain salient features that such offenses have in common. These features can then be used as a basis on which to go back and assess whether particular existing offenses are in fact properly thought of as sexual offenses after all. In attempting to develop a coherent and principled understanding of the norms that inform the sexual offenses, it will often be necessary not only to describe the various approaches the law takes but also to advocate for a conception that departs from one or more prevailing formulations. The project can thus be thought of as a kind of "normative reconstruction," in which (as Neil MacCormick put it) we attempt to "dismantle" legal sources and make them "comprehensible," "imaging and describing . . . the found order," and deciding what fits into a "coherent whole," and what needs to be "discarded or abandoned or at least revised."[5]

A. The Sexual Offenses as an Umbrella Category

So what should count as a sexual offense? I am skeptical (because I have tried) that we could ever find a meaningful set of necessary and sufficient conditions that would cover every offense that has a plausible claim to being classified as such. We could say, in general terms, that an offense should be regarded as "sexual" if and only if it criminalizes sexual or sex-related activity, but that definition seems too conclusory and circular to be of much use. A better approach would be to think of the sexual offenses as a kind of umbrella category that links a collection of at least three, partially overlapping subcategories of offenses, all of which criminalize sex-related activity.

One central subgroup of sexual offenses involves the prohibition of one or more kinds of sexual conduct. This is true of nonconsensual offenses such as rape, sexual assault, statutory rape, and abuse of position of trust, as well as consensual or arguably consensual offenses such as fornication, adultery, prostitution, sodomy, adult incest, sadomasochism, bestiality, and necrophilia. As we shall see next, the manner in which the prohibited sexual conduct is defined varies significantly from offense to offense. In some cases, it is defined with almost clinical specificity; other times, it is left vague or is entirely implicit. In some cases, sex functions as a necessary conceptual element of the conduct prohibited, while elsewhere it seems to be merely contingent.

A second group comprises sexual offenses that prohibit conduct that is presumed to be preparatory of, or conducive to, future (illicit) sexual conduct. Offenses of this type include solicitation, pandering, child grooming, bigamy, polygamy, failing to register as a sex offender, and (the English offense of) administering a substance with intent to commit a sexual offense. As is the case with other "preventive justice"–type criminal statutes, one of the concerns about such offenses is whether the conduct prohibited by such provisions is too attenuated from the supposed harms sought to be prevented to justify criminalization.[6]

A third, also highly significant, way in which sexual offense statutes can function is by prohibiting conduct that infringes on some aspect of another's right to what I shall tentatively refer to as sexual autonomy. In many cases, prohibiting conduct of this sort also involves the prohibition of a sexual act (as in the case of the first category of offenses). Indeed, the reason the acts underlying rape and sexual assault are prohibited is precisely because they infringe on others' rights to sexual autonomy. Other autonomy-infringing offenses, such as voyeurism (involving the infringement of a victim's right to sexual privacy), indecent exposure and obscenity (infringing a victim's right to avoid witnessing others' sexuality), and necrophilia (which arguably involves an infringement of a victim's presumed posthumous right to sexual autonomy), also require the performance of a sexual act. There are some cases, however, in which a victim's right to sexual autonomy is infringed in the absence of a sexual act. This is true, for example, of female genital mutilation, which infringes on a victim's future ability to enjoy sex, though it involves no sexual act per se. There are also cases, as we shall see, in which an offender satisfies the elements of rape or sexual assault by engaging in conduct that, though it infringes on a victim's sexual autonomy, does not necessarily qualify as "sexual."

B. Sex as a Type, Rather Than Token

Under my account, an offense will be sexual only if sex plays a role in how it is defined (as a type), rather than how it is carried out at the level of a token. For example, John Hinckley was alleged to have attempted to assassinate President Reagan out of an erotomanic fixation on the actor Jodie Foster.[7] Even though Hinckley's crime arguably involved an act that was sexual (at least to him), it would not qualify as a sexual offense on my account, since the offense which was committed—attempted murder—is not defined in a way that implicates sexual interests. The same would be true of a case in which an offender stole a sex toy, a bottle of Viagra, or even sexual services (from a prostitute).

For similar reasons, I would exclude from my account violent assaults not specifically aimed at reducing or eliminating sexual capacity, but which have such an incidental effect. For example, the shooting of pornographer Larry Flynt by white supremacist serial killer (and recently executed) Joseph Paul Franklin was intended to kill Flynt, but ended up causing him, apparently, to lose his ability to have an erection (as well as walk). Unlike female genital mutilation, which is specifically intended to reduce the victim's sexual capacity and pleasure, and therefore properly regarded as a sexual offense, Franklin's shooting of Flynt does not qualify as such, since it did not have such a specific purpose.

III. DEFINING SEXUAL CONDUCT

In the remainder of this chapter, I will be concerned primarily with offenses that fall into the first subcategory identified previously—namely, offenses involving the prohibition of one or more forms of sexual conduct. I thus leave to the side offenses that do not involve sexual conduct as such but instead involve conduct that is preparatory of future sexual conduct (such as child grooming) and offenses that involve an infringement of a victim's right to sexual autonomy (such as female genital mutilation).[8] I also defer until later in the chapter a discussion of offenses in which sex plays a role as a form of identity rather than as a form of conduct.

Defining the sexual offenses partly in terms of prohibited sexual conduct raises an even more fundamental question: namely, what should count as *sexual conduct* in the first place? Although I acknowledged what I regarded as the futility of trying to find a set of necessary and sufficient conditions that define the class of sexual *offenses*, I am more sanguine about the possibility of finding a set of necessary and sufficient conditions that define the class of sexual *conduct*. Moreover, more is at stake here from a practical perspective: Unless we have some clear criteria for defining sexual conduct per se, we will have difficulty in saying what constitutes sexual conduct in more specific cases—such as when it is forced (as in sexual assault), performed with someone other than one's spouse (as in adultery), bought and sold (as in prostitution), or performed with an animal or corpse (as in bestiality and necrophilia, respectively).[9]

A. "Sexual Conduct" versus "Having Sex"

For a start, I would distinguish between "sexual conduct" and "having sex." Consider in this connection an empirical study published in 1999, not long after Bill Clinton implied, in grand jury testimony, that he had not "ha[d] sex" with Monica Lewinsky (who, it turns out, had fellated, but apparently not had intercourse with, him). In the study, approximately six hundred American college students were asked what kinds of behaviors they would regard as "having sex."[10] (Specifically, they were asked, "Would you say you 'had sex' with someone if the most intimate behavior you engaged in was . . . (mark yes or no for each behavior).") While there were some modest differences between the responses of men and women, a basic hierarchy emerged: More than 99 percent said they would be "having sex" if they had engaged in penile-vaginal intercourse; 81 percent, penile-anal intercourse; 40 percent, oral contact with genitals; 15 percent, having a person touch the genitals; and less than 5 percent, oral or digital contact with breasts or nipples, or deep kissing.

The authors concede that their study does not explain the reasoning behind these responses.[11] But we can speculate: Perhaps the young subjects in the study were thinking about whether they could engage in such contact and still, for better or worse, consider themselves virgins. Perhaps they were concerned with issues of "fidelity" to boyfriends or girlfriends. Perhaps their answers varied depending on their sexual orientation. In assessing their responses, it would be helpful to know what the subjects understood as the costs and benefits (to their mental health, self-esteem, reputation among their peers, and the like) of labeling some behavior as "having sex." Would their answers have differed if they had been asked to make judgments about the conduct of others, rather than themselves? What if the person they were making a judgment about was their own regular sexual partner, who had been intimate with a third party? Would it matter if the conduct was performed in the context of a "hook-up" or "one-night stand" rather than in a long-term relationship? What assumptions did the subjects make based on the minimal description of the conduct given? Did the subjects assume that the contact was consensual? Would their answers have differed if they had been told that they had been forced or tricked or coerced into having such contact?

I expect to return to studies of this sort in future work, but for the moment, three points are worth making: First, while common or conventional usage is worth considering, it can hardly be viewed as conclusive in critical projects of this sort. Second, in deciding what constitutes "sexual conduct," context and audience matter. Perhaps the subject students' answers to the question "would you say you 'had sex'" would have differed had it been posed in some forum other than a social science study—say, by a doctor taking a medical history or in a late night dormitory "bull session." Third, and more specifically, the terms "having sex" and "sexual conduct" almost certainly refer to different phenomena: "Having sex" is commonly understood as a euphemism for sexual intercourse, and as such is best understood as a (centrally important and in some respects preeminent) subset of what I shall now suggest is the broader category of "sexual conduct."

B. Previous Accounts of Sexual Conduct

Historically, theorists have been concerned less with the question "what is sex" or "what is sexual conduct" than with what is "natural" or "normal" or "morally worthwhile" sex or sexual conduct. And they have invariably answered this second question in terms of one or another purpose or end—whether it is procreation, love, communication, pleasure, or something else.[12] Judeo-Christian authorities have historically defined sex in terms of procreation: human beings are commanded to be fruitful and multiply.[13] Activity that is directed toward that end, and performed within the framework of marriage, was regarded as normal or natural sex. Other conduct was considered deviant, perverse, or unnatural. Thus, for commentators such as Augustine and Aquinas, the question of what constitutes sex was driven by what were essentially normative considerations.

Modern, secular scholars have tended to focus on goals other than procreation. For example, Roger Scruton's theory of sex focused on notions of intimacy, love, and "mutuality of desire," while Thomas Nagel's focused on sex as a kind of language—a complex, multilayered process of mutual perception and arousal.[14] Conduct that failed to achieve, or at least aim at, such ends—for Scruton, masturbation and bestiality; for Nagel, voyeurism and sadomasochism—was considered suboptimal, or even perverse. For present purposes, however, such a means-end approach presents problems. Although a comprehensive theory of the sexual offenses will at some point need to deal with the concept of "deviant sex," our more immediate concern is with defining the larger category of "sex," of which "natural" and "unnatural" sex must logically be subsets.

One particularly influential response to the more general "what is sex" question is provided by Alan Goldman.[15] Goldman says that we should define sex on its own terms, rather than as a means to something else. According to Goldman's definition, "sexual desire is desire for contact with another person's body and for the pleasure which such contact produces; sexual activity is activity which tends to fulfill such desire of the agent."[16] Although Goldman's approach lacks the limitations of Scruton's and Nagel's, it nevertheless presents problems of its own. First, despite Goldman's disavowal of a teleological approach, it appears that his approach is itself framed in terms of a means to an end—that is, having contact with another's body *as a means to* pleasure. Second, Goldman's approach to defining sexual activity seems to apply to conduct that should not properly be regarded as sexual; as such, it is overinclusive. Goldman himself voices concern about cases such as contact sports and cuddling with a baby. Goldman concedes that both involve having contact with another's body as a means to pleasure, but maintains that "the desire is not for contact with another body per se, it is not directed toward a particular person for that purpose, and it is not the goal of the activity."[17] In the case of contact sports, the goal is "winning or exercising or knocking someone down or displaying one's prowess." In the case of cuddling with a baby, the goal is to demonstrate "affection, tenderness, or security."[18]

Perhaps. But even if Goldman is right about contact sports and baby cuddling, there remains the problem of (ordinary, non–"happy ending") massage, which Goldman himself does not consider. Surely, getting a massage is an "activity which tends to fulfill" the "desire for contact with another person's body and for the pleasure which such contact produces." And while massage can certainly have therapeutic value, it is hard to deny that the basic point of a massage is the pleasure of physical contact. So, either massage is a form of sexual activity or Goldman's account is too broad.

Third, Goldman's physical-contact-leading-to-pleasure definition of sexual activity is also *under*inclusive, inasmuch as it requires a (1) touching of (2) another person. There are some kinds of presumptively sexual activity that do not involve touching: think of phone sex, voyeurism, exhibitionism, viewing pornography, and even perhaps flirting. There are also forms of presumptively sexual activity that do not necessarily involve another person, such as masturbation, and, again, viewing pornography.

Goldman himself recognizes the difficulty his definition of sexual activity has in applying to such conduct. His solution is an awkward one:

> While looking at or conversing with someone can be interpreted as sexual in given contexts it is so when intended as preliminary to, and hence parasitic upon, elemental sexual interests. Voyeurism or viewing a pornographic movie qualifies as a sexual activity, but only as an imaginative substitute for the real thing. . . . The same is true of masturbation as a sexual activity without a partner.[19]

I am not sure I really understand what Goldman means when he says that certain kinds of activity "qualif[y]" as sexual activities, but only as "imaginative substitute[s] for the real thing." It seems to me that masturbation and pornography viewing are such ubiquitous activities that they should be able to stand on their own as discrete forms of sexual behavior. It seems odd, in other words, to insist that "real" sex necessarily involves physical contact with a partner when so much sex-like behavior seems to involve neither.

C. A Subjective Approach to Defining Sexual Activity

So far, I have criticized Goldman's hedonic account of sex on the grounds that it would include presumptively nonsexual activities like massage, and exclude, or at least downgrade to "substitutes," presumptively sexual activities like masturbation, viewing pornography, voyeurism, phone sex, and flirting. Can I offer an account that is more consistent with common usage?

I agree with Goldman that the definition of sex should be closely tied to the notion of pleasure, but I would propose two major changes to his account. Goldman says that "sexual desire is desire for contact with another person's body and for the pleasure which such contact produces." I would modify this to say that *sexual desire is desire for sexual pleasure; sexual activity is activity that tends to fulfill such desire of the agent*. I would thus (1) eliminate the requirement that desire be for contact with another person's body, and (2) specify that sexual desire is desire for *sexual* pleasure.

So what do I mean by sexual pleasure? Is it not circular to define sexual "desire" as a desire for sexual "pleasure"? How exactly would my account distinguish the pleasure of a lover's caress from the pleasure of a massage therapist's effleurage?

I would say that the difference between massage and a lover's caress is a phenomenological one, a matter of how each activity is perceived. Unlike massager and massagee, caresser and caressee (ordinarily) feel sexually aroused. Moreover, such subjective feelings of arousal typically manifest themselves in a range of objectively measurably ways. In men, arousal typically involves the swelling and erection of the penis and changes in hormone levels. In women, sexual arousal involves vaginal wetness, swelling and engorgement of external genitals, internal enlargement of the vagina, and increases in testosterone levels. Other changes include an increase in heart rate and blood pressure, a feeling of being hot and flushed. Evidence of sexual arousal has also been observed in images of the amygdala and hypothalamus.[20] This is not to say that every sexual thought, image, or activity will trigger all of these responses in all people, or that these physical symptoms cannot in some unusual cases result from nonsexual feelings.[21] It is only to recognize that there is an unmistakable subjective feeling that virtually everyone can recognize as sexual. And as neuroscience progresses, it will increasingly be possible to observe the neural bases on which such feelings supervene. Under this approach, what is perceived as sexual *is* sexual.[22]

If I am right, this would explain why neither massage nor baby cuddling should normally qualify as sex. Though physically pleasurable, neither of these activities is typically attended by the subjective feeling or physiological indicators of sexual activity.

My account would also eliminate Goldman's requirements of touching and sharing. The question here is largely a definitional one. We could say, along with Goldman, that masturbation and viewing pornography are merely "imaginative substitutes" for genuine sexual contact; and at some level that is certainly true. But it seems likely that masturbation and pornography viewing often involve subjective feelings and physiological responses that are similar to those experienced during intercourse, foreplay, and other shared forms of sexual contact and its precursors.

Another advantage of the subjective approach is that it allows us to account for objects and situations that are not normally regarded as sexual, but which evoke an idiosyncratic sexual response in one or more persons—such as fetishes and paraphilia. Often, these involve everyday objects and situations that are not thought of as sexual by the general public—say, running shoes, or frotteurism—but become viewed as sexual by some individuals. When these objects and situations trigger a sexual response, it makes sense to think of them as sexual.

This, in turn, brings us back to cases like that involving John Hinckley. On my account, Hinckley's shooting of Reagan *was* a sexual act, since it presumably felt sexual to him. But this does *not* necessarily mean that his act should be classified as a sexual offense. Classification of crimes occurs at the level of types, not tokens, and involves generalizations about the harms and wrongs that such conduct typically entails. We could decide that homicides motivated by sexual motives posed such a distinctive set of wrongs and harms that they should be classified as sexual offenses.[23] But I am not aware of any jurisdictions having done so to date.

D. Nonpleasurable Sex

If I am correct that conduct should be regarded as sexual if and only if it tends to fulfill the desire for sexual pleasure, we then face a question concerning the status of some sex-like conduct (including some that is important in the realm of the sexual offenses) that does not involve pleasure for one or both parties.

Consider first the case of prostitution. One can easily imagine that, while sexual contact with a prostitute tends to fulfill *customers'* desire for sexual pleasure, it does not normally serve the same function for prostitutes themselves. If that is so, it would seem to point to the possibility that intercourse could constitute sexual activity for the former, but not for the latter. And perhaps that is the right to think about such cases. Alternatively, we might consider amending the definition offered here to say that "sexual desire is desire for sexual pleasure," and that "sexual activity is activity that tends to fulfill such desire of the agent *or the agent's partner*."

Rape presents an even more puzzling case. Let us assume not only that very few, if any, victims of rape derive sexual pleasure from the act of intercourse or other putative sexual activity but also that there are cases in which the rapist himself also derives no sexual pleasure from the act.[24] For example, consider a recent case in which soldiers in Congo engaged in the atrocity of torturing a young woman by ramming a small tree into her vagina.[25] Because the perpetrators had taken drugs that made them temporarily incapable of having an erection, it is possible that they had no intention to achieve sexual gratification. Their victims, needless to say, also derived no sexual pleasure from the act. On my account, this would likely not constitute a sexual act. It would, however, constitute a sexual offense, since the horrific act obviously violated the women's sexual autonomy and was clearly intended to inflict humiliation of a specifically sexual (and especially grotesque) sort.

IV. SEXUAL CONDUCT IN SEXUAL OFFENSES

The question of what constitutes sexual conduct turns out to be quite relevant within the context of the sexual offenses. Many offenses specifically enumerate those activities that will be considered "sexual." Others leave that determination to the finder of fact, based on the defendant's motives or intent.

A. Sexual Offences Act 2003

A good example is provided by the United Kingdom's Sexual Offences Act 2003, which on some occasions enumerates specific activities that will be regarded as sexual and on other occasions leaves that determination to the finder of fact.[26] Consider Section 4, which makes it a crime to cause a person to engage in "sexual activity" without consent. "Sexual activity" in turn is defined quite explicitly. It consists of penetration of the victim's anus or vagina, penetration of the victim's mouth with a person's penis, penetration of a person's anus or vagina with a part of the victim's body or by the victim with anything else, or penetration of a person's mouth with the victim's penis. This provision of the statute could hardly be more specific or categorical about what kinds of "sexual activity" are covered.

What constitutes "sexual activity" in other provisions of the act, however, is defined in a much less categorical manner. For example, the offense of sexual assault (Section 3) criminalizes nonconsensual touching of any part of the victim's body with any part of the offender's body or with anything else, provided that the "the touching is sexual." A touching would, in turn, be considered "sexual" "if a reasonable person would consider that" it was of a sexual "nature" or that its "circumstances" or "purpose" were sexual.[27]

So what does it mean for a touching to be of a sexual nature, have a sexual purpose, or occur in sexual circumstances? To decide that, I would apply something like the test articulated above. I would ask whether the activity is of the sort that a reasonable person would think "tends to fulfill" the "desire for sexual pleasure."

Consider in this context the English case of *Court*.[28] The defendant ("*D*") pulled the victim ("*V*"), a twelve-year-old girl, across his knees and smacked her buttocks with his hand through her shorts. Had *V* been a parent or schoolmaster, he might have been doing so for nonsexual, disciplinary purposes. But in the actual case, *D* was a store clerk and *V* was a customer, and when asked by the police why he had done what he did, *D* admitted that he had a "buttock fetish." For this reason, *D* was held to have had a "sexual" motive, and therefore to have committed indecent assault. This seems to me the right result.

Now contrast the case of *Tabassum*.[29] *D* carried out what may have been genuine research into breast cancer, aware that women he examined mistakenly assumed he was a medical doctor. The court held that their mistake vitiated the women's consent and that, even assuming the research was genuine and done without a sexual motive, the examinations were inherently sexual and therefore constituted indecent sexual assaults rather than mere assault.

I am skeptical that the reasoning in *Tabassum* is correct. Though obviously wrongful, touching a woman's breast for the purpose of unconsented-to medical research does not appear to qualify as a sexual act. It is not an activity that tends to fulfill the desire for sexual pleasure. Indeed, there are many acts that involve contact with "sexual" bodily parts that are not, in the normal course of things, sexual. These include not only medical research involving such body parts but also certain therapeutic acts (such as gynecological exams, urological exams, mammograms, and certain forms of surgery), and perhaps certain kinds of "hands on" sex education.[30] Touching those parts without informed consent is certainly a violation of the victim's rights to bodily autonomy, but it does not seem to be a violation of any specifically sexual rights.

B. Sex as a Necessary or Contingent Element

Another question that needs to be asked about the role sexual conduct plays in defining various sexual offenses concerns the extent to which the sexual nature of such conduct is necessary, or merely contingent. In some cases, the infringement of a right to sexual autonomy serves to inform the offense and distinguish it from otherwise similar nonsexual crimes. For example, sexual assault differs from other assaults in the particular wrongs it entails; unjustifiably touching someone who does not want to be touched is morally wrong, but forcing someone to engage in sexual contact is almost invariably treated as a distinct offense. Female genital mutilation follows a similar pattern; although non-lethal mutilation involving nonsexual organs is a very serious crime, mutilation of the sexual organs has physiological and psychological effects on a victim's life that are distinctive, and for this reason female genital mutilation deserves to be treated as a distinct offense. Offensive exposure of any sort can make observers uncomfortable, but indecent exposure that involves sex arguably involves a distinctive kind of wrong. As Joel Feinberg explains, "Nudity and sex acts have an irresistible power to draw the eye and focus the thoughts on matters that are normally repressed."[31] When a person forces others to witness his nudity or sexual activity, he forces them to be a kind of unwilling "participant" in his sex life. Similarly, all voyeurism involves an infringement of the victim's privacy, but voyeurism that intrudes on a victim's sexual privacy is arguably distinctive and worthy of specialized legislation. Sex is an inherently and quintessentially private act. For most people, nothing is more likely to extinguish sexual desire and even induce shame than the realization that one's sexual activities are being spied on.[32] And though there are many ways for teachers, coaches, and clergy to exploit the young people over whom they have authority, using their position to obtain sex seems especially wrongful and therefore worthy of special criminalization.

But there is also a range of offenses that, though sometimes classified as sexual, prove, on inspection, to be only contingently so. For example, using sex to transmit disease is wrongful, but it is not clear that it is qualitatively worse than doing so by means of a (nonsexual) blood transfusion, provided that both underlying acts are voluntary, or involuntary, as the case may be.[33] Necrophilia is also typically classified as a sex offense, but I am skeptical that corpse desecration involving sex is qualitatively different from nonsexual forms of corpse desecration, such as dismemberment. And to the extent that bestiality is properly thought of as a form of cruelty to animals, it is not clear that it should be viewed as involving a form of cruelty that is qualitatively different from subjecting an animal to beating, abandonment, or confinement.

V. THINKING ABOUT SEX NORMATIVELY

So far we have been considering the sexual offenses mainly in definitional terms: we have been looking in particular at the role that sexual conduct plays in defining such offenses. Now, I want to say a bit about why the sexual offenses are deserving of a distinct place in the criminal code.

A. The Value of Sex

Sex, of course, plays a highly valued role in our lives. Many people regard the decisions whether, when, how, and with whom to have sex to be among the most meaningful kinds of choice they must make.[34] A major reason sex is so valued is that it holds the potential for a range of significant benefits that ordinarily cannot be obtained by other means. Without sexual intercourse, of course, most people (or at least those without access to costly technologies such as in vitro fertilization and artificial insemination) could not reproduce, and under evolutionary theory, we would expect human beings to place a priority on controlling their reproductive autonomy.[35] Sex also provides significant hedonistic benefits—both as a relief from the carnal demands of sexual desire, and in what Richard Posner has called the more refined sense of "*ars erotica*, the deliberate cultivation of the faculty of sexual pleasure; the analogy is to cultivating a taste for fine music or fine wine."[36] Finally, and perhaps most complexly, sex can satisfy deep-seated needs for human connection, intimacy, and communication (as well as, in some cases, for domination and submission).

Simply tabulating the many benefits of sex, however, probably doesn't fully account for the importance we place on it in our lives. For one thing, not all sexual acts produce these benefits equally. Obviously, only sexual intercourse has the potential for procreation; and only certain kinds of sexual activity performed with a partner hold the potential for human connection and intimacy. Yet, even those sexual acts with few clear benefits are still considered to be within the realm of privileged conduct. As Foucault and others have observed, there seems to be something about sexual conduct and sexual identity that, at least in our era, helps us define our most basic sense of self.[37]

B. Hierarchies in Sexual Conduct

Given the wide range of activities that would qualify as sexual on my account, it is worth asking whether, within the category of sexual conduct, some activities should be regarded as more central or highly valued than others. The answer to that question, of course, will depend on the criteria by which such acts are judged. Some sexual acts are more conducive than others to pleasure, intimacy, procreation, communication, or other goals. In a system that judged the value of a given sexual act by its ability to produce X, those sexual activities that produced more X would be judged as more valuable than those that produced less.

These judgments are important because they affect not only how we choose to conduct some of the most important aspects of our lives, but also how we classify and grade the sexual offenses, and whether various offenses should be crimes to begin with. In the case of nonconsensual sexual offenses such as rape and sexual assault, we can observe the following pattern: the more central or significant or highly valued the form of sex in which *V* is compelled to participate, the greater the infringement, and, consequently, the more serious the offense.[38] For a variety of reasons—cultural, physiological, hedonic, and historical—sexual intercourse seems to enjoy a special moral and legal status. It typically involves a higher level of intimacy than, say, kissing or fondling.[39] So forcing *V* to have sexual intercourse will normally be viewed as entailing a more wrongful and harmful act than forcing *V* to submit to a kiss or caress.

In the case of consensual or aconsensual sexual offenses, such as voluntary adult incest and sadomasochism, a different sort of pattern exists. Here, we might say that, the more valuable the form of prohibited sex is to its practitioner, the greater we would expect the burden on the government to justify the prohibition.

VI. SEX AS A FORM OF IDENTITY

To this point, the discussion has focused on offenses that criminalize a collection of human behaviors we refer to as "sexual" as well as infringements of autonomy rights associated with such behavior. But there is another important sense of the word *sex* that also needs to be considered. In addition to referring to activities that hold the potential to produce a distinctive form of pleasure, the term also refers to an aspect of a person's identity typically defined by a suite of biological differences (including differences in chromosomes, hormonal profiles, and internal and external sex organs) and which mark a person out as male or female.[40] This duality of meaning—between sex as an activity or subject of autonomy, on the one hand, and sex as an aspect of identity, on the other—leads us to ask if the concept of sexual offenses should be understood to include not only offenses that relate to sexual activity or autonomy but also offenses that relate to a person's sex (in the sense of being male or female).

A couple of examples will help illustrate what I have in mind: First, consider a provision in Israel's innovative Prevention of Sexual Harassment Law, which makes it a crime, inter alia, to make "an intimidating or humiliating reference directed towards a person concerning his sex."[41] Second, imagine that, in response to a rash of misogynistic killings of women, a law was enacted making it a crime to kill someone "because of their sex."[42] Should such laws be classified as sexual offenses despite the fact that they make reference only to a person's identity as male or female, and not to her sexual conduct or sexual autonomy? The question is one that goes to the heart of how we conceive of the sexual offenses. It will not be possible to resolve the issue definitively here, but I would like to offer some preliminary thoughts on how it should be approached.

A closely analogous (if converse) question arises in the context of the American (civil) law of sexual harassment and sexual discrimination. Title VII of the Civil Rights Act of 1964 states that it "shall be an unlawful . . . to discriminate against any individual . . . *because of such individual's* race, color, religion, *sex*, or national origin."[43] By referring to discrimination on the basis of an "individual's . . . sex," it seems obvious that the statute is intended, at least in the first instance, to prohibit discrimination based on the fact that a person is male or female, in the same way that it would prohibit discrimination based on the fact that a person is African American or Latino or Jewish. But is Title VII also intended to prohibit discrimination on the basis of a person's sexual preferences or practices? Is it intended to prohibit discrimination based on a person's being gay or lesbian, straight or bisexual? Should it protect against discrimination directed toward a person who was considered "effeminate" or "butch"? Should it protect people who are transgender? Would it prohibit discrimination against a person who was promiscuous or celibate or who favored sadomasochistic sex?

The case law, legislative history, and scholarly literature regarding such questions are highly complex and contested.[44] I offer no views on how Title VII should be interpreted. For present purposes, my only point is that sex as an identity and sex as an activity (or as the subject of autonomy) should be understood as conceptually distinct, even if they sometimes overlap in practice.

Consider a case in which an employer decided not to hire, or even interview, a prospective employee simply because she was a woman. Assume that he did so without any knowledge of her sexual practices or preferences. In such a case, the employer would have discriminated against the prospective employee because of her status as a woman and not because of her sexual activities or preferences. This would be discrimination in the same sense that denying a person a job because of his race or religion would be discrimination.

Now contrast a case in which an employer repeatedly propositioned a female employee to have sex she did not wish to have, made unwanted comments about her appearance or sex appeal, or subjected her to pornography she did not wish to see. Unlike the previous case, this treatment *would* involve an infringement of the woman's sexual autonomy. (It might simultaneously involve discrimination because of her sex as well: the employer might be motivated to engage in such acts precisely because of his animus towards women.)

What about denying a person a job because he's gay or bisexual (or straight)? That question is a bit trickier. Being gay, bisexual, or straight are also kinds of identity, but they are identities that are inextricably tied to one's sexual identity. Being gay or lesbian means being sexually attracted to persons of one's own sex. Being heterosexual means being sexually attracted to persons of the opposite sex. Being bisexual means being sexually attracted to persons of both sexes. Discriminating against or harassing a person because he is gay, straight, or bisexual would thus seem to infringe on his sexual autonomy.

How about discriminating against someone because he's transgender—that is, because his gender identity is different from the gender assigned to him at birth? Being transgender seems to have to do mostly with sexual identity rather than any particular sexual preference. To say that a person is transgender tells us nothing more about the person's sexual practices than saying that a person is male or female. A transgender male or female could be straight, gay, bisexual, or asexual. So, from this perspective, discriminating against or harassing a person because he or she is transgender should not necessarily be categorized as a sexual offense. It is analogous to discriminating against the person because of his race or religion. At the same time, it should be recognized that much harassment of trans persons takes the form of unwanted questions or remarks about such persons' anatomy or sexual practices.[45] Behavior like that certainly could infringe on a person's sense of sexual autonomy, in the same way that similarly unwanted remarks to a non-trans person would infringe on her autonomy.

The question raised in this section has mostly been a theoretical one. In our current system, conduct of this sort is not normally criminalized. But there is no reason in principle why certain serious acts of discrimination based on a person's sex alone could not be treated as a crime. If we were to enact such an offense, should it be classified as a "sexual offense"? I have offered some reasons for treating offenses that involve sex as a form of identity as conceptually distinct from offenses that involve sex as a form of conduct.

NOTES

1. Distinguished Professor of Law, Rutgers School of Law. This chapter is part of a larger book-length work in progress, tentatively titled *Criminalizing Sex: A Unified Theory*. An earlier version was presented as the Second Annual Hugo Adam Bedau Memorial Lecture in the Tufts University Department of Philosophy, and at workshops at the Universities of Cambridge, Durham, London, Oxford, and South Carolina. I am grateful for the many helpful comments and questions I received. Special thanks to Thom Brooks, Chad Flanders, James Chalmers, Tommy Crocker, Michelle Dempsey, Audrey Guinchard, Jonathan Herring, Zach Hoskins, Erin Kelly, Suzanne Kim, Matt Kramer, John Stanton-Ife, Rebecca Williams, and Lucia Zedner.

2. *See, e.g.*, Sexual Offences Act 2003, c. 42 (Eng.), http://www.legislation.gov.uk/ukpga/2003/42/pdfs/ukpga_20030042_en.pdf (includes rape, assault, child sex offenses, abuse of position of trust, prostitution and related offenses, indecent exposure, indecent photographs of children, voyeurism, bestiality, necrophilia); MODEL PENAL CODE Art. 213 (includes rape and related offenses, deviate sexual intercourse by force or imposition, corruption of minors and seduction, sexual assault, and indecent exposure). Sexual offender registration is dealt with in Part 2 of the Sexual Offences Act and in numerous state and federal Megan's Laws.

3. For a useful account, see ESTELLE B. FREEDMAN, REDEFINING RAPE: SEXUAL VIOLENCE IN THE ERA OF SUFFRAGE AND SEGREGATION (2013).

4. Consider, for example, the fact that kidnapping of a minor is one of the offenses included in the Sex Offender Registration and Notification Act (SORNA), the federal version of Megan's Laws. Without a theory as to what the sexual offenses are, it's hard to explain exactly why this offense may be misconceived. SORNA, 42 U.S.C. §§ 16901–16945, http://ojp.gov/smart/pdfs/42_usc_index.pdf.

5. Neil MacCormick, *Reconstruction after Deconstruction: A Response to CLS*, 10 OXFORD J. LEGAL STUD. 539, 556 (1999).

6. *See generally* ANDREW ASHWORTH & LUCIA ZEDNER, PREVENTIVE JUSTICE (2014).

7. Thanks to Matt Kramer for the example. For further discussion of such crimes, see *infra* note 23 and accompanying text.

8. Both kinds of offense are considered in Stuart P. Green, *Lies, Rape, and Statutory Rape*, *in* LAW AND LIES IN THE UNITED STATES: DECEPTION AND TRUTH-TELLING IN THE AMERICAN LEGAL SYSTEM 194, 205–14, 238–51 (Austin Sarat, ed., 2015).

9. *See* Alan Soble, *Activity, Sexual*, *in* 1 SEX FROM PLATO TO PAGLIA: A PHILOSOPHICAL ENCYCLOPEDIA 15, 15 (2006) (making similar point).

10. Stephanie A. Sanders & June M. Reinisch, *Would You Say You "Had Sex" If . . . ?*, 281 JAMA 275 (1999). Although the study was published after the Lewinsky scandal broke, the data were obtained prior.

11. *Id.* Though some later studies have attempted to explore these questions. *See, e.g.*, Ava D. Horowitz & Louise Spicer, *"Having Sex" as a Graded and Hierarchical Construct: A Comparison of Sexual Definitions among Heterosexual and Lesbian Emerging Adults in the U.K.*, 50 J. SEXUAL RES. 139 (2013).

12. For a helpful summary, see IGOR PRIMORATZ, ETHICS AND SEX 9–49 (1999).

13. Of course, there are significant differences both between the Jewish and Christian views of sexuality and within the two traditions. For a useful discussion, see DAVID M. FELDMAN, BIRTH CONTROL IN JEWISH LAW (1998).

14. ROGER SCRUTON, SEXUAL DESIRE: A PHILOSOPHICAL INVESTIGATION (reprint 2006)(1986); THOMAS NAGEL, *Sexual Perversion*, *in* MORTAL QUESTIONS 39 (1979). *See also* Robert Solomon, *Sexual Paradigms*, 71 J. PHIL. 336 (1974) (describing linguistic theory of sexuality).

15. Alan H. Goldman, *Plain Sex*, 6 PHIL. & PUB. AFF. 267, 268 (1977). Primoratz calls Goldman's the "best philosophical statement of the hedonist understanding." Primoratz, *supra* note 12, at 41. Alan Wertheimer also adopts Goldman's definition of sex as his own. ALAN WERTHEIMER, CONSENT TO SEXUAL RELATIONS 37–38 (2003).

16. Goldman, *supra* note 15.

17. *Id.* at 269.

18. *Id.*

19. *Id.* at 270.

20. *Sexual Arousal*, WIKIPEDIA, http://en.wikipedia.org/wiki/Sexual_arousal (last visited June 21, 2015).

21. Simon Blackburn offers the case of priapism as involving the physical manifestations of lust or desire, but without the usual psychological triggers. SIMON BLACKBURN, LUST 16 (2004).

22. A somewhat similar subjective approach is suggested in Margo Kaplan, *Sex-Positive Law*, 87 N.Y.U. L. REV. 89 (2014), though Kaplan would apparently go even further and include in the definition of sex not just sexual pleasure produced by physical, visual, or auditory stimuli, but also "mere thoughts and fantasies without any external stimulation." *Id.* at 95.

23. *See generally* JOHN E. DOUGLAS, ET AL., SEXUAL HOMICIDE: PATTERNS AND MOTIVES (1995) (empirical study of serial sex murderers).

24. *But see* Diana T. Sanchez, et al., *Eroticizing Inequality in the United States: The Consequences and Determinants of Traditional Gender Role Adherents in Intimate Relationships*, 48 J. SEX RES. 168 (2012) (postulating that male rapists typically experience sexual pleasure).

25. The case was described to me by Matthew Kramer during the discussion following a talk I gave at the Cambridge Forum for Legal & Political Philosophy, in October 2013. Kramer recalls that he originally heard about the case in a "From Our Own Correspondent" report on BBC4 during the summer of 2010.

26. *See generally* PETER F.G. ROOK & ROBERT WARD, ROOK & WARD ON SEXUAL OFFENCES: LAW AND PRACTICE (4th ed. 2010).

27. *See* Sexual Offenses Act of 2013 § 78. Note that the language in neither Section 3 nor Section 4 is broad enough to cover a range of activities that would be regarded as sexual under the analysis of sexual activity offered above, including, for example, voyeurism, indecent exposure, possession of child pornography, bestiality, and necrophilia. Most of these offenses are dealt with in a separate part of the Act, titled simply "other offenses." Sexual Offences Act of 2013, §§ 66–71.

28. R. v. Court [1989] AC 28, 44.

29. R. v. Tabassum [2000] 2 Cr. App. R. 328.

30. Thanks to John Stanton-Ife for his help in sorting this out.

31. JOEL FEINBERG, OFFENSE TO OTHERS: THE MORAL LIMITS OF THE CRIMINAL LAW 17 (1985).

32. *See generally* Richard D. Mohr, *Why Sex Is Private: Gays and the Police*, 1 PUB. AFF. Q. 57 (1987).

33. English law views transmission of this sort as a nonsexual assault. R. v. B. [2006] EWCA CRIM 2945, [2007] 1 W.L.R. 1567; Sharon Cowan, *Offenses of Sex or Violence? Consent, Fraud, and HIV Transmission*, 17 NEW CRIM. L. REV. 135 (2014) (contrasting English, American, and Canadian approaches to the question).

34. For an interesting take on the decision to abstain from sex, see Elizabeth F. Emens, *Compulsory Sexuality*, 66 STAN. L. REV. 303 (2014).

35. *See* Jeffrie G. Murphy, *Some Ruminations on Women, Violence, and the Criminal Law*, *in* IN HARM'S WAY: ESSAYS IN HONOR OF JOEL FEINBERG 209, 214 (Jules L. Coleman & Allen Buchanan, eds., 2004).

36. RICHARD A. POSNER, SEX AND REASON 111 (1992).

37. MICHEL FOUCAULT, THE HISTORY OF SEXUALITY: VOLUME 1 AN INTRODUCTION 155–56 (Robert Hurley, trans., 1978), https://suplaney.files.wordpress.com/2010/09/foucault-the-history-of-sexuality-volume-1.pdf.

38. John Gardner and Stephen Shute make a similar point, in John Gardner & Stephen Shute, *The Wrongness of Rape*, *in* OXFORD ESSAYS IN JURISPRUDENCE, FOURTH SERIES, VOLUME FOUR 212 (Jeremy Horder ed., 2000). For an empirical study that tends to support this intuition, see Carol McNaughton Nicholls et al., *Attitudes to Sentencing Sexual Offences*, 193 SENTENCING COUNCIL RESEARCH SERIES (2012), http://www.natcen.ac.uk/media/24273/attitudes-sentencing-sexual-offences.pdf.

39. Though it is worth noting that refraining from mouth-to-mouth kissing appears to be a common practice among prostitutes. SHERIL KIRSHENBAUM, THE SCIENCE OF KISSING: WHAT OUR LIPS ARE TELLING US 121–22 (2011).

40. *Sex* in this sense is also contrasted to *gender*, which describes the characteristics that a society or culture delineates as masculine or feminine, or as somewhere along the continuum.

41. Prevention of Sexual Harassment Law, 5758-1998, SH 166, https://www.jewishvirtuallibrary.org/jsource/Politics/PrventionofSexualHarassmentLaw.pdf, Art. 3(a)(5), Art. 5.

42. *Cf.* ROSA-LINDA FREGOSO & CYNTHIA BAJARANO, TERRORIZING WOMEN: FEMINICIDE IN THE AMERICAS (2010).

43. 42 U.S.C. § 2000e–2(a)(1).

44. For a small sampling, see Anita Bernstein, *Treating Sexual Harassment with Respect*, 111 HARV. L. REV. 445 (1997); Katherine M. Franke, *What's Wrong with Sexual Harassment?*, 49 STAN. L. REV. 691 (1997); Vicki Schultz, *Reconceptualizing Sexual Harassment*, 107 YALE L. J. 1683 (1998).

45. *Cf.* Anna Kirkland, *What's at Stake in Transgender Discrimination as Sex Discrimination?* 32 SIGNS: J. WOMEN CULTURE SOC'Y 83 (2006).

Part II

Authority and Legitimacy

Chapter Four

Conditions of Legitimate Punishment

Alice Ristroph

The methods by which theorists evaluate state violence vary by context. Compare the long tradition of just war arguments to the more recent investigations of state-administered torture. Just war arguments set forth conditions under which war is ethically permissible. "Just cause," usually self-defense, is the condition most often identified and discussed; other conditions include a principle of last resort and proportionality constraints.[1] The aim, at least of the best known and most influential philosophical studies of war, is to specify all the conditions that must be satisfied before a state may use military force. Whether any or all of the conditions are met in a given conflict is an open question, to be assessed with reference to actually existing circumstances.

Torture apologists of the early twenty-first century, in contrast, have evaluated the moral permissibility of torture by imagining away most of the circumstances that surround torture in the real world.[2] The ticking time bomb hypothetical that so captured public and scholarly attention began with several stipulations: state officials have a known terrorist in custody; they are certain that a bomb is ticking and lives will be destroyed if the state does nothing; and they are certain that the terrorist knows the location of the bomb and will provide the information if, but only if, he is tortured. With these stipulations, we are asked, isn't torture justified? Perhaps, in some contexts, there may be intellectual value in such fancies. In the months after the September 11, 2001, attacks on the United States, however, the ticking bomb arguments were deeply dishonest, purporting to justify a violent practice by stipulating away the very problems that inescapably plague the practice in the real world. Put differently, the ticking bomb touts got everyone arguing about an imaginary form of violence—torture under conditions of certain-ty—while the only torture humans will ever know—torture under conditions of uncertainty—continued on.

In these philosophical arguments about war and torture, there is a difference in structure, usually accompanied by a difference in terminology. One approach evaluates the legitimacy of violence by looking closely at existing practices and identifying the *conditions* for permissible violence. A second approach speaks more often of *the justification* for a given state practice. On this approach, those who seek justification for state violence may use the same label that is applied to actual practices (e.g., torture), but their theorizing addresses a rather different enterprise, one framed by a number of counterfactual stipulations.

Like the apologists for torture, theorists of punishment have too often adopted the latter approach, seeking a single principle of justification rather than a complete list of necessary conditions. Punishment theorists tend to ignore, or stipulate as satisfied, conditions for legitimate punishment that are demonstrably unsatisfied in the real world, and focus instead on just two criteria: desert and utility. For several decades, much of the action in punishment theory consists of efforts to explain whether the offender's desert or some form of social utility offers the best justification for punishment.[3] Theorists occasionally do speak of necessary and sufficient conditions for punishment, we should note, but desert and utility are almost always the only conditions identified or considered. Thus, some scholars claim that desert is both a necessary and sufficient condition for punishment. Other "hybrid" theories argue that desert is a necessary condition, but it is not sufficient; punishment is justified only when we can also establish the existence of some consequentialist benefit, such as deterrence or incapacitation. Still another view, attributed to various strawmen but rarely directly defended today, denies the relevance of desert and argues that utility is itself a sufficient condition to impose punishment.

As the violence of the American criminal justice system has proliferated, and as it has been directed disproportionately at racial minorities and the poor, theorists of punishment have kept arguing about desert and utility. Some have suggested that the expansion of punitive violence includes many undeserved sentences, and they have appealed to desert as a limiting principle to scale back American punishment. But since desert assessments are both deeply contested and non-falsifiable, the invocation of desert as a limiting principle has accomplished little.[4] Other scholars have sought to demonstrate that some types of lengthy sentences produce disutility rather than net social benefits.[5] Utility claims are, in principle, more easily demonstrable than desert claims, but in practice, empirical evidence of deterrence and empirical explanations for crime rates have yielded little consensus. So far, arguments of disutility have not generated significant scalebacks in American punitive violence. And truth be told, most punishment theorists direct their arguments at each other more often than they address the public or policy makers. On and on, which flavor of retributivism or which hybrid varietal, the philosophers argue while Ferguson and Baltimore burn.

With its unrelenting and myopic focus on desert and utility, punishment theory becomes increasingly irrelevant and perhaps even irresponsible. Punishment in the United States is deeply illegitimate, but desert and utility do little to explain why that is. The most problematic features of existing punishment practices are the ones that the theorists have stipulated away or simply ignored. This chapter offers a more complete list of the conditions of legitimate punishment, and highlights some ways in which those conditions are presently unsatisfied. More broadly, my aim is to expand the horizons of punishment theory—to make clear that neither desert nor utility standing alone, nor again the two concepts together, can "justify punishment." Indeed, the very references to "*the* justification of punishment" may have contributed to the field's myopia by suggesting that a single principle or concept will resolve all of our normative questions about punishment.[6] "Conditions for punishment" more accurately describes what the theorist needs to identify, and this phrase helps make clear that several independent criteria must be established before we can label punishment just or legitimate.

Four conditions for legitimate punishment merit discussion now precisely because there are reasons to doubt that these conditions are satisfied. First, as a general background principle, legitimate state punishment requires the existence of a legitimate state.[7] State legitimacy is deeply complex, and best measured on a continuum, and I will not try to establish conclusively that the United States is or is not a legitimate state. But some of the pathologies of American criminal justice stem from deeper problems of political legitimacy, and it is helpful to bring that to the fore. Second and more narrowly, legitimate punishment depends upon fair substantive criminal laws. If the process of criminalization is flawed, or its substantive outcomes unjust, then punishment as a mechanism of enforcement is illegitimate. Third, legitimate punishment requires legitimate policing. And finally, legitimate punishment (like legitimate military force) depends upon a determination that the state's violence does not inflict unacceptably high levels of collateral damage.

Importantly, the first three conditions focus upon the agents of punishment rather than its targets. I have complained elsewhere that punishment theory focuses nearly exclusively on the target of punishment—the wrongdoer—and neglects the various persons and groups that authorize, impose, and administer punishment.[8] Here I demonstrate an approach to punishment theory that does keep the agent firmly in view.

A last preliminary note: I suspect that most scholars currently working in punishment theory will agree with at least two, and probably three, of the conditions for punishment discussed in this chapter. Some authors have already been explicit that a legitimate state and a legitimate substantive criminal law are necessary conditions for legitimate punishment.[9] My third condition, legitimate policing, has received less attention but may not prove controversial. With respect to these three conditions of punishment, my argument here is largely a critique of the practice of counterfactual stipulation. That is, I doubt my interlocutors and I will disagree that political legitimacy, legitimate substantive criminal laws, and legitimate police practices are criteria for just punishment. Instead the dispute is whether punishment theorists should stipulate these criteria as satisfied, and then give them no further attention. The fourth condition identified here—a proportionality constraint on the collateral damage of punishment—may provoke substantive and not just methodological disagreement. My suggestion that punishment is not legitimate if its collateral consequences are too high is directly at odds with at least some scholars' claims about the scope of factors relevant to the legitimacy of punishment. I will contest those claims, with the hope of generating a better framework for the normative evaluation of punishment.

I. A LEGITIMATE STATE

May state punishment be justified if the state that imposes it fails to meet more general standards of political legitimacy?[10] For example, were any criminal punishments imposed by the Nazis justified? Much of the literature that purports to justify punishment tends either to ignore questions of political legitimacy or to stipulate the existence of a legitimate punishing authority. A small but growing branch of punishment theory specifically tackles questions of political legitimacy, but usually stops short of direct engagement with the question whether the justifiability of actual punishments is compromised by existing political circumstances.[11] Without adopting a particular set of criteria for political legitimacy, and without offering a full evaluation of the overall political legitimacy of the United States, I suggest in this section that these issues must be addressed (rather than stipulated out of sight) by any purported justification of punishment.

It may be useful at the outset to identify a few distinct accounts of the relationship between political legitimacy and the legitimacy (or justification) of punishment. First, one might believe that political legitimacy and the legitimacy of punishment are actually one and the same question. Some work in political theory seems to express this view.[12] A closely related possibility is that the legitimacy of punishment necessarily follows from political legitimacy. If a state meets minimal standards for democratic legitimacy, on this view, the state's criminal law and its enforcement of that law is necessarily justified. A third possibility is that political legitimacy is one, but only one, condition for justified punishment. This is, I suspect, the position that most punishment theorists would endorse, although it is not always clear, since many theorists of punishment do not address the state or its legitimacy at all. Still another possibility reverses the order of priority, and holds that justified punishment is one, but only one, condition for political legitimacy.[13] Finally, one might believe that the legitimacy of the state is simply irrelevant to the justifiability of punishment—a sentence imposed for murder in the Third Reich was justified if the offender deserved it, even if the state's power was otherwise illegitimate.

I am going to set aside the last of these possibilities, because I think few subscribe to it. So long as there is some relationship between the legitimacy of punishment and more general political legitimacy, may the punishment theorists ignore the latter issue? May the theorist take as given the legitimacy of the state, then proceed to investigate desert and social utility as criteria for punishment in individual cases? Is such a method comparable to the strategy of the torture apologists, positing as satisfied conditions they know to be false or at least not demonstrably true?

My suggestion here is simply that theorists of *state* punishment should engage, rather than stipulate to, the overall legitimacy of the state. Punishment might be the fundamental expression of political authority, in which case the legitimacy of punishment and the legitimacy of the state seem almost the same question, or punishment might be just one among many functions to be carried out by the ruling authority. Either way, the state's background authority to rule shapes the legitimacy of its penal practices. This simple point is obscured by punishment theories that claim desert or deterrence (or some combination of the two) can "justify" punishment. Without attention to the identity and authority of the punisher, such theories have no principled grounds to differentiate between official penal practices and the violence of a lynch mob.

Happily, a number of scholars have directly or indirectly identified political legitimacy as a condition for justified punishment. For example, Antony Duff has argued that punishment is legitimate only when meted out by an actor or authority with standing to punish, and a state that perpetrates injustices against its own citizens lacks standing to punish them.[14] Other thinkers connect political legitimacy to the specific issue of punishment via social contract theory. With some variations that are not essential to this chapter, these thinkers identify the conditions under which the institution of punishment would be acceptable to all rational or reasonable persons; those conditions for legitimate punishment tend to track the theorist's conditions for political legitimacy.[15] Some form of consent, widely viewed as the "gold standard" for political legitimacy, is posited as a necessary condition for penal legitimacy.[16] Notably, none of these theories claim that actual criminals give literal consent to their punishments; instead, each of these accounts uses some form of constructive consent to justify punishment.

I note for the record my skepticism that these accounts are successful, but readers should look elsewhere for the full articulation of my doubts.[17] I do not aim to settle these issues within the scope of this chapter. Instead, the point is simply that political legitimacy does matter to the justification of punishment, and the various social contract theories (along with Duff's more republican account) are right to treat punishment theory as a branch of political theory.[18] More broadly, any purported justification of state punishment must address the legitimacy of the punishing state. Any scholar who claims to justify punishment solely on the basis of desert, or deterrence, or a desert-deterrence amalgamation, has oversold what he has to offer.

The broad principle that state legitimacy matters to penal legitimacy suggests two narrower areas of concern that merit more attention from punishment theorists. First, to the extent that our prevailing conceptions of political legitimacy are democratic, requiring some minimal opportunity for self-government, widespread disenfranchisement in the United States raises serious doubts about the legitimacy of punishment. A felony conviction simultaneously increases the likelihood and magnitude of future punishment and decreases opportunities for political participation. In short, we preemptively exclude from the democratic process the very people we are most likely to punish. If political legitimacy is democratic legitimacy, this approach needs far greater attention than punishment theorists have given it. Second, to the extent that political legitimacy is linked to some conception of distributive justice, profound socioeconomic inequality also calls into question the legitimacy of punishment. The point goes beyond Duff's observation that a state that has perpetrated affirmative injustice has lost standing to punish. Theorists who wish to construe criminal offenses as a claim of unfair advantage, corrected by the disadvantages of punishment, need to take seriously the baseline against which the effects of crime are measured. If the baseline is one of socioeconomic inequality, and if indeed the socioeconomically disadvantaged are more likely to commit crimes, egalitarian theories of retribution are simply fantasies with little bearing on actual criminals and actual punishments. As Jeffrie Murphy observed years ago, "criminality is, to a large extent, a phenomenon of economic class," and accordingly, as "upsetting" as it is to admit, "everything we are ordinarily inclined to say about punishment (in terms of utility and retribution) [is] quite beside the point."[19]

II. FAIR CRIMINALIZATION

For half a century or more, commentators have worried about the expanding scope of the substantive criminal law in the United States.[20] Many have called for constraints on what may be permissibly criminalized, arguing, for example, for a ban on status or morals offenses, or for a principle of limitation based on concepts of harm. In an important recent book, Doug Husak has argued that the massive (and excessive) scale of punishment in the United States can be traced to our failure to establish an adequate theory of criminalization and adequate limitations to the substantive criminal law.[21] There is widespread consensus, I believe, around the principle of fair and limited criminalization. But two specific points have received inadequate attention, and I highlight those points here. First, theories of criminalization and theories of punishment are interrelated, and one cannot justify punishment without attention to the substantive criminal law. Second, our inquiries into criminalization should address not only the content of the law's prohibitions but also the process by which those prohibitions are put in place. Fair criminalization has a procedural as well as a substantive component. Put differently, a procedurally and substantively just criminal law is another condition for legitimate punishment—and given existing circumstances in the United States, it makes little sense to stipulate that this condition is satisfied.

Criminalization and the normative justification of punishment are sometimes identified as separate branches of criminal law theory. It is conceptually possible to distinguish the inquiries, of course, but doing so is costly to each inquiry. The question of what to criminalize is ultimately a question of what may be punished. Punishment is painful and burdensome, and we risk overuse of the criminal sanction if we think only about what we'd like to prohibit and not about the specific mechanisms of prohibition. From the other side, as we evaluate the practice of punishment it is essential to ask the criteria by which persons are selected for punishment. In no existing legal system is desert (or consequentialism) a direct principle of selection. Instead, persons are punished for violations of the criminal law—which may or may not accord with one's theory of desert or utility. Thus, the justice of punishment depends upon the justice of the substantive criminal law. Or, a just substantive criminal law is a necessary condition—albeit not a sufficient one—for just punishment.[22]

Many punishment theorists would agree in principle, I suspect. For example, Jeffrie Murphy writes that punishment is permissible only after "the liberal state has a criminal properly in its clutches (i.e., after he has been found guilty of what has properly been made a crime)."[23] My emphasis here is on the dangers of stipulation, and of the language of justification. If a theorist stipulates that the criminal law is properly defined, and then proceeds to offer a justification of punishment that is contingent on that stipulation, he has obscured some of the most pressing contemporary problems in criminal justice. Mass incarceration is, or should be, a concern of punishment theorists, and mass incarceration is partly a product of the unconstrained proliferation of substantive criminal prohibitions.

Doug Husak has illustrated nicely the relationship between theories of the substantive criminal law and theories of just punishment. To sketch a theory of fair criminalization, Husak identifies four constraints "internal" to the criminal law and three additional "external" constraints. Internal constraints, as Husak uses the term, are those that come "from within criminal theory itself: from the general part of the criminal law, and from reflection about the nature and justification of punishment."[24] Specifically, criminal offenses must be designed to address a nontrivial harm or evil; they must address wrongful conduct; they must impose only deserved punishment; and finally, those who wish to criminalize conduct bear the burden of proof of showing that the other constraints are satisfied.[25] External constraints on the criminal law are derived from political theory rather than the criminal law itself, Husak explains, and they specify conditions that must be satisfied in order to overcome the important right not to be punished.[26] Drawing inspiration from so-called intermediate scrutiny in American constitutional law, Husak enumerates three requirements of criminal legislation: it must serve a substantial state interest; it must directly advance that interest; and it must do so by means no more extensive than necessary.[27]

In his discussion of the burden of proof constraint—the requirement that those who favor criminal legislation bear the burden of proof of defending it—Husak emphasizes the burdens of the criminal law and of punishment in particular. He imagines a proposed criminal prohibition of doughnut consumption, motivated by a state interest in reducing obesity.[28] To justify such a law, it is not enough to say that the law will actually reduce obesity and persons have no right to eat doughnuts. Persons have a right not to be punished, Husak emphasizes, and it is not at all clear that reducing obesity can justify the infringement of that right.[29] In other words, we ask not only whether the conduct in question is conduct we wish to eliminate but also whether a criminal prohibition is worth the costs of enforcement. (Husak does not emphasize, but I would, that punishment is not the only burden imposed by the criminal law. A theory of criminalization, and a theory of legitimate punishment, must address other enforcement costs, including the costs of policing. I elaborate this point in the next section.)

I am not sure whether Husak's constraints could effectively discipline the substantive criminal law in practice. One of his constraints is desert, and as I have noted previously and in other work, desert has not served as an effective limiting principle in American criminal justice. Husak also suggests "nontrivial harm" as a principle of limitation, and several commentators have described the failure of the harm principle to constrain criminal law.[30] But if indeed the substantive criminal law continues to evade constraint, then the punishments it authorizes will be illegitimate. Husak's work is thus an important antidote to claims that desert or utility, standing alone or as a pair, can provide "the justification" of punishment.

A final note on fair criminalization as a condition for punishment merits mention. Arguably, the legitimacy of the substantive criminal law depends not only on its substance but also on the process by which the law is formed. As discussed in previous section, the exclusion of convicted persons from the electorate arguably delegitimizes all legislative decisions, including of course changes to the criminal code. Perhaps other procedural constraints are also applicable. Husak's work initially seems to hint at a system that guarantees heightened judicial scrutiny of criminal legislation, but Husak then disavows that approach and suggests that legislatures themselves should apply "intermediate scrutiny" to their own criminal laws as a mechanism of self-restraint.[31] Other calls for internal constraints on legislatures have failed, and Husak acknowledges the possibility that legislatures may ignore key principles of criminalization or misapply them. Perhaps fair criminalization requires greater judicial scrutiny of criminal legislation or some other procedural mechanism to check legislative power. I leave that question open here; for the purposes of this chapter, it is enough to emphasize that legitimate punishment requires a legitimate criminal law. And a legitimate criminal law, in turn, requires a political process that offers those who will be punished opportunities for meaningful participation, and perhaps it also requires externally enforced substantive constraints on criminal laws.

III. LEGITIMATE POLICING

Punishment theorists do not typically address policing or issues of investigative procedure. Some scholars have related adjudicative procedures to the legitimacy of punishment,[32] but the more common approach is to leave procedure out of the picture altogether. Instead, the punishment theorist begins with a guilty defendant and asks what justifies the punishment of that defendant. Thus punishment theory doesn't usually take up questions about how the defendant was identified or how his guilt was established—how the defendant came to be in the state's clutches, to borrow Jeffrie Murphy's phrase. This is a mistake, I suggest; legitimate police practices are among the conditions for legitimate punishment.[33] And, like the fair criminalization requirement discussed earlier, legitimate policing is a condition for punishment that remains unsatisfied in current practice.

The philosophical question is whether official misconduct on the path to punishment undermines the justice of the eventual penalty. A familiar complaint about exclusionary remedies implies a negative answer—when courts exclude evidence obtained by illegal policing, the complaint goes, the criminal goes free because the constable has blundered. Implicit in the complaint is the suggestion that the blunders of constables are irrelevant to the legitimacy of punishment. But why should that be? State punishment claims distinctive normative status precisely because it is a kind of *state* action, produced by trained, authorized, and regulated officials rather than vigilantes. Whether those officials comply with their training, or act within the scope of their authority, is central to the legitimacy of the criminal justice process. Moreover, we should view the criminal justice process holistically rather than as a series of isolated, discrete episodes. The entire point of many police activities is to identify and detain wrongdoers so they may be punished. We authorize police forces as mechanisms to make punishment possible. The legitimacy of punishment depends, in part, on the policing that provides the targets of punishment.

Interestingly, although this holistic view of criminal justice is not well established in philosophical literature, it seems implicit in American constitutional structure. The U.S. Constitution shows a special regard for those facing punishment. It offers these individuals specific protections against the state; it sets a variety of conditions that must be satisfied before the state may punish. Some of these conditions relate to the substantive criminal law and the adjudicative process; others relate to the police and the investigative process. For example, in order to punish, the state must first define prohibited conduct in advance and give notice of its prohibition.[34] Criminal prohibitions must be both forward-looking and generally applicable, rather than targeted at specific individuals for past acts.[35] (Of course, criminal prohibitions are also subject to the constitutional constraints that apply to all state action, such as the protections for speech and religion in the First Amendment.) Before the state may punish, it must establish guilt at a jury trial, if the defendant so elects, and must ensure that the defendant has adequate legal counsel.[36] At that trial, or in other adjudicative proceedings to establish guilt, the state must avoid reliance on compelled self-incrimination.[37] Any punishment eventually imposed must not be cruel or unusual.[38] And, of course, individuals must not be deprived of life, liberty, or property without due process of law, a requirement that has been interpreted to imply various further conditions on punishment, such as the state's obligation to prove each element of a crime beyond a reasonable doubt.[39]

Not surprisingly, courts and commentators readily and frequently recognize that the threat of punishment frames the *adjudicative* process and imposes distinctive constitutional requirements on it. For example, this basic idea has underwritten recent Sixth Amendment sentencing jurisprudence: increases in punishment have triggered appellate scrutiny of the preceding fact-finding process and led courts to conclude that juries, not judges, must determine the facts that authorize more severe sentences.[40] But it bears emphasis that punishment looms on the horizon of the *investigative* process as well. The constitutional provisions that have been applied most often to the police have, by and large, been so used because the police facilitate the imposition of punishment. The Fourth Amendment prohibition of unreasonable searches and seizures is not limited to criminal cases, but it (like the First Amendment) restricts the power to punish nonetheless. By prohibiting unreasonable searches and seizures, the amendment prohibits the state from using certain tactics to gather the evidence that it is required (by other constitutional provisions) to present to establish guilt and impose punishment.[41] Similarly, the Fifth Amendment privilege against self-incrimination suggests that legitimate interrogation procedures are a condition for legitimate punishment; the state may not establish guilt by relying on a compelled confession.

Given this constitutional structure, there is arguably a substantial role for judicial enforcement of legitimate policing as a condition for punishment. The previous section left open the questions whether and to what degree courts should enforce limits on the substantive criminal law. With respect to police practices, though, specific constitutional provisions invite judicial inquiry in each defendant's case. We should understand motions to suppress unconstitutionally seized evidence as defendants' claims that the conditions for legitimate punishment have not been satisfied.[42] Exclusion, rather than a complete bar to prosecution, is a remedy that gives the state an opportunity to show that it can satisfy the conditions for punishment independently of the police misconduct. If the state fails to make that showing, the defendant will go free—as he should whenever the conditions for punishment are not satisfied.

IV. *JUS IN POENA* PROPORTIONALITY

I have argued so far that in order to establish the legitimacy of state punishment, we must establish the legitimacy of the punishing state, the legitimacy of the substantive criminal law, and the legitimacy of the police practices that led to the defendant's conviction. Obviously this set of conditions extends far beyond an inquiry into the offender's desert or the social utility to be gained by punishment, though desert and utility might be subsidiary requirements of a legitimate criminal law. But is this set complete, or sufficient? Does the legitimacy of punishment depend on still further conditions?

The philosophy of war suggests one further principle for consideration: a proportionality constraint that assesses the collateral damage of state violence. Contemporary theorists of the morality of war identify multiple criteria governing the permissibility of military force.[43] No single concept serves as "the justification" of war, even among those who believe war can sometimes be justified. Indeed, a conceptual approach that arguably did flirt with "the justification" of war has been mostly supplanted by a framework that emphasizes various independent criteria for permissible force. I am referring to the shift from *jus ad bellum*, or the justice of war, to *jus in bello*, justice in war.[44] *Jus ad bellum* is sometimes used interchangeably with the phrase "just war"; the central inquiry is whether a nation is justified in going to war. The focus is on the war as a whole, and although there are several conditions of a just war, the looser rhetoric sometimes suggests that a single "just cause" can serve as the justification of a war. *Jus in bello* refers to restrictions on the conduct of hostilities, or conditions that govern the permissibility of specific uses of force. *Jus in bello* is undoubtedly the more influential framework today. As I have explained elsewhere, scholars and commentators came to realize that to look for "the" justification of war was an ineffective strategy for limiting war's violence, and they began to emphasize instead restraints on the conduct of hostilities that were independent of claims about the war's overall justifiability.[45] And I have suggested that punishment theory has been unprofitably mired in what we might call the *jus ad poena*, or questions of the justification of punishment. Scholars' efforts would be better directed at the development of a *jus in poena*, or principles of limitation and restraint that are independent of a theory of the justification of punishment.[46]

One of the central tenets of the modern *jus in bello* is a principle of proportionality that juxtaposes the expected benefits of an attack with its overall costs, including its foreseeable but unintended consequences.[47] If a planned attack on a military target will cause substantial collateral damage to civilians, the attack may be impermissible. This principle may be understood to reflect a judgment that good intentions are not dispositive when we evaluate state violence; effects, even unintended effects, are relevant to the moral analysis. To be sure, a great deal then rides on the assessment of proportionality—on the determination of how much collateral damage is an acceptable price to pay for a given military advantage.[48] There are complaints, seemingly well founded, that states interpret the *jus in bello* proportionality rule too permissively and thus perpetuate excessive harm to civilians. At least at the level of principle, though, *in bello* proportionality serves as an important model for punishment theory insofar as it makes collateral consequences relevant to the ethical analysis of violence.

In addition to the conditions for legitimate punishment identified earlier in this chapter, I suggest a requirement of *jus in poena* proportionality. This proportionality inquiry focuses not on the relationship between crime and penalty, but on the relationship between the benefits of a penalty and the collateral damage it inflicts. Punishment inflicts intended suffering on the target of punishment (rightly so, retributivists argue), but it is also typically produces further harms to its target, some intended and some merely foreseen. For example, a criminal conviction generates many collateral consequences, including denial of opportunities for employment and political participation. Prison sentences often lead to harms beyond the intended deprivation of liberty, such as assaults by other inmates. Punishment also inflicts tremendous harms on third parties—the families of prisoners, the local communities from which prisoners may be removed, and even the broader society that operates and accommodates mass incarceration. Racial and socioeconomic disparities in the distribution of punishment inflict further social damage. At some point, all of this collateral damage suggests a violation of our proportionality condition—and I would suggest that when "mass incarceration" has become a household term, we have reached that point.

This suggestion may be prove more objectionable to punishment theorists than the conditions identified earlier in this chapter. Indeed, some scholars have explicitly denied that the sheer number of prisoners in the United States, or the demographic composition of the prisoner population, is relevant to the legitimacy of punishment.[49] Others emphasize that foreseeable but unintended consequences of a state-imposed criminal sentence, such as assaults in prison or post-release deprivations, are not properly called "punishment" and are thus irrelevant to retributive claims about the justification of punishment.[50] But it is not clear why the burden of justification should be set so low. Punishment, like war and like other state actions, generates substantial secondary and tertiary and still more remote harmful effects. We do not believe that individual persons should always be held liable for the indirect effects of their actions, but that principle has little bearing on the question of the legitimacy of state action. State action, and state violence in particular, is distinctive in part for its far-reaching impact. Justifying state punishment, then, or showing it to be legitimate, requires an analysis of its collateral damage.

CONCLUSION

Punishment stands in need of justification, scholars say, and then they purport to offer that justification, almost invariably by appealing to desert, utility, or a combination of the two.[51] But the practice justified by philosophers of criminal law is not one that our criminal justice system actually implements. The "punishment" justified by philosophers seems to assume, explicitly or implicitly, a legitimate punishing authority, an appropriately defined substantive criminal law, and legitimate policing. The "punishment" justified by philosophers is like the "torture" justified by the ticking bomb hypothetical: a construct of counterfactual stipulations that borrows the terminology of the real world but eschews its difficulties.

"Ideal theory" is the phrase sometimes used to describe this type of analysis: it stipulates a number of utopian conditions and then examines a specific institution or practice against that utopian background. As John Rawls used the term, ideal theory referred to a world of compliance, in which each person was motivated by a sense of justice and compliant with its demands.[52] Rawls used the method to discern principles of distributive justice, but he made it clear that crime, punishment, and other issues of noncompliance lay beyond the scope of ideal theory. And it is difficult to see why theorists posit punishment, or torture or war, as ideals. If we are willing to stipulate to utopian conditions, why not stipulate crime, terrorism, and war out of existence? What sadism drives a thinker to conjure the perfect world—and place within it torture, war, and punishment?

I have little doubt that most theorists of criminal law and punishment are not sadists but decent and conscientious people. They might argue that it is important to identify the ideal in order to measure the gap between the ideal and the real, the better then to close that gap. But punishment theory has not in fact served as an inspiration for criminal justice reform, and it's difficult to see how it could. Again, punishment theory tends to stipulate out of existence or simply ignore the most substantial and persistent problems of actual criminal justice—failures of the democratic process, racial injustice, abusive policing, and substantial harm to third parties. If theorists are to contribute to the amelioration of those problems, then the problems must become part of the theorists' conversations. Instead of pretending that either desert or utility could carry the enormous burden of justifying an institution as weighty as state punishment, the philosopher should be honest and explicit about the many conditions that would have to be satisfied before we call punishment legitimate.

NOTES

1. For details and examples, see Alice Ristroph, *Just Violence*, 56 ARIZ. L. REV. 1017 (2014). I am for the moment glossing over the distinction between two strands of thought—between the *jus ad bellum* and *jus in bello*. I discuss that distinction in part IV.

2. *E.g.*, ALAN DERSHOWITZ, WHY TERRORISM WORKS (2002).

3. There is little point in summarizing (again) a voluminous literature. For my own earlier survey of the field, see Alice Ristroph, *Desert, Democracy, and Sentencing Reform*, 96 J. CRIM. L. & CRIMINOLOGY 1293 (2006). For a more recent review, see Marc O. DeGirolami, *Against Theories of Punishment: The Thought of Sir James Fitzjames Stephens*, 9 OHIO ST. J. CRIM. L. 699, 703–706 (2012). Curiously, the suggestion that punishment could be justified by either desert or utility standing alone (or some combination of the two) has persisted notwithstanding the repeated and forceful rejection of that claim by Antony Duff and Doug Husak. *See, e.g.*, DOUG HUSAK, *Why Punish the Deserving*, *in* THE PHILOSOPHY OF THE CRIMINAL LAW: SELECTED ESSAYS 393 (2010) ("A political theory is required in addition to a moral theory if we hope to identify the conditions in addition to desert that must be satisfied in order to justify state punishment"). Duff and Husak are otherwise two of the most influential criminal law theorists of the twentieth and twenty-first centuries.

4. Ristroph, *supra* note 3.

5. *See, e.g.*, FRANKLIN ZIMRING, GORDON HAWKINS & SAM KAMIN, PUNISHMENT AND DEMOCRACY: A HARD LOOK AT THREE STRIKES' OVERBLOWN PROMISES (2001).

6. For a slightly different but related critique, see DeGirolami, *supra* note 3, at 708–711.

7. Thus, for the purposes of this chapter, I am setting aside the possibility that there is some natural or pre-political right to punish that may be exercised by individuals or other non-state actors. *See, e.g.*, JOHN LOCKE, SECOND TREATISE OF GOVERNMENT 4–6 (Jonathan Bennett, ed., Early Modern Texts 2010)(1690), (describing a natural and pre-political right to punish).

8. Ristroph, *supra* note 1; *see also* Alice Ristroph, *Responsibility for the Criminal Law*, *in* PHILOSOPHICAL FOUNDATIONS OF CRIMINAL LAW 107 (R. A. Duff & Stuart Green eds., 2011),

http://www.gbv.de/dms/spk/sbb/recht/toc/65514773X.pdf. "To say in the passive voice that D ought to be punished ducks the question of who ought to do this punishing and by what process." Donald Dripps, *The Priority of Politics and Procedure over Perfectionism in Penal Law, or, Blackmail in Perspective*, 3 CRIM. L. & PHIL. 247, 254 (2009).

9. *E.g.*, John Bronsteen, *Retribution's Role*, 84 IND. L. J. 1129, 1149 (2009) ("The reason the state has the right to punish is that a criminal has broken a legitimate law").

10. Two distinctions merit brief mention here; one matters to my discussion and one does not. First, in the context of this chapter the term "legitimacy" refers to normative legitimacy rather than sociological legitimacy. In other work I argue that the relationship between normative and sociological legitimacy is more complex than the usual distinction between these terms acknowledges. *See* ALICE RISTROPH, THE LAW OF VIOLENCE (forthcoming) (chapter 2) (on file with author). For the purposes of this chapter, however, I simply adopt the widely recognized terminology of moral or normative legitimacy. Second, I do not distinguish here between the terms "(normative) legitimacy" and "justification," but in other contexts scholars have sometimes thought it important to distinguish those concepts. *See, e.g.*, A. JOHN SIMMONS, JUSTIFICATION AND LEGITIMACY 123–130 (2001) (describing state justification as a question of prudential rationality or moral acceptability and distinguishing it from state legitimacy, a question of political obligation).

11. Much of this work appears inspired by John Rawls and his renewed focus on social contract theory. *See* Richard Dagger, *Social Contracts, Fair Play, and the Justification of Punishment*, 8 OHIO ST. J. CRIM. L. 341 (2011) (surveying theories of punishment based on contractarian and contractualist accounts of political legitimacy). Sharon Dolovich directly addresses both abstract standards of political legitimacy and the extent to which current practices satisfy those standards. *See* Sharon Dolovich, *Legitimate Punishment in a Liberal Democracy*, 7 BUFF. CRIM. L. REV. 307 (2004).

12. Under this approach, political legitimacy is framed as a question about the legitimacy of state coercion, especially state punishment. *See, e.g.*, ROBERT NOZICK, ANARCHY, STATE AND UTOPIA 134 (1974) (legitimacy as "entitlement" to punish); Allen Buchanan, *Political Legitimacy and Democracy*, 112 ETHICS 689, 689–90 (2002) (legitimacy as "moral justification" to make and apply laws and enforce them via punishment); David Copp, *The Idea of a Legitimate State*, 28 PHIL. & PUB. AFF. 3, 4 (1999) (legitimacy as "moral authority" to govern by means of laws enforced through punishment); A. John Simmons, *Justification and Legitimacy*, 109 ETHICS 739, 746 (1999) (state legitimacy as "complex moral right" to impose duties and "to use coercion to enforce the duties"). Markus Dubber has suggested a similar interdependence of political and penal legitimacy, although he seems to prioritize the legitimation of punishment as a means to legitimize the state. *See* Dubber, *Legitimating Penal Law*, 28 CARDOZO L. REV. 2597 (2007).

13. Adil Haque contemplates this possibility, but ultimately rejects it in favor of the view that "while criminal justice is neither necessary nor sufficient for political legitimacy, criminal injustice substantially undermines political legitimacy and can provide independent reasons for revolution." Adil Ahmad Haque, *The Revolution and the Criminal Law*, 7 CRIM. L. & PHIL. 231, 233 (2013). Haque defends a "non-statist" account of criminal law and punishment, in which individuals sometimes have not just the power but the duty to impose punishment. I believe such a view improperly naturalizes the social and legal constructions of crime and punishment, but I leave aside that debate here and simply assert a focus on *state* punishment.

14. *E.g.*, R. A. DUFF, ANSWERING FOR CRIME (2007).

15. Corey Brettschneider, *The Rights of the Guilty: Punishment and Political Legitimacy*, 35 POL. THEORY 175 (2007); Dolovich, *supra* note 11; Claire Finkelstein, *A Contractarian Approach to Punishment, in* THE BLACKWELL GUIDE TO THE PHILOSOPHY OF LAW AND LEGAL THEORY 207 (Martin P. Golding & William A. Edmundson eds., 2005).

16. Allen Buchanan, *Political Legitimacy and Democracy*, 112 ETHICS 689, 699 (2002).

17. If we take consent seriously, we cannot simply construct it as convenient. Whatever the social benefits of punishment (themselves often overstated), to the condemned person punishment is typically an act of violence that is at best incompletely legitimate. *See* Alice Ristroph, *Respect and Resistance in Punishment Theory*, 97 CAL. L. REV. 601 (2009); Ristroph, *The*

Imperfect Legitimacy of Punishment, *in* HOBBES TODAY: INSIGHTS FOR THE 21ST CENTURY (Sharon Lloyd ed., 2014).

18. Guyora Binder, *Punishment Theory: Moral or Political?* 5 BUFF. CRIM. L. REV. 321 (2002); Pablo de Greiff, *Deliberative Democracy and Punishment,* 5 BUFF. CRIM. L. REV. 373 (2002).

19. Jeffrie Murphy, *Marxism and Retribution*, 2 PHIL. & PUB. AFF. 217, 241 (1973).

20. *E.g*., Henry M. Hart, Jr., *The Aims of the Criminal Law*, 23 LAW & CONTEMP. PROBS. 401 (1958); Herbert L. Packer, *Mens Rea and the Supreme Court*, 1962 SUP. CT. REV. 107 (1962).

21. DOUGLAS HUSAK, OVERCRIMINALIZATION: THE LIMITS OF THE CRIMINAL LAW (2008).

22. "A theory of criminalization provides the set of conditions under which the state is permitted to resort to punishment. Of course, additional conditions must be satisfied before punishment is warranted; I do not pretend that a theory of criminalization generates a comprehensive justification of punishment. But I insist that principles to limit the criminal law are important because we need principles to limit the circumstances under which the state is allowed to inflict punitive sanctions." Douglas Husak, *Reservations about Overcriminalization*, 14 NEW CRIM. L. REV. 97, 98–99 (2011).

23. Jeffrie G. Murphy, *The State's Interest in Retribution*, 5 J. CONTEMP. LEGAL ISSUES 283, 296 (1994).

24. Husak, *supra* note 22, at 103.

25. *See id.* at 66 (nontrivial harm and wrongfulness constraints); 82 (desert constraint); 100 (burden of proof constraint).

26. *See id.* at 120.

27. *See id.* at 132.

28. *Id.* at 101–102.

29. *Id.* at 102.

30. Avani Mehta Sood & John M. Darley, *The Plasticity of Harm in the Service of Criminalization Goals*, 100 CAL. L. REV. 1313 (2012); Bernard Harcourt, *The Collapse of the Harm Principle*, 90 J. CRIM. L. & CRIMINOLOGY 109 (1999).

31. Husak, *supra* note 22, at 130–131.

32. *See* DUFF, *supra* note 14 and accompanying discussion.

33. I develop similar claims, with a more extensive discussion of constitutional doctrine, in Alice Ristroph, *Regulation or Resistance? A Counter-Narrative of Constitutional Criminal Procedure*, 95 B.U. L. REV. (forthcoming 2015).

34. These general principles of legality and notice underlie the ex post facto clause, and they are also understood as implications of the due process clause. U.S. CONST. art. I, § 9; amend. XIV.

35. U.S. CONST. art. I, § 9 (prohibition of bills of attainder).

36. U.S. CONST. amend. VI.

37. U.S. CONST. amend. V.

38. U.S. CONST. amend. VIII.

39. U.S. CONST. AMEND. XIV; *In re* Winship, 397 U.S. 358 (1970).

40. *See, e.g.*, Alleyne v. United States, 133 S. Ct. 2151, 2162 (2013) ("[T]he essential Sixth Amendment inquiry is whether a fact is an element of the crime. When a finding of fact alters the legally prescribed punishment so as to aggravate it, the fact necessarily forms a constituent part of a new offense and must be submitted to the jury"); *see also* Kate Stith, *Crime and Punishment Under the Constitution*, 2004 SUP. CT. REV. 221, 221 ("[T]he essential holdings of *Apprendi v. New Jersey* and *Blakely v. Washington* seem constitutionally obvious. . . . [W]hen a legislature decides that certain conduct warrants an increase in criminal punishment, such conduct is part of the 'crime' that must be charged and proven in accordance with the requirements of the Fifth, Sixth, and Fourteenth Amendments of the Constitution") (internal citations omitted).

41. *See Winship*, 397 U.S. at 368 (interpreting the Fourteenth Amendment due process clause to require the state to prove each element of a crime beyond a reasonable doubt). Again, the Fourth Amendment is not limited to criminal investigations, but courts have repeatedly recognized that investigations aimed at detecting crime trigger particular Fourth Amendment scrutiny. This premise is at least as old as *Boyd v. United States*, where the Court applied the

Fourth Amendment in a civil forfeiture proceeding but felt it necessary to emphasize that the government action, "though technically a civil proceeding, is in substance and effect a criminal one." Boyd v. United States, 116 U.S. 616, 634 (1886). Today, the Fourth Amendment's heightened concern with criminal investigations is most often expressed in discussions of the special needs doctrine, which relaxes constitutional requirements for searches that serve needs other than criminal law enforcement. *See, e.g.*, Ferguson v. City of Charleston, 532 U.S. 67, 74 n. 7 (2001) ("[I]n limited circumstances, a search unsupported by either warrant or probable cause can be constitutional when 'special needs ' other than the normal need for law enforcement provide sufficient justification").

42. Ristroph, *supra* note 33.

43. *E.g.*, Thomas Hurka, *Proportionality and Necessity*, *in* WAR: ESSAYS IN POLITICAL PHILOSOPHY (Larry May ed., 2008).

44. I describe this shift in greater detail in *Just Violence*. Ristroph, *supra* note 1, at 1029–1037.

45. *See id.*

46. *See id.* at 1020–1022; 1052–1062.

47. *See, e.g.*, Robert W. Tuttle, *Death's Casuistry*, 81 MARQ. L. REV. 371, 375 (1998).

48. *Cf.* MICHAEL WALZER, JUST AND UNJUST WARS: A MORAL ARGUMENT WITH HISTORICAL ILLUSTRATIONS, 151–154 (2d. ed. 1992).

49. *See* Dolovich, *supra* note 11, at 311 ("[V]iewed in isolation, the race and class position of America's inmate population tells us nothing regarding the legitimacy of the sentences being served"); *id.* at 419 (arguing that the number of prisoners, by itself, "tells us nothing about the legitimacy of the sentences being served").

50. *See, e.g.*, Dan Markel, Chad Flanders & David Gray, *Beyond Experience: Getting Retributive Justice Right*, 99 CAL. L. REV. 605, 618–620 (2011).

51. *See, e.g.*, Mitchell N. Berman, *Punishment and Justification*, 118 ETHICS 258, 258 (2008) (describing "a consensus approach[ing] unanimity" around the claim that "punishment stands in need of justification"); *id.* at 271–289 (developing an "integrated dualist" justification of punishment that appeals to both desert and consequentialist benefits).

52. JOHN RAWLS, A THEORY OF JUSTICE 7–8 (rev. ed. 1999); *see also* Alice Ristroph, *When Freedom Isn't Free*, 14 NEW CRIM. L. REV. 468, 484 (2011).

Chapter Five

Does the State Have a Monopoly to Punish Crime?

Douglas Husak

INTRODUCTION

My topic is not how punishment is justified. I will take quite a bit for granted with respect to whether punishment is justified. Instead, I ask why authority to punish is vested in the state—and whether this authority is or ought to be exclusive. A philosopher has good reason to be apprehensive when he believes a set of problems is fairly simple even though they seem to have baffled others and given rise to a massive literature. In fact, however, I think the problem of why it is *the state* that has the authority to punish crime can be solved relatively easily. Since I believe this problem is pretty straightforward, I will need to devote only a small amount of time and effort to resolve it. Of course, an allegation that so many other competent philosophers are fundamentally mistaken had better diagnose the source of their error. In the course of presenting my answer to why the authority to punish crime is vested within the state, I will address why other philosophers disagree with me. Although my critics can and do take issue with any number of steps in my argument, I hope to identify several of the particular places where confusion is most likely to arise. But one source of confusion will merit special emphasis at the outset. Legal philosophers may think the basic problem is to explain why the state has a *monopoly* on punishment, or the *sole* authority to punish. This source of confusion is easily rectified. Quite simply, the state does *not* have the sole authority to punish. Many arguments to the contrary transform what initially appears to be an important substantive claim into an uninformative tautology. Or so I will contend.

I. A STATE MONOPOLY ON JUSTIFIED PUNISHMENT?

To begin, we must specify what punishment *is*. That is, we must be able to recognize when given treatments are instances of punishment. This topic is extraordinarily important in its own right. Persons are entitled to many protections when the state threatens to punish them, and these protections may be unavailable when the state proposes to treat them in ways that do *not* count as punishments. Moreover, unless we say what punishment is, we may fail to recognize exactly what it is *about* punishment that requires a justification. For present purposes, however, a definition is important for a different reason. My ensuing positions may seem objectionable because some of my examples—those in which someone other than the state inflicts a sanction—might be held not to involve *punishment* at all. If these examples do not involve punishment, the arguments in favor of my position are obviously unsound. But if any of these examples do not involve punishment, we should be able to explain why this is so by pointing to one or more conditions in the definition that are not satisfied.

According to my account, a response amounts to a punishment when it deliberately imposes a stigmatizing deprivation or hardship. Each of these components is crucial. A treatment is not punitive because it *happens* to deprive and stigmatize. The very *purpose* of a response must be to deprive and to stigmatize before it qualifies as a punishment. That is, punishments *intentionally* impose a stigmatizing deprivation. Clearly, if a treatment does not result in a deprivation—that is, a hardship—we would not categorize it as a punishment. In addition, the deprivation must convey censure and impose some sort of stigma. If the treatment does not involve a mark of disapproval, we would not classify it as punitive. To the extent this definition is problematic, difficulties probably inhere in borderline cases of application. Can a person stigmatize himself? By what baselines (e.g., temporal or counterfactual) are deprivations determined? Is it important that the hardship typically or actually produces a negative psychological state—a state that might be described as *suffering*? Can a treatment amount to a hardship if it happens to improve the welfare of the person on whom it is imposed? Whose intentions count in deciding whether treatment has the purpose to deprive and stigmatize, and what if these intentions are mixed? Reasonable minds disagree about these matters. It is not always clear whether a given treatment deprives and stigmatizes, and it may be even more unclear whether it is intended to do so. We should not be surprised to find that this definition produces quite a bit of vagueness. States frequently have enormous incentives to administer treatments that come close to the borderline of what constitutes punishment without actually crossing it.[1]

Armed with a suitable definition of punishment, we can clarify the question to be addressed. The question why (or whether) it is the state that has the authority to punish is equivalent to the question why (or whether) it is the state that is permitted to deliberately impose a stigmatizing deprivation on persons. In the course of addressing this question, we might ask why (or whether) it is the state that has the *sole* authority to punish, that is, has a *monopoly* on punishment. It is hard to say whether this latter question should be raised only after the former is answered and we understand why the state has the authority to punish in the first place. On the other hand, maybe the key to a solution to why the state has any authority to punish is to be found by examining the rationale of its alleged monopoly powers. In any event, I will argue that the state does *not* have the sole authority to impose all treatments correctly categorized as instances of punishment. In fact, treatments designed to deprive and stigmatize are frequently imposed by all sorts of persons and institutions, and it is clear that many of these treatments are justified. Punishments are routinely dispensed by schools, by parents, and by many other authority figures—even by friends and acquaintances.[2] The conditions that justify these punishments are so diverse that I doubt we are able to say much that is informative about all of them. For present purposes, however, the important point is that no one should believe that states have the *sole* authority to punish or possess a *monopoly* on punishment.

Examples help to illustrate my point. Suppose Susan is a student in a university that initiates an intercollegiate basketball program. All students are eligible to compete for a place on the team. Susan wins the competition and begins to play. She is subsequently caught cheating—she knowingly and inexcusably uses a banned substance to enhance her performance that is explicitly prohibited by the rules of the governing body. Surely the governing body that oversees intercollegiate athletics would be justified both in deliberately stigmatizing her for her conduct and in depriving her of the place to which she is otherwise entitled. For example, she might be banned from further competition, and her name might be publicized to the media to try to deter other athletes who are tempted to emulate her. In other words, the institution would be justified in *punishing* her. In case it is important, I add (but will not argue) that Susan would *deserve* to be punished.

Why would anyone doubt that such examples demonstrate that states lack a monopoly on justified punishments? I suppose legal philosophers might contest the adequacy of my definition of punishment or question whether the school would really be justified in imposing a stigmatizing deprivation on Susan. In all probability, however, their response will be different. Legal philosophers would probably respond that they are interested in *state punishment* rather than punishment per se. The fact that institutions other than states impose punishments is beside the point and irrelevant to the topic. Of course, I admit that the historically important question for legal philosophers involves the justification of state punishment. This response, however, reveals that the answer to the question I have posed is an uninformative tautology.

Obviously, the state has the sole authority or a monopoly to impose *state punishment.* Schools have a similar monopoly to administer school punishments and families have the sole authority to inflict family punishments. If we retreat behind the pragmatic stipulation that the only kind of punishment with which we are interested is *state punishment*, we may be misled into thinking we have claimed something significant when we say that only states have the authority to punish.

I suspect the suggestion that we should focus only on *state punishment* rather than on punishment per se can be traced to the enormous influence of H. L. A. Hart. His celebrated definition stipulates that "the standard or central case of 'punishment'" is "imposed and administered by an authority constituted by a legal system."[3] Armed with this definition, legal philosophers can proceed directly to the topic that interests them. But it is unclear exactly why Hart regarded *state* punishment as central or standard. It is not central or standard in a statistical sense. I am confident that non-state institutions impose far more punishments than states. Nor is state punishment central or standard in a historical sense. Punishments existed long before states were formed. It seems wildly implausible to say that any treatment administered by anyone other than a state must be deviant according to an adequate definition of punishment.

What other response might legal philosophers offer? They might modify their initial claim and thereby dispute the *significance* of my example. They might contend that the question is not whether states have the sole authority to punish, but rather whether states have a monopoly to administer punishments *for crime.* But this response cannot be quite right. Surely the state does *not* have exclusive authority to punish persons for crime. Recall again that justified punishments are imposed by all sorts of persons and institutions for a wide range of behaviors. Surely some of the behaviors that make persons eligible for nonstate punishments are crimes. The force of my example is probably enhanced and at worst is unchanged if we stipulate that the performance-enhancing substance Susan has taken is proscribed by the penal law. Thus the punishment the institution is justified to impose on Susan *is* for conduct that constitutes a crime. But legal philosophers may not yet concede. Although Susan is clearly punished for conduct that constitutes a crime, legal philosophers might deny that she is punished *for* her crime, or that her conduct is punished *qua* crime. She is punished for violating a rule to ensure fairness in intercollegiate sports. Perhaps these legal philosophers have a point. Once again, however, they come dangerously close to transforming what initially seems to be an important substantive point into an uninteresting tautology. What exactly does it mean to punish persons *for* crime? That is, to punish conduct *qua* crime? According to a plausible answer, persons can only be punished *for* crime, that is, their conduct can only be punished *qua* crime, when their punishment is administered by the state. But if *this* is what these claims mean, it again becomes trivially true that only the state has the authority to punish for crime, or to punish conduct qua crime. Perhaps these claims have a different meaning. If so, however, it is incumbent on those legal philosophers who offer this response to tell us how to construe these claims as informative.

Legal philosophers might hazard yet a different response. They might admit that states lack the sole authority to punish, and thus lack a monopoly on punishment. But they might allege that states have the sole authority to punish *beyond a specified limit of severity*. According to this response, the state monopoly on punishment involves only stigmatizing deprivations that exceed a given threshold. Arguably, this threshold is the point at which punishments involve *violence*. After all, whatever sanctions Susan's school may justifiably impose on her cannot be especially severe. They cannot justifiably incarcerate her, require her to pay a fine, confine her to a given space, or impose any of the other modes of punishment available to modern states. Again, these legal philosophers have a point. Most importantly, their latest response does not threaten to transform the dispute into an uninformative tautology. Instead, it represents an important consideration seldom noticed explicitly. Maybe the debate about whether states have the sole authority to punish, or possess a monopoly on punishment, should apply only to sanctions that exceed a given threshold of severity. It is *these* punishments, and not less serious sanctions, that states have the sole authority to administer.

Here, at last, is a significant substantive claim. Is it really true that states have the sole authority to administer severe punishments (perhaps those involving violence), whereas other persons and institutions possess only the authority to administer punishments less serious (or nonviolent)? Perhaps. Of course, if we are to decide whether the state has the sole authority to impose severe punishments, we must have criteria to measure the relative severity of alternative modes of sanctions (and to determine whether they involve violence). Intuitively, it seems clear that a jail sentence is a more punitive *type* of response than a disqualification from intercollegiate athletics. But why must the focus be on *types* of punishments rather than on particular tokens? Susan might well prefer to be fined or incarcerated for a short period of time than to be permanently banned from further competition. From her perspective, the sanction imposed by the state is far less severe.[4] It is surprisingly difficult to devise a metric by reference to which one form of punishment can be assessed to be more or less serious than another.

In any event, if I am correct so far, some old controversies might be cast in a new guise. For example, *abolitionist* positions about punishment—which have always attracted a large following on the European continent and have become increasingly popular in Anglo-American jurisdictions—become less plausible.[5] It is one thing to deny that *states* can ever be justified in punishing persons for *crime*. It is quite another to hold that *no one* can ever be justified in punishing *anyone* for *anything*. The claim that no one can ever be justified in deliberately imposing a stigmatizing deprivation on another is quite remarkable and is far more radical than most contemporary abolitionists seem to appreciate. If the more radical interpretation of the abolitionist position were true, several familiar practices would need to be rethought and abandoned. In particular, the school would not be justified in punishing Susan for violating the rules of the competition when she is caught knowingly using a banned performance-enhancing substance. Abolitionist positions presumably are meant to deny only the permissibility of state punishment and not punishment per se.

In addition, we might gain a new perspective about the conditions under which the authority to punish might be delegated. If parents may punish their children—as seems clear—they might also transfer their authority to others. A baby sitter, for example, gains the authority to impose punishments on children through a contractual arrangement with their parents. I have already conceded that these punishments may not exceed a given threshold of severity, but that is not the point. Some commentators seemingly believe that the existence of a state monopoly on the power to punish creates problems for institutions such as private prisons.[6] Admittedly, something seems peculiar about delegating a power over which one ought to possess a monopoly. In the absence of a monopoly, however, these peculiarities evaporate. Nothing about the authority to punish per se renders delegation especially problematic. Of course, we might object to private prisons on any number of grounds—but not because the authority to punish is delegated.[7]

I propose to put questions about delegation aside. I hope to have shown that our central question should *not* be why the state has the sole authority to punish crime, or has a monopoly on justified punishments. No answer to *this* question can be found. Instead, the issue is why the state has *any* authority to punish. I now turn to this issue. I discuss how it can be resolved easily, why many competent legal philosophers have been mistaken in finding it to be difficult, and what my critics are likely to regard as suspicious about my reasoning.

I begin by noting that questions about the justification of state punishment for crime are intimately connected to questions about criminalization. That is, we cannot begin to justify impositions of punishment without knowing *what* persons are punished *for*. To some extent, this point is almost universally acknowledged. Virtually all legal philosophers accept the *principle of legality* according to which only conduct that amounts to a preexisting crime may justifiably be punished by the state. Exactly *why* this point is almost universally acknowledged is somewhat mysterious. Several theorists, as I will explain next, have difficulty explaining why the state should conform to the principle of legality and punish only preexisting crimes. For now, I simply point out that nearly everyone concedes that questions about whether state punishment is justified depend to some extent on what persons are punished for.

But the principle of legality has little or no substantive content and does not exhaust the intimate connection between criminalization and justified punishment. When the state enacts a penal statute, it should anticipate that some persons will violate it. In only a handful of unusual cases is compliance universal. If the state means what it says in denominating this law as criminal, offenders will become eligible for state punishment. These punishments must be justified. I claim that these punishments will *not* be justified if the conduct should not have been criminalized in the first place. Why else should philosophers bother to produce a theory of criminalization unless the laws that fail to satisfy the constraints in this theory are unjustified and result in punishments that are unjustified as well? Obviously, attempts to understand this limitation on the scope of justified state punishment depend on the content of the constraints in a normative theory of criminalization. I have defended such a theory elsewhere, but the controversial details of my theory need not detain us.[8] I could be mistaken about the criteria that preclude the state from criminalizing conduct. What I *cannot* be mistaken about, however, is that *some* such criteria are needed if we hope to become clear about what punishment is justifiably imposed *for*. Conduct that has been criminalized by the state but fails to satisfy the correct normative theory of criminalization—whatever the content of that theory may be—is not justifiably punished.

It seems apparent that an attempt to justify a punitive response to conduct (or, indeed, to anything else to which it is possible to respond punitively) must ensure that the conduct in question merits that response. Although this claim may seem obvious, I must admit that most of the voluminous philosophical commentary on the justification of punishment devotes little or no attention to what persons are punished for. It would be easy to infer that philosophers believe the question of what persons are punished for is immaterial to the justification they produce. In fact, however, I regard their neglect of this issue as an indication of what most of them take for granted. That is, the great majority of philosophers simply assume without comment that any justification of state punishment fails unless the punishments to be justified are imposed for conduct that is properly criminalized.[9] Some philosophers include this requirement within a broad stipulation that the state in which a justification of punishment is sought must be "basically just."

Thus we must attend to what persons are punished *for*. According to my theory of criminalization, the state enters the picture of what it can justifiably punish in two related places. First, the state may enact penal statutes only to punish *public wrongs*. The state neither does nor should punish *all* wrongs—even when these wrongs are egregious.[10] Instead, the state should proscribe only public wrongs—that is, conduct that wrongs and thus concerns the whole community and not merely those persons who are immediately victimized.[11] Second, the state must have a *substantial* interest in proscribing conduct before it subjects offenders to state punishment. The requirement that the state interest must be substantial is designed to support the intuition that trivial state interests, however real, do not warrant a punitive response. If I am correct about these two claims, it follows that a theory of the state—in particular, a theory of which wrongs concern it and to what extent—is needed in order to determine what crimes the state may enact and whether it is justified in imposing punishment. Thus a theory of justified punishment is intimately connected to a political theory of the state. No legal philosopher can hope to provide an adequate theory of the former in the absence of normative presuppositions about the latter.

More importantly for present purposes, the foregoing claims make it relatively easy to answer my central question and understand why the state has the authority to punish crime. Since any conduct the state is justified to proscribe must concern the citizens on whose behalf it is created—and implicate a substantial interest of the polity—its authority to punish is no more mysterious than the authority of any person or institution to deliberately impose a stigmatizing deprivation on those who commit wrongs against it. Admittedly, *all* punishments require a justification, and legal philosophers continue to divide about how this fundamental problem should be solved. But the question I address is not the broad and general issue of how punishment per se is justified. I do not allege that punishment itself is easy to justify, but that the authority of the state to punish is no more in need of explication than the authority to punish in other kinds of cases in which wrongs are committed against whoever inflicts a punitive sanction. Almost certainly the authority to punish is vested in persons or institutions *other* than those victimized by wrongs. But the authority to punish is most clearly vested in those against whom substantial wrongs are committed. The basic question I pose here is not especially difficult to answer.

II. OBJECTIONS AND COMPETING ANSWERS

I anticipate that theorists who regard the problem of state authority to punish as difficult will raise any number of objections to my account. In most of the remainder of this chapter, I identify and respond to possible misgivings. I also discuss why a few competing theories of state authority to punish encounter greater problems than my own. I conclude with brief remarks about some implications of my view that require further thought.

First, legal philosophers might challenge my claim that legitimate statutes must proscribe *public* wrongs and violate a substantial state interest. Which wrongs are public, and which interests are substantial? My response is incomplete in the absence of a substantive account of the features that make wrongs public and state interests substantial. The former claim is especially controversial. Indeed, a number of prominent legal philosophers purport to find baffling the very idea of a private wrong. Obviously, the best way to persuade skeptics is to defend a theory of public wrongs. As I have said, any theory of public wrongs presupposes a theory of the state. Alas, I have no theory of the state to offer. I lack more than the barest outline of a view according to which we can identify the wrongs that are public. One explanation for my failure is that no single theory can possibly be adequate in all times and places. Wrongs that are public in some locale may be private elsewhere, and wrongs that are private at some time may be public in another. Thus we cannot say that actions X, Y, and Z are private wrongs; private wrongs are whatever our procedural criteria identify as private wrongs, and the application of these criteria produce different outcomes from one time and place to another. At any rate, the contrast between public and private wrongs is just as elusive as the contrast between the public and private itself. Many theorists would confess to lacking a theory to demarcate public from private realms. The boundaries of these domains are hotly contested, most recently in such contexts as social media and targeted advertising. Nonetheless, few theorists would go so far as to deny that such a distinction exists. Among the most important defining features of a liberal state—the kind of state I believe is most clearly defensible—is its commitment to take seriously a sphere of privacy. It is especially important to protect this realm from interference through the *criminal* law. In short, if we recognize a distinction between the public and the private elsewhere in our political theory, the contrast is no more obscure when applied to actions that are wrongful and justifiably criminalized.

In addition, it is easy to provide examples of wrongs that are public and wrongs that are private. Acts of unjustified violence, for example, concern more than their immediate victims. These acts alarm members of the public and cause them to alter their behavior in ways that are deleterious. Acts of infidelity, by way of contrast, are private wrongs, at least in contemporary Western communities.[12] Unless I have personal ties to the participants, I have no cause for alarm when my neighbor is unfaithful to her spouse. Of course, skeptics who purport not to understand the contrast will not be content with mere examples; they will demand to know *why* the latter is a private and not a public wrong. What principles explain the contrast? Without pretending to answer this question directly, I respond by posing an equally difficult challenge my opponents have just as much reason to meet. On what principled grounds do these skeptics explain why no sensible modern theorist (including, in all likelihood, the skeptic himself) advocates the criminalization of marital infidelity? We should not believe that such a proscription could not be enforced; infidelity is probably no more difficult to detect than domestic violence. Instead, the answer is that such a law prohibits conduct that does not wrong or concern the community.

A more general challenge to these skeptics might be posed: The entire contrast between criminal and civil wrongs is jeopardized if no principled contrast between private and public wrongs could be drawn. When a civil wrong is perpetrated, third parties have no cause for complaint when immediate victims forgive or elect not to pursue civil remedies. But the discretion not to punish is not vested in immediate victims when public wrongs—that is, crimes—are perpetrated. The commission of a public wrong concerns the entire community, so decisions to forgive by immediate victims should not be decisive against prosecutorial decisions to charge.

Unfortunately, I also lack a detailed theory of which state interests are sufficiently weighty to qualify as substantial—a second constraint that putative criminal laws must satisfy in order to be justified. Fortunately, constitutional adjudication in the United States has developed an enormous body of precedent to decide when given state interests qualify as substantial. The state is permitted to discriminate on the basis of gender, for example, only when it has a substantial interest in so doing. The rights implicated by punishment are at least as valuable as those implicated by gender discrimination. Thus legal philosophers are well advised to consult this body of precedent to develop a theory of the conditions under which the state has a substantial interest that would justify subjecting persons to the deliberate infliction of a stigmatizing deprivation. Although I have no illusions that it will be easy to produce such a theory, one should not be overly pessimistic about the prospects of defending criteria to show that some state interests are far more important than others. Somewhere along this continuum, a line must be drawn and state interests should be deemed substantial.

Suppose, however, that my opponent is willing to concede (at least for the sake of argument) that it is possible to contrast public from private wrongs and trivial from substantial state interests. A *second* objection is that the need for these limitations on state authority to criminalize is unmotivated and suspiciously ad hoc. Of course the state has the authority to punish conduct that wrongs political communities and violates substantial state interests, but why is its authority limited to the proscription of *only* these wrongs? My account would be question-begging if my only answer is that the state must enter the picture somehow in order to explain how it gains its authority to punish. Can we do better?

I think so. Although the constraints in my theory of criminalization are defensible as a matter of principle, a complete rationale would also draw from instrumentalist considerations. According to my account, only public wrongs that implicate substantial state interests may be proscribed and punished because the state has finite resources. Unlike punishments imposed in a divine realm, the institutions of penal justice established in the real world inevitably involve huge moral and nonmoral costs. I have referred (perhaps inelegantly) to three of these costs as the *drawbacks* of punishment.[13] First, institutions of penal justice are funded through taxation and are extraordinarily expensive. Many other valuable goods—schools, arts, a social safety net, and the like—compete for the scarce revenue taxpaying citizens are forced to provide. Second, institutions of criminal justice are prone to error and mistake. No one knows for certain how many persons have been punished unjustly, but any plausible estimate should give citizens pause before they create a system of penal justice. Third, officials who administer an institution of criminal justice are subject to corruption and may be tempted to abuse the power they are given. Again, the extent of corruption and abuse is difficult to ascertain, but no one doubts the amount to be considerable. Why, then, should taxpaying citizens incur these moral and nonmoral costs and create institutions of criminal justice? They are warranted in refusing to do so unless the state, on their behalf, proscribes conduct that concerns them and implicates a substantial state interest. Even if persons who commit private wrongs or violate trivial state interests deserve some modicum of retribution—a matter on which I reserve judgment—the case for actually *treating* them as they deserve and inflicting punishments must overcome the enormous drawbacks that inevitably plague systems of penal justice in the real world. In fact, I believe citizens should create and fund a system of penal justice only if they have good reason to believe it would significantly reduce levels of serious crime. This consequence, if it could be achieved, would overcome the foregoing drawbacks and allow the creation of a system of penal justice. Thus I hope to have provided a noncircular basis for allowing the criminalization only of public wrongs that implicate substantial state interests.

I have argued that the correct theory of criminalization is needed to show why the state has the authority to punish crime. With the right theory in place, the question of why the state has the authority to punish crime is answered easily. Most legal philosophers who find this question to be difficult presuppose the wrong theories of criminalization and punishment. Many of these deficient theories attempt to justify criminalization and punishment without immediate reference to the state, and thus need to furnish an independent ground to explain why the state is in the business of punishing. Not surprisingly, this task is difficult. I will briefly mention two theories that encounter this problem.

First, consider *legal moralism*—or at least that "immodest" version of legal moralism defended by Michael Moore. According to Moore, institutions of criminal law and punishment are justified because and to the extent that they implement a principle of retributive justice. Retributive justice, in turn, demands that all and only culpable wrongdoers are punished.[14] These legal moralists derive a theory of crime and punishment solely from moral philosophy without the need for political theory. Thus they must struggle to explain why the state has the authority to create crimes and to punish persons who commit them.[15] This difficulty is formidable.[16] Even if legal moralists are correct that punishing all culpable wrongdoers implements a principle of retributive justice, I contend that a theory of public wrongs and substantial state interests is needed to explain why taxpaying citizens should care very much about whether their state conforms to this principle. The value of implementing a principle of retributive justice is not especially great.

Second, consider the *duty view* recently defended by Victor Tadros.[17] According to the duty view, the justification of punishment is derived through an ingenious series of steps from the right of personal self-defense. To oversimplify a bit, Tadros contends that aggressors who harm their victims breach duties and thus incur a new duty to rectify what they have done. But why should victims of wrongful aggression give up what is owed to them to achieve higher levels of protection throughout all of society—which Tadros identifies as the primary objective of institutions of penal justice? If the central problem in justifying punishment consists in showing why *wrongdoers* may be used for the benefit of others, as Tadros alleges, it seems that taking the duty owed to victims and using it for general deterrence amounts to an impermissible use of *victims*. But if we are *not* permitted to use victims in this way, the duty view does not explain how states gain the authority to punish.[18]

Moreover, adherents to both the duty view and to immodest legal moralism are committed to the existence of a general *duty* to punish criminals. Recall that Moore believes retributive justice requires *all* culpable wrongdoers be punished, while Tadros grounds punishment in a duty aggressors incur by wrongfully harming their victims. A retributive injustice is done, or a duty is unfulfilled, whenever criminals are *un*punished. The problem with these positions is evident: no *duty* to punish actually exists. It is no secret that many and probably most criminals evade detection. Moreover, exercises of police and prosecutorial discretion routinely allow many guilty persons to evade punishment. No philosopher of criminal law, to my knowledge, explicitly argues that these results are unjust or violate a duty. Of course, discretion not to impose punishment can be exercised arbitrarily or unfairly. But the objection to such an abuse of discretion is not that it fails to recognize a general duty to punish. My theory avoids this worrisome implication. I do not ground state authority to punish crime in a duty to implement a principle of retributive justice or a duty to compensate victims of wrongful aggression. Even if desert provides a reason *to* punish, conformity with this reason does not discharge a duty.

In addition, as I have indicated, legal moralists or defenders of the duty view encounter difficulty upholding the principle of legality. Much wrongful conduct is not proscribed by law; isn't the legal moralist case for punishment equally strong in such cases? And persons incur duties to others through wrongful aggression even when their acts are not crimes; may the state enforce these duties by using such persons to further its end of general deterrence?[19] A theory of criminalization and punishment that draws heavily from political philosophy (and not simply from moral philosophy) is bound to have an easier time accounting for the centrality of a principle of legality. Political communities, not constructs built wholly from moral philosophy, have the authority to punish crime. This authority is conferred in the same way it is conferred when nonstate actors such as schools impose punishments—that is, when political communities are wronged.

These difficulties aside, how *do* these theorists believe the state gains the authority to punish? Although instrumentalist accounts of why the state has the authority to punish are typically associated with utilitarianism, adherents of legal moralism or the duty view tend to embrace instrumentalist accounts as well. Instrumentalists allege that punishment of wrongdoers by anyone other than the state is unlikely to be as effective as state punishment in protecting victims of crime.[20] Alon Harel is correct, I think, to contend that all such views are problematic.[21] I add to his objections that such accounts include a tremendous amount of unwarranted speculation. Critiques of alternative ways to deter crime and protect victims are mere conjectures, and no one should profess to know whether they are correct. Social scientists have consistently found that the deterrent force of a sanction is affected most dramatically by how swiftly it is imposed. We know the wheels of criminal justice turn slowly; victims or vigilantes could respond far more quickly. In addition, private actors would not be burdened by the nonexculpatory public policy defenses that some commentators allege to have eroded general deterrence. Thus there is at least *some* reason to suspect that immediate victims or vigilantes might do a better job than the state protecting the public and deterring crime. We simply lack confidence in the empirical hypotheses that would vindicate or undermine an instrumental defense of state authority to punish.

Despite my agreement with this part of Harel's position, my sentiment extends no further. He seems to believe that only states *can* punish. He writes, "It is not that it is impermissible for non-state agents to punish; it is rather that no other agent can punish, and any attempt to punish on the part of such agents is bound to fail, and constitute a mere (impermissible) act of violence."[22] His support for this curious claim consists in his *integrationist* account of criminal sanctions, by which he means that "the same agent who is the source of criminal prohibitions must also administer the sanctions for the violation of these prohibitions."[23] But Harel cannot believe, I hope, that the athletic department of an educational institution *does not* punish or *cannot be justified* in punishing Susan because it is not the *source* of the criminal prohibition against the use of performance-enhancing substances. It is one thing to say that someone must be wronged to gain the authority to punish, and quite another to say that someone must be the source of the wrong before such authority is conferred.

Although he does not describe his view as *integrationist*, Malcolm Thorburn concurs with Harel's position. He writes, "There is something in the nature of criminal sentencing that requires that it be administered by state officials."[24] As far as I can see, however, his claim that there is something in the *nature* of criminal sentencing that requires it to be imposed by the state amounts to the kind of tautology I identified earlier. If someone other than the *state* tried to sentence criminally, they simply would not be involved in *criminal sentencing*. Of course, only *states* can impose *state* punishment. This conclusion is true but uninformative. Thorburn seemingly is aware that the disputed issue is not resolved by a tautology, because he is tempted to say that parental punishments are really not punishments at all, at least not in the relevant sense. "One might put the point even more strongly and say that parental discipline is not really punishment at all in the sense understood by criminal justice theorists. It is not the infliction of hard treatment against fully responsible agents."[25] We need to know more about "the relevant sense" of punishment before we should be persuaded by this response. If punishment in the relevant sense is necessarily imposed by the state, Thorburn has returned to the tautology he sought to avoid. In any event, I hope Thorburn would not make the same response about Susan, who is clearly a responsible agent. He cannot believe that whatever the school does to her for her act of cheating "is not really punishment at all." Even though the school cannot administer *state* punishment, it certainly can administer punishment.

I want to conclude with a problem that has received too little attention from legal philosophers but seemingly arises as a result of the position I have defended. Retributivists (as I like to call myself) tend to believe that punishments must be *proportional*, which I take to require (*ceteris paribus*) that the severity of punishment must be a function of the seriousness of the crime. I have contended that all sorts of institutions and individuals may be justified in imposing punishments, that some of the behavior that merit such punishments may be crimes, and that the punishments inflicted for such behaviors may be deserved. If so, should any quantum of punishment inflicted by non-state actors for given instances of criminal behavior count against the severity of the punishment the state is subsequently authorized to impose?[26] Let me provide an illustration of the problem I have in mind by turning to a new example. Suppose Jack deliberately, unjustifiably, and inexcusably rapes Jill. I assume that Jill would be justified in deliberately imposing a stigmatizing deprivation on Jack. Suppose Bill perpetrates an equally wrongful rape against Elizabeth, who elects not to respond to Bill at all. Both Jack and Bill are subsequently prosecuted and convicted. They now await the sentence to be imposed by a judge persuaded of the merits of the foregoing principle of proportionality. *Ex hypothesi*, Jack (but not Bill) has already been punished to some extent for his wrong. If the judge imposes an identical sentence on Jack and Bill, it follows that Jack is punished more severely than Bill. How can this outcome be compatible with a retributivist penal theory that embraces proportionality?

The case for allowing what Jill does to Jack to count against the severity of the sentence a judge should impose is strongest when Jill impermissibly inflicts a stigmatizing hardship on Jack that is equal in severity to the stigmatizing hardship he deserves according to the principle of proportionality. Suppose Jill kidnaps Jack and imprisons him in a makeshift prison for the same period of time a judge would authorize on behalf of the state, and this treatment is designed to stigmatize him to the appropriate degree. Eventually, however, Jack is freed and apprehended and convicted by the state. On what ground should the law subsequently neglect what has already been done to Jack and sentence him as though Jill had behaved like Elizabeth and ignored the rape altogether?[27] I suspect that many penal theorists would respond by stipulating that nothing that is done to Jack by nonstate actors should be allowed to count against the severity of the sentence the state is authorized to impose—even if what is done to Jack is the punishment he deserves for the crime he has committed, and is imposed *for* that very crime.[28] To my mind, this stipulation is no more plausible than the claim that what is done to Jack by Jill is not an instance of punishment at all. But the question must be answered even if we categorize what Jill has done to Jack as something other than punishment. We still should ask whether any stigmatizing deprivation that is *not* punishment should ever be allowed to reduce the quantum of hardship that *is* punishment when an offender is sentenced by the state.[29]

I am uncertain how the foregoing problem should be resolved. I am content at present if readers are persuaded that the question is genuine and demands a thoughtful answer. But the problem of why it is the state that has the authority to punish crime is different. *That* problem is easily solved. Moreover, the problem of why the state has the *sole* authority to punish crime is easily resolved as well. As I hope to have shown, the state *lacks* a monopoly on the authority to punish crime.[30]

NOTES

1. *See, e.g.*, Andrew Ashworth & Lucia Zedner, *Preventive Orders: A Problem of Undercriminalization? in* THE BOUNDARIES OF THE CRIMINAL LAW 59 (R.A. Duff, et al., eds., 2010).

2. *E.g.*, LEO ZAIBERT, PUNISHMENT AND RETRIBUTION 16–25 (2006). *See also* Neil MacCormick & David Garland, *Sovereign States and Vengeful Victims: The Problem of the Right to Punish, in* FUNDAMENTALS OF SENTENCING THEORY 11, 23 (Andrew Ashworth & Martin Wasik, eds., 1998).

3. *See* H.L.A. HART, PUNISHMENT AND RESPONSIBILITY 4, 5 (1968).

4. At the time of this writing, a good deal of publicity has surrounded the quantum of punishment that should be imposed by professional sports leagues on players who commit acts of domestic violence. In many of these cases, states have declined to prosecute at all. Even when state prosecution occurs, the punishments they inflict are far less severe than those imposed by the league.

5. Several defenses of abolitionism are available. The most philosophically sophisticated is MICHAEL J. ZIMMERMAN, THE IMMORALITY OF PUNISHMENT (2011).

6. *See* Alon Harel, *Why Only the State May Inflict Criminal Sanctions: The Case Against Privately Inflicted Sanctions*, 14 LEGAL THEORY 113 (2008).

7. *See* Alon Harel & Ahivay Dorfman, *The Case Against Privatization*, 41 PHIL. & PUB. AFF. 67 (2013), *but see* Malcolm M. Feeley, *The Unconvincing Case Against Private Prisons*, 89 IND. L. J. 1401 (2014).

8. *See* DOUGLAS HUSAK, OVERCRIMINALIZATION (2008).

9. For a possible exception, see J.D. Mabbott, *Punishment*, *in* THE PHILOSOPHY OF PUNISHMENT 115 (H.B. Acton, ed., 1969).

10. *See* Leo Katz, *Villainy and Felony*, 6 BUFF. CRIM. L. REV. 100 (2003).

11. *See* R.A. Duff, *Towards a Modest Legal Moralism*, 8 CRIM. L. & PHIL. 217 (2014).

12. *But see* Jens D. Thaysen, *Infidelity and the Possibility of a Liberal Legal Moralism*, 9 CRIM. L. & PHIL. (forthcoming 2015).

13. Douglas Husak, *Why Punish the Deserving?*, *in* PHILOSOPHY OF CRIMINAL LAW: SELECTED ESSAYS 393 (Douglas Husak, ed., 2010).

14. MICHAEL S. MOORE, PLACING BLAME: A THEORY OF THE CRIMINAL LAW (1997).

15. *See* Jeffrie Murphy, *The State's Interest in Retribution*, 5 J. CONTEMP. LEGAL ISSUES 283 (1994).

16. For further thoughts, see Michael S. Moore, *A Tale of Two Theories*, 28 CRIM. JUST. ETHICS 27 (2009); Douglas Husak, *Convergent Ends, Divergent Means: A Response to My Critics*, 28 CRIM. JUST. ETHICS 119 (2009).

17. VICTOR TADROS, THE ENDS OF HARM: THE MORAL FOUNDATIONS OF CRIMINAL LAW (2011).

18. *See* Kimberly K. Ferzan, *Rethinking the Ends of Harm*, 32 L. & PHIL. 177 (2013).

19. *See* Patrick Tomlin, *Innocence Lost: A Problem for the Duty View of Punishment* (June 26, 2015) (unpublished manuscript) (on file with author).

20. "My views about legitimacy and authority are primarily instrumentalist—the agent who has legitimacy and authority to punish is that which best serves the aims of punishment, whilst satisfying constraints that apply." Victor Tadros, *Punishment and the Appropriate Response to Wrongdoing*, 9 CRIM. L. & PHIL. (forthcoming, 2015).

21. Harel, *supra* note 6.

22. ALON HAREL: WHY LAW MATTERS 81 (2013).

23. Harel, *supra* note 6, at 127.

24. Malcolm Thorburn, *Proportionate Sentencing and the Rule of Law*, *in* PRINCIPLES AND VALUES IN CRIMINAL LAW AND CRIMINAL JUSTICE 269, 276 (Lucia Zedner & Julian V. Roberts, eds., 2012).

25. *Id.* at 277 n.26.

26. One commentator usefully calls this issue the *boundary problem*. *See* Larry Alexander, *You Got What You Deserved*, 7 CRIM. L. & PHIL. 309 (2013). *See also* Douglas Husak, *The Philosophy of Criminal Law: Extending the Debates*, 7 CRIM. L. & PHIL.351 (2013).

27. *See* Douglas Husak, *Already Punished Enough*, *in* PHILOSOPHY OF CRIMINAL LAW: SELECTED ESSAYS, *supra* note 13, at 433.

28. That the punishment is imposed *for* the crime is probably crucial to our thoughts about this issue. *See* Dan Markel & Chad Flanders, *Bentham on Stilts: The Bare Relevance of Subjectivity to Retributive Justice*, 98 CAL. L. REV. 907 (2010).

29. *See also* Shawn J. Bayern, *The Significance of Private Burdens and Lost Benefits for a Fair-Play Analysis of Punishment*, 12 NEW CRIM. L. REV. 1 (2009).

30. Thanks to Chad Flanders and Zachary Hoskins for helpful suggestions in improving this paper.

Chapter Six

Universal Jurisdiction and International Criminal Law

Jovana Davidovic

In recent years, there has been growing scholarly interest in the question of legitimacy of international criminal law (ICL), especially in providing justifications for ICL's right to rule. Such justifications are meant not only to provide the normative ground for ICL's right to rule but also to circumscribe a scope of criminal actions over which the international criminal law could govern.[1] For many scholars a starting question is this: what makes some spheres of action such that some of the time one can override state sovereignty in claiming the right to rule with respect to them? This partly explains why literature on the legitimacy of ICL often focuses on the question of universal jurisdiction—the question of whether there are some crimes any state can prosecute regardless of where they were committed or by whom.

Making sense of universal jurisdiction is valuable not only for answering the question of ICL's legitimacy, but also for answering more foundational questions about criminal law in general. For example, analyses of universal jurisdiction can ground a better understanding of sovereignty and its instrumentality.[2] Also, answering the question of universal jurisdiction one way rather than another can set limits on possible interpretations of many legal documents, including the Geneva Conventions. Furthermore, making sense of universal jurisdiction for some crimes requires that we address what could ground such authority in the first place. This gives rise to familiar questions about what makes something a crime, what makes something a public wrong, what are the aims of punishment and criminal justice, and so on. Thus questions about universal jurisdiction can also help make sense of these more foundational questions.

Universal jurisdiction permits states or possibly international bodies to prosecute perpetrators of some of the worst crimes independent of where such crimes occurred, to whom and by whom. The central question about universal jurisdiction is under which circumstances and for which crimes (if any) can a state (or an international court) prosecute an individual who neither is their national (or national of the member state), nor had committed the crime on their territory, nor against their citizens, nor against their vital interests.[3] In this chapter, I argue that universal jurisdiction for some crimes can be justified. In particular, I argue that universal jurisdiction can be justified for *jus cogens* crimes, that is, violations of *jus cogens* norms.[4] By *jus cogens* norms, scholars usually mean the kinds of norms that are "of such transparent bindingness that no individual can fail to understand that he or she is bound by them."[5] To say that an international legal norm rises to the level of *jus cogens* is to say that it is peremptory and that it prevails over any conflicting international rule. I believe that failing to prosecute *jus cogens* crimes would undermine the international rule of law and in that way threaten peace and security of the international community. This is why I argue that international crimes that fall under universal jurisdiction are crimes for which failing to prosecute would be a special kind of a wrong by the international community. I start, in section I, by trying to provide a clearer understanding of universal jurisdiction and the problems of justification to which it gives rise. I address the current status of universal jurisdiction in the international law. In this first section, I also address the proper relationship between normative arguments, such as the one I am providing here, and possible legal arguments one could provide for or against universal jurisdiction.

In section II, I consider some of the proposed justifications for universal jurisdiction, including those of David Luban, Antony Duff, Jiewuh Song, and Win-chiat Lee.[6] Most of the arguments in support of universal jurisdiction start from the intuition that there are some crimes that are so heinous, so grave that they could justify universal jurisdiction. This is where the similarities among various accounts end, since there is significant disagreement regarding which other conditions, in addition to the starting intuition, need to be met to justify universal jurisdiction. For example, while Luban thinks the heinousness of these crimes is, together with a fair procedure, sufficient to justify an institution in prosecuting such crimes, Duff insists on a particular relationship between the crime and the institution or the community asserting the right to prosecute. To establish jurisdiction, Duff argues, we also need to explain why exactly *this* court rather than another is justified in calling a perpetrator to account. Different, albeit just as relevant, disagreement exists between Song and Lee, who both pay close attention to the historical standing of universal jurisdiction and its relationship to the crime of piracy. While Song takes the case of piracy and reasons behind universal jurisdiction in the case of piracy as essential for making sense of universal jurisdiction for the crimes of genocide and crimes against humanity, Lee argues that piracy couldn't possibly satisfy that starting intuition that some crimes are so heinous that they could justify universal jurisdiction. I discuss both of these debates as a way of situating my argument for universal jurisdiction.

Finally, in section III, I develop an argument for universal jurisdiction for the worst of crimes. I start from the intuition that it is the heinousness of these crimes that even raises the question of universal jurisdiction. This means, I argue, that we must accept heinousness as a relevant element for defining which crimes are even to be considered for possible universal jurisdiction. Next, I argue that universal jurisdiction crimes are those crimes that are covered by the *jus cogens* norms, which commonly include norms against aggression, apartheid, slavery, torture, and genocide. The fact that (rather than the reasons why) the international community recognizes and accepts some crimes as *jus cogens* can define a moral community around those norms. The impunity for violations of such norms then can be understood as giving rise to a different and larger set of reasons for prosecution for the international community than for some state. Impunity for *jus cogens* crimes undermines the functional role these norms can play in establishing and strengthening the international rule of law, which plays a significant role in promoting sustainable peace and protecting human rights. It is for these reasons that I conclude that universal jurisdiction can be justified as a right of the international community as a whole, explained by the fact that the type of a wrong that arises from the international community's failure to prosecute *jus cogens* norms is different from the type of a wrong that comes from failing to prosecute such violations by some state or another.

I. UNIVERSAL JURISDICTION AND ITS RELATIONSHIP TO THE INTERNATIONAL CRIMINAL LAW

Commonly, most states accept a set of principles that governs when a state might transgress borders to legislate behavior in another state. These include the territoriality principle, the nationality principle, the passive personality principle, the protective principle, and more controversially the universal jurisdiction principle.[7] Under the universal jurisdiction principle, a state (or possibly an international body) might prosecute an individual even when none of the other principles apply. For a state, this would mean it could prosecute a noncitizen, who is not in its territory, for a crime committed against someone other than its citizens, for a crime that did not directly harm or undermine that state's vital interests. For an international body, it would mean prosecutions of individuals from states or for crimes committed in states that are not signatories of the relevant treaty. This gives rise to a worry about the possible justification behind such prosecutions. Commonly the relationship between citizens and their government or state is a necessary condition in most accounts explaining why the state is justified in prosecuting, punishing, and in general acting coercively. By definition, any justification for universal jurisdiction will not be able to rely on the relationship between the victim or offender to the state or international court that seeks to prosecute such a crime.

While there is widespread acceptance (legally speaking) of universal jurisdiction for the crime of piracy, there is a significant amount of disagreement regarding whether or not universal jurisdiction is a customary norm with respect to crimes of genocide, torture, slavery, and other heinous crimes. While universal jurisdiction with respect to piracy has been practiced in the past, universal jurisdiction with respect to many of these other proposed universal jurisdiction crimes has not—until recently. For example, in 2002 Belgium issued an arrest warrant for the Congolese minister of foreign affairs, Abdoulaye Yerodia Ndombasi, in an attempt to prosecute him under Belgium's new universal jurisdiction laws governing war crimes, crimes against humanity, and genocide.[8] In the *Arrest Warrant Case*, which was brought before the International Court of Justice (ICJ), the court decided against Belgium, based not on the issue of universal jurisdiction, but immunity. Nonetheless several dissenting opinions provide useful groundwork for the current legal stance on the issue of universal jurisdiction.[9] In a joint dissenting opinion judges Higgins, Kooijmans, and Buergenthal argue that immunity cannot be established without establishing jurisdiction and that the court should have made a decision on the question of jurisdiction as well. The judges assert that although, as a matter of practice, there is no custom of universal jurisdiction, nonetheless "[t]his does not necessarily indicate . . . that such an exercise would be unlawful."[10] In fact they argue that not only is there "nothing in this case law which evidences an *opinio juris* on the illegality of [universal] jurisdiction," but also there are "certain indications that a universal criminal jurisdiction for certain international crimes is clearly not regarded as unlawful."[11] They further acknowledge that in fact there is a tendency to grant states universal jurisdiction with respect to the most heinous of crimes, entitling them to act as agents of the international community. Among these crimes they include war crimes and incitement of racial hatred.

Clearly whether law permits universal jurisdiction seems to be an open question. But even had the law decided on this question, one could obviously still argue that the law should be changed. The goal of any normative argument in support of universal jurisdiction is to provide a philosophical framework that might inform or give reasons to accept universal jurisdiction. In what follows, I will not be providing legal reasons to interpret relevant law one way or another. Instead I will be giving conceptual and moral reasons to do so. Clearly, conceptual and moral reasons can and do inform legal interpretations of relevant statutes and practice all the time, and that is the hope for the argument discussed here as well.

II. UNIVERSAL JURISDICTION DEBATES

Largely due to the recent attempts by some states to exercise universal jurisdiction over at least some crimes against humanity and war crimes, there has been an uptick in interest regarding the moral and legal grounding of universal jurisdiction. Most accounts, if not all, start from the assertion that what gives rise to consideration of universal jurisdiction is the presence of heinous acts for which impunity from prosecution is unacceptable. But problems arise. These come in a number of varieties, two of which I focus on here.

First, there are worries that the heinousness of the act cannot possibly be sufficient to establish a right to prosecute and violate sovereignty. Instead one must establish why a particular court or community is entitled to prosecute; in other words, jurisdiction, by definition, requires a particular claim of relationship between the community prosecuting the perpetrator and her or her crimes. This problem focuses on deciding on the correct type of reasons one must give to establish jurisdiction and is primarily normative in nature.

Second, there are worries about the relationship between current arguments for universal jurisdiction and traditionally accepted arguments for it—namely, in the case of piracy. For some scholars, any arguments we give for universal jurisdiction for crimes of genocide and crimes against humanity must be continuous with arguments that explain universal jurisdiction in the case of piracy, while for others this is not necessary. In fact, some even argue that the crime of piracy doesn't share the main impetus behind even proposing universal jurisdiction over crimes of genocide and crimes against humanity—namely, the level of heinousness.

I start here (in A) by addressing the first set of worries regarding what types of reasons in addition to the heinousness of a crime we must give so as to be able to assert a right to universal jurisdiction over certain crimes. Next I turn (in B) to the relationship between justifications of universal jurisdiction for the crime of piracy and for more heinous crimes.

A.

David Luban starts off his argument for the legitimacy of international law by acknowledging that international criminal law can be understood to give rise to different problems in at least three different contexts: domestic, treaty-based, and international.[12] In international law and for international tribunals, the key question is whether we can legitimately assert jurisdiction over certain crimes, in particular over "pure international crimes." For Luban, these are crimes whose "criminal character originated in international rather than domestic law, and international rather than domestic legal institutions."[13]

Luban argues that unlike in domestic criminal contexts where justificatory focus is on justifying punishment, in the case of international criminal courts, the justificatory focus ought to be on justifying trials. This is because, in his view, the primary aim of ICL is norm projection. Given this expressive aim of law, the focus of our justification of ICL and its institutions ought to be on the practice of prosecuting rather than punishing, even though "punishment following conviction remains an essential part of any criminal process that aims to project a no-impunity norm."[14]

But whether or not punishment is central to the aims of ICL and international tribunals, the main question nonetheless remains: what could justify prosecutions across borders, prosecutions that infringe on sovereignty? Luban argues that the manifest fairness of procedures and punishments provides just such a justification. The conditions that a mechanism needs to meet to be considered fair and therefore legitimate in this case include the familiar rights to a speedy and public trial, to an impartial tribunal, to be informed of charges, and to have access to witnesses for and against you, as well as a ban on double-jeopardy and self-incrimination, and the like. Luban thinks that to meet most of these conditions, we need an organization such as the United Nations and agreement by the state, so that state authorization is "contingently indispensable to achieve procedural justice."[15] Ultimately, Luban argues that for the most heinous crimes a mechanism that meets the conditions of procedural justice also meets the conditions that are sufficient to assert a right to try in an international tribunal.

A central element of procedural justice is the principle of legality, which requires that "conduct may be criminalized and punished only if the crimes and punishment are explicitly established by publicly-accessible law."[16] There are at least two interpretations of why we ought to care about the principle of legality so stated. On the one hand, we ought to care about giving fair notice to would-be violators, and on the other hand, these legality conditions are meant to curb state power. Luban seems sympathetic to the idea that the role of the conditions of legality is to provide fair notice, and he further argues that when a crime is particularly heinous there are no reasonable expectations of defendants that are violated if they are prosecuted for such offenses.[17]

The problem with Luban's account is that it fails to provide sufficient justification for why it is that some international tribunal rather than a domestic court is justified in prosecuting these heinous crimes. His answers seem to be that an international tribunal can do so fairly and that for certain sorts of crimes everyone seems to be a potential victim. These answers seem insufficient, as Antony Duff points out.[18] Duff argues that fairness is not sufficient to establish jurisdiction:

> If a criminal court is to be morally justified in convicting a defendant, it must be able to sustain three claims: that the conduct constituting the alleged crime was criminal under a system of law binding the defendant; that the court has authority to try him; and that his guilt has been proved through a fair process which respected the demands of natural justice.[19]

In other words, one needs to establish a particular relationship between defendants or their crimes, on the one hand, and the court which seeks to prosecute them on the other. Duff rightly points out that to assert a right to prosecute it is not sufficient that the crime be so grave that it needs prosecuting and that there is a mechanism that might fairly prosecute that crime. The constant focus on the passive "that crimes should be punished," rather than the active "we ought to call them to account," Duff argues, is what leads scholars wrongly to focus on the heinousness of the act and ignore the more important question—what entitles the international community to call perpetrators of such crimes to account.[20]

For those crimes that we assert fall under universal jurisdiction, we are also asserting that they in some sense are of concern to the international community as a whole. For Duff, to say that a crime is a public wrong is not to say that a particular action actually wrongs the public, but that it is of concern to the public as a whole. In the case of domestic prosecutions it is easy to explain or justify what makes a particular community the relevant public that is concerned with that crime—namely, these wrongs concern the public as a whole in virtue of citizens' shared membership in a polity. But what makes an international community the body to whom a perpetrator should answer?[21] In what sense can we argue that a perpetrator must answer to "humanity"?[22] Duff points out that we need not establish humanity as a political community—it clearly is not—but that it is sufficient that humanity be a moral community arranged around certain norms. Duff further argues that we need not seek nor find some shared interests. This is because for Duff we are not after the claim that these crimes actually undermine the interests of all of humanity, but that they are of concern to humanity as a whole. He argues that "[w]e recognize others . . . as fellow human beings—which is to recognize that they have a claim on our respect and concern simply by virtue of our shared humanity."[23]

What the debate between Luban and Duff brings forth is that we must answer whether the heinousness of the crimes that are considered for universal jurisdiction is sufficient to ground and make sense of other conditions necessary to assert universal jurisdiction. I will argue that Duff's criticism of Luban is correct; we need to show that the international community is properly speaking an entity that one could be accountable to, and furthermore that there is something about these most heinous crimes that explains why the international community is entitled as a whole to infringe on sovereignty.

I will contend that the international community does in fact make up a moral community around certain shared norms—namely, the *jus cogens* norms. I will further argue that it is not necessary that we establish that *jus cogens* norms protect the interests of all of humanity to be able to use that notion to justify universal jurisdiction. In particular, I will argue that the very recognition of these norms (even if it is on disparate grounds) plays a significant role in strengthening and establishing the international rule of law which in turn is essential for promoting peace and human rights. This is why I think the international community has an added interest in prosecuting *jus cogens* crimes, explaining thus the unique relationship between the international community as a whole and the right of universal jurisdiction. Before I move on to that argument, I quickly turn to a separate issue regarding the relationship between the justification of universal jurisdiction in the case of piracy and in the case of other crimes, such as those covered by *jus cogens* norms.

B.

In her "Pirates and Torturers," Jiewuh Song argues that we ought to take very seriously the arguments that ground universal jurisdiction in the case of piracy and that we ought to attempt to develop arguments for universal jurisdiction in all other cases from reasons consistent with those that explain piracy as a universal jurisdiction crime. She argues, like Duff, that appealing simply to the heinousness of certain crimes, which gives rise to what she calls "the standard account" of universal jurisdiction, is not sufficient to justify it. Instead she argues that universal jurisdiction can only be justified as a way of filling enforcement gaps for some international norms that are prone to such gaps. In this way her justification for universal jurisdiction is continuous with previous justifications for the crime of piracy as a universal jurisdiction crime.

The "standard account," which Song rejects, she attributes to cases such as the *Arrest Warrant Case* and to scholars such as Luban. Song argues that one of the reasons the "standard account" fails is that the appeal to the most heinous of crimes invites worries about the scope of universal jurisdiction, primarily because it is hard to draw a principled line separating out "the most heinous of crimes."

In addition to worries about the scope of universal jurisdiction, Song, like Duff, insists that we must establish a uniquely justified relationship between the crime and those who seek to prosecute it. Even if we could somehow settle the worries about the scope of universal jurisdiction and heinousness of crimes, we would still have to explain the unique relationship between the community that seeks to prosecute and the crime. She examines several proposals for this unique relationship, including Luban's and Duff's. She rejects Luban's suggestion regarding this relationship—namely, the suggestion that the international community is entitled to prosecute those crimes for which every human is a potential victim. Luban's proposal that some crimes are a general threat and that we all thus have an interest in not allowing perpetrators of such crimes to get away with impunity is not sufficient, Song insists. She argues that we would want to justify universal jurisdiction for some crimes even if we were not all potential targets (for one reason or another).[24]

Alternatively, we could, like Duff, suggest that it is not an actual threat to our security that explains the relationship between the international community and crimes for which we want to justify universal jurisdiction, but instead that "we recognize others as fellow human beings—which is to recognize that they should have a claim on our respect and concern simply by virtue of our shared humanity."[25] This, however, Song argues, leaves us back where we started—with worries about the scope of universal jurisdiction. We are left with too many crimes that might fall under universal jurisdiction.

Heinousness, Song concludes, is clearly not enough—after all how could differences in the heinousness of the act explain why the appropriate venue for trial and punishment expands? Why would, for example, domestic battery in Massachusetts only concern Massachusetts residents, while murder in Boston would concern the whole country or the world?[26]

All of this points to the fact, Song argues, that even if we could agree on the sorts of crimes that affect the interests of all in the international community, this would not be sufficient to assert a right to universal jurisdiction. Instead of these "standard account" arguments, Song proposes that, continuous with arguments for piracy as a universal jurisdiction crime, universal jurisdiction for other crimes be justified as filling an enforcement gap. In the case of piracy, what really justified the right to universal jurisdiction is the common location of where piracy crimes occur. Song argues that

> by institutionalizing a legal practice that gives any state that captures any pirate jurisdiction over him, states can increase the chances of capturing pirates, and so increase compliance with the international legal prohibition of piracy. That is, universal jurisdiction over piracy is a response to an enforcement gap, rather than a jurisdictional gap.[27]

I think this attempt is mistaken. The universal jurisdiction with respect to piracy seems to be grounded in a very different principle from universal jurisdiction in the case of crimes against humanity or genocide. It is not obvious that we must insist on the same types of justifications in both the case of piracy and the case of genocide, and attempting to do this puts legal history above moral reasons which often are meant to independently criticize a proposed legal framework. In other words, the proposal that Song puts forth is correct, it seems to me, in suggesting that universal jurisdiction for piracy is best explained as well as justified by the gap in enforcement, but it is not clear to me why we ought to think that universal jurisdiction in cases of genocide and crimes against humanity ought to be as well.[28] Even though heinousness of the crimes cannot on its own justify universal jurisdiction for such crimes, it is nonetheless this heinousness, which piracy doesn't embody to the same extent, which gives rise to an interest in universal jurisdiction for such crimes in the first place. To ignore this, it seems to me, is to ignore the very question of universal jurisdiction for the worst of crimes. Win-chiat Lee seems to agree, as he argues against insisting on continuity between arguments for universal jurisdiction in the case of piracy and in the case of genocide or crimes against humanity.[29]

Lee argues that there is a set of "international crimes proper" and that membership in that set can be defined by looking at what justifies universal jurisdiction. For Lee, universal jurisdiction is explained, and thus the category of international crimes proper is defined, by those crimes that we ought not to leave for the states to prosecute—namely, those crimes that undermine the political authority of the very states that would try to prosecute them, such as crimes against their own people. He argues that the universal jurisdiction is explained by the nature of the crimes that it prosecutes, rather than solely by the harm those crimes inflict on individuals.[30] In other words, it is not a question of the level of harm a particular crime inflicts, rather it is against whom and by whom the crime is perpetrated.

On Lee's view, there are some international crimes that may be explained by policy considerations and gaps in enforcement, but the membership of those crimes in the international crime pool is ad hoc. For other crimes, the ones he focuses on, it is a matter of moral obligation that we treat them as international crimes. The role of international crimes proper and international criminal mechanisms with respect to those crimes is not simply to enhance law enforcement and prosecutions domestically. Instead, the role of prosecuting such crimes is to protect some international (rather than domestic) value. This leads him to think that piracy, even though commonly considered a universal jurisdiction crime, is not an international crime proper.[31]

Lee argues that piracy is ultimately a crime against states and that the suppression of piracy might require coordination, and that in this sense it is not a crime that is against the international community as a whole. For a crime to be against the international community as a whole, it is not sufficient that some commonly shared value is violated; for example, it is not sufficient that a murder is committed. Instead what is essential is that the murder is committed by a state (or an individual because of lack of protection by the state). This view together with the focus on the undermining of political authority by committing heinous acts commits Lee to a view that the central cases of international crimes proper are those committed internally rather than those across borders (although his account, he believes, can accommodate those across borders as well).

Lee and Song clearly disagree about the role that arguments for piracy as a universal jurisdiction crime ought to play for arguments in support of, for example, genocide as a universal jurisdiction crime. As I have mentioned, while it seems obvious that we might learn valuable lessons about universal jurisdiction by looking at previous laws such as piracy laws, we ought not to rest our arguments on the existence or content of such laws (in this case). This is because of the obvious differences, morally speaking, between crimes against humanity, for example, and the crime of piracy. I think we ought to decouple the intuition that we ought to have universal jurisdiction with respect to the worst of crimes from the often misguided and failed attempts to establish universal jurisdiction via past piracy laws. Whether or not this should be done will depend on what exactly we think justifies calls for universal jurisdiction independent of laws regarding piracy.[32] So then instead of focusing on attempts to make sense of piracy as a universal jurisdiction crime, we should turn our focus to the relationship between the particular set of crimes that we propose ought to be considered universal jurisdiction crimes and the international community. It is this relationship that needs to be explained so as to establish universal jurisdiction for the worst of crimes.

III. JUSTIFYING UNIVERSAL JURISDICTION

With all of the above in mind, what would we need to justify universal jurisdiction? The shared starting intuition is that there are some crimes that are so grave, so heinous, that they ought not to go unpunished.[33] In this starting claim there seems to be an (often unspoken) assumption that not punishing such crimes is a wrong in itself in a sense different from the crimes for which such prosecutions are considered. It might very well be the case that for anything that is a crime leaving it unpunished is a separate wrong. That is why we ought to examine whether the wrong in allowing perpetrators to get away with impunity for *these sorts of crimes* is somehow different.

In what follows, I argue that we can circumscribe and define an international moral community around *jus cogens* norms. Furthermore, I argue that universal recognition of *jus cogens* norms (whether or not recognition and acceptance is what grounds their moral salience) is sufficient to explain why impunity for violations of such norms is a unique wrong for the community circumscribed by recognition of those norms—namely, the international community. *Jus cogens* norms play a unique functional role for the international community in strengthening the international rule of law. Impunity for *jus cogens* crimes undermines the functional role of these norms for the international rule of law. This is why we, as an international community, have an interest in ensuring that these norms retain their role in the international arena. I conclude that universal jurisdiction can be justified as a right of the international community as a whole, explained by the fact that the type of a wrong that arises from the international community failing to prosecute a *jus cogens* crime is different from the wrong of failing to prosecute such violation by some state or another (that has a jurisdictional relationship to that crime). This does not mean that the international community should prosecute such crimes in international tribunals, however, there are some reasons (akin to the ones Luban provides as well as higher visibility reasons) to prefer international prosecutions for *jus cogens* crimes.

I start from the claim that failing to prosecute a crime is a separate wrong from the wrong that the commission of that crime entailed, and that failing to prosecute a *jus cogens* crime is a particular type of such separate wrong. This assertion is not unfamiliar; it simply acknowledges that failing to punish or try a crime is a wrong with respect to whatever justifies such punishment (or trial).[34] When punishment is, all things considered, justified, then failing to punish is a wrong against the people whom such punishment is meant to protect, or whom the justification of such punishment considers to be the beneficiaries of such punishment. But what then would it mean to say that the wrong committed by failing to punish and try *jus cogens* crimes is in type different from failing to punish or try perpetrators of other types of crimes? To answer this I turn to the way in which *jus cogens* norms are uniquely related to the international community.

Jus cogens norms are the kinds of norms that are "of such transparent bindingness that no individual can fail to understand that he or she is bound by them."[35] Larry May argues that *jus cogens* norms ground the central justification for international prosecutions. For May, they capture crimes that are covered by what he calls the "international harm principle" and the "security principle." The international harm principle suggests that certain crimes, which have a group character either with respect to the perpetrators or with respect to victims, harm the international community as a whole.[36] The security principle provides a justification for a permission to interfere in a sovereign state's affairs in cases when the state deprives its citizens (or fails to protect them from violations) of physical security or ability to subsist.[37] May can be understood as suggesting that certain types of crimes (those covered by *jus cogens* norms) are in fact harmful to the international community because of the risk they imply for any member of the international community. This sort of an account would be in theory sufficient to explain why the international community might be justified in prosecuting *jus cogens* crimes under universal jurisdiction via the courts of some state or another. But this is also the sort of account, as Duff (persuasively) suggests, that requires that the international community can be harmed or wronged as a whole. Possibly more seriously, this account, like Luban's, depends on the claim that there are certain crimes that it is in everyone's interest to protect against because everyone is a potential victim (because we must live in groups, Luban might add). But accounts that depend on the potentiality or risk of harm fail to explain why we should care if the risk of harm was only with respect to certain group characteristics.[38]

It seems to me that we can assert a much simpler and less controversial relationship between the international community, *jus cogens* crimes, and universal jurisdiction, if we start from the claim that the recognition of *jus cogens* norms circumscribes and defines an international moral and normative community. What is central to this account is that varied moral justifications behind *jus cogens* norms are compatible with it. In other words, we need not assert that humanity has shared interests, other than the interest in the rule of law that protects their varying other interests. On this view, an unpunished violation of a universally recognized non-derogable norm is a wrong committed by the international community in virtue of the fact that it undermines the international rule of law, which protects our varying interests.

As we saw, a common worry regarding universal jurisdiction is trying to explain why for some crimes the appropriate community to call perpetrators to account is the international community, or some state as its agent. Duff, for example, argues that humanity ought not to be seen as a community that can actually be wronged. But it seems to me that a more central question is whether we have reasons to think that the international community has reasons above and beyond those that individual states might have to prosecute offenders of *jus cogens* norms, and, as I have argued, the role *jus cogens* norms play in the sustainability of the international rule of law is just such a reason. In other words, the international community would commit a different type of a wrong in failing to prosecute a perpetrator of *jus cogens* norms than some other entity (such as a traditionally jurisdictionally related state). This is because of the status and the role *jus cogens* norms play for the international community as a whole.

As I have mentioned, my account does not depend on the argument for justification of *jus cogens* norms. My argument is consistent both with the view that their normativity arises out of agreement and with the view that it arises out of some kind of a natural law. Instead, what is central for my account is that as a matter of fact, and possibly for disparate reasons, *jus cogens* norms *are recognized* by the international community as a whole and as such play a particular role in not only defining a unique normative community but also establishing a *rule of law* for that community. This sort of approach also dissolves worries about the scope of our argument; on this account, the recognition of a crime as a *jus cogens* crime defines the scope of universal jurisdiction.

Some scholars, including May, argue that *jus cogens* norms are different from customary laws since if they were simply customs then one could opt out of them. Scholars who argue in this way worry that if recognition and consent grounded *jus cogens* norms, then they would lose their non-derogable status.[39] *Jus cogens* norms are non-derogable norms, and while their instantiation in moral theories might very well be properly grounded in natural law or principles of justice, it is the role they play in international law and for international community that matters here. The Vienna Convention on the Law of Treaties states that

> [a] treaty is void if, at the time of its conclusion, it conflicts with a peremptory norm of general international law . . . [that is] a norm accepted and recognized by the international community of States as a whole as a norm from which no derogation is permitted and which can be modified only by a subsequent norm of general international law having the same character.[40]

My argument doesn't depend on the moral grounding for *jus cogens* norms, only on their recognition as universal, because it is that recognition that I believe strengthens the international rule of law and in that way further promotes sustainable peace and protection of human rights. Furthermore, it is the recognition of *jus cogens* norms that defines a normative community that has a particular set of obligations with respect to those norms (because of their unique role for that community), and as such their recognition is sufficient to explain why it is an obligation of the international community to prosecute such crimes. Simply put, the universal acceptance and recognition of certain norms as non-derogable and universally binding defines a community which is then entitled to assert that impunity from prosecutions for violation of such norms is a matter for *that community* rather than some more localized community because and when such norms establish scaffolding for other rules that govern the same community, as it is in this case.

One might still possibly wonder why we think that prosecutions under universal jurisdiction are essential. If we take the earlier argument seriously, it is because suggesting that one has violated a norm that we all hold dear says something different from saying that one has violated a norm that a particular polity holds dear. This is in part because we, as an international community, hold them dear to a different extent and for different reasons. The assumption is that all the reasons that are relevant for justifying prosecuting some particular *jus cogens* crime in the name of a state are also relevant internationally, but, in addition, the international community has further reasons to prosecute in its name.

I have suggested that not prosecuting violations of these norms undermines the role they can and do play for the international community. As I have argued, whether or not the recognition or acceptance of these norms is the source of their normativity, it is without a doubt a main element in their role for the international community. In other words, *jus cogens* norms play a particular functional role for the international community in virtue of their recognition as *jus cogens*. This role is partially to act as scaffolding for the establishment of international rule of law. For a number of reasons, I take it as obvious that the international rule of law can play a significant role in sustaining peace and protecting human rights. This is why it seems in everyone's interest to retain all these norms as *jus cogens* and to reaffirm the recognition of them as non-derogable. But if *jus cogens* crimes ought not to go unpunished because of the unique functional role they play for the international community and the international rule of law, then it would be a different kind of wrong for the international community not to prosecute those crimes than it would be for a state.

It doesn't follow from this that the *jus cogens* crimes must be prosecuted by international courts, but it does follow that *jus cogens* crimes are crimes of universal jurisdiction and as such ought to be prosecuted in the name of humanity; that is, they are the sorts of crimes for which one is accountable to the international community. There might be very good reasons to prosecute such crimes in international courts, but the argument here only attempts to establish the universal jurisdiction for such crimes.[41]

It is important to note that I am not suggesting that *jus cogens* crimes are wrong or particularly wrong because they undermine international rule of law. What I am suggesting is that *jus cogens* norms' functional status in the international community for the international rule of law can explain why they rise to the level of universal jurisdiction. In fact, ultimately I do think that *jus cogens* crimes wrong humanity, not because anyone could be subject to such crimes, but because (and when) they undermine the international rule of law. Once again, this doesn't mean that a *jus cogens* wrong is simply a wrong of undermining international rule of law—that would be preposterous—but *jus cogens* crimes give the international community defined by recognition of those norms an *extra reason* for prosecution which can justify universal jurisdiction. This should also lead us to consider that when states prosecute such crimes, they should prosecute them on universal jurisdiction grounds (even in cases when other jurisdictional grounds are available).

NOTES

1. For more, see, for example, Allen Buchanan, *The Legitimacy of International Law*, *in* Philosophy of International Law 79 (Samantha Besson & John Tasioulas eds., 2010); John Tasioulas, *The Legitimacy of International Law*, *in id.* at 97.

2. For more on the relationship between the role of national and international prosecutions, see, for example, Andrew Altman & Christopher Wellman, *A Defense of International Criminal Law*, 115 Ethics 35 (2004).

3. The common justifications include "(a) the territoriality principle, which gives states jurisdiction over crimes committed in their territories, as well as crimes committed elsewhere with effects in their territories. (b) the nationality principle, which give states jurisdiction over crimes committed by their own nationals. (c) the passive personality principle, which gives states jurisdiction over crimes committed against their nationals. (d) the protective principle, which gives states jurisdiction over crimes committed against vital government interests-crimes like espionage." David Luban, *Fairness to Rightness: Jurisdiction, Legality, and the Legitimacy of International Criminal Law*, *in* PHILOSOPHY OF INTERNATIONAL LAW, *supra* note 1, at 570.

4. I use the term "*jus cogens* crime" to describe a crime that is prohibited by a norm that rises to a level of a *jus cogens* norm.

5. LARRY MAY, CRIMES AGAINST HUMANITY: A NORMATIVE ACCOUNT 64 (2004).

6. In the case of Luban and Duff, I extend their arguments about legitimacy of international criminal law to universal jurisdiction. *E.g.*, David Luban, *Fairness to Rightness*, *in* PHILOSOPHY OF INTERNATIONAL LAW, *supra* note 1, at 569; Antony Duff, *Authority and Responsibility in International Criminal Law*, *in* PHILOSOPHY OF INTERNATIONAL LAW, *supra* note 1, at 589; Jiewuh Song, *Pirates and Torturers: Universal Jurisdiction as Enforcement Gap-Filling*, 23 J. POL. PHIL. (forthcoming 2015); Win-chiat Lee, *International Crimes and Universal Jurisdiction*, *in* INTERNATIONAL CRIMINAL LAW AND PHILOSOPHY 15 (Larry May & Zachary Hoskins eds., 2010); David Luban, *A Theory of Crimes against Humanity*, 29 YALE J. INT'L L. 85 (2004). At a later time I also address Larry May's argument for universal jurisdiction. MAY, *supra* note 5.

7. *See supra* note 3.

8. *Arrest Warrant Case* (*Dem. Rep. Congo v. Belg.*), 2002 I.C.J., http://www.icj-cij.org/docket/index.php?p1=3&p2=3&case=121&p3=4.

9. In the *Arrest Warrant Case* the ICJ decided against Belgium saying that "the arrest warrant of 11 April 2000, and its international circulation, constituted violations of a legal obligation of the Kingdom of Belgium towards the Democratic Republic of the Congo, in that they failed to respect the immunity from criminal jurisdiction and the inviolability which the incumbent Minister for Foreign Affairs of the Democratic Republic of the Congo enjoyed under international law." *Id.*

10. Joint Separate Opinion of judges Higgins, Kooijmans, and Buergenthal, art. 44, at 76–77, http://www.icj-cij.org/docket/files/121/8136.pdf.

11. *Id.*, art. 45, 46, at 77. Judges Higgins, Kooijmans, and Buergenthal cite the following sources as relevant support for their view: M. Cherif Bassiouni & Benjamin B. Ferencz, *The Crime Against Peace and Aggression: From Its Origin to the ICC*, *in* INTERNATIONAL CRIMINAL LAWS, VOL. III: INTERNATIONAL ENFORCEMENT 207, 228 (M. Cherif Bassiouni ed., 2nd ed. 1999); Theodor Meron, *International Criminalization of Internal Atrocities*, 89 AM. J. INT'L L. 554, 576 (1995). They go on to argue that "the duty to prosecute under those treaties which contain the *aut dedere aut prosequi* provisions opens the door to a jurisdiction based on the heinous nature of the crime rather than on links of territoriality or nationality (whether as perpetrator or victim). The 1949 Geneva Conventions lend support to this possibility, and are widely regarded as today reflecting customary international law." Judges Higgins, Kooijmans, and Burgenthal in their joint opinion and Judge Van den Wyngaert in her separate dissenting opinion all endorsed an exercise of universal jurisdiction for the most heinous crimes (even *in absentia*). Joint Separate Opinions, *supra* note 10, art 60, at 82; Mattias Goldman, *Arrest Warrant Case (Democratic Republic of the Congo v Belgium)*, OXFORD ENCYCLOPEDIA OF INTERNATIONAL PUBLIC LAW (2015), http://opil.ouplaw.com/view/10.1093/law:epil/9780199231690/law-9780199231690-e1249.

12. Luban, *supra* note 6. With respect to the first, Luban argues that universal criminal jurisdiction in domestic laws can only be justified "if states have distinctively moral interests in repressing crimes (or at least certain crimes) wherever they occur." *Id.* at 571. Most importantly, Luban argues that what can justify universal jurisdiction is that these crimes are literally crimes against humanity. Treaty-bases of universal jurisdiction are in his mind a hybrid between domestic and international universal jurisdiction and don't independently give rise to philosophically interesting questions about universal jurisdiction, according to Luban.

13. *Id.* at 572.

14. *Id.* at 576.

15. *Id.* at 583.
16. *Id.* at 581.
17. *Id.* at 584. So for Luban the perpetrators tried in Nuremberg did no worse than they should have expected given the heinousness of their crimes. This is particularly interesting as a solution to the well-known worry about retrospective laws and prosecutions in Nuremberg.
18. Duff, *supra* note 6.
19. *Id.* at 590.
20. *Id.* at 594.
21. If we argue that she is to answer to her political community, then any justifications that can be derived from delegating such accountability will not be a justification of universal jurisdiction.
22. The question of what we mean by "humanity" and whether it can play the same or parallel role as "public" in the "public wrong," which is an essential step in making sense of what we mean by saying something is a "crime," is an important question and has received significant discussion in literature including in May, *supra* note 5; Duff, *supra* note 6; Antony Duff, *Theorizing Criminal Law*, 25 OXFORD J. L. STUD. 353 (2005).
23. Duff, *supra* note 6, at 601.
24. Song, *supra* note 6.
25. Duff, *supra* note 6, at 601; Song, *supra* note 6, at 10.
26. Song, *supra* note 6, at 11.
27. *Id.* at 12.
28. A clear argument in support of such continuity in argumentation might take the form of suggesting that any proposals for universal jurisdiction must have some relevant relationships to the body of law we are trying to analyze or criticize. So the argument often goes that philosophers are not sensitive to the actual laws and Song seems to be quite responsive to that worry.
29. Lee, *supra* note 6.
30. As he argues, "They all involved serious harm to individuals." *Id.* at 18.
31. Lee follows Cassese's argument in rejecting piracy as an international crime. For Cassese, piracy is not an international crime because it fails one of the four conditions that he says are necessary for a crime to be international. These include "1. Violation of customary international rules that often originate in or are clarified by treaties, 2. Violations of rules "intended to protect values considered important by the whole international community and consequently binding all states and individuals, 3. A universal interest in suppressing these crimes, manifested in the universal jurisdiction that states can claim in principle over these crimes, 4. No functional immunity of perpetrators who are de jure or de facto state officials form the civil or criminal jurisdiction of foreign states." *Id.*; ANTHONY CASSESE & PAOLA GAETA, CASSESE'S INTERNATIONAL CRIMINAL LAW 23 (1st ed. 2003).
32. I ought to be clear here that I am not suggesting that we call for a particular set of laws ignoring the laws that are there, but if there are moral reasons to have universal jurisdiction in some cases that analysis should be done separately from the legal analysis of sets of reasons that apply. It might turn out that jointly the legal reasons and extra-legal reasons tell us that all things considered we cannot have universal jurisdiction, but the biggest flaw of the arguments that have attempted to argue for universal jurisdiction was to try to assert that their properly speaking extra-legal analysis is legal in a sense.
33. I too start from the belief that it is the heinousness of certain crimes that makes them such that they would even be considered for inclusion in what Lee calls "international crimes proper" or in other words for inclusion into the types of crimes that we might prosecute under universal jurisdiction. As I mentioned previously, this assertion alone should explain why I think we are justified in putting arguments that ground universal jurisdiction for piracy aside. Whether or not universal jurisdiction is of a single kind remains to be seen; it is not a foregone conclusion that everything that scholars define as arguments for universal jurisdiction must share the same grounding. What is clear is that the sort of intuition that even gives rise to suggestions for domestic and international universal jurisdiction laws is that certain crimes ought to be punished by the international community.

34. Whether it be retributive, consequentialist, rehabilitative, expressive, or communicative justification.

35. May, *supra* note 5, at 64.

36. More formally, "Only when there is serious harm to the international community, should international prosecutions against individual perpetrators be conducted, where normally this will require a showing of harm to the victims that is based on non-individualized characteristics of individual, such as the individual's group membership, or is perpetrated by, or involves, a State or other collective entity." *Id.*

37. More formally, "If a State deprives its subjects of physical security or subsistence, or is unable or unwilling to protect its subjects form harms to security or subsistence: a) then that State has no right to prevent international bodies from 'crossing its borders' in order to protect those subjects or remedy their harms; b) and then international bodies may be justified in 'crossing the borders' of a sovereign State when genuinely acting to protect those subjects." *Id.*

38. I addressed this criticism by Song above. Song argues that if human psychology were different and we only exhibited persecutory tendencies towards a single group, we would live in a world where we would not have an interest in "suppressing these crimes qua potential victims." She goes on to argue that how we should respond does not depend on potential victimhood. Song, *supra* note 6, at 10.

39. As I mentioned, one concern regarding this account of *jus cogens* norms is that it supposedly suggests that were there not to be recognition of these norms as *jus cogens*, they would lose their status. This is why scholars such as May insist that *jus cogens* norms are non-consensual. There is a sense in which this is right, but there is also a sense in which this seems mistaken. They are non-consensual in the sense that whether or not one consented or decided to abstain from consent, these norms would be binding to one. So it is not necessary that we give consent for these norms conceptually speaking to have the status of a *jus cogens* norm. That being said, it also seems obvious that much of the language surrounding *jus cogens* norms seems to imply they are in fact agreed upon and that states do in fact use them as grounds for behavior and more importantly for criticism of others. In other words, while we might agree with May that the ultimate source of *jus cogens* norms is morality, this seems less relevant—it is the recognition and the practice of these norms that defines the community and that explains why failing to prosecute violations of those norms would constitute a unique wrong. I ought also to mention that it doesn't at all seem obvious to me that one could fail to recognize apartheid, slavery, genocide, or torture (the crimes May discusses as central cases of *jus cogens*) as wrong. This is because all four of these have built into the very concept the normative elements suggesting one could not fail to recognize them as wrong. So even though May is right in the claim that "the fact that . . . States consent to these norms does not seem itself to be the source of their validity since even if many States withdrew their consent the norms against apartheid, slavery, and genocide would seemingly still have universally binding status," it nonetheless follows that the recognition of these as *jus cogens* norms defines a community with a particular interest in the role such norms can play in rule-of-law establishment and thus furthering the security of the community as a whole. Larry May, *Habeas Corpus as* Jus Cogens *in International Law*, 4 Crim. L. & Phil. 249, 252 (2010).

40. Vienna Convention on the Law of Treaties, May 23, 1969, https://treaties.un.org/doc/Publication/UNTS/Volume 1155/volume-1155-I-18232-English.pdf.

41. But there are good reasons—moral, legal, and historic—that explain why nonetheless most such crimes have been prosecuted domestically. These include facts such as having access to location of crimes and victims of such crime, the unique benefits to the victims and the wronged community and the state from a highly visible local prosecution, etc.

Part III

Offenders and Victims

Chapter Seven

Historicizing Criminal Responsibility

Arlie Loughnan[1]

Individual responsibility for crime is the central organizing principle of the criminal law in the current era. Responsibility in criminal law is typically understood as denoting answerability, the capacity to account for oneself or one's actions. As such, it refers to those to whom the criminal law—as a normative system—"speaks," and thus who may be properly called to account for their conduct via criminal law processes such as the criminal trial.[2] Criminal responsibility concerns the scope or reach of the criminal law—measured not in terms of the types of conduct prohibited, but in terms of who is, or who should be, subject to the law. As I discuss in this chapter, this conception of criminal responsibility is informed by the legal-philosophical scholarly tradition, which views criminal law a system of official censure and sanction or punishment for certain types of conduct.[3]

In this chapter I consider the value of a socio-historical approach to scholarly understanding of criminal responsibility principles and practices. I suggest that a socio-historical approach to criminal responsibility helps to contextualize or situate the (rather abstract) conceptual concerns of legal-philosophical studies of criminal responsibility. I then examine the state of play in socio-historical scholarship, which, broadly, has focused on the period up to the nineteenth century, and consider why the twentieth century has been somewhat difficult for scholars to grasp. From this basis, it is possible to sketch out a socio-historical study of criminal responsibility in the twentieth century. I propose an approach to the study of the twentieth century that sets criminal responsibility norms against broader extra-legal responsibility practices. This approach makes it possible to appreciate the wider social and political significance of criminal responsibility practices.

I. STUDYING CRIMINAL RESPONSIBILITY

Looking across the scholarly terrain, it appears that scholarship on criminal responsibility is, broadly, of two types—legal-philosophical and socio-historical. Here, I provide a brief assessment of the former and make a case for the value of the latter. I suggest that a socio-historical approach to criminal responsibility is useful in that it helps to contextualize the conceptual concerns of legal-philosophical study of criminal responsibility.

The first of the two broad camps of scholarly work on criminal responsibility comprises what I call legal-philosophical scholarship. I use the term "legal-philosophical" in a broad way to denote the type of criminal law scholarship that invokes normative philosophical thinking. Broadly speaking, the idea at the heart of the scholarly work in this tradition is that the application of the ordinary principles of liability and punishment to an individual is an acknowledgement or affirmation of their subjectivity.[4] Reflecting its connection to liberal moral and political philosophy, and its overarching concern with justifications for state punishment, this scholarly tradition places individual responsibility for crime at the heart of the "general part" of criminal law—the rules and doctrines that apply across the terrain of criminal law (i.e., that are "generalizable")[5]—and indeed at the heart of normative criminal law theory more generally.[6] The importance of criminal responsibility in this respect means that it has formed the focus of a dynamic body of legal-philosophical work, which continues to inform and enrich scholarly understanding of responsibility in criminal law. As I discuss below, this approach to the study of criminal responsibility currently dominates the field.

The legal-philosophical approach is associated with a particular conception of criminal responsibility, as mentioned at the outset of this chapter. According to this conception, there is a correspondence (weaker or stronger in the work of different scholars[7]) between moral understandings of responsibility and individual responsibility for crime such that the latter is constructed in psychological terms, centered on an *abstract*, rational entity that is *abstracted* from his or her social and political context.[8] In legal-philosophical accounts, the focus is on the minimal conditions of criminal responsibility, which are typically conceptualized as either a particular set of individual (moral, cognitive, or volitional) capacities or a set of opportunities.[9] So, as H. L. A. Hart argues, to assert that a person is responsible for his or her actions is to assert that a person has "normal" capacities—those of "understanding, reasoning and control of conduct: the ability to understand what conduct rules or morality require, to deliberate and reach decisions concerning these requirements, and to conform to decisions when made."[10] As this suggests, according to legal-philosophical approaches, the key questions for criminal responsibility are questions regarding the individual offender—"her acts, her brain, her self-control, her blameworthiness"[11]—with other "agents" or responsibility dynamics placed beyond the scholarly frame.

As even this short overview reveals, for scholars working in the legal-philosophical tradition, what we might call the responsibility question is generally framed positively—as a positive precondition for liability ("Who is responsible under criminal law for their conduct?"). Thus, as part of an argument about responsibility as answerability, Antony Duff argues that responsibility requires an individual to have "capacity both to respond to reasons and then to answer for oneself."[12] Another such approach is offered by John Gardner, who argues that criminal responsibility is being able to offer an account of oneself as a rational being, where such account-giving is instantiated in the legal process.[13] But, as I discuss below, viewed in historical light, the responsibility question operated as a negative one—responsibility was the *absence* of conditions of nonresponsibility ("Who is not responsible under criminal law?"). Indeed, as a practical matter, this is still the case because responsibility at trial (in the narrow terms of the legal-philosophical scholarship, as capacity) is assumed not proved.[14] Interrogating the framing of the responsibility question is not a matter of mere semantics but raises queries about the way in which the legal-philosophical discussion of criminal responsibility has taken place (and continues to take place) almost wholly in the absence of consideration of issues of evidence and proof.

In legal-philosophical approaches to criminal responsibility, responsibility and liability are conceptually distinct: it is possible to be responsible but not liable, for instance, if one has a defense to a criminal charge. As Duff argues, liability—to criminal punishment or to moral blame—is grounded in responsibility.[15] But what is a meaningful conceptual distinction has, in extant literature, hardened, arguably to the point of reification. This reification risks obscuring as much as it illuminates because, at least in its positive formulation (i.e., in relation to ascriptions of responsibility as opposed to ascriptions of nonresponsibility), it is difficult sharply to separate criminal responsibility and criminal liability. Despite the clear conceptual distinction, intention, recklessness, or knowledge are the "concrete concepts" out of which criminal responsibility is crafted, or, put another way, mens rea and actus reus is a "prevalent and continuing way of doing criminal responsibility."[16] The interrelation of responsibility and liability in this way risks being discounted in legal-philosophical work on criminal responsibility.

Legal-philosophical approaches to criminal responsibility also exclude significant developments in criminal law that would be helpfully included in studies of criminal responsibility. As Nicola Lacey argues, a legal-philosophical type approach brackets off a set of questions related to the institutional, social, and other conditions of existence of concepts of responsibility.[17] Such an approach also discounts what Lacey calls the "operational principles of criminal responsibility"—including policing, prosecution, and plea bargaining—and effectively quarantines the more obviously politically charged question of exactly what conduct can be criminalized.[18] In addition, this exclusion feeds into, and reflects, the subsisting marginality of noncore offenses in criminal law theory, and the associated neglect by scholars of the local or summary jurisdiction. This jurisdictional space is populated by, but not coextensive with, strict liability or outcome-based principles of criminal liability, and it forms the procedural context for the massive expansion of the criminal law in recent decades.[19] In the summary jurisdiction, the high profile of questions of fact has meant that scholars have seen little space for law (and thus for criminal law theory). And, as Lacey points out, the lack of attention to the summary jurisdiction serves to perpetuate the myth that a coherent set of general principles animates the criminal law.[20] Overall, the forms of criminal responsibility or liability that do not fit the dominant legal-philosophical story have been marginalized, creating a (growing) gap between the scholarly self-narrative through which the legal principles and practices of criminal law are understood, explained, and justified, and the reality of criminal law practices.

Over the last two decades or so, criminal responsibility has also come to the attention of socio-historical scholars, enlivening the academic field. Socio-historical approaches to criminal responsibility take legal concepts and principles as objects of study, and examine them in light of the substantive social, political, temporal, and institutional conditions under which they are realized.[21] Here, criminal responsibility is approached more broadly than in legal-philosophical scholarship. It is regarded as a social practice or a "thick" legal "thing"—the product of a network of laws, processes, institutions, and actors—rather than as a "thin" product of certain rules or moral norms.[22] This means these scholars are concerned with conceptions of criminal responsibility, but also with wider processes, including practices of evidence and proof, related to finding individuals (and others) responsible or nonresponsible in criminal law. The socio-historical approach has generated deep insights into criminal responsibility norms and practices—including regarding the dynamic relationship between ideas about criminal responsibility and the development of the modern state,[23] the changing coordination and legitimation requirements of criminal law into the current era,[24] the role of the police power,[25] and the influence of Enlightenment liberalism on the structures and operation of the criminal law.[26]

A closer look at just two aspects of extant socio-historical work on criminal responsibility illustrates the value of this type of scholarship. First, referring back to the way the responsibility question is framed (mentioned previously), socio-historical examination reveals the significance of nonresponsibility and diminished responsibility in the historical development of criminal responsibility principles and practices. It is generally recognized that a positive conceptualization of criminal responsibility, and any sense of the requirements of criminal liability (in terms of mens rea and actus reus), was absent from the early modern criminal law and process.[27] This meant that the mode of the criminal trial was exculpatory, with the defendant's responsibility (understood in a loose sense) assumed rather than an object of inquiry for the court, and defendants in effect presumed guilty and required to prove their innocence.[28] Up to and including the eighteenth century, individual defendants were assumed to be accountable for their actions, unless exceptional factors, such as insanity, existed.[29] This meant that legal elaboration of the necessary conditions for criminal responsibility-cum-liability (as yet incompletely separated) took place in cases in which those conditions appeared to be absent, as with defendants raising insanity. As a result, claims to exculpation based on incapacity were crucial in the development of criminal responsibility norms, in the formalization of criminal law defenses (the cleaving apart of defenses and factors in mitigation), and in the development of the particular rules of evidence and procedure that accompanied this movement.[30]

A second valuable contribution offered by socio-historical work on criminal responsibility is that it has demonstrated that individual mental states have come to occupy their central place in criminal law only relatively recently. At the end of the eighteenth century, it was still not yet necessary to appeal to individual responsibility to legitimize criminal law, reflecting, as Lacey writes, the "relative weakness of liberal, democratic and humanist sentiments" of the period.[31] Even after individual and subjective standards of responsibility started to be recognized in specific legal rules (such as murder), individual criminal responsibility did not yet provide a "basis for the conceptual organisation of the law."[32] The formalization of principles and practices of criminal responsibility—by which standards encoded in specific rules came to be thought of as generally applicable—continued into the twentieth century. In this dynamic context, and as one of the features of the modern law, the "ascription of responsibility was reformulated as a technical-legal question, a matter of positive law."[33] Later, the rise to prominence of a capacity-based concept of criminal responsibility was advanced by the development of psychological notions of mental states and personhood more generally, and this would come to have a profound effect on concepts of mens rea and ideas about fault in criminal law.[34]

Socio-historical work on criminal responsibility is valuable, as it helps to contextualize or situate the (rather abstract) conceptual concerns of legal-philosophical scholarship. A historicized analysis of criminal responsibility reveals that ideas about responsibility are "modulated" over time.[35] It is clear that, as Lacey argues, the institutional framework of criminal responsibility "conditions and shapes the contours of responsibility as an operational idea in criminal law and criminal justice."[36] And as I have argued in relation to the terrain of mental incapacity in criminal law, and based on a socio-historical analysis of the law, older ideas about the way in which "madness" (an aspect of nonresponsibility) becomes known, and may be proved for criminal law purposes—the means by which certain types of human behavior are evaluated, and the confidence with which evaluative judgments are made—continue to inform legal principles and practices grounded in mental incapacity.[37] Of course, it must be acknowledged that thinking about the history of criminal responsibility (or criminalization, or the principle of legality) is a different task from conceptualizing criminal responsibility in legal-philosophical terms.[38] But nonetheless it is useful (arguably even vital) for legal-philosophical scholars to get a sense of what the socio-historical approach has to offer in framing questions about, and advancing understanding of, criminal responsibility.

II. SOCIO-HISTORICAL STUDIES OF CRIMINAL RESPONSIBILITY

Despite the richness of socio-historical work on criminal responsibility overall, the twentieth century has been subject to less attention by these scholars than other periods. I suggest that three factors relating to the state of the academic field help to explain this: the structure and periodization of the historical narrative of criminal responsibility, the extant dominance of the legal-philosophical approach in criminal law theory, and, two intimately associated developments, the pluralization of bodies of knowledge about responsibility and the politicization of responsibility. I discuss each of these in turn.

A. The Structure and Periodization of the Historical Narrative(s)

The first factor that helps to explain why the twentieth century has been relatively difficult for socio-historical scholars of criminal responsibility to grasp is the structure of the historical stories told about criminal responsibility. The socio-historical narrative typically given about criminal responsibility is structured in broad chapters; current principles and practices of criminal responsibility are depicted as the products of developments playing out over large periods of time, with major changes occurring during the seventeenth and eighteenth centuries, and again over the nineteenth century. According to this narrative, the major developments that gave rise to relevant legal and procedural distinctions—such as the distinction between conduct (actus reus) and fault (mens rea), fact and opinion, liability and responsibility, and conviction and sentencing—which now govern the way we think about criminal responsibility, had largely played out by about the beginning of the 1900s. The study of criminal legal history framed by these distinctions perpetuates the view that this period is determinative of a historicized understanding of criminal responsibility. Narrating a socio-historical account of criminal responsibility in this way—a particular but, I would suggest, not necessary periodization, or division of historical time—encourages scholars to focus on earlier periods as most crucial for understanding criminal responsibility principles and practices as we now know them.

It is only the last chapter of the socio-historical narratives of criminal responsibility that is given over to the twentieth century, and, generally, only the first half of the century is in view. This chapter is brief, and perceived as significant mostly for the consolidation of major changes introduced in the earlier periods. Thus, as Lacey argues in relation to the changing coordination and legitimation requirements of the criminal law, this is a period in which factors such as regularized criminal case reporting and a formal appeals system enabled a more thorough realization of a capacity-based conception of individual responsibility—a development sometimes assumed to have occurred earlier.[39] Similarly, for Lindsay Farmer, after Kenny's *Outlines of Criminal Law* at the beginning of the century, Glanville Williams's work in the mid-twentieth century is something of an end point for developments in legal scholarship that have their origins in the nineteenth century.[40] As the twentieth century is not a period in which one type of criminal trial superseded another, or one in which radical shifts in our understanding of individuals (such as that relating to a capacity conception of fault) played themselves out, it is reduced to a sort of codicil to the main criminal responsibility narrative.

The risk of this sort of approach is that it renders parenthetical developments that may bear on our understanding of criminal responsibility in the current era. The twentieth and twenty-first centuries witnessed seismic social, economic, and political transformations (each of which has ontological and epistemological dimensions), the enormity of which resists neat cataloging. Shaped by these transformations, the realm of criminal law and criminal justice changed dramatically over the twentieth century. In terms of substantive law, the twentieth century is marked by the (possibly exponential) proliferation of criminal offenses, almost exclusively by statute,[41] and strict liability offenses have been created in significant numbers.[42] The postwar era signaled the arrival of new criminal law norms through the introduction of international human rights schemas and international criminal justice from the Nuremberg Trials to the ongoing prosecutions of the International Criminal Court. In terms of punishment, the prison became decentered within the penal system with the diversification of penal sanctions and the advent of new state agencies (such as the probation service and juvenile courts).[43] Procedurally, independent prosecutorial bodies have been established in many jurisdictions, and specialist courts (such as drug courts) have appeared and risen to prominence. With "new types of offense, new courts and procedures and even new bodies of criminal law," these developments may be understood not just as an intensification of the pace of change, but as a qualitative shift.[44] Approaching criminal responsibility broadly, to countenance at least some of these developments is to treat the twentieth century not so much as a postscript but as a new act—the twentieth century as its own drama.

B. The Dominance of Legal-Philosophical Approaches to Criminal Law Theory

The second factor that helps to explain why the twentieth century has proved relatively difficult for socio-historical scholars to grasp is the dominance of legal-philosophical approaches to criminal law theory from the second half of the twentieth century. There is comparatively little criminal law theory in the first half of the twentieth century, at least in the United Kingdom. As Farmer notes, when Glanville Williams was writing *The General Part* in the mid-century (it was first published in 1953), practitioners were mostly using nineteenth-century criminal law texts.[45] In the decades prior to the middle of the twentieth century, law was yet to acquire robust academic credibility within the English university system, thus circumscribing the possibilities for scholarly theorizing about law.[46] In the second half of the century, by contrast, and as is well known, jurisprudence experienced a heyday, with, prominently, the scholarly work of H. L. A. Hart heralding (and contributing to) the current vitality of the discipline.[47]

Criminal responsibility occupies a central place within the legal-philosophical approach to criminal law, as mentioned earlier, and the strong connection between criminal responsibility and the liberal moral and political philosophy that informs that approach suggests that it is playing a particular role. As Farmer suggests, responsibility has come to be thought to be central to the conceptual order and the self-understanding of the criminal law in the current period, expressed through the idea that responsibility can act as a constraint on criminalization via mens rea.[48] However, as Farmer argues, responsibility was not in fact foundational to the modern criminal law, but a commitment to its foundational character reflects the way in which responsibility is now part of the modality of law—the way civil order is secured. This civil order rests on the generalizability of the juridical person—a person who can self-regulate/self-reflect, and appreciate the importance of general norms of conduct for self and others—as the modern subject.[49] As this persuasive analysis suggests, an academy which is dominated by legal-philosophical approaches to criminal law theory is thoroughly invested in criminal responsibility. Indeed, arguably, any socio-historical study of criminal responsibility should encompass reflection on the significance of its current popularity among scholars.

The dominance of legal-philosophical approaches to criminal responsibility risks redefining what are most accurately regarded as questions of approach or method (understood as a type or mode of theorizing) as substantive questions (the content of theorizing). That is, it seems it is only possible to "do" criminal law theory in a particular way, and one approach becomes coextensive with the category of criminal law theory as a whole. Put another way, and at some risk of exaggeration, this tends to render all legal theory questions of legal-philosophy. Thus, it is not merely that legal-philosophical approaches eschew historically grounded analyses, but that their dominance has so far influenced the scholarly debate on criminal responsibility that the insights generated by socio-historical research tend to be, in effect if not by intention, pushed into a scholarly corner—as lacking weighty analytical purchase, or, because such assessment is interpretive rather than normative, of marginal significance or interest only.

C. The Pluralization of Bodies of Knowledge about Responsibility and the Politicization of Responsibility

The third factor making the twentieth century relatively difficult for socio-historical scholars of criminal responsibility is the pluralization of bodies of knowledge about responsibility and the politicization of responsibility, two closely related phenomena. By contrast with the first two factors, this factor relates not to the features of legal discourses, but to their position in relation to other scholarly discourses, and to the place of responsibility in the social system of which the legal order is a part. Put another way, here I am concerned both with the position of legal knowledge in the wider scholarly field, and the nature of responsibility as an object of study.

The pluralization of knowledges about responsibility and the politicization of responsibility relate to the broad, epochal shift, from modernity—a distinct "mode of life," centered on the state, rather than local or religious institutions[50]—to "late" modernity—a period associated with a loss of confidence in totalizing narratives of progress, science, and human rights—that occurred in the twentieth century.[51] This shift marks a fundamental change—in time/space relations, in relationships between self and other—that has played out on both historical or sociological, and epistemological levels. This shift, including whether it has occurred at all, has been much debated by social theorists and others, but its relevance to criminal law scholarship has not been considered as thoroughly as it might be.[52] I suggest that this shift has affected our ability to study criminal responsibility by making it more difficult to carve out the terrain that forms a ready or "natural" subject matter of socio-historical studies of criminal responsibility.

One of the hallmarks of the shift to from modernity to "late" modernity is the rise to prominence of a range of expert social knowledges about individuals and groups (e.g., social work, sociology, psychology, criminology), and their enlistment in the projects of state organization.[53] The rise of social knowledges, which both reflected and enhanced a more interventionist social reform agenda on the part of states, diversified the array of juridical, penal, social and therapeutic measures tailored to individual offenders.[54] These social knowledges also produced a pluralization of knowledges about responsibility, which has decentered *legal* knowledge of crime and criminality, and thus contributed to the difficulty of grasping criminal responsibility practices as they have played out over the twentieth century. The prominence of expert social knowledges in "late" modernity is challenging because law, which developed first as a practice rather than a scholarly discipline, rests on the "absolute authority" of text and court,[55] and does not necessarily sit easily alongside the social sciences, which rely on the empirical proof structures associated with scientific method.[56] This makes it hard to integrate legal knowledges with social science knowledges, and this impacts on the ready viability—the scope and significance—of studies of "traditional" or "core" legal subject matter, such as criminal responsibility. Arguably, this decentering of legal knowledge of responsibility is part of the decentering of legal knowledges more broadly, as law's premises of rationality, coherence, and objectivity are subject to increasing challenge.[57]

The pluralization of knowledges about responsibility both reflects and contributes to the politicization of responsibility that has taken place under conditions of "late" modernity. By the term *politicization*, I mean that responsibility has been denaturalized. As social knowledges found a place in penal institutions and practices alongside legal knowledge, they contributed to the reconstruction, under modern penality, of the individual offender as someone with a particular character ("normal," "defective") and an "uncertain degree of rationality."[58] The effect of this was both to champion and problematize individual responsibility.[59] On the one hand, techniques of liberal governance produced a dynamic of "responsibilization," while, on the other hand, and when viewed in a criminological frame, "*responsibility thus became a presumption which was always put in doubt.*"[60] While the extent to which this dynamic has impacted on criminal law directly, as opposed to criminal justice more broadly, is debated, it seems clear that individual responsibility for crime (and indeed for other acts or conditions) is now thoroughly politicized—rhetorically associated with "tough on crime" criminal justice policies and conservative political discourse about "rights and responsibilities."[61]

Taken together, the pluralization of knowledges about responsibility, and the politicization of responsibility, has meant that it has become more challenging to carve out, and defend, the terrain that would form the subject matter of a socio-historical study of criminal responsibility. Criminal responsibility now has what I call a socio-political complexity that goes beyond its legal existence, and thus it has become more difficult to determine a ready or "natural" subject matter of socio-historical studies of criminal responsibility.

For instance, it may be that, studied via a socio-historical approach, criminal responsibility trespasses on terrain hitherto now analyzed under the label criminalization, or, more broadly, as part of larger processes of identity construction or the formation of subjectivity in "late" modernity.[62] In this respect, it is perhaps not merely coincidental that the period in which criminal responsibility accrues this socio-political complexity coincides with the rise to prominence of legal-philosophical approaches to its study, which are, in relative terms, acontextual and atemporal, and focused on the abstract and abstracted individual of law.

III. AN APPROACH TO CRIMINAL RESPONSIBILITY IN THE TWENTIETH CENTURY

The socio-political complexity of criminal responsibility in the current era demands a revitalization of the study of criminal responsibility. While presenting challenging terrain for socio-historical scholars of criminal responsibility, for the reasons discussed above, the twentieth (and twenty-first) century is an important focus for scholarship. In the spirit of revitalizing contemporary socio-historical study of criminal responsibility, I suggest that a useful approach to such a study is to set developments in criminal responsibility norms and practices against, or within the context of, extra-legal responsibility norms and practices. By extra-legal responsibility norms and practices, I refer to social and political responsibility attribution practices broadly.

My starting point here is the conviction that, in the twentieth century, the core idea of individual responsibility for crime confronts new conditions of possibility. Developments in medical and scientific knowledge give rise to powerful challenges to traditional criminal law precepts.[63] Further, the twentieth century has seen greater (both institutionalized and routinized) use of predictive knowledges, such as actuarial knowledge,[64] to inform criminal law practices. At the same time, as Lacey argues, the massive expansion of the criminal law makes accommodation of "unequally situated defendants" more difficult.[65] As Farmer suggests, changes in temporal and spatial relations under conditions of "late" modernity have manifold implications for criminal law, relating to both criminalization and criminal responsibility.[66] Taken together, these new conditions furnish challenges to our thinking (and the traditional concepts on which we continue to rely), and faith in the traditional idea of individual responsibility for crime—where the ordinary principles of liability and punishment apply, and where the application of these ordinary principles to an individual is an acknowledgment or affirmation of his or her subjectivity—comes under some pressure.

How might we grasp the ways in which these changed conditions of possibility affect criminal responsibility principles and practices? One way is to view (developments in) criminal responsibility norms and practices in the context of extra-legal responsibility norms and practices. This involves taking social ideas about responsibility seriously. "The social" is a prominent aspect of critical and socio-historical legal scholarship, which, broadly, might be characterized by scholarly effort to hold both the individual and his or her social context (or agency and structure) in the frame at the same time, without losing sight of either one or the other.[67] The scholarship points to the significance of the social for criminal responsibility. For example, Alan Norrie, who exposes the ideological aspects of the focus on the individual in criminal law practices, argues that, in criminal law, individual responsibility is always intermixed with social responsibility for wrongdoing.[68] As Norrie writes, "To talk of agency, subjectivity or responsibility *is apparently paradoxically, also to talk of what appears to deny it: the role of community in constituting agency, subjectivity and responsibility*."[69] "The social" is an important, if sometimes neglected, part of criminal responsibility practices.

It has proved challenging to find concrete ways to grasp the relevance of "the social" to practices of criminal responsibility, however. One way of grasping the social is to adopt different units of analysis to those usually employed in criminal law—that is, social rather than traditional or standard legal units of analysis (such as "all defendants charged with sex offenses"), which generally consist of acts which can be committed by anyone. Of course, social norms are not (merely) represented in law but taken up (or not) in complex and dynamic ways within the legal sphere;[70] however, studying a social unit presents a way of potentially making "the social" visible in criminal legal practices which otherwise focus on the (more or less abstract) individual. This approach exposes significant dimensions of criminal responsibility practices, because, as Farmer writes, "the language of legal responsibility [is] one way in which the relations between legal and political organization are mediated."[71] As this suggests, criminal responsibility is implicated in larger discourses of citizenship, community, and society, each of which takes on distinct contours in different places and at different moments in time.

There are multiple examples of (more self-evidently) "social" units of analysis that might be of interest to socio-historical and critical legal scholars,[72] but in this chapter, I present a study of just one. My case study involves veteran defendants—those defendants who have served in the military, and often in combat, and face serious criminal charges after returning home. Military or war veterans are a social category rather than a legal category. Veterans are a particularly interesting case study of criminal responsibility for three main reasons. First, as agents of the state, they bring the state into the criminal courtroom in distinctive ways, complicating the standard criminal law dynamic of "state versus individual." Second, in the Australian context, this group enjoys a high social profile, meaning that veterans are a focus of public attention and debate. Over the course of the twentieth century, war has loomed large on the Australian social landscape, and it has proved to be important in Australia's self-understanding.[73] War has played a crucial role in development of Australian national identity, and has been integral to the project of nation building in the period following Federation in 1901.[74] Third, the category of veterans charged with criminal offenses after war or military service has already garnered some attention from criminal responsibility theorists.[75] For my purposes here, this case study allows me to open novel ways of exploring the social dimension of criminal law responsibility principles and practices.

Through a close examination of the case law on veterans who face serious criminal charges, I assessed the ways in which, over the twentieth century (and the first years of the twenty-first century), such individuals have been treated for criminal law purposes. As I discuss in detail elsewhere, veterans emerge as a special group—a specialness which I suggested rests on the (changing) social meanings of war, soldiers, and soldiering.[76] Premised on the status of veterans as a distinct social category, ex-soldiers are accorded special standing in criminal adjudication and sentencing practices—as "veteran defendants." Different ideas about criminal responsibility run through these cases—centering on the ex-soldier as a complex figure, simultaneously agentic and victim-like, courageous and vulnerable, both more and less than other defendants.[77] In my analysis, the special status of "veteran defendants" has two main aspects: "veteran defendants" as *über-citizens*, civic models, or exemplars, and "veteran defendants" as having "diminished capacity" whereby they have impaired or reduced responsibility for crime. I found that there is a historical interplay between these two aspects of the specialness of "veteran defendants," with the latter becoming more prominent over the course of the twentieth century (particularly after the Vietnam War).

My study also revealed that, in relation to the responsibility of "veteran defendants," the practice of sentencing was especially significant. While sentencing is not typically a focus of criminal responsibility scholarship, there have been some calls for its inclusion within the bounds of responsibility studies.[78] My study of Australian cases revealed that veteran status is taken into account at sentencing in multiple ways—both for and against the defendant—and indeed, that judicial sentencing practices revealed a rather nuanced accounting of responsibility for crime. For instance, in *R. v. Hicks*[79] the Crown appealed the sentence of the defendant, who had served in the army in World War II and had been given a sentence of two years suspended for causing death by dangerous driving, having killed two people in another car. Hicks argued that it was right that he was subject to the more lenient provisions of the Offenders Probation Act 1913 (South Australia) on the basis of the personal or subjective factors of his case. The appellate court allowed the appeal but stated that Hicks "had to be given full credit for his service to his country in time of war."[80] According to the Chief Justice, who gave the leading judgment, "[a]ctual exposure to prolonged danger to life in the course of service to one's country must, in my view, carry special weight in the sentencing process."[81] This seems to suggest that it is not just that there is a "residue of mitigating factors," such as character, which does not fit neatly within dominant sentencing theory,[82] but that wider currents of meaning—in this instance, relating to duty, bravery, and obedience, extending beyond but impacting on criminal justice—are playing a role in evaluation and adjudication of criminal responsibility.

The nuanced accounting for responsibility for crime revealed in my study exposed the ways in which actors other than the defendant are implicated in responsibility discourses within criminal process. Ascribing greater agency to "veteran defendants" as *über-citizens* generated responsibility in *others* involved in the adjudication and evaluation process. I suggested that judges assumed responsibility for weighing up the sacrifices involved in war or military service to the state, on the one hand, and the seriousness of the offense on the other ("responsibility for responsibility"). By contrast, courts considered veteran defendants with "diminished capacity" to blame for their war or military trauma: with mental illness characterized as an individual failing rather than a consequence of war or military service to the state, society's responsibility for them is reduced. This complex economy of individual and social responsibility became apparent in adopting a social rather than a traditional or typical legal unit of analysis.

Appreciating this complex economy of responsibility involves thinking differently about individual defendants, and taking into account the broader institutional, social, and political context in which they are located. What is significant about something like the criminal responsibility of veterans is the ways in which it maps onto particular social norms, that is, non- or extra-legal norms, about responsibility. That is, the conditions of possibility of criminal responsibility for this cohort lie outside the criminal law (and outside law more generally). In material ways, the way in which responsibility is configured within and through legal forms seems to depend on particular ideas about relationality, citizenship, the state, and masculinity (in my case study), each of which is historically and culturally contingent. It seems crucial to understand the ways in which particular (dynamic) social relations give rise to criminal responsibility in order to understand criminal responsibility in a thorough manner. Examining relevant social and political or extra-legal responsibility norms and practices promises to generate an alternative picture of criminal responsibility, in a particular moment and over time.

What is the value of a study such as this in the broader context of research on criminal responsibility? This sort of study is useful because it makes it possible to assess the wider social and political significance of criminal responsibility, and to cast critical light on responsibility in criminal law in the twentieth (and twenty-first) century. It helps us genuinely to appreciate that criminal law is not "just" a normative system of censure and sanction, but a way of ordering social relations.[83] This sort of study of criminal responsibility can tell us something about these broader cultural currents, and, indeed, it seems only possible to fully understand criminal responsibility in light of these broad and dynamic relations—between the citizen and the state, the self and the collective. In doing so, we are encouraged to reflect on the ways in which we understand these dynamics—what language we use to capture them, and what expert knowledges we bring to bear on the practice of evaluating and adjudicating criminal responsibility.

CONCLUSION

This chapter looks somewhat different from the other chapters that compose this collection. By contrast with other chapters, this chapter occupies an extra-mural position: it is situated in a socio-historical, rather than a legal-philosophical, scholarly tradition. Nonetheless, given the importance for legal-philosophical scholarship of the context in which intellectual ideas are given life,[84] and growing awareness among legal-philosophical scholars of changing institutional and other conditions for the development of concepts and principles,[85] I suggest that the discussion contained in this chapter bears on the development of scholarly knowledge about criminal law beyond the confines of the socio-historical scholarly tradition, and augments the variety of disciplinary resources harnessed to the task of addressing key questions for the criminal law in the current era.

Reliance on traditional modes of analysis seems to limit our ability to grasp the deep complexity of the criminal responsibility in a way that the conditions—intellectual, social, and political—of the current era demand. Having made the case for the value of a socio-historical approach to criminal responsibility, this chapter outlined one such approach to the study of criminal responsibility in the twentieth century—in which legal norms are set against extra-legal norms. Taking seriously the idea that legal knowledge now shares its influence on the organization of social and political relations with social science knowledge, and acknowledging that it is increasingly difficult to fit lived reality within a strict understanding of criminal responsibility, demands a revitalized approach to criminal responsibility. I suggested that setting criminal legal practices against extra-legal practices is useful because it provides a means of assessing the wider social and political significance of criminal responsibility. It is this broader significance of criminal responsibility that legal scholars must aim to grasp in order to foster sophisticated understandings of criminal responsibility.

NOTES

1. Faculty of Law, University of Sydney. This research is supported by the Australian Research Council (ARC) (Grant No. DE130100418). The ideas presented here benefited from discussion at the Criminal Law and Legal Theory Seminar, London School of Economics, and at the Centre for Criminal Law, University College London, December 2013. I would like to thank Ian Dennis, Lindsay Farmer, Nicola Lacey, Manolis Melissaris, David Omerod, Sabine Selchow, and all those present at the seminars for helpful comments. I would also like to thank Mikah Pajaczkowska-Russell for assistance in the preparation of this chapter for publication.

2. *See* Nicola Lacey, *Response to Norrie and Tadros*, 1 CRIM. L. & PHIL. 267, 268 (2007).

3. *See* ANDREW ASHWORTH & JEREMY HORDER, PRINCIPLES OF CRIMINAL LAW 1 (7th ed. 2013).

4. *See, e.g.,* R.A. DUFF, ANSWERING FOR CRIME: RESPONSIBILITY AND LIABILITY IN THE CRIMINAL LAW (2005).

5. *See* Nicola Lacey, *Legal Constructions of Crime*, *in* THE OXFORD HANDBOOK OF CRIMINOLOGY 179, 185–86 (Mike Maguire et al. eds., 2007).

6. Nicola Lacey, *Character, Capacity, Outcome: Towards a Framework for Assessing the Shifting Pattern of Criminal Responsibility in Modern English Law*, *in* MODERN HISTORIES OF CRIME AND PUNISHMENT: CRITICAL PERSPECTIVES ON CRIME AND LAW 14–41 (Markus D. Dubber & Lindsay Farmer eds., 2007).

7. The work of Michael Moore represents something of the epitome of the moral philosophy approach to criminal responsibility. *See, e.g.,* MICHAEL S. MOORE, PLACING BLAME: A GENERAL THEORY OF THE CRIMINAL LAW (2010).

8. *See* ALAN NORRIE, CRIME, REASON AND HISTORY: A CRITICAL INTRODUCTION TO CRIMINAL LAW (2nd ed. 2001). For a critique, see Lacey, *supra* note 5, at 14–41.

9. This distinction relates to theories of punishment. *See* J. Deigh, *Responsibility*, *in* THE OXFORD HANDBOOK OF PHILOSOPHY OF CRIMINAL LAW 194 (John Deigh & David Dolinko eds., 2011).

10. H.L.A. HART, PUNISHMENT AND RESPONSIBILITY 227 (2nd ed. 2008).

11. *See* Alice Ristroph, *Responsibility for the Criminal Law*, *in* PHILOSOPHICAL FOUNDATIONS OF CRIMINAL LAW 107, 109 (R.A. Duff and Stuart P. Green eds., 2011). *See also* LINDSAY FARMER, CRIMINAL LAW, TRADITION AND LEGAL ORDER: CRIME AND THE GENIUS OF SCOTS LAW, 1747 TO THE PRESENT 181 (1997).

12. Duff, *supra* note 4, at 41; *see also* R. A. DUFF, TRIALS AND PUNISHMENTS (1986).

13. *See* John Gardner, *The Mark of Responsibility*, 23 OXFORD J. L. STUD. 157, 166–168 (2003).

14. *See* M'Naghten (1843), 10 CL. & FIN. 200 (Eng.); Bratty v Att'y Gen. for N. Ir. (1963) AC 386 (N. Ir.).

15. Duff, *supra* note 4, at 15–16.

16. Nicola Lacey, *Institutionalising Responsibility: Implications for Jurisprudence*, 4 JURISPRUDENCE 4, 1, 11 (2013); Alan Norrie, *Legal Form and Moral Judgement: Euthanasia and Assisted Suicide*, *in* THE STRUCTURES OF CRIMINAL LAW 139 (R. A. Duff et al. eds., 2011).

17. Lacey, *supra* note 16, at 2.

18. *See* Lacey, *supra* note 6, at 26. On criminalization, *see also* Lindsay Farmer, *Criminal Law as an Institution: Rethinking Theoretical Approaches to Criminalization, in* CRIMINALIZATION: THE POLITICAL MORALITY OF THE CRIMINAL LAW 80 (R.A. Duff et al. eds., 2014); Lindsay Farmer, *Territorial Jurisdiction and Criminalization*, 63 U. TORONTO L. J. 225 (2013).

19. *See* James Chalmers & Fiona Leverick, *Tracking the Creation of Criminal Offences*, CRIM. L. REV. 543 (2013).

20. *See* Lacey, *supra* note 5, at 179, 190.

21. *See also* Markus D. Dubber & Lindsay Farmer, *Introduction: Regarding Criminal Law Historically*, *in* MODERN HISTORIES OF CRIME AND PUNISHMENT 1 (Markus D. Dubber & Lindsay Farmer eds., 2007); Markus D. Dubber, *Historical Analysis of Law*, 16 LAW & HIST. REV. 159 (1998).

22. *See* PETER CANE, RESPONSIBILITY IN LAW AND MORALITY 4, 25 (2002); SCOTT VEITCH, LAW AND IRRESPONSIBILITY: ON THE LEGITIMATION OF HUMAN SUFFERING 36–37 (2007).

23. FARMER, *supra* note 11.

24. Nicola Lacey, *Responsibility and Modernity in Criminal Law*, 9 J. POL. PHIL. 249 (2001); Nicola Lacey, *In Search of the Responsible Subject: History, Philosophy and Social Sciences in Criminal Law Theory*, 64 MOD. L. REV. 350 (2001); Lacey, *supra* note 6, at 14.

25. Markus D. Dubber, *Policing Possession: The War on Crime and the End of Criminal Law*, 91 J. CRIM. L. & CRIMINOLOGY 829 (2001).

26. *See* NORRIE, *supra* note 6.

27. JOHN H. LANGBEIN, THE ORIGINS OF ADVERSARY CRIMINAL TRIAL 59 (2003).

28. Lacey, *In Search of the Responsible Subject*, *supra* note 24, at 369.

29. Lacey, *Responsibility and Modernity*, *supra* note 24, at 256.

30. *See* ARLIE LOUGHNAN, MANIFEST MADNESS: MENTAL INCAPACITY IN CRIMINAL LAW (2012).

31. Lacey, *supra* note 6, at 21.

32. FARMER, *supra* note 11, at 138.

33. *Id.* at 139–42, 159; Lacey, *Responsibility and Modernity*, *supra* note 24, at 267–68.

34. *See* Nicola Lacey, *Space, Time and Function: Intersecting Principles of Responsibility Across the Terrain of Criminal Justice*, 1 CRIM. L. & PHIL. 233, 240–43, 246–49 (2007).

35. Lacey, *supra* note 16, at 8.

36. *Id.* at 11.

37. I argued that this gives the terrain of mental incapacity distinctive features, which I conceptualized as broad ontological and epistemological contours. See further LOUGHNAN, *supra* note 30, at chap. 3.

38. *See* Lacey, *supra* note 16, at 18; Farmer, *supra* note 18.

39. *See* Nicola Lacey, *Contingency, Coherence and Conceptualism: Reflections on the Encounter between "Critique" and "Philosophy of the Criminal Law," in* PHILOSOPHY AND THE CRIMINAL LAW: PRINCIPLE AND CRITIQUE 9 (R. A. Duff ed., 1998).

40. *See* Farmer, *supra* note 9, at chap. 6; Lindsay Farmer, *The Modest Ambition of Glanville Williams*, *in* FOUNDATIONAL TEXTS IN CRIMINAL LAW 263 (Markus D. Dubber ed., 2014).

41. *See* Chalmers & Leverick, *supra* note 19.

42. *See* Farmer, *supra* note 19. Farmer argues that this as a "qualitative change" when compared with the long-established existence of strict liability in common law.

43. *See* DAVID GARLAND, PUNISHMENT AND WELFARE: A HISTORY OF PENAL STRATEGIES 1 (1985).

44. Lindsay Farmer, *Time and Space in Criminal Law*, 13 NEW CRIM. L. REV. 333, 335 (2010).

45. *See further* Farmer, *supra* note 40.

46. *See* Neil Duxbury, *English Jurisprudence Between Austin and Hart*, 91 VA. L. REV. 1 (2005).

47. H. L. A. HART, THE CONCEPT OF LAW (3rd ed. 2012); *see also* NICOLA LACEY, A LIFE OF H.L.A. HART: THE NIGHTMARE AND THE NOBLE DREAM (2006).

48. *See* LINDSAY FARMER, THE MAKING OF THE MODERN CRIMINAL LAW (forthcoming 2016).

49. *Id.*

50. *See* ANTHONY GIDDENS, THE CONSEQUENCES OF MODERNITY 4 (1990). For an intellectual history, see Joshua Getzler, *Law, History and the Social Sciences: Intellectual Traditions of the Late Nineteenth- and Early Twentieth-Century Europe*, *in* 6 LAW AND HISTORY, CURRENT LEGAL ISSUES SERIES, 215 (Andrew Lewis & Michael Lobban eds., 2003).

51. *See* Couze Venn & Mike Featherstone, *Modernity*, 23 THEORY CULTURE & SOC'Y 457 (2006); NIKOLAS ROSE, INVENTING OUR SELVES: PSYCHOLOGY, POWER, AND PERSONHOOD (1996); DAVID GARLAND, THE CULTURE OF CONTROL: CRIME AND SOCIAL ORDER IN CONTEMPORARY SOCIETY (2001); ULRICH BECK, RISK SOCIETY: TOWARDS A NEW MODERNITY (1992); GIDDENS, *supra* note

50; ANTHONY GIDDENS, MODERNITY AND SELF-IDENTITY: SELF AND SOCIETY IN THE LATE MODERN AGE (1991).

52. For an exception, see ALAN NORRIE, LAW AND THE BEAUTIFUL SOUL (2005), chap. 6 (where Norrie considers the relevance of Giddens's ideas about "late modern" society to our understanding of guilt).

53. *See* GIDDENS, *supra* note 50, at 40, 51.

54. *See* GARLAND, *supra* note 43; PAT O'MALLEY, CRIME AND THE RISK SOCIETY (1998); GARLAND, *supra* note 51.

55. *See* Peter Goodrich, *Intellection and Indiscipline*, 36 J. L. SOC'Y 460 (2009); Geoffrey Samuel, *Interdisciplinarity and the Authority Paradigm: Should Law Be Taken Seriously by Scientists and Social Scientists?* 36 J. L. SOC'Y 431 (2009).

56. *Cf.* ROGER COTTERRELL, LAW, CULTURE, AND SOCIETY: LEGAL IDEAS IN THE MIRROR OF SOCIAL THEORY 23–26 (2006).

57. *See, e.g.*, MARIANNE CONSTABLE, JUST SILENCES: THE LIMITS AND POSSIBILITIES OF MODERN LAW (2005); Peter Goodrich, *Law and Modernity*, 49 MOD. L. REV. 545 (1986).

58. *See* GARLAND, *supra* note 43, at 26, 31.

59. *See generally*, GIDDENS, *supra* note 50; Nikolas Rose, *supra* note 51; NIKOLAS ROSE, GOVERNING THE SOUL: THE SHAPING OF THE PRIVATE SELF (2nd ed. 1999).

60. GARLAND, *supra* note 43, at 185, 187 (emphasis in original).

61. *See* Lucia Zedner, *Security, the State and the Citizen: The Changing Architecture of Crime Control*, 13 NEW CRIM. L. REV. 397 (2010) (where this is discussed in the context of security and citizenship).

62. An illustration might be parental responsibility for offenses committed by their children: while often viewed as an issue of criminalization, this practice relies on and reproduces particular social ideas of responsibility, which themselves encode attitudes to and beliefs about gender, familial relationships, and the place of the family in contemporary society.

63. *See* Nicole A. Vincent, *On the Relevance of Neuroscience to Criminal Responsibility* 4 CRIM. L. & PHIL. 77 (2010). *See also* Nicola Lacey & Hanna Pickard, *From the Consulting Room to the Court Room? Taking the Clinical Model of Responsibility Without Blame Into the Legal Realm*, 33 OXFORD J. L. STUD. 1 (2013).

64. On the development of statistical knowledge, see IAN HACKING, THE EMERGENCE OF PROBABILITY: A PHILOSOPHICAL STUDY OF EARLY IDEAS ABOUT PROBABILITY, INDUCTION AND STATISTICAL INFERENCE (2006).

65. Nicola Lacey, *Community, Culture, Criminalization, in* CRIME, PUNISHMENT, AND RESPONSIBILITY: THE JURISPRUDENCE OF ANTONY DUFF 292–310, 306 (Rowan Cruft et al. eds., 2011).

66. *See* Farmer, *supra* note 44, at 333. On "time-space compression" under conditions of modernity, see GIDDENS, *supra* note 50, at 17–21.

67. *See, e.g.*, ALAN NORRIE, PUNISHMENT, RESPONSIBILITY AND JUSTICE (2000); JENNIFER NEDELSKY, LAW'S RELATIONS: A RELATIONAL THEORY OF SELF, AUTONOMY, AND LAW (2011).

68. *See* Alan Norrie, *Simulacra of Morality? Beyond the Ideal/Actual Antinomies of Criminal Justice*, *in* PHILOSOPHY AND THE CRIMINAL LAW, *supra* note 39, at 101, 117.

69. *Id.* at 101 (emphasis in original). *See also* NORRIE, *supra* note 67.

70. On this point, see Lindsay Farmer, *Criminal Wrongs in Historical Perspective*, *in* THE BOUNDARIES OF THE CRIMINAL LAW 214 (R. A. Duff et al. eds., 2010).

71. FARMER, *supra* note 11, at 12.

72. *See, e.g.*, Simon Bronitt & Wendy Kukulies-Smith, *Crime, Punishment, Family Violence and the Cloak of Legal Invisibility*, 37 J. AUSTL. STUD. 390 (2013) (making a plea for legal focus on "crimes against the family").

73. *See generally*, R. White, *War and Australian Society, in* AUSTRALIA: TWO CENTURIES OF WAR AND PEACE 391 (M. McKernan and M. Brown eds., 1988); Susanne Davies, *Women War and the Violence of History: An Australian Perspective, in* 2 VIOLENCE AGAINST WOMEN 359 (1996).

74. *See, e.g.*, Ken Inglis, *The Anzac Tradition*, 24 MEANJIN Q. 25 (1965); GRAHAM SEAL, INVENTING ANZAC: THE DIGGER AND NATIONAL MYTHOLOGY (2004). On gender and nation-building, see Stephen Garton, *War and Masculinity in Twentieth Century Australia*, 22 J. AUSTL.

STUD. 86 (1998); Marilyn Lake, *Mission Impossible: How Men Gave Birth to the Australian Nation—Nationalism, Gender and Other Seminal Acts*, 4 GENDER & HIST. 305 (1992).

75. *See* Youngjae Lee, *Military Veterans, Culpability, and Blame*, 7 CRIM. L. & PHIL. 1 (2013); Victor Tadros, *Poverty and Criminal Responsibility*, 43 J. VALUE INQUIRY 391 (2009).

76. *See* Arlie Loughnan, *"Society Owes Them Much": Veteran Defendants and Criminal Responsibility in Australia*, 2 CRITICAL ANALYSIS L. 106 (2015).

77. *Id.*

78. *See* Lacey, *supra* note 16.

79. R. v. Hicks (1987) 45 SASR 270 (Austl.).

80. *Id.* at 278. The Court of Appeal upheld the sentence of two years imprisonment, but removed the suspension, and reduced the non-parole period from twelve months to six months.

81. *Id.* at 285.

82. *See* A. Manson, *The Search for Principles of Mitigation: Integrating Cultural Demands*, *in* MITIGATION AND AGGRAVATION AT SENTENCING 40, 45 (*Julian v. Roberts* ed., 2011).

83. *See* Lacey, *In Search of the Responsible Subject*, *supra* note 24.

84. *See* Lacey, *supra* note 16; Farmer, *Criminal Law as an Institution*, *supra* note 18.

85. *See* ANTONY DUFF ET AL., THE TRIAL ON TRIAL (Oxford: Hart, 2007).

Chapter Eight

Victims of Crime: Their Rights and Duties

Sandra Marshall

I. INTRODUCTION: PUTTING VICTIMS FIRST

In his classic book, *The Culture of Control*, David Garland mapped the development of "our social response to crime during the last thirty years and . . . the social, cultural and political forces that gave rise to them."[1] One aspect of that development that is central to this chapter is the way in which victims of crime have come to figure in the criminal justice process, particularly the criminal trial and punishment.[2] So, as Garland puts it,

> In the penal-welfare framework, the offending individual was center-stage: the primary focus of criminological concern. Sentencing was to be individualized to meet the offender's particular needs and potential for reform. . . . The individual characteristics of the offender were, in theory if not always in practice, to be the key determinant of all penal action. In vivid contrast, the individual victim featured hardly at all. For the most part, he or she remained a silent abstraction: a background figure whose individuality hardly registered, whose personal wishes and concerns had no place in the process.
>
> In contemporary penality this situation is reversed. The processes of individualization now increasingly center on the victim.[3]

These developments raise crucial questions about the way we think of the nature of crime, and the way we characterize the relationship between individual citizens, and between citizens and the state. These are fundamental questions of political theory which impinge upon the very nature of crime. Of course, the developments in penal practice have not been deliberate attempts to take forward such philosophical theories, but, nevertheless, the concepts and ideas contained in such theories form a crucially illuminating context for the critical analysis of our criminal justice practices and procedures.

The change in perspective captured by Garland is not unique to the United States: it is in evidence in Canada, Australia, and the United Kingdom most obviously, but also in other European jurisdictions such as the Netherlands. However, the ubiquity of these developments does not mean that they are unproblematic, seeming, as some do, to conflict with other, fundamental normative features of the criminal law and process. This is particularly so where the shift to a more "victim-centered" approach involves claims of *right* for victims.

This chapter explores some of the ramifications of this shift in perspective and argues that the concentration on victims' rights fails adequately to capture the most significant aspect of what it means to be an active participant in the criminal process, for it says nothing about victims' duties. It is *duties*, I shall argue, that form the core of the victims' formal role as a vital participant in the criminal process. I take these firstly to be civic duties: what we owe to each other as citizens in a democratic republic—a society that is, or aspires to be, a political community of free and equal citizens. It will be a further question as to whether and when they should be legal, enforceable, duties. We should then see some of the rights currently attributed to victims as arising from these civic duties.

II. THE RISE OF "VICTIMS' RIGHTS"

To set the scene, I begin with a brief discussion of some of the rights which are now claimed for victims.

Perhaps the least contentious of the rights afforded to victims in the criminal process are those best viewed as rights to services designed to meet victims' needs.[4] So, systems will be put in place to make sure that victims are kept informed about the progress of "their case": whether a suspect is to be charged, or cautioned; the nature of the charge; whether it is altered at any stage, including, in the United States particularly, a plea bargain; the date of any trial; the verdict; the sentence. If we wish to speak of rights here, then, the right in play would be a right to be informed. Other rights to service provisions might have to do with support for vulnerable victims, including protection against intimidation; general support of victims who are required to stand as witnesses in court; compensation for injuries caused by the criminal acts.[5] Furthermore, some may argue that victims have a right to be informed about parole decisions and release dates for those who have served a prison sentence.[6] What might justify such an extension is by no means obvious.[7]

Important though all these rights are, they are not the rights provisions which most sharply signal the shift in perspective indicated by Garland's analysis: the significant move has been in the direction of what may be called claims of "rights to participation"—most obviously rights which involve some participation in the criminal trial. These rights fall, roughly, into two categories: rights to be consulted and rights of veto, and jurisdictions vary as to the extent of such rights. In some European jurisdictions, for example, victims may have a considerable role in the bringing of a prosecution, prosecutions may proceed only at the request of the victim, or only with their consent; or victims may have a right to insist on a prosecution, join in as a co-prosecutor, or initiate the prosecution themselves.[8] All these provisions go far beyond the limited right in England for the victim to seek a review of prosecutorial decisions not to proceed, and the provisions made in the English and U.S. trial process for Victim Impact Statements (VIS), Victim Personal Statements (VPS), or victims' opinions or preferences at the sentencing. Each of these provisions may figure at different stages in the criminal process: in the trial, at sentencing stage, or post-trial. But wherever they figure, they are not unproblematic.[9] It is enough for my purposes here, though, to reflect briefly on sentencing in the English courts.

The VPS scheme gives victims a formal opportunity to give an account, most importantly in their own words, of how the crime has affected them—emotionally, physically, and financially. In deciding on a sentence, "The court must pass what it judges to be the appropriate sentence having regard to the circumstances of the offense and of the offender, taking into account, so far as the court considers it appropriate, the consequences to the victim."[10] So, the VPS may or may not carry weight, but the fact that it *can* figure in decision-making raises questions about the fairness and consistency of the process. Not all victims will submit a VPS—it is a voluntary matter—and the emotional or financial impact of a crime on victims will vary. (We should be clear here that the discussion concerns victims of *crime*, not just victims of very serious or monstrous crimes.) I may be annoyed by the theft of my handbag but not distressed, while another victim of handbag theft might be deeply pained by it. I might, however, be aggrieved if "my thief" were to receive a lighter sentence, for I am the victim of the same criminal wrong, as characterized in the act description—the act of theft. My property right has been infringed in just the same way whether I am distressed by it or not. The situation will be even worse in more serious cases, such as rape, where the emotional and physical impact on victims can be markedly different.

This brings into sharp focus a fundamental problem: the VPS system has been introduced as a way of increasing participation for victims, of facilitating their being heard and taken into account, but crucially this scheme does not allow for their account to be tested or challenged, even though the VPS might have some influence on punishment. In these ways the aim of doing justice is put at risk.

(Given the extensive rights that are now claimed for victims, it is important to ask who the victims of crime are—how wide is the category of "victims"? Does it include corporations and collectives of other kinds, for example? There is not space to consider this question here, but see Marcus D. Dubber's *Victims in the War on Crime* for a useful starting point.[11])

III. ROLES AND DUTIES

Now, we should examine more carefully the formal role that victims should play in the criminal law process.

Consider the case of "Sarah," prosecuted and jailed for a false retraction of claim of rape—that is, the *retraction* was a lie, and she was prosecuted for perjury. Those who were outraged by the conviction, including "Sarah" herself, wished to argue that she had "done nothing wrong" and that in any case it was she who was the victim—although this had been something which she had, of course, at one stage denied.[12] I will argue in what follows that, to the contrary, she had done something wrong—she had failed to fulfill a duty, one which she had in virtue of being a victim.[13]

One thing to keep clearly in view is that "Sarah's" claim is that she is the victim of a *crime* and not simply the victim of wrongdoing or misfortune. Thus her claim and the arguments surrounding it get part of their sense from being located within a particular institution. Law, of which criminal law is a part, is a political institution, through which political communities express the decisions of the community regarding the way people should behave, the entitlements they have, and so on, and the views about these matters, however sound and however popular, which do not have the imprimatur of the community. By and large the law represents those standards which are considered in that community as expressing the decisions of that community.[14]

Attention needs to be paid, therefore, to the roles and status of the participants in that institution. Citizens can play three kinds of role in relation to the criminal law. Some are official and professional: those who fill them are employed by the polity to do so, and are meant to bring professional skills to the job. Examples include civil servants engaged in drafting legislation; police officers engaged in preventing and investigating crimes; prosecutors determining who to charge with what, and bringing cases to court (or otherwise disposing of them); defense counsel; judges and other court officials; and correctional officials. We must ask in each case how the role should be understood; what ends those who fill it should pursue, what responsibilities and rights they should have, how they should deliberate about what to do. We must also ask whether the role should exist at all, and (if so) how people should come to occupy it (whether, for instance, by election or by appointment).[15]

A second kind of role is official in that it brings legal authority, but it is filled by lay citizens rather than by professionals. Obvious examples are the roles of juror and lay magistrate or judge. But we could also consider lay roles related to policing—special constable, for instance; and we could ask why we should not create lay roles in the administration of punishments—beyond such modest roles as that of prison visitor. One general question that I cannot pursue here concerns the proper relationship between these first two kinds of role. How far should a democratic system of criminal law be administered by professional officials, whether elected or appointed? How far should it be controlled by lay citizens?

A third kind of role is acquired by citizens who have, or are thought to have, a relevant connection to a particular alleged crime, and who therefore acquire distinctive sets of legal, or civic, rights and responsibilities—victims being the central case for this chapter, though a full account of such roles will need to say a great deal more about the interrelations between the victim's role and the other roles, including those of officials.

Roles are located within particular institutions or practices, and are to be understood in terms of their contributions to the goals of the practice within which they fall. They consist in patterns of rights, responsibilities, and duties, which together specify the distinctive activities that belong to the role. To understand a role is therefore also to understand the practice within which it functions. Further, the role bearer has an interest in being able to fulfill the role; that is, to carry out the duties of that role. Just as officials have a role-based right to perform their duties,[16] so citizens have a right to carry out theirs. That in turn will reflect on the role duties of others—especially, but not exclusively, the officials—to enable the role bearer to carry out that role and not to impede them.

How, then, should we characterize the role of the victim of crime in terms of the duties that partly constitute it? Let us return to the case of "Sarah": the core of the wrongdoing for which she was prosecuted—perverting the course of justice—and for which she was convicted, was the lying nature of her retraction of her complaint against her husband. The case is complicated by the fact that she initially faced two (mutually incompatible) accusations of lying. First, when she not only withdrew her original complaint that her husband had raped her but also "then proceeded to assert and reassert that her complaint had been false," proceedings against him were stopped, and she was charged with perverting the course of justice by making a false complaint of rape. Then, when after discussing her position with her counsel and solicitor, "she reasserted the truth of the original complaint," she faced a further indictment alleging that she had perverted the course of justice by "ma[king] and pursu[ing] a false retraction":[17] she pleaded "not guilty" to the first indictment and was acquitted when the prosecution offered no evidence; it was the second indictment (to which she pleaded guilty) that became the focus of the prosecution and her subsequent appeals.

Suppose instead that she had merely withdrawn her complaint; surely she would then have done no wrong? There might be all sorts of reasons why someone would choose to withdraw a complaint, or just not make a complaint at all, without any implication that the complaint was false. Surely the most that their role demands of victims is that they, like all other participants in the legal process,[18] engage in it honestly and do not stand in the way of others' performance of their proper duties. While not making a complaint (perhaps) does not amount to "standing in the way," however, withdrawing what I *know* to be a true charge might well amount to standing in the way of police and prosecutors who are trying to carry out their duties; though this will undoubtedly depend on our conception of the officials' duties. On one view these might be no more than to investigate only, but not all, allegations that are made to them. On a more expansive view the role might be to investigate all, or most, potential criminal wrongdoing, however it might come to their attention. (I cannot tackle these issues here; I only note that they speak to my point that the roles which form the legal process are interdependent.)

Still, whether a victim chooses to participate in the legal process in the first place is surely up to them. A particular kind of focus on victims' rights might, indeed, bolster this thought. The demand for the recognition of "victims' rights" has increasingly focused on demands for greater participation by victims in the judicial processes of criminal law and punishment; however, the right to participate is typically portrayed as the right to participate *if they wish to do so*, rather than as a right to participate because it is their *duty* to do so.

We can see here a similarity with those versions of restorative justice inspired by Nils Christie's early claim that, as he somewhat (over-) dramatically put it, the criminal law "steals" our conflicts: taking away the "conflict," which he claimed is the real nature of what we call "crime," from those whom it directly concerns and transferring it to the professional world of the law.[19] Thus, those we call the "victim" and the "offender" are deprived of the chance to deal with the "conflict" themselves. The solution should then be to put matters back into the hands of those whose concern crimes (or rather "conflicts") properly are. The only role for any formal process would be to facilitate the discussion between the parties. Whether this kind of position could generate a *duty* on the part of victims to take part in the process of conflict-resolution is perhaps arguable, although it seems implausible at first sight.

The connection between restorative justice and the more familiar conceptions of "victims' rights" should not be overplayed: one very marked difference would certainly be that part of some classical restorative justice arguments was that the very concept of "crime" should be rejected and that what need to be addressed are simply "harms" or "conflicts." The outcome to be achieved was the "repair" of a broken relationship between the parties—"punishment" was rejected as barbaric and pointless. However, the development of "victims' rights" does not necessarily involve any such attempt at reconceptualization. Quite to the contrary, appeals to "victims' rights" more commonly involve a demand for greater participation by victims in the *criminal* processes of investigation, prosecution, trial, and sentencing. So, from this perspective, "Sarah's" claim to have "done nothing wrong" is best understood as an assertion of her right to take the case forward or not, since it is essentially *her* conflict. What business is it of anyone else whether she chooses to make the allegations or not, whether she requires her husband to be subject to punishment through the criminal law or not? Maybe a choice not to request a criminal prosecution would be seen by others as a foolish choice, but there would be nothing that should count as any kind of *wrongdoing*. Perhaps a better way for her to proceed, and one which she might even have preferred had the option been available to her, would have been to sue her husband for compensation for the harms done,[20] and to secure a rapid divorce with an order preventing any attempt on his part to contact her.

I have argued elsewhere that a more developed version of this conception of the criminal law makes it more like a civil process.[21] In doing so it does not adequately account for the idea of *criminal* wrongdoing and for the process which puts the political community in charge of responding to such wrongs. It does not capture the sense in which, in the criminal law context, the relevant wrongdoing precisely *is* others' business. Of course, it is not meant to do so, being rather a reformist account that proposes change and the elimination of much that currently falls under the concept of crime. Similarly inadequate is what one might think of as the directly opposing view: that the criminal law is one of the central and legitimate forms of coercive state power, since it is the *state* which is, as it were, the "victim" of crime; it is *its* laws that are attacked. On such a view crimes, even those involving individual victims, are to be understood as attacks on the state. (I call this "the statist view," recognizing, of course, that I give a singularly crude version of it here). On the statist view the individual victims stand as the *occasions* for crime, and thus any role that they might have in the process will be only such as is necessary to fulfill the state's interest.[22]

This does not mean that the state is anything other than a legitimate body, or that it has no right to exercise coercive power, though some states may indeed be illegitimate, in which case they have no right to exercise coercive power.[23] It does not follow either from the statist view that victims should be kept out of the criminal process—there might, for instance, still be room for victim impact statements as aspects of the punishment, so that the offender is required to hear the statement, the better to grasp the full nature of their actions. The important difference lies in the *reasons* for such inclusion: on the statist view, these reasons are instrumental reasons which focus on the way in which the participation of the victim serves the state's interest. One advantage, however, that the statist view has over the civilizing account here is that it takes *wrongdoing* to be at the core of the characterization of crime, and gives some content to the idea that the criminal law is concerned with "public" rather than "private" wrongs. It is in the light of the idea that criminal law is concerned with "public wrongs" that not just the victims' rights but, crucially, victims' duties, must be understood. My criticism is that the statist view construes "public" in quite the wrong way.

IV. SHARING WRONGS AND SHARING RESPONSIBILITIES

To understand the nature of law, we have to understand its role as partly constitutive of a political community and therefore as an object for identification, as playing an important role in a people's sense of who they are.[24]

The state, on the account on which I rely in what follows, is "the institutional manifestation or mechanism of . . . a political community."[25] Citizens are responsible both *to* the state (insofar as they are responsible to one another in their roles as citizens) and *for* the state. Seen in this light, the criminal law and its processes are something for which citizens, qua citizens, are responsible not merely as subcontractors of responsibilities to officials, but as participants sharing responsibility for the criminal law with the officials. In this way the different role-based duties of citizens and officials are interconnected and give the criminal law its institutional form.

In order to get clearer about the victim's role in the criminal law of a political community, let us return to a seemingly simple difference between civil and criminal cases. A civil case is listed as *"Smith v. Jones"*: a plaintiff, Smith, brings a case against Jones, a defendant, complaining that Jones has wrongfully harmed her; if the court finds for Smith, it upholds that complaint, thus validating Smith's account of what happened. It is up to Smith whether to sue Jones or not, whether to settle without going to trial, and whether to enforce a judgment in her favor. A criminal case, by contrast, will be listed as *"People v. Jones"* or *"State v. Jones"* or *"Commonwealth v. Jones"*: by a title that portrays the complainant not as an individual but as the polity. In a polity that aspires to be democratic, this means that the complainant is not just the individual victim (if there is one), not just a singular "I," but the polity, a collective "we." *We*, who include the victim, complain that Jones has wronged Smith in a way that properly concerns *us* as a violation of the values that go to define us as a political community. Upon proof of his guilt in a fair trial (one that summons Jones to answer the charge, and gives him a fair hearing), that complaint becomes an authoritative condemnation of Jones's conduct as a wrong that was in a certain sense public. A trial thus calls a defendant to answer not just to an alleged individual victim, though it does indeed do that, but also to the whole polity for the wrong that he allegedly committed; and it constitutes, in part, an expression, articulation, and application of what are purported to be the shared, "public" values of the polity. It is also an expression of solidarity with the victim and with the alleged offender, for they are both fellow citizens. Such articulation and application involves, of course, the interpretation of those values in relation to the particular series of events that constituted the crime; in this way the individuals involved get to be recognized as individuals.

Values are shared in that they are the values that are internal to the structure of the institutions and practices that go to form the political community and the nature of citizenship within that community. Such a characterization of these values as part of the structure of the polity is to a degree abstract: it says nothing at all about what those values might be, or how rich a range of values there might be, or what importance any particular value has in the structure. All of this will vary from one political community to another. There will be some limits on what values could form this structure, but these limits are given only by what can intelligibly count as a political community—they are conceptual limits. Moreover, in this sense of the "shared values" of a political community, it does not follow that there is no scope for disagreement as to how those values are to be interpreted in their particular applications. Nevertheless, without some shared and roughly agreed upon conceptions there will not *be* a political community (or any other kind of community, for that matter). However, I shall suppose that we are concerned with a roughly liberal polity, with shared values of, for instance, liberty and equality. We can see that even here there is plenty of room for people to disagree about what those values amount to and how they are to be weighed against one another: the crucial point is that it is because these are the shared values in the sense I have specified that disagreement is possible at all.

In a liberal polity the range of values constituting the public domain will be limited. They will not seek to govern all aspects of citizens' lives; rather they specify the quite limited, normative terms of our cohabitation as citizens. Moreover, liberal polities may instantiate different interpretations of those values and there may be, from time to time, disagreement as to how best to express those values in the criminal law. Nevertheless, what is claimed for those values understood as the polity's *public* values is that they both protect and bind us. They protect us from being victimized by criminal wrongs and bind us in requiring us to refrain from criminal wrongdoing. They protect us not only as actual or potential victims but also, just as importantly, as actual or potential offenders. We can all be assured that we will be called to public account through a coercive and condemnatory criminal law, but only for the wrongs defined by the criminal law, as authoritatively interpreted by the courts. The criminal law constituted by these publicly defined wrongs binds us, furthermore, not only as actual or potential offenders but also as witnesses, as jurors, and as victims: those values demand our allegiance and respect not just in requiring that we do not directly violate them by committing crimes, but in requiring us to play our part in their application and enforcement.

This is what is involved in seeing the criminal law, as citizens in a democracy should be able to see it, not as a law to which we are subjected by "the state," but as our law—a law by which we bind ourselves and each other. Then, if it is indeed our law, we must be ready to play our part in the activities that make up this political institution: activities that include not just legislation but also the roles indicated earlier.

V. TAKING PART

The account of the relationship between citizens, between citizens and the state, and between citizens and the law, sketched above clearly has some affinities with the republican tradition of political thought which emphasizes active citizenship and the idea that citizenship is an office which brings with it public duties, an important one of which will be the duty to speak out. Wenar argues that "this picture of the citizen as the bearer of public duties has faded in common sensibility."[26] Still, even if he is right that such a conception of citizenship no longer resonates in "common sensibility" as strongly as it once might have done—living on only, as he notes, in some contemporary republican theory[27]—nevertheless I suggest that it still whispers to us through the institution of criminal law. Thus, citizens are *summoned* to jury *service*, not merely invited to participate, and are excused only under certain circumstances—that is to say, reasons need to be given, not simply an RSVP declining an invitation. Jurors, once they are engaged, then participate in proceedings which include a shared interpretative responsibility: they have to share in the interpretation of the law in applying it to the particular case. In making these determinations, the jury has to make normative judgments as a collective "we" whose responsibility is to determine the meaning of the polity's public values as they apply to the instant case. Furthermore, in line with account of roles discussed previously, the role of juror is partly structured by the desire to perform the role well, and with this comes the right to be enabled to perform the task and not be obstructed. Officials, including judges, then have responsibilities to the jury to aid it in its deliberations.[28]

The jury is thus one example of the way in which citizens and officials share responsibility for the criminal process, but there are other roles for citizens—witnesses and victims—which are crucial in the response to criminal wrongdoing, and which though less formally structured are nonetheless structured by duty. So, while the actualization of the response to criminal wrongdoing is largely the responsibility of various kinds of official (police, prosecutors, the judiciary, penal officials), citizens also have a responsibility to assist in that response: to report crimes, to assist in their investigation, to give evidence in court. These responsibilities are, I suggest, grounded in a general duty to bear witness, to "speak out." This way of putting it is related to the ideal, alluded to earlier, of an active citizenry whose responsibility is to hold *its* government and state to account. However, citizens have a duty not just to hold their government to account but, as members of the political community, to hold themselves and one another to account: bearing witness to wrongdoing by reporting crime is one way in which they discharge this duty. (There is, of course, ample room for disagreement both about how extensive and stringent such responsibilities are, and what force they should have.)

So, just what responsibilities do citizens have, for instance, to report crimes or to assist in their investigation? One kind of answer might have to do with the prevention of crime: someone who has knowledge of a planned crime has a duty to report it in order to prevent the crime from actually taking place; someone who witnesses a crime in progress has a duty to report it in order that the crime be frustrated; someone who knows of a past crime has a duty to report it in order that the offender be prevented from committing crimes in the future. There are certainly arguments to be had about all three of these putative duties and the way in which they may, or may not, infringe liberty or undermine human dignity or undermine trust in such ways as to outweigh their preventative value.[29] My argument, however, grounds the duty to bear witness, or to speak out—and thus the duty to report—not in prevention but in the requirement to address public wrongs. It is not limited, therefore, to cases where crime might be prevented. We must also bear in mind, of course, that such responsibilities could be unqualifiedly asserted only in polities whose criminal laws and procedures were wholly legitimate.[30] To the extent that the criminal law is radically imperfect in its content, in its procedures, in the claim it has on the allegiance and obedience of all citizens, those citizens' responsibilities become more complex and more qualified.

What needs to be clear at this point is that the citizen's duty to report crime, as one form of the general duty to bear witness to criminal wrongdoing, is *not* a duty to seek out or investigate crimes. Any claim to a duty to seek out crime, or even to a general habit of watchfulness, would be in tension with, and would more than likely undermine, the kind of civic trust on which a genuinely communal life for citizens depends.[31] So, "neighborhood watch" schemes, often characterized as a commendable form of citizens' engagement in their local community, would require a different form of justification (crime prevention, for example), and even then what gets justified should be something very limited indeed. Certainly such a justification seems unlikely to sanction a permission, let alone a duty, to investigate.

So, to the extent that a liberal polity's criminal law can properly claim to speak in the voice of its citizens, who share in the values it embodies, they must recognize that they have responsibilities to support and assist it that go beyond the responsibility not to commit what it defines as crimes. In meeting such responsibilities citizens will most certainly be required to exercise judgment: not all breaches of the law, even of the criminal law, are equally serious; just as officials exercise discretion in carrying out their duties, so must citizens in carrying out theirs. It will not make sense to suppose, and it does not follow from my account, that every time I spot another driver committing a driving offense, however trivial, I should report what I see to the police: being overzealous in the performance of duties is as much a (moral) failing as being indifferent to them. Equally, however, this is not to say that I should never report a driving offense, and there may be some offenses the reporting of which is never discretionary, even where there is some risk to the witnesses themselves.

VI. BACK TO VICTIMS

On the account I am offering here, the witness's and victim's duties to report, to testify and give evidence in court, are grounded not simply in the need to prevent crime, but in the importance of addressing public wrongs and calling offenders to account. Indeed, in the case of the victims it is particularly inappropriate to rest such duties in prevention. It would seem odd to suggest that the duty of the rape victim to report and testify is simply grounded in the need to prevent further rapes—this would make the victim primarily of instrumental interest. The best way to focus the preventive aspect would be to talk in terms of her responsibility to help protect her fellow citizens against this person. The duty to bear witness to wrongdoing, as I am characterizing it, is better seen as something which victims owe both to themselves and their fellow citizens as a matter of civic solidarity,[32] and civic dignity. We need then to notice that among the "fellow citizens" to whom the duty is owed are the accused offenders themselves—to call a wrongdoer to account is to acknowledge the wrongdoer *as* "one of us" with equal standing, where that means being equally bound by the law as well as protected by it.

How, then, does this reflect on the role that victims have in the criminal law process? To flesh the account out a little further, consider "Sarah," with whom I began my discussion. Clearly, in falsely claiming that the rape did not take place, she at least failed in her civic duty not to impede the officials—police and prosecutors—in the performance of their duties, but more than that she failed in her duty to bear witness to wrongdoing. She had a duty not just to not make false claims that she had not been raped, but also a duty to report the rapes in the first place and not to withdraw the claim. Notice too that, insofar as she owes these duties to her fellow citizens, she also owes the duty *to her husband*—not because he is her *husband* but because he is a fellow citizen. In failing to report his wrongdoing she failed to take him seriously as a responsible citizen whose actions need to be addressed both by him and the community of fellow citizens.

This is not yet to say that we should give these civic duties the force of law, or criminalize failures to discharge them. A fully developed account would need to be part of a larger discussion about which of our civic duties should be legal duties, and whether the victim's duty to report is more stringent than that of other witnesses. Still, since my argument has stressed the role-based, active, and participatory nature of these duties, there seems to be at least a prima facie case for arguing that victims' duties should be legal duties. In this respect their role will be similar to that of jurors and other witnesses, whose roles involve legal duties with which we are already familiar. It might, at this point, be argued that we could at least start by distinguishing between failures to engage in the process of responding to crime—failures to report, or withdrawals of claims that amount to a withdrawal from the process—and engagements that aim to impede or pervert that process. But this distinction is not quite as straightforward as it at first appears, for at least some failures to engage with the process will be ways of impeding it. So, where there is a legal duty to bear witness—for example, the legal duty to appear as a witness if one is summoned—then failure to turn up to court will impede the trial process and undermine it, although failing to turn up looks like one form of just not engaging with the process.

It might also look as if, where a victim is not required as a witness, the duty to bear witness will nonetheless require the victim to make a VIS,[33] which would turn what is currently a right that the victim may choose not to exercise into an enforceable duty. However, this change will then surely require the VIS to be subject to challenge and that would change its status quite radically.

But whether we are talking only of civic duties or also legal duties, what I say might seem unduly or harshly demanding of victims. (This might be the real burden of the protests from "Sarah" and her supporters.) Now the fact that duties can be burdensome is not a reason for denying that there is a duty, though it might be a reason for us to try to minimize the burden as far as possible. It must certainly be recognized that victims can be, though not inevitably, under considerable pressure not to report or not to testify and that victims, when they do fail in their duty, may have a reasonable excuse which can provide grounds for a plea in mitigation, or even a defense. Nevertheless,

I am less inclined to think that victims would have a *justification* for not reporting a case that ought to be reported (bearing in mind what I said about the exercise of judgment by citizens here), even in the face of strong pressure, short of necessity. Holding firm against such pressures may indeed take courage, but it is not unreasonable to expect citizens to be brave in the face of adversity. Moreover, as I argued earlier, even in the face of strong pressure, victims have rights of an enabling kind. And it is precisely in the context of pressures not to report that we see the importance of these rights. If victims have the kinds of role duty I am ascribing to them, then they also have the right, first of all, not to be obstructed in the performance of that duty; furthermore, they have the right to positive assistance from their fellow citizens and, most importantly, from officials. Apart from some very general role-derived rights—to be taken seriously when they report crimes, to be protected from intimidation, for examples—the precise form which such assistance should take will depend upon the nature of the criminal justice processes: the differences between adversarial and inquisitorial systems, for instance, will impose different obligations on officials as to the treatment of witnesses and victims in the trial process. Thus a full account of these rights will need to show how and in what ways the roles of officials—police, prosecutors, court officials, judges—articulate with the citizens' roles in the whole criminal justice process. If *these* victim rights are properly recognized within the system, then the failure to fulfill those duties is one for which even a victim can be held accountable.

At this point it might strike one that the stress I have placed on keeping in mind that the accused/offenders, as well as their victims, are citizens, invites the question of how the duty to bear witness to criminal wrongdoing applies to offenders, with respect to their own crimes. I cannot do proper justice to the important question of the accused/offender's responsibilities here, but a simple beginning might go as follows:

I ought to recognize my crime as a wrong, and to recognize it as a wrong is to recognize it as something for which I should answer to those whose business it is. As a public wrong, a crime is the business of the polity as a whole, and the criminal trial is the public forum in which criminal wrongdoers are formally called to answer; I therefore have a civic duty to answer for my crime in that forum, which I can do by reporting myself to the appropriate authorities, and pleading "guilty" when I come to trial.[34]

The two caveats to this answer are, first, that it holds good as an unqualified "Yes" only if I am living under a tolerably just system of law; and, second, that this is not (yet) to say that this civic duty should be turned into a legal duty. As to the first caveat, it is important that the offense I committed was indeed a public wrong, whether in virtue of its intrinsic precriminal character as a *malum in se*, or in virtue of its violation of a legal regulation that I had a real obligation to obey. If my conduct did not constitute a public wrong, it should not have been defined as a criminal offense for which I can be called to such public account; and it is then at least questionable whether I have a civic duty to report myself or to plead "guilty." It also matters whether what I face if I plead "guilty" will be a just and appropriate punishment: I am certainly not suggesting that someone whose guilty plea would expose him to some harshly inhumane and unjust mode of punishment has any such duty. But if a guilty plea would only make me liable to an appropriate, inclusionary kind of punishment, the civic duty is real.

As to the second caveat, however, we might still see very good reason not to turn such a civic duty into a legal duty—for instance by making it a criminal offense not to report one's own crime, or not to plead "guilty" if one knows that one is guilty. For one thing, a person could be convicted of such an offense only if he was also convicted of the offense to which he failed to confess, since only then could he proved guilty of failing to confess; so he would face two convictions, two punishments, relating to the same underlying offense. That might seem reasonable, since he would be guilty of two distinct violations of civic duty; compared to an offender who did confess his crime, this offender would be guilty of something more. However, a decent system of criminal justice will also leave room for dissenting citizens to enact their dissent, and will make such allowance as it can for its own fallibility. A dissenting citizen, who denies the authority of the law or the court, might for that reason refuse to play her allotted part in the process—refuse to cooperate with the investigation or trial. If we are to take the law seriously, we cannot allow that to bar her trial and (given proof) conviction for the crime with which he was charged, but we can refrain from also convicting and punishing her for her very defiance. We must also recognize that any human system will sometimes get it wrong, and in particular that even if we set a demanding standard of proof for the criminal trial, innocents will sometimes be mistakenly convicted: it is bad enough that such innocents are punished for crimes that they did not commit; it would be even worse to punish them as well for failing to confess to those crimes (a confession that would of course be false).[35]

It is worth noting a corollary to the civic duty to plead "guilty" if one knows one is guilty: a civic duty to plead "not guilty" if one knows that one is not guilty (or even if one is not sure). This might look like an odd duty: why would an innocent even think of pleading "guilty"? One answer is that in a system based on plea bargaining to the extent that, for instance, the U.S. system is based, and in which insisting on going to trial brings a real risk of a much harsher punishment on conviction, it might well be prudent for an innocent to accept a plea bargain, rather than face the danger of a mistaken conviction. There is, however, no space to pursue these questions further here.

Finally, I have argued, so far, only that we should see the victims' and offenders' duties as civic duties. More argument is required to make a case for these to be legal duties. I have no space to argue for that here, except to make clear that it will not follow from there being such legal duties that the failure to fulfill them must attract *punishment*. It may well be that a firm reminder from the court that citizens do have legal duties, and that we should not take such duties lightly, is all that is reasonable in polities like our own which fall as far short of the ideal as they do.

NOTES

1. David Garland, The Culture of Control vii (2001); *see also* Lucia Zedner, *Victims*, *in* The Oxford Handbook of Criminology (Mike Maguire, Rod Morgan & Robert Weiner eds., 1997).
2. Note that the focus here will be somewhat parochial, concentrating as it does on aspects of the adversarial trial in the Anglo-American tradition, although some of what follows should be relevant to more inquisitorial traditions.
3. Garland, *supra* note 1, at 179.
4. I am not here, or anywhere else in this chapter, concerned with the financial *cost* of implementing such rights, contentious though those costs might be.
5. *See* Zedner, *supra* note 1.
6. The U.K. Victim Charter (2006), for instance, includes the right to such information.
7. So far as I know, no one has argued for a right to be informed about the paying of fines or completion of other non-custodial sentences, though consistency might require such a right.
8. Germany, France, and Poland have such provisions.
9. For some of the potentially perverse consequences, see Marcus D. Dubber, Victims in the War on Crime 214 (2002).
10. Practice Direction (2001), 4 All E.R. 640.
11. Dubber, *supra* note 9.
12. R. v. A. (2012), 2 Cr App R 8 (Eng.).
13. For a fuller discussion, see S. E. Marshall, "*It Isn't Just About You": Victims of Crime and Their Associated Duties*, *in* Criminalization: The Political Morality of the Criminal Law 291 (Antony Duff, Lindsay Farmer, Sandra E. Marshall, Massimo Renzo, & Victor Tadros eds., 2014).
14. *See* Joseph Raz, Between Authority and Interpretation 101–102 (2009).
15. On officials, see Kimberley Brownlee, *Responsibilities of Criminal Justice Officials*, 27 J. Applied Phil. 123 (2010); John Gardner, *Criminals in Uniform*, *in* The Constitution of Criminal Law 97 (Antony Duff, Lindsay Farmer, Sandra E. Marshall, Massimo Renzo, & Victor Tadros eds., 2011); Malcolm Thorburn, *Criminal Law as Public Law*, *in* Philosophical Foundations of Criminal Law 21 (2011).
16. *See* Leif Wenar, *The Nature of Claim Rights*, 123 Ethics 202 (2013).
17. *R. v. A.*, 2 Cr. App. R. 8, para. 2.
18. I use the term "legal process" very broadly here to cover more than just court proceedings.
19. *See* Nils Christie, *Conflicts as Property*, 17 Brit. J. Criminology 1 (1977).
20. Or indeed to sue him as a matter of "civil recourse" for the wrongs that he did to her—the key point being that it is for the wronged victim to decide whether or not to pursue such redress. *See* John C. P. Goldberg & Benjamin C. Zipursky, *Torts as Wrongs*, 88 Tex. L. Rev. 917 (2010).
21. *See* S. E. Marshall & R. A. Duff, *Criminalisation and Sharing Wrongs*, 11 Can. J. Juris. 7 (1998); R. A. Duff & S. E. Marshall, *Public and Private Wrongs, in* Essays in Criminal Law in Honour of Sir Gerald Gordon 70 (James Chalmers ed., 2010).

22. Note that statist view might focus more on harms than on wrongs, although this would not make a difference to the substance of my argument at this particular point.

23. The argument about what grounds the legitimacy of state power is one of the deep questions of political theory and not one I address here. All that is necessary to my argument here is that there is a clear enough distinction between "the state" and what I, along with others, call a "political community."

24. Raz, *supra* note 14, at 106.

25. *See* Criminalization: The Political Morality of the Criminal Law, *supra* note 13.

26. Wenar, *supra* note 16, at 221.

27. *Cf.* Philip Pettit, Republicanism: Theory of Freedom of Government (1997); Richard Dagger, Civic Virtues: Rights, Citizenship, and Republican Liberalism (1997).

28. For a discussion of the duty to do jury service which is close to the spirit of my account here, see Sherman Clark, *The Courage of Our Convictions*, 97 Mich. Crim. L. Rev. 2381 (1999); Albert W. Dzur, Punishment, Participatory Democracy, and the Jury (2012). For an interestingly ambitious account of the interpretive role of the jury, see Robert Burns, A Theory of the Trial (1999).

29. In some jurisdictions, e.g., Israel and the United States, there is a legal duty, in some form, to report. In the United Kingdom, there is a duty to report in special cases: for example, to report information about terrorist offenses (Terrorism Act 2000, s. 38B). An extensive discussion of the duty to report can be found in Miriam Gur-Ayre, *A Failure to Prevent Crime: Should it Be Criminal?* 20 Crim. J. Ethics 3 (2001).

30. *See* Alice Ristroph, *Conditions of Legitimate Punishment.*

31. This is not to say that there are never any, particular, circumstances in which "watchfulness" is appropriate. The public notice warnings seen at large railway stations to "watch out for" pickpockets are not unreasonable as guides to tourists—though such warnings do not impose duties on travelers. But still, there may be some argument to be had about warnings to "watch out for" and "report" sightings of "unattended bags" at, e.g., airports.

32. "Solidarity" is a complex notion which requires more unpacking than I have space for here, but an intriguing discussion of it has been started in Alan Norrie, Address at the the IARC Annual Conference at Rhodes University, South Africa: The Man Who Will Turn the World Upside Down: Critical Realism, Freedom and Political Theory (July 2012).

33. Or a "Victim Personal Statement" in England; *see* Crown Prosecution Service, *Victim Personal Statements*, http://www.cps.gov.uk/legal/v_to_z/victim_personal_statements/index.html.

34. Reporting myself does not of course guarantee that I will be put on trial: the prosecuting authority might decide to take no further action, or divert me from the criminal process, or impose a prosecutorial penalty that preempts the need for a trial. I cannot embark here on a discussion of when (alleged) offenders should be sent to trial.

35. The issue here resembles that which arises when release from prison is conditioned on the prisoner "facing up to" his crime, and is refused if he continues to protest his innocence, which makes the plight of someone who was wrongly convicted even more tragic.

Part IV

Criminal Procedure

Chapter Nine

Reforming Plea Bargaining

Richard L. Lippke

Adversary criminal trials have distinctive proof structures according to which those accused of crimes are to be presumed innocent, the burden of establishing their guilt is on the government, and the standard of proof—beyond a reasonable doubt—is formidable. The accused, with the aid of legal counsel, are afforded opportunities to confront the government's witnesses, challenge its evidence, and call witnesses of their own, which the government must compel to appear. All of this occurs in a public setting, before an impartial judge, who either determines the verdict or regulates and oversees the process by which citizen jurors reach a verdict. If a convicted defendant is not satisfied that the trial process was fair, he or she can challenge it by filing appeals to the higher courts.

There are competing accounts of why we set up criminal trials to be such rigorous tests of the government's case against the individuals it has accused of crimes. Some theorists argue that we do so because we prefer, and indeed strongly prefer, to avoid convicting the innocent to convicting the guilty.[1] Other theorists maintain that trials should be conceived as complex, moral, assurance procedures, designed to ensure that our punishment of individuals, with its grave and enduring consequences for them, is fully and appropriately justified.[2] Beyond such outcome-based accounts, other values—human dignity, the rule of law, and fundamental fairness—are served by carefully designed and administered public trials. If we are going to accuse individuals of serious wrongdoing and present evidence in support of these accusations, then it matters considerably how we go about doing so if we are to avoid the appearance of partiality, corruption, or insensitivity regarding what is at stake for the accused in such proceedings.

Yet in many countries, the United States foremost among them, most persons accused of crimes decline to put the government's accusations against them to the test of a criminal trial. In the United States, more than 95 percent of those accused of crimes waive the right to trial and enter guilty pleas. The process that leads to this surprising result—known as plea bargaining—exists in other countries as well, though usually in more restrained forms.[3] In the United States, trial avoidance takes a distinctive, and many believe worrisome, form. My first task will be to provide an overview of this unique form, with special emphasis on the myriad pressures to waive the right to trial to which accused persons are subjected, the relative indifference of the courts to the quality of the government's evidence against the accused, and the seeming disconnect between plea bargaining and the aims of legal punishment.

In the second section, various reforms in U.S.-style plea bargaining are urged, ones that would have the effect of bringing it more in line with forms of trial avoidance that are found elsewhere in the world. In particular, I urge the adoption of smaller and less negotiable concessions on sentences in exchange for guilty pleas. Bargaining about the charges to be filed or maintained in a case should be discouraged, as should bargaining about the facts of a case, especially when this distorts the nature of the criminal activity in which persons can be proven to have engaged. Judges should be encouraged to police the charging process to a greater extent and to ensure that the evidence against persons about to plead guilty meets a minimum standard of sufficiency. We should move toward a system of fixed and modest sentence concessions for guilty pleas, one that ensures that police and prosecutors have conducted themselves responsibly and in accordance with the larger aims of the criminal justice system.

But would the adoption of such reforms make much difference, especially in reducing the extent to which the United States relies, and arguably overrelies, on legal punishment as a device for reducing undesirable conduct? It is tempting to portray unfettered plea bargaining as the "engine" of mass incarceration, or more generally, mass punishment. After all, if every person charged with a crime demanded or had to be given a full-on adversary trial, the criminal justice system would, the Supreme Court, among others, has assured us, quickly grind to a halt.[4] In the third section, I take up the vexed question of the role of plea bargaining in producing the bloated criminal justice system of the United States. Though reformed plea-bargaining procedures would likely slow the production of mass punishment, I contend that the main reasons for modifying those procedures have more to do with the promotion of other values. These include substantive and procedural justice, as well is ensuring that the sanctions assigned criminal offenders comport with the aims of legal punishment.

I. THE DISTINCTIVE FORM OF TRIAL AVOIDANCE IN THE UNITED STATES

Well-established procedures for avoiding trials are not unique to the United States. In particular, sentencing concessions for accused persons willing to admit their guilt, and in some cases concessions with respect to charges, exist in numerous other countries. What is unique about trial avoidance in the United States is the magnitude, variety, and manipulability of the concessions granted to accused persons who are prepared to plead guilty, along with the minimal oversight exercised by members of the judiciary over the plea process. Plea bargaining, U.S. style, might not be akin to haggling at a street bazaar, as some have alleged, but it comes closer to it than many scholars believe is appropriate.[5]

What makes plea bargaining in the United States so distinctive? What follows is a partial listing of its features, along with some brief comment on each of them:

1. The magnitude of the sentencing concessions: Plea bargaining in the United States is driven by what has been termed the "sentencing differential," the difference in sentences assigned to those who plead guilty and the sentences assigned those who, charged with similar crimes, are convicted after trials. Part of this differential stems from the sentencing concessions granted to accused persons who tender guilty pleas. Though estimates vary, it seems clear that such sentencing concessions can exceed 50 percent of the statutorily available sentences—that is, the sentences that prosecutors could legally recommend at the conclusions of trials at which accused persons are convicted and which judges might legally assign. It is widely agreed that sentencing concessions are greatest for misdemeanors, relatively minor crimes for which sentences rarely exceed a year's confinement and often include no custody at all.[6] Prosecutors (and judges) are eager to clear such cases off their dockets and so offer generous sentencing concessions in exchange for guilty pleas. Subsequently, I will say more about the problems raised by misdemeanors.
2. The existence of charge bargaining: Along with sentence concessions, one of the other main contributors to the sentencing differential is the willingness of prosecutors to reduce charges in exchange for guilty pleas. Charge reductions typically produce lighter sentences, especially since most U.S. jurisdictions eschew concurrent approaches to sentencing. Importantly, prosecutors can also add charges to increase the sentences to which the accused are vulnerable if they believe them to be reluctant to plead.

3. The existence of trial penalties: Criminal defendants who refuse to enter guilty pleas, but who instead go to trial and are convicted, are very unlikely to receive the sentence or charge concessions on offer from prosecutors pretrial, assuming that prosecutors saw fit to offer any. Such concessions were proffered as rewards for guilty pleas. But do persons convicted after trials suffer more than the loss of such "waiver rewards"? Many observers believe that they do, that prosecutors often recommend longer sentences than they might have initially deemed appropriate or fair, given the nature of the accusations against persons, simply to punish the convicted for having exercised the right to trial. These vindictively-motivated sentence add-ons are "trial penalties." Not only can they be substantial, but judges might also go along with them. Judges likewise do not appear to appreciate exercise of the right to trial by many criminal defendants.[7] Assuming they exist, trial penalties swell sentencing differentials.
4. The existence of cooperation rewards: Another factor that contributes to sentencing differentials is the existence of rewards (in the form of reduced sentences, charges, or both) for accused persons who cooperate with the authorities in testifying or otherwise providing evidence against their accomplices in crime.[8] These rewards can be substantial and sometimes go to the first defendant to be arrested or to recognize the benefits of cooperation, regardless of his or her relative culpability among those collectively involved in one or more criminal acts.
5. Charging discretion of prosecutors: The U.S. criminal justice system affords prosecutors enormous discretion in initially determining and subsequently altering charges. Judges are generally reluctant to second-guess prosecutors on these matters. This discretion facilitates charge bargaining. Prosecutors can drop charges without judges asking pesky questions about why they did so. Prosecutors can also add charges, to better motivate accused persons to plead, without much judicial scrutiny beyond the weak "probable cause" standard.
6. The existence of fact bargaining: Beyond sentence and charge bargaining, prosecutors and defense attorneys sometimes engage in negotiations about the "facts" of cases in ways that bear on sentencing outcomes.[9] For instance, sentencing under U.S. drug laws often depends crucially on the amount of contraband found in a person's possession. In exchange for guilty pleas, prosecutors might agree to charges that effectively misrepresent the quantity of drugs found in a defendant's possession. This misrepresentation will be made to the judge overseeing the plea hearing. Judges have little ability to detect such misrepresentations of the facts of cases, as they are not typically provided with full case dossiers containing all of the police reports and other evidence relevant to cases.

7. Lax judicial oversight of the evidence: By U.S. law, the judges who oversee the hearings at which accused persons enter guilty pleas (known as "plea colloquies") are supposed to ensure that there is a "factual basis" for any guilty plea. However, most legal observers concur in the judgment that U.S. judges are far from diligent in performing this vital task.[10] Many judges seem to believe that prosecutors know more about specific cases than they do; add to this a general reluctance to tamper with plea agreements already worked out between prosecutors and defense attorneys (the latter of whom might be assumed to satisfactorily see to the protection of their clients' interests), and judges understandably exercise a "light touch" when it comes to their oversight of guilty pleas.
8. Inadequacies in the indigent defense system: Many if not most of the individuals charged with crimes in the United States are poor. They cannot afford to hire their own defense attorneys and so must be supplied with them by the government. But few observers regard the indigent defense system in the United States as anything but an unqualified disaster.[11] At best, indigent defendants are represented by public defenders who have many more clients than they can effectively counsel and serve, and who therefore implicitly or explicitly encourage (some would say "pressure") most of their clients to enter guilty pleas. Few defendants have attorneys willing and able to perform their own investigations of alleged crimes or mount stalwart defenses to the government's charges.
9. High process costs: Fewer efforts are made in the United States, compared with other countries, to contain the "process costs" of going to trial. These are costs, exclusive of legal punishment, that those accused of crimes have to endure: pretrial detention, numerous required court hearings, delays in the onset of trials, the public embarrassment involved in having to appear and answer to charges, foregone earnings from work, and stress on familial and other social relations.[12] Some process costs are unavoidable, but all of them increase the pressure on accused persons to plead guilty and get their cases resolved. In particular, pretrial detention is arguably overused in the United States, with detrimental impact on the willingness of those charged with crimes to contest the charges, especially when they are relatively minor. A not insignificant number of accused persons held in pretrial detention will plead guilty in exchange for recommended sentences of "time served" (that is, time served in pretrial detention).
10. No limits on the kinds of cases subject to plea negotiations: In other countries in which sentencing concessions for guilty pleas exist, serious cases (typically denominated as such by the sentences to which accused persons are potentially subject) must be subjected to trial

adjudication.[13] No such limits exist in the United States. All kinds of criminal cases are subject to plea negotiations, no matter how serious the charges and therefore (it would seem) how sorely needed is close scrutiny of the evidence against the accused. Prosecutors might be more reluctant to plea bargain when the charges are serious, but these are decisions governed more by politics or their own preferences than any formal legal requirements.

These features of trial avoidance in the United States provide the basis for a telling critique of plea bargaining. First, the magnitude of the sentencing differential should undermine our confidence that when accused persons plead guilty, they do so because they really are guilty or because the government can prove their guilt beyond a reasonable doubt in a court of law. The sentencing differential might, in fact, make the evidence that the government can muster in a given case of only marginal relevance to its ability to generate guilty pleas. This is most worrisomely true in misdemeanor cases involving defendants with existing criminal records. Legal scholars have shown that many such defendants plead guilty at their first court appearances, before any real investigation of their alleged crimes occurs beyond their initial arrests by police officers.[14] Why would those charged with misdemeanors do this? Because many of them face prolonged pretrial detention, are demoralized by their previous dealings with the criminal justice (and wider social) system, lack effective legal counsel, and can trade their right to trial for substantially reduced punishment—all of this even if they are, in fact, innocent of the current charges against them. Even if most who are charged with crimes are guilty, and the evidence against them is strong, the size of the sentencing differential limits the ability of the charge adjudication system to determine the appropriateness of the charges against them. If few accused persons are willing to contest the government's case against them, there is little effective regulation of the actions of police and prosecutors in arresting persons and charging them with crimes.

Second, the United States plea bargaining system provides too much scope for variation in the punishment meted out to individuals who have committed roughly similar crimes. Plea bargained outcomes depend to a significant extent on an array of factors that have little to do with the gravity of the criminal misconduct in which individuals have engaged or which the government can prove.[15] These factors include the quality of the defense counsel available to accused persons, the extent to which the accused can offer useful information to the authorities or are the first to do so, the risk-aversion profile of accused persons (less risk-averse defendants might wrangle better offers from prosecutors), how busy the prosecutor is or whether he or she is on friendly terms with the defense counsel in a given case, and the abilities of accused persons to pay bail and thus remain free of detention while charges against them are pending. These seemingly irrelevant factors produce significant variations in the sentences assigned to like offenders who are willing to admit their guilt.

The objection based on the comparative injustices produced by plea bargaining feeds into a further criticism of the practice: It produces sentencing outcomes that are not reliably related to the sentencing goals of the criminal justice system, whether these are conceived in retributive, crime reduction, or other terms. Charge and fact bargaining should especially undermine our confidence in the penal outcomes of plea negotiations. Additional or more serious wrongdoing by persons might be downplayed or swept under the rug by prosecutors eager to attract guilty pleas. Cooperation rewards might likewise enable individuals who have engaged in serious wrongdoing to minimize their punishment. Conversely, trial penalties or stacked charges that are not negotiated away might produce disproportionately harsh or counterproductive criminal sanctions for those defendants who are brave or foolish enough to put the government's charges to the test of trial adjudication. And cooperation rewards might expose some individuals to more than their deserved or optimal punishment because their accomplices are eager to implicate them for crimes of which they are less or only marginally guilty.

The preceding points against plea bargaining would all hold, for the most part, even if the United States was a reasonably just society with normatively defensible criminal prohibitions and a rational sentencing scheme. But add in concerns about rising inequality in the United States, combined with overcriminalization and unduly harsh sentences for many crimes, and a different critique of plea bargaining emerges. Consider, again, the point that misdemeanor case processing constitutes the bulk of the work done by the criminal justice system. Many of the crimes for which individuals are arrested and charged are so-called public order offenses: trespassing, disorderly conduct, prostitution, marijuana possession, and the like.[16] As legal scholars have shown, a majority of the individuals charged with such offenses are poor or members of racial minorities.[17] In such cases, police decisions about whom to arrest loom large and there is lax oversight of these decisions. Given the casual approach to the processing of such cases that we have already seen, the more or less inevitable outcome is that persons whose lives are already difficult, and arguably unjustly so, suffer further setbacks because of their entanglement with the criminal justice system. At least some of that entanglement might be limited if more poor and minority defendants had better legal representation, were more able to avoid or absorb the process costs of trials, and there was proper judicial screening of the evidence in their cases. In short, U.S. plea bargaining operates in a distinctive context, one created by the society's peculiar history of race relations, deep ambivalence toward social policies designed to minimize social deprivation, harsh sentencing policies, and minimal oversight of criminal justice officials. Plea bargaining's brusque treatment of many offenders further degrades their lives and likely alienates them from the social order.

II. REFORMING PLEA BARGAINING

Numerous reforms to plea bargaining have been proposed by those who study it, though some scholars urge its abolition. Space does not permit me to discuss all of the reforms that have been proposed nor fully defend the ones I support.[18] My view is that we should seek to rein in plea bargaining, so that it becomes a more judicially supervised system of modest and fixed sentencing concessions for those accused persons willing to admit their guilt. Charge and fact bargaining should be strongly discouraged and cooperation rewards should be kept small. Trial penalties should be prohibited. How might we go about implementing these changes?

Part of doing so involves encouraging judges to take more active roles in nontrial charge adjudication, something that is the norm in other countries with more constrained forms of plea bargaining. The U.S. system of plea bargaining effectively turns judges into spectators. They conduct plea colloquies during which plea agreements, previously worked out by prosecutors and defense attorneys, are passively acquiesced in. As we have seen, judges at such hearings are disinclined to scrutinize the government's evidence, though they are supposed to. In place of such a scheme, I propose a different one. Once charged with crimes, individuals who indicate a willingness to plead would be given settlement hearings before a judge. Prior to such hearings, there would be no negotiations permitted between prosecutors and defense attorneys about charges or sentences. The first task of the judge during a settlement hearing would be to determine whether there is sufficient evidence to support the tendering of a guilty plea by the accused. To aid in accomplishing this task, I would have full case dossiers provided to judges in advance of the hearing. Then, at the hearing, both the prosecution and the defense would be given the opportunity to briefly present their cases before the judge. In particular, the defense could urge a reduction in charges (either their number or severity) or their complete elimination. I would also permit the judge to question the accused, to determine whether and to what extent his or her account of the events in question coheres with the accounts presented by the prosecutor and defense attorney.[19] Only charges supported by at least a preponderance of the evidence should then be sustained by the judge.

The settlement hearing judge's second main task would be to set a presumptive sentence on any and all remaining charges.[20] This would provide the accused person with a sense of the worst sentence he or she could reasonably expect if convicted after a trial. It would also provide a benchmark against which to detect and thus discourage trial penalties—posttrial sentence increases recommended by prosecutors and imposed by judges the purpose of which is solely to punish the convicted for having elected trial adjudication. Any posttrial sentencing increases over the presumptive sentence would have to be explained, in writing, by the sentencing judge and would be subject to appeal. Once a presumptive sentence had been determined by the judge at or shortly after the settlement hearing, accused persons would face a stark choice: either enter guilty pleas, in which case they would receive modest and fixed discounts from the presumptive sentence, or go to trial and risk no more (in most cases) than the presumptive sentence if they were convicted. I would keep the sentence discounts in the 10 percent range. Accused persons willing to admit their guilt and thus spare the government, witnesses, and jurors the burdens of trials (and subsequent appeals) ought to be given some consideration for this, in the form of modestly reduced sentences. At the same time, keeping such waiver rewards small would ensure that the sentencing differential did not render the strength of the government's evidence of little import in the accused's decision to plead guilty. Such rewards would also help to ensure that guilty pleas served the larger sentencing aims of the criminal justice system. Keeping them fixed would reduce the comparative injustices produced by the kinds of negotiations between prosecutors and defense attorneys that are currently the norm. Cooperation rewards should also be kept in the 10 percent range, though in combination with sentence discounts, the result might be sentences reduced by 20 percent.

Charge and fact bargaining could be discouraged in a number of ways. First, settlement hearing judges would have case dossiers against which to assess the current charges against the accused. Such dossiers should include not only summaries of the evidence against the accused but also histories of any charges filed and subsequently altered or dropped by prosecutors. Prosecutors could thus be queried by settlement hearing judges if it appeared that charges had been altered in some way. I would not permit judges to add charges if they believed that prosecutors had engaged in significant undercharging in order to attract guilty pleas. The judge's role should be limited to eliminating excessive charges or ones for which the evidence is too weak to warrant going forward. But judges could refuse to accept guilty pleas to charges that they believed downplayed the crimes committed by the accused. By doing so, they would place the ball back in the prosecutor's court. The prosecutor would have to determine whether to bring the charges more in line with what the evidence suggests about the crimes of the accused or to drop all charges. There is no use denying that this approach would produce acute dilemmas in some cases. Prosecutors might doubt their abilities to prevail on more serious charges, and accused persons might not agree to plead guilty to them. But I believe that we should not have our courts aid and abet misrepresentations of the crimes which individuals have committed, even if by doing so prosecutors can thereby gain more convictions.[21]

Second, I would prohibit, as matters of professional ethics, presettlement hearing negotiations about charges and sentences between prosecutors and defense attorneys. Defense attorneys should be permitted to provide prosecutors with evidence of their clients' innocence or reduced culpability, but doing so should be distinguished from bartering about charges and sentences in exchange for guilty pleas. This change in the standards of professional ethics would be radical by U.S. standards. But in many other countries, negotiations about charges and sentences are frowned upon (which is not to say they never occur).[22] This suggests that reform of U.S. standards and practices is at least feasible.

Third, the victims of crimes should be permitted to file affidavits disputing the prosecutor's charges if victims believe that the charges misrepresent what the accused did to them.[23] Indeed, such affidavits might lead settlement hearing judges to refuse to accept defendants' guilty pleas. Again, such refusals by judges would effectively force prosecutors to reconsider, and perhaps redraw, the charges against the accused. Of course, many crimes lack direct victims, so this constraint on charge or fact bargaining would then be unavailable. Nonetheless, the case dossier should work to keep such practices in check, to some extent.

How would the preceding scheme work to counter the critique of U.S.-style plea bargaining adumbrated in the previous section? First, it would substantially reduce the sentencing differential as between plea-bargained and trial outcomes. The contribution of trial penalties to this differential would be a thing of the past. It would be harder to ferret out and discourage charge bargaining, but the proposed scheme should work to keep it in check. Large sentence concessions in exchange for guilty pleas would not be on offer. All of this would mean that we could be much more confident that the incentives to plead guilty that are independent of the evidence that the government can muster against the accused would be greatly reduced.[24] Add to this the more active role of judges in determining the sufficiency of the evidence against the accused, and concerns about whether individuals plead guilty simply because they wish to minimize their punishment, as opposed to because they are guilty or believe the government well capable of proving their guilt, should be minimized.

Second, comparative injustices in sentencing would be substantially reduced by my proposed scheme. The differences in sentences between accused persons who pled guilty and those who were convicted after trials would be slight (typically, no more than 10 percent). No longer would the sentences of those who elected trial adjudication be swelled by the loss of substantial waiver or cooperation rewards or the imposition of trial penalties. Moreover, charges and sentences for those who pled guilty would not be determined by negotiations between prosecutors and defense attorneys. This means that many of the extraneous factors that currently affect such negotiations—how busy the prosecutor is, how friendly an accused person's attorney is with the prosecutor, how risk-averse a defendant is—would cease to have much influence over sentencing outcomes. Once a settlement hearing was requested, charges were sustained by a judge, and a presumptive sentence was issued, accused persons who wished to plead guilty would receive modest and fixed sentence discounts. There would be much less wiggle room for all of the parties, with the inevitable sentencing inequities it creates.

Third, we would have greater assurance that the outcomes of guilty pleas were in accordance with the principal aims of legal punishment. Fact and charge bargaining would be discouraged, with their attendant possibilities for significant disconnects between the crimes that individuals have committed and the crimes for which they are punished. Limited cooperation and sentencing rewards would keep sentencing outcomes better in line with the crimes to which individuals admitted. Defense attorneys who were more motivated, skilled, or better positioned to negotiate deals on behalf of their clients would be much less able to affect sentencing outcomes. Granted, all of this presupposes that the sentencing scheme is itself set up to achieve defensible penal aims in ways that employ appropriate means—an ideal against which existing sentencing schemes might come up considerably short. If existing schemes are too harsh or too lenient, then a reformed approach to guilty pleas will not produce optimal results. But that is no fault of the reformed plea system. Neither should it be taken as a strong argument against such a reformed system that it might prove less capable than current forms of plea bargaining of ameliorating the excessive criminal sanctions that many scholars believe United States legislators have authorized the courts to employ. True, current forms of plea bargaining might produce greatly discounted sentences for some offenders. But it will not do so systematically for all offenders; when prosecutors can freely engage in charge stacking, outcomes are hardly certain to be lenient or fair. And current forms of plea bargaining clearly produce significant sentencing inequities. The only solution to a defective sentencing scheme is to fix the scheme, not to rely on a defective charge adjudication process to repair it, which the process will only accomplish in a haphazard way in any case.

Fourth, and relevant to the immediately preceding point, the reformed plea adjudication scheme would go some way toward limiting the damage done by misdemeanor charges and convictions in the United States. No longer would persons accused of such crimes be permitted to hurriedly plead guilty in the absence of a determination by a judge that there is sufficient evidence to sustain their pleas. Part of the problem with the current scheme is precisely its casual processing of such cases. Not only might the reforms I have proposed weed out weak cases, but they also would discourage police from harassing the poor or prosecutors from filing charges against them to begin with. If little is likely to come of such conduct by police and prosecutors, then they might be less inclined to engage in it. Also, the ban on plea negotiations would reduce the kinds of inequities in misdemeanor enforcement that plague our current system, whereby the rich or better-positioned can effectively evade punishment for their minor crimes, whereas the poor cannot.[25] Where plea negotiations determine sentencing outcomes, those with better attorneys get better outcomes. Under my proposed scheme, which eschews such negotiations, rich and poor alike would get outcomes more constrained by the evidence against them and the decisions made by settlement hearing judges.[26]

Nonetheless, I must concede that one seeming advantage of the current form of plea bargaining is that it produces steeply discounted sentences in many misdemeanor cases, with those willing to plead guilty assigned sentences well below the statutorily available maximums. Such discounts will not be available on my proposed scheme, though we should not assume that settlement hearing judges would routinely set presumptive sentences at the statutorily available maximums. Robust and negotiable charge and sentence discounts can produce large reductions in sentences for misdemeanants; that much is clear. Again, it will do so in ways that are highly uneven and will likely produce convictions of more persons against whom the government's evidence is flimsy. Reforms in charge adjudication are not a panacea. They will not magically fix other grave and largely independent defects in the criminal justice system. But will such reforms really do much good at all if we take a larger view of the United States criminal justice system and its flaws? Or are plea concessions, in any form, the root of these flaws because they keep the wheels of justice turning, however lamentable their outcomes? It is to these questions that we turn in the third section.

III. SHOULD PLEA CONCESSIONS BE PRESERVED?

There is a venerable line of argument according to which plea bargaining, in its current U.S. forms, is vital to keeping the criminal justice system functioning effectively. The U.S. Supreme Court has taken this view in some of its rulings in support of plea bargaining, as have some legal scholars.[27] The idea is that the system simply cannot provide all accused persons with full-on trials, whether bench or jury trials.[28] The demands on the system would be too great, so we must acquiesce in the status quo, with its substantial and negotiable sentencing differentials which are designed to induce guilty pleas from the vast majority of criminal defendants. The gap between the major premise of this argument and its conclusion is vast. Even if we cannot provide all or most of those accused of crimes with trials, it hardly follows that the current scheme, with all of its worrisome features, is the only alternative. I have not proposed to eliminate plea concessions, only plea bargaining as it currently exists. Whether my scheme would likewise cause the criminal justice system to become hopelessly bogged down is an interesting question, albeit one which I will not attempt to answer.

Instead, I want to focus on a different line of argument concerning plea bargaining, one according to which it is the lynchpin of mass punishment, such that without it, we would not be able to punish so many people with all of its costly and destructive effects. This line of argument embraces the same major premise as the previous one but turns it on its head: Instead of casting plea bargaining as the savior of the criminal justice system, it casts it as the vital cog in a bloated and damaging state punishment regime. Look at the United States, it says, with its 2.3 million people in prison. Would this ghastly state of affairs have been remotely possible without the crass and casual approach to charge adjudication of which plea bargaining consists? And will anything short of the complete elimination of plea bargaining in all of its forms—including modest and fixed plea concessions of the sort I propose—have any realistic prospect of reducing the overuse of legal punishment in the United States?

In addressing this line of argument, we should begin by distinguishing mass incarceration from mass punishment. The U.S. criminal justice system both sends many people to prison and inflicts other forms of criminal sanctions on many others. Over two million people are in U.S. prisons and jails at present, but almost seven million are in some way or other currently serving criminal sentences.[29] Since we punish many people in ways other than by sending them to prison, we should be cautious about assuming that the factors responsible for the incarceration boom of the last forty years are the same as the ones responsible for mass punishment. Most scholars trace the beginnings of the incarceration boom to the early to mid-1970s, with the most significant escalation in imprisonment rates occurring during the 1980s and 1990s. Plea bargaining in its current forms was in place considerably before this time period. By the 1920s, guilty pleas were the main form of charge adjudication in many jurisdictions.[30] By the 1960s, plea bargaining was, far and away, the dominant form of charge adjudication throughout the country.[31] This suggests that something other than plea bargaining explains the huge increases in incarceration that the United States experienced in the latter two decades of the twentieth century. Indeed, if one examines the literature on mass incarceration, one rarely finds plea bargaining mentioned as one of its principal causes.[32] Instead, one finds changes in sentencing policies as the dominant explanation for the incarceration boom, along with changes in attitudes towards the poor, the politicization of crime and criminal justice policy, and residual racism. If plea bargaining is the engine of mass incarceration, then it is one to which most scholars of the topic pay scant attention.

However, as we have seen, the majority of the crimes actually processed by the criminal justice system are misdemeanors. Many of these prosecutions produce noncustodial sentences of one kind or another and their targets are overwhelmingly persons living at the social margins. Perhaps it is mass punishment of the poor of which plea bargaining is the "engine." It makes their harassment and control by the authorities too easy, especially with the pressure to plead guilty that it generates and the cursory examination of the evidence for crimes that it provides. Granted, the reforms in plea bargaining I have proposed might slow down the processing of misdemeanor cases. Settlement hearing judges would have to determine whether there was evidence sufficient to warrant the acceptance of guilty pleas. Not only is this considerably more than judges overseeing most plea colloquies appear to do at present, but it also might force the authorities to do more than simply arrest and charge people in order to gain convictions.[33]

Still, it might be argued that any form of plea concessions—even modest and fixed ones available subsequent to settlement hearings—would sustain misdemeanor case processing. Only a requirement of full-on criminal trials in every case would have the potential to "crash the system," over-burdening it in ways that would force police and prosecutors, and the legislators whose decisions determine what conduct to criminalize and to what extent, to stop and rethink what they are doing.[34] Trial avoidance is the root of the problem with our approach to misdemeanors. Somewhat independently of this, it might also be claimed that criminal trials comport better with the dignity of accused persons, norms of fair process, and the rule of law. Trials give accused persons notice of the charges against them, the opportunity to respond (with the aid of legal counsel) to those charges, and an exacting standard of proof as a barrier to easy or mistaken conviction. Plea bargaining is a "cattle call," where intimidated defendants are quickly herded through the courts with only a perfunctory glance at the evidence against them and little concern about how they are treated in the rush to punish them.

I concur with these latter points. We should reform plea bargaining to reduce the pressure on accused persons to plead and to ensure that judges scrutinize the evidence against them before accepting their pleas. This will slow down and render more exacting non-trial case processing. If such reforms were combined with substantial improvements in indigent defense, the result would be a system that provided accused persons a meaningful opportunity to contest the charges against them before they pled guilty.[35] In response, it might be claimed that the case pressure of the misdemeanor courts will inevitably erode the increased procedural protections I propose. Harried misdemeanor court judges will quickly revert to superficial scrutiny of the evidence against the accused, and prosecutors will find other ways beyond the sentencing differential to pressure them to plead. In particular, the process costs of punishment might be manipulated by prosecutors.

The objection that settlement hearings will not survive the caseload pressure of misdemeanor courts is not without merit, but it constitutes a two-edged sword for enthusiasts of criminal trials. For it is equally plausible to believe that trial adjudication in the lower courts would eventually be degraded by caseload pressure, such that trials would gradually become little more than quick and casual affairs.[36] The only real solution is to try to make sure that any enhanced procedural protections we adopt for individuals accused of misdemeanors are not quickly abandoned. My sense is that because settlement hearings are more modest in their demands upon the system than full-on criminal trials, their prospects are comparatively better for resisting the depredations of caseload pressure.

As for manipulating process costs in lieu of manipulating the sentencing differential, the solution is to limit the abilities of prosecutors to do so. Strongly persuasive arguments already exist to reduce reliance on pretrial detention in the United States, and this for reasons that go beyond the pressure such detention exerts on the accused to plead guilty.[37] Also, any undiluted trial requirement is bound to increase process costs, as it will mean that final case adjudication is delayed. It is a virtue of settlement hearings that they are less rigorous than trials and therefore less time-consuming. Many persons charged with misdemeanors want to get their cases resolved sooner rather than later. Trials are unlikely to vindicate them, because many of them are, in fact, guilty more or less as charged. Trials would expose the accused to unwanted public scrutiny, and the elimination of plea concessions would mean that the convicted would suffer more punishment. In light of all of this, it is not clear who exactly is supposed to benefit from the trials of persons who want to plead guilty in exchange for modest and fixed sentence discounts consequent to settlement hearings.

Perhaps the idea is that trials will weed out a few more factually innocent defendants than will settlement hearings—a benefit not only to the defendants themselves, but also to the public who must foot the bill for their unjust punishment. In response, three quick points might be made: First, one wonders how many type-1 errors (that is, errors of mistaken conviction) full-on trials will prevent, compared with the modified plea approach I support, especially if (a) charges have to first survive a settlement hearing, and (b) the rewards for pleading guilty are kept modest. Second, even if trials will significantly reduce type-1 errors, they will do so at considerably increased costs to the public and produce type-2 errors, that is, acquittals of some guilty persons who might have pled guilty in exchange for modest and fixed sentencing concessions. Third, there might be some materially innocent defendants for whom trial exoneration is not worth the costs and risks. As legal scholars have noted, this is arguably true for individuals who already have criminal records and who are charged with misdemeanors. For some of them, another mark on their records is insignificant, whereas avoiding process costs, gaining reduced punishment, and getting their punishment over with are perceived by them to be more valuable.[38] To this, I would add that any innocent accused whose settlement hearing has not resulted in the dismissal of all charges against her faces a realistic prospect of conviction after a trial. It seems to me that whether such persons should persist in their claims of innocence all the way through a trial ought to be their call. If the pressures to plead are kept modest, the process costs of going to trial are minimized, accused persons are provided adequate legal counsel, and a settlement hearing judge certifies the charges against them, then it might seem that we have done enough to ensure that any "false" guilty pleas are neither coerced nor wholly misguided.

I would be more sympathetic to proposals to eliminate plea concessions in cases in which the potential penal consequences faced by accused persons are grave. Perhaps any person facing a prison sentence of more than five years ought to be given a full-on criminal trial. The potential consequences for the accused in the event of conviction are simply too momentous to tolerate anything less than full and exacting scrutiny of the government's evidence against them. Also, we could probably provide trials in such cases without too many additional financial burdens on the public. Still, there is another possibility here, one that is consistent with providing modest and fixed plea concessions in these kinds of cases. We could require settlement hearing judges to employ more exacting evidence-sufficiency standards in such cases. They could be required to find that the government's evidence was "much more likely than not" to prove the guilt of the accused or, stronger yet, was "clear and convincing" before any accused person would be allowed to tender a guilty plea. If the enhanced evidence-sufficiency standard was not found to be met by the settlement hearing judge, accused persons would have no choice but to submit to trial adjudication of the charges against them.

This leaves us with "system crashing" argument for requiring trials in all cases, even when the charges against persons are relatively minor. Proponents of an unqualified trial requirement might hope that its costs and delays would be so great that government officials would be forced to confront overcriminalization in all of its guises, but especially of minor forms of misconduct. There is, of course, a powerful case to be made for reducing overcriminalization in the United States.[39] But I am not convinced that a trial requirement would produce the requisite resolve to take on the task. There are plenty of other reasons to do so, the burgeoning costs and patent destructiveness to too many people's life-prospects of the penal policy choices we have made foremost among them. Also, there is the practical problem of figuring out how to get political officials to take a trial requirement seriously.

It will be difficult enough to get the reforms in plea adjudication I have urged adopted, though they are less ambitious. Those who believe that the way to slow down the punishment machine is to insist that all accused persons be provided criminal trials have to answer a difficult question: How would we go about getting such a proposal implemented though few of the people who would have to see to its implementation seem committed to easing off on the punishment throttle?

My own proposal might appear vulnerable to this kind of objection. There seems little support outside of academia for significant reforms in plea bargaining. However, at least my defense of such reforms is not premised on "crashing the system," a goal that few politicians or legislators are likely to embrace. Instead, it is based on the desirability of reducing adjudication errors by giving the evidence in cases more salience, treating accused persons with more dignity by not compelling their guilty pleas, and ensuring that the sentences meted out to offenders cohere with the aims of legal punishment. These are not radical ideas, even if they are not, at present, politically popular. Also, if such reforms produced or were combined with a reexamination of the punitive path down which we have gone, so much the better.

NOTES

1. Larry Laudan, Truth, Error, and the Criminal Law: An Essay in Legal Epistemology (2006); Erik Lillquist, *Recasting Reasonable Doubt: Decision Theory and the Virtues of Variability*, 36 U.C. Davis L. Rev. 85 (2002); Michael L. DeKay, *The Difference Between Blackstone-Like Error Ratios and Probabilistic Standards of Proof*, 21 L. & Soc. Inquiry 95 (1996).

2. Richard L. Lippke, *Justifying the Proof Structure of Criminal Trials*, 17 Int'l J. Evidence & Proof 323 (2013); The Trial on Trial, Volume Three: Towards a Normative Theory of the Criminal Trial 284 (Antony Duff, Lindsay Farmer, Sandra Marshall & Victor Tadros eds., 2007).

3. For overviews of plea bargaining in other countries, see Yue Ma, *Prosecutorial Discretion and Plea Bargaining in the United States, France, Germany, and Italy*, 12 Int'l Crim. Just. Rev. 22 (2002); Máximo Langer, *From Legal Transplants to Legal Translations: The Globalization of Plea Bargaining and the Americanization Thesis in Criminal Procedure,* 45 Harv. Int'l L. J. 1 (2004).

4. Santobello v. New York, 404 U. S. 257, 260 (1971).

5. The street bazaar metaphor comes from Robert E. Scott & William J. Stuntz, *Plea Bargaining as Contract*, 101 Yale L. J. 1909, 1912 (1992). Scott and Stuntz are critical of plea bargaining but do not urge its abolition. Harsher critics of plea bargaining include Albert Alschuler and Stephen Schulhofer. *E.g.*, Albert W. Alschuler, *The Prosecutor's Role in Plea Bargaining*, 36 U. Chi. L. Rev. 50 (1968); Albert W. Alschuler, *The Changing Plea Bargaining Debate*, 69 Cal. L. Rev. 652 (1981); Stephen J. Schulhofer, *Is Plea Bargaining Inevitable?* 97 Harv. L. Rev. 1037 (1984); Stephen J. Schulhofer, *Plea Bargaining as Disaster*, 101 Yale L. J. 1979 (1992). For my take on plea bargaining, see Richard L. Lippke, The Ethics of Plea Bargaining (2011).

6. Josh Bowers, *Punishing the Innocent*, 156 U. Pa. L. Rev. 1117, 1122 (2008), https://www.law.upenn.edu/journals/lawreview/articles/volume156/issue5/Bowers156U.Pa.L.Rev.1117(2008).pdf.

7. Milton Heumann, Plea Bargaining: The Experiences of Prosecutors, Judges, and Defense Attorneys 140 (1977).

8. Lippke, *supra* note 5, at 146–66.

9. Nancy J. King, *Judicial Oversight of Negotiated Sentences in a World of Bargained Punishment*, 58 Stan. L. Rev. 293 (2005), http://papers.ssrn.com/sol3/Delivery.cfm/SSRN_ID839746_code603.pdf?abstractid=839746&mirid=1.

10. *See* Jenia I. Turner, *Judicial Participation in Plea Negotiations: A Comparative View*, 54 Am. J. Comp. L. 199, 212–23 (2006).

11. *See, e.g.*, Stephen B. Bright & Sia M. Sanneh, *Fifty Years of Defiance and Resistance after* Gideon v. Wainright," 122 Yale L. J. 2150 (2013), http://www.yalelawjournal.org/essay/fifty-years-of-defiance-and-resistance-after-gideon-v-wainwright.

12. *See* Malcolm M. Feeley, The Process Is the Punishment: Handling Cases in a Lower Criminal Court (1979); Bowers, *supra* note 6, at 1132.

13. *See* Langer, *supra* note 3, at 50.

14. *See* Alexandra Natapoff, *Misdemeanors*, 85 S. Cal. L. Rev. 1313 (2012), http://lawreview.usc.edu/wp-content/uploads/slideshow/85SCalLRev_Natapoff.pdf.

15. For the best discussion of the many factors affecting plea bargained outcomes, see Stephanos Bibas, *Plea Bargaining Outside the Shadow of Trial*, 117 Harv. L. Rev. 2463 (2004), http://www-tc.pbs.org/wgbh/pages/frontline/shows/plea/etc/bargain.pdf.

16. Natapoff, *supra* note 14, at 1321. *See also* Jenny Roberts, *Why Misdemeanors Matter: Defining Effective Advocacy in the Lower Courts*, 45 U. C. Davis L. Rev. 277, 280 (2011), http://lawreview.law.ucdavis.edu/issues/45/2/Articles/45-2_Jenny_Roberts.pdf.

17. Natapoff, *supra* note 14, at 1368.

18. For a more complete defense, see Lippke, *supra* note 5.

19. Such questioning might be objected to on the grounds that it will preclude judicial impartiality in the event that accused persons ultimately decline to plead but instead elect trial adjudication of the charges against them. For further discussion of this issue, see *id.* at 27–28.

20. Trials might reveal features of the conduct of convicted defendants that should be taken into account at sentencing. Hence, judges at settlement hearings should announce "presumptive" sentences, ones that could be modified subsequent to trial conviction. I would make such modification subject to appeal by the convicted. Notice, however, that trials could reveal the accused's conduct to have been less culpable than it was initially believed, in which case post-trial sentences should be reduced.

21. For more on the trade-off between higher conviction rates and more accurate adjudications, see Lippke, *supra* note 5, at 63–96, 119–45, 191–215.

22. For discussion of the more restrained form charge bargaining takes in Germany, see Ma, *supra* note 3, at 38.

23. As is common practice in countries such as Germany and France. *Id.*

24. The National Registry of Exonerations claims that of the 1600 persons officially exonerated after having been convicted of crimes, 209 had pled guilty. *The First 1,600 Exonerations*, National Registry of Exonerations, http://www.law.umich.edu/special/exoneration/Documents/1600_Exonerations.pdf.

25. Natapoff, *supra* note 14, at 1341–43.

26. Still, there is no use denying that accused persons who have better attorneys will fare better, even under a reformed plea system. Such attorneys will work harder or more intelligently to better position their clients ahead of settlement hearings.

27. *Santobello*, 404 U.S. 260. *See also* Bibas, *supra* note 15, at 2527; Douglas D. Guidorizzi, *Comment, Should We Really "Ban" Plea Bargaining? The Core Concerns of Plea Bargaining Critics,* 47 Emory L. J. 753, 776 (1998).

28. For the contrary view, see Albert W. Alschuler, *Implementing the Criminal Defendant's Right to Trial: Alternatives to the Plea Bargaining System*, 50 U. Chi. L. Rev. 931 (1983), http://chicagounbound.uchicago.edu/cgi/viewcontent.cgi?article=1987&context=journal_articles; Schulhofer, *Is Plea Bargaining Inevitable?*, *supra* note 5.

29. Lauren E. Glaze, & Danielle Kaeble, *Correctional Populations in the United States, 2013*, Bureau of Justice Statistics (Dec. 19, 2014), http://www.bjs.gov/index.cfm?ty=pbdetail&iid=5177.

30. Albert W. Alschuler, *Plea Bargaining and Its History*, 79 COLUM. L. REV. 1, 26 (1979), http://chicagounbound.uchicago.edu/cgi/viewcontent.cgi?article=2005&context=journal_articles.

31. Alschuler, *The Prosecutor's Role in Plea Bargaining*, *supra* note 5, at 50.

32. The literature is vast. *E.g.*, Marc Mauer, *The Causes and Consequences of Prison Growth in the United States*, 3 PUNISHMENT & SOC'Y 9 (2001); Todd R. Clear & James Austin, *Reducing Mass Incarceration: Implications of the Iron Law of Prison Populations*, 3 HARV. L. & POL'Y REV. 307 (2009), http://www.naacpldf.org/files/case_issue/Reducing Mass Incarceration. Implications of the Iron Law of Prisons (00033885).PDF; Mona Lynch, *Mass Incarceration, Legal Change, and Locale: Understanding and Remediating American Penal Overindulgence*, 10 CRIMINOLOGY & PUB. POL'Y 673 (2011), http://onlinelibrary.wiley.com/doi/10.1111/j.1745-9133.2011.00733.x/epdf; Milton Heumann, *A Note on Plea Bargaining and Case Pressure*, 9 L. & SOC'Y. REV. 515 (1975).

33. That something like this is the norm in misdemeanor case processing, see Natapoff, *supra* note 14, at 1328.

34. I borrow the "crashing the system" expression from Jenny Roberts, *Crashing the Misdemeanor System*, 70 WASH. & LEE L. REV. 1089 (2013), http://papers.ssrn.com/sol3/Delivery.cfm/SSRN_ID2516475_code817486.pdf?abstractid=2512918&mirid=1. Roberts's focus is on providing those charged with misdemeanors better defense attorneys, rather than the elimination of plea bargaining.

35. Without improved indigent defense, trials would not be much better at effectively screening cases.

36. Scott & Stuntz, *supra* note 5, at 1950.

37. Marc Miller & Martin Guggenheim, *Pretrial Detention and Punishment*, 75 MINN. L. REV. 335 (1990–91).

38. Bowers, *supra* note 6, at 1125.

39. DOUGLAS HUSAK, OVERCRIMINALIZATION: THE LIMITS OF THE CRIMINAL LAW (2009).

Chapter Ten

Presumptions of Innocence

R. A. Duff

I. INTRODUCTION

An explanation of the presumption of innocence (PoI) must tell us what is to be presumed, of whom, by whom, to what effect, and what can defeat that presumption. In the criminal trial, where the PoI has its most familiar home, initial answers to these questions are quite easy. The court that is to reach a verdict must presume that the defendant is innocent of the crime charged, with the effect that he must be acquitted, unless the prosecution proves his guilt.[1]

Even in that context questions arise about the foundations and implications of the PoI: sections 2 and 3 discuss these. Further questions then arise if we ask whether the PoI has a role outside the trial. Some argue that it does not: it should be understood simply as a rule of trial procedure that lays the burden of proof on the prosecution.[2] Others argue that it should apply throughout the criminal process, at least from the time when a person is formally charged with a crime, in line with Article 6(2) of the European Convention on Human Rights (ECHR): "Everyone charged with a criminal offense shall be presumed innocent until proved guilty according to law";[3] section IV will discuss this extension of the PoI. Others argue that we should recognize a wider role for the (or a) PoI in the state's dealings with its citizens: that it is undermined, for instance, when DNA samples are retained from people who have not been convicted,[4] or that it has implications for criminalization,[5] or for the treatment of those who have completed their punishments.[6] We cannot discuss these further suggested extensions here, but I should say something about the debates between broad and narrow readings of the PoI.

There are considerations that favor each of these readings, narrow or wide, of the PoI. Advocates of a narrow reading can argue that this gives the PoI a tolerably clear, determinate meaning, expressing what can be plausibly portrayed as a categorical right: more expansive readings risk turning it into empty rhetoric that can do no substantial work in constraining the exercise of state power. Advocates of a wider reading can argue that if we are to understand the significance of the PoI within the criminal trial, we must see it as an expression of deeper values that should structure the state's dealings with its citizens; and that since the question of whether we are criminally guilty or innocent bears on the treatment we can expect both from the state and from our fellow citizens in contexts well beyond the criminal trial, the PoI must be relevant in these other contexts too. The PoI as it functions in the particular context of a criminal trial protects a particular group of people, those who appear in court as defendants, against a particular kind of state coercion or imposition—against conviction and punishment for a criminal offense. But we face other kinds of coercion, other kinds of imposition, as the state exercises its powers in the investigation and prevention of crime: surely we can expect to be protected against these other kinds of coercive imposition as well—protected, we might expect, by something like the PoI.

Perhaps, however, this controversy is to some extent misconceived, at least if our concern is with normative theorizing about the PoI. The controversy would matter if we had to assume that there is such a thing as "*the* PoI": a single principle whose scope we must determine. That assumption makes sense if we are interpreting a specific statute: if, for instance, our concern is with the legal interpretation of Article 6(2) of the ECHR, we must talk about "the PoI," as the principle enshrined in that article, and determine its proper scope. But if we are not thus bound to a specific statutory provision, we can take a more relaxed approach, and talk of not one but many PoI: of different presumptions made by and about different people in different normative contexts, with different effects, defeasible in different ways. Such presumptions will be connected to each other in a larger web of values, but we will not need to argue that they can be unified into a single PoI. We can recognize a distinctive PoI that applies in the criminal trial: but we will not suppose that this is the only context in which we can talk of a demand that people be presumed innocent.

This is the approach that I will pursue in what follows: although the discussion will have to be limited to presumptions that operate within the criminal process (broadly understood), it should help to show that we can fruitfully view the PoI that operates within the criminal trial as just one of a range of presumptions of innocence that should constrain the state's dealings with its citizens, and citizens' dealings with each other. We must begin, however, by looking more closely at the PoI that operates within the criminal trial.

II. THE PRESUMPTION OF INNOCENCE IN THE CRIMINAL TRIAL[7]

The first point to note is that in its classical formulation, the PoI concerns the burden, but not the standard, of proof. The prosecution must bear the burden of proving the defendant's guilt, rather than the defendant having to prove her innocence, but to what standard must guilt be proved if the PoI is to be defeated and conviction warranted? Would it be consistent with the PoI to convict a defendant if the prosecution proved her guilt "on the balance of probabilities" (the standard of proof in civil cases)? The rhetoric of the PoI suggests that a more stringent standard is required: guilt must be proved "beyond reasonable doubt." To see whether such a demanding standard is implicit in the PoI, however, we must inquire into the PoI's grounds: *Why* should courts be required to presume the innocence of those who appear before them?

One answer to this question is found in Blackstone's dictum: "It is better that ten guilty persons escape than that one innocent suffer."[8] It is much more serious to convict and punish an innocent person than to fail to convict a guilty person, given not just the burdens, material and psychological, that conviction brings, but the injustice perpetrated (albeit unintentionally) by condemning as a criminal wrongdoer one who is actually innocent of the crime: so we should tilt the balance at the trial firmly in the defendant's favor, and allow conviction only if the prosecution has put guilt beyond reasonable doubt; "*in dubio pro reo*."[9] This is indeed a plausible grounding for a "beyond reasonable doubt" rule, which reflects a general principle that the greater the burden that state action imposes on those subjected to it, the more certain those who implement it should be that it is warranted. But it does not completely explain the persuasive power of the PoI—the demand that the court must begin from the position that the defendant is innocent.

What would it be for a criminal court to begin with either the opposite presumption—that the defendant is guilty unless she can prove her innocence—or an open mind on whether she is guilty or innocent?[10] How would such a court view the citizens who appeared before it as defendants?[11] It would view them as suspicious characters who might well be criminals, who must clear their names if they are to avoid conviction or the remaining suspicion of guilt. Since, in a democracy, the courts act in the name of all citizens, that is then how we would collectively, as a polity, be viewing defendants; and since any of us could be a defendant, that is then how we would be formally viewing each other and ourselves. But that is not a viable basis for civic life. If we are to live together in civic peace, rather than a state of nature, we must be able to display a modest civic trust toward each other.[12] We must be able to behave toward each other not, certainly, as if we are angels who can do no wrong, but as responsible agents who are able and willing to guide their conduct by good reasons, including the reasons that the criminal law offers for refraining from crime.

It might seem, however, that even if this is how we should treat each other in our civic lives (and there is much more to be said about what such civic trust requires), it cannot justify making the PoI a binding principle for the criminal trial. A citizen who appears in a criminal court as a defendant is not an ordinary citizen who can claim to be "beyond reproach": he is someone against whom there is some evidence of guilt—or else the prosecuting authority would have had no good reason to bring him to court. Thus once he becomes a defendant, we and the court already have some reason to doubt his innocence, and to question whether the civic trust to which he was entitled was misplaced. What this shows, however, as we will see, is not that the PoI cannot be grounded in the idea of civic trust, but that its operations cannot be limited to the criminal trial.

If criminal trials are constrained by the PoI, this has obvious implications for prosecuting authorities. If the burden of proof will lie on the prosecution, it will be worth bringing a case only if there is a real prospect of being able to discharge that burden by proving guilt; and if the standard of proof is a strict one, such as "beyond reasonable doubt," this too will constrain prosecutors' decisions about which cases to bring to court.[13] The point here is not simply the pragmatic point that a prudent prosecutor will not waste resources on bringing cases to court if she cannot offer persuasive evidence of the defendant's guilt: it concerns the prosecutor's duty as an officer of the law. To bring a person to court as a defendant is to cast formal doubt on his innocence; he now stands accused of a criminal offense. This is both psychologically and materially burdensome; prosecutors should impose those burdens only when they have very good reason to do so. Quite apart from such burdens, however, it is a serious matter to bring such a formal public accusation of criminal wrongdoing against a citizen; it is to cast formal doubt on his standing as a law-respecting member of the polity. We must, therefore, ensure that such accusations are only made if there is very good reason to do so—only when there is strong evidence of their truth; that is an implication of the requirement of civic trust as a feature of the state's relationship to its citizens and of citizens' relationship to each other.

We can express this point about the prosecutor's duties by saying that a PoI also applies before the actual trial, to the activities of prosecuting authorities in deciding whether to bring a case. This is not the PoI that operates in the trial: it concerns what must be presumed not by the court, but by the prosecutor, and what must be presumed not of the defendant (for as yet there is none) but of a suspect; the effect is to ward off not conviction, but a formal charge of criminal wrongdoing; and what can defeat this PoI is not proof of guilt, but evidence of guilt sufficiently strong to justify putting the matter to a criminal court. This PoI, like the PoI that applies within the trial, is an offshoot of the civic trust that is vital to a functioning polity: as public officials acting in the name and on behalf of the whole polity, prosecutors must start from the presumption that those with whom they have to deal are law-abiding citizens.

When the defendant comes to court, the prosecutor should therefore have evidence that at least creates a strong suspicion of his guilt. But why then, it might again be asked, should the court be expected to begin with the presumption that he is innocent, when that presumption has clearly been undermined? The answer is that it is the court that will pass formal, public judgment on the defendant. On such a serious matter, it must not simply take it on trust from the prosecutor that the defendant is (probably) guilty; it must come to its own judgment, on the basis of its own evaluation of the evidence; it must start from scratch, dealing with a citizen whom it must see as being "beyond reproach." Only once the prosecution has actually led the evidence of guilt is the PoI put in doubt.

To understand the PoI as it operates in the criminal trial, we must therefore connect it to other parts of the criminal process (so far, to prosecutorial decisions about whether to bring a person to trial), and to deeper values that structure the law and the political community whose law it is—to the idea of civic trust, as an essential dimension of a functional polity.

This opens the way to asking whether the PoI, or principles connected to it, can play any wider role, either within the criminal process or more broadly. Before tackling that question, however, we should note two questions that we cannot pursue here about the implications of the PoI for the criminal trial, and a methodological point about my approach in this chapter.

The methodological point is that the account of the PoI sketched here is oversimplified, idealized, and parochial. It is oversimplified and idealized in part because issues of criminal guilt and innocence are often not dealt with by the courts. Many cases are dealt with, as cases of guilt, without going to court, for instance, by police cautions or by penalties imposed by prosecutors without a court hearing;[14] in most cases that come to court, the defendant pleads guilty (often as the result of a plea bargain), so that he appears in court not as a presumptively innocent person, but as one who is formally admitting guilt.[15] It is parochial because, in its illustrations, it draws on the Anglo-American style of criminal procedure, whereas in other jurisdictions (notably those with "inquisitorial" rather than "adversarial" styles of investigation and adjudication) the procedures differ significantly. Another issue that I cannot discuss here is how far theorizing about criminal law can transcend the parochial. All we need note here is that the PoI is recognized in international conventions as expressing a right that is taken to be universal;[16] that the grounding suggested for it here should apply in any polity that aspires to be a democracy of citizens; and that the precise institutional form that it takes must depend on the local character of each polity's practices.

The two questions to be noted concern, first, whether it can be consistent with the PoI to shift any kind of probative or evidential burden from the prosecution to the defense, and second, what "innocent" should mean in this context.

If the prosecution must prove the defendant's guilt, beyond reasonable doubt, it would be clearly inconsistent with the PoI to require the defendant to prove any matter on which her acquittal depended—to prove either the absence of an element of the offense or the presence of a defense;[17] this would remain true even if the standard of proof for the defendant was only proof on the balance of probabilities, rather than proof beyond reasonable doubt. Courts have held, however, that it can be consistent with the PoI to shift onto the defense the formal evidential burden of adducing evidence either of the absence of some element of the offense, or of the existence of a defense: evidence that need not prove the matter in question, but that suffices (if not rebutted by the prosecution) to raise a reasonable doubt about the defendant's guilt.[18] Such provisions might also seem to be inconsistent with the PoI, since they appear to relieve the prosecution of the burden of proving everything on which conviction depends—that is, of proving the defendant's guilt, but some might be justifiable if we can read them as specifying what is to count as "reasonable doubt."[19]

As to the meaning of "innocence" in this context, the simple view, endorsed by English courts, is that it means legally innocent of the offense charged, as that offense is defined by the law—"of whatever may be the elements of a criminal offense." One must not confuse innocence of a criminal offense with innocence of blameworthy conduct."[20] However, some have argued that we should interpret the PoI in richer terms, as a presumption of substantive rather than of merely formal innocence: on this view, the PoI is violated if, even though the prosecution proves beyond reasonable doubt that the defendant's conduct fitted the law's definition of a crime, it does not prove the defendant to be guilty of the substantive mischief at which the law must be taken to be aimed.[21] The point here is that legislatures sometimes deliberately define offenses too broadly: to ensure that the definition of the offense covers, and makes possible the effective prosecution of, the "really" guilty, the legislature enacts a definition that also covers conduct which does not merit conviction and punishment. A good example is provided by sections 9–13 of the Sexual Offenses Act 2003, one effect of which is to criminalize any consensual sexual activity between two young people aged fifteen, although the government made it clear that this was not the kind of mischief at which these sections of the act were aimed (they were rather concerned with coercive or exploitative sexual activity involving children):[22] on the substantive reading of the PoI, the conviction of two such young people would violate the PoI; on the formal reading it would not.[23]

Both these questions raise interesting issues about the scope and meaning of the PoI, but we cannot pursue them here; we must instead turn to consider some ways in which the scope of the PoI might be extended.

III. THE VERDICT AND ITS AFTERMATH

We have so far been discussing the narrowest version of the PoI, as it operates within the criminal trial, to constrain the way in which the court reaches its verdict: it must acquit unless the prosecution proves guilt (beyond reasonable doubt). We must now consider the role that the (or a PoI) might play beyond that narrow context, and can turn first to what happens once the verdict is reached and pronounced (which could still count as part of "the trial").

Suppose first that the defendant has been convicted. It might seem that since the PoI has been defeated, it can no longer play any role: the defendant can now be treated as guilty. But matters are not that simple, since we must consider the sentencing process. Sentencers may be required or permitted to attend to specified sets of "aggravating factors" in determining the appropriate sentence for a convicted defendant: Is it then consistent with the PoI for a judge to pass sentence on the basis that an aggravating factor obtains, if that factor was not proved by the prosecution beyond reasonable doubt? The U.S. Supreme Court has held that if the aggravating factor served to increase the sentence beyond the maximum that could be imposed in its absence, it must be proved to the jury, beyond reasonable doubt—that is, it must be treated as if it was an element of the offense.[24] We can see that this is indeed required by the PoI, once we are clear about what it requires a court to presume. During the pre-verdict trial, the defendant must be presumed innocent of the offense charged. The specification of aggravating factors that serve to increase the sentence can be seen as in effect defining a new, more serious offense: the defendant is sentenced not just, for instance, for "second-degree kidnapping involving domestic violence and use of a firearm," but also for committing that offense "with deliberate cruelty."[25] Now, if the PoI is taken seriously, the court must presume, before the verdict, that the defendant is innocent of kidnapping, domestic violence and use of a firearm, and it must also presume him innocent of the deliberate cruelty; proof of his guilt on the basic charge is not proof of guilt in relation to the aggravating factor. Therefore, if the PoI is to apply (as it should) to the crime for which the defendant is liable to be convicted *and to be sentenced*, it should apply to all the elements of that crime—to the "with deliberate cruelty" as well as to the other elements.

Suppose next that the prosecution fails to prove the defendant's guilt, so that the court must acquit him—which typically involves bringing a verdict of "not guilty." This verdict might seem strange. The trial might have established, at least on the balance of probabilities, that the defendant is innocent—in which case "not guilty" would be appropriate. But given the PoI, the defendant is entitled to an acquittal even if the court reasonably concludes that it is more likely than not that he is guilty, if there remains a reasonable doubt about his guilt. "Not guilty" might seem inappropriate in such cases: for it seems to assert the defendant's innocence, when the most that can be said is that the prosecution has failed to prove his guilt. A more accurate verdict might be "not proven guilty." This is what Scots law allows: it allows not just two verdicts, but three—"guilty," "not guilty," and "not proven."[26] Laudan has also argued that the "not guilty" verdict, in systems that allow only two verdicts (and set a high standard of proof for convictions), is "neither very informative nor very exculpatory," for it means only that guilt has not been proved to the requisite standard, and leaves an acquitted defendant with most of "the stigma already arising from being arrested, charged with, and tried for, a crime."[27] He suggests instead a four-verdict system: courts would find a defendant "guilty," or "probably guilty," or "probably innocent," or "innocent."

Now someone who has been acquitted is in fact likely to suffer social stigma, in the eyes of those who "know" that the acquitted are very often actually guilty; the law itself sometimes allows a charge on which a person was acquitted to count against her subsequently.[28] Such social reactions and such legal provisions, however, are manifestly inconsistent with the PoI. If a person is presumed innocent, that presumption remains effective until it is defeated; an acquittal marks a formal judgment that it has not been defeated; so an acquitted defendant must be presumed, as she was presumed during her trial, to be innocent of the charge. If we take the PoI seriously, an acquittal is as "informative" as it needs to be: it tells us that the PoI has not been defeated. It is not "exculpatory," but, given the PoI, no exculpation is needed: what matters is the absence of inculpation, of proof of guilt, since that leaves the PoI intact.

Were it the court's job simply to arrive at a detached judgment about a defendant's guilt or innocence, Laudan's suggestion might be plausible. It is often hard to come to a confident judgment either that *p* or that *not-p*—either that *D* is guilty or that he is not guilty; often the most accurate way to express a judgment is "probably *p*," or "perhaps *p*." But the court's job is not to produce a detached record of the facts; it is to determine whether this citizen is to be condemned as a wrongdoer or to retain her standing as a citizen who is presumed innocent.

We could, perhaps, adopt a more nuanced approach. We could say that if the prosecution offers plausible, albeit not conclusive, evidence of the defendant's guilt, and the defendant is unable (or unwilling) to rebut this evidence, then the PoI with which the trial began is indeed undermined or qualified: the defendant who fails to clear her name is not now "innocent," but "suspected," or "suspected but not proven guilty"; her innocence remains formally in doubt. It might be argued that this would recognize social reality: for many acquitted defendants are in fact (or so we confidently believe) actually guilty; allowing a "not proven" verdict enables us to mark this important fact. However (and leaving aside the question of what difference such a formal provision for lasting suspicion would make to the defendant's future dealings with the state and its agents), we should reject this suggestion, as inconsistent with how we should aspire to treat each other as fellow citizens. Basic to citizenship in a well-functioning republic is, as noted earlier, a modest civic trust, which is reflected in the PoI: the status of continuing suspect would be inconsistent with such trust. Suspects and defendants do admittedly suffer some qualification of that trust: but their roles are strictly time-limited; they end with a trial and verdict, or with an official decision not to proceed with the case. To permit such an open-ended, indefinitely extended status of "continuing suspect" would be to abandon the principle of civic trust on which a civilized polity depends—the principle that citizens are entitled to be trusted unless and until they show, by their own conduct, that such trust is unwarranted.

Courts have not always taken this implication of the PoI seriously. In *Davis, Rowe and Johnson*, the Court of Appeal overturned the appellants' convictions for murder and other offenses, because of "material irregularities" in the trial that rendered the convictions unsafe. However, the court said firmly that "the case against all three appellants was formidable," and that "this is not a finding of innocence, far from it."[29] Now an acquittal (or an overturning of a conviction) is indeed not "a finding of innocence," as noted above: given the PoI, no such "finding" is required; the court need find only that the PoI has not been defeated. But it is hard to read the court's comment as anything other than a version of "not proven": the defendants were probably guilty, but must be acquitted because of those "material irregularities." It might be hard to resist the temptation to make such remarks when defendants must be acquitted on such grounds: but if we are serious about the PoI, and about procedural justice, we must insist that defendants are to be presumed innocent by the court unless and until their guilt is proved, beyond reasonable doubt and by due process. So when the court acquits defendants on the grounds that their guilt has not been thus proved, it must affirm that that presumption remains undefeated; the defendants are to be treated still as innocent. That is why the European Court of Human Rights held, rightly, that the PoI is violated when a court refuses to award costs to an acquitted defendant on the grounds there was "compelling evidence" of his guilt: for it is violated when any "statement of a public official concerning a person charged with a criminal offense reflects an opinion that he is guilty unless he has been proved so according to law," so long as there is "a sufficient nexus" between that statement and the "criminal proceedings" to which the PoI applies—a nexus which clearly obtains here.[30]

These points apply directly to the court that acquits a defendant: it must not make formal comments that imply doubt about his innocence. But they must also apply to other courts, and to other legal officials: for courts act not as isolated agents, but as parts of a whole system of law in whose name they speak; their decisions must be taken as decisions of, and be binding on, the system as a whole. Thus, when the police say (as they have been known to say) after a defendant's acquittal that they are "not looking for anyone else" in connection with the crime, or if a government minister says in a public forum that the acquitted defendant was probably guilty,[31] they violate the PoI. This is another indication of the way in which the PoI cannot be narrowly confined to the criminal trial itself: it bears at least on the conduct of the officials of the system in which the defendant is acquitted.

One further complication should be noted here. In many legal systems, one who claims to have been the victim of a criminal act can bring a civil case for damages against the person who allegedly wronged them; and while the burden of proof lies on the plaintiff, to prove the defendant liable, the standard of proof is lower than it is for the prosecution in criminal cases: typically, the plaintiff need only prove liability "on the balance of probabilities," rather than "beyond reasonable doubt." Now sometimes a verdict for the plaintiff in such a civil case implies that the defendant was guilty of the relevant crime:[32] so would it be at odds with the PoI for the court to find for the plaintiff, if the defendant has been acquitted on the criminal charge?[33] Such cases highlight a tension between criminal law, understood as focused on whether defendants can properly be convicted and punished for the commission of a public wrong; and tort law, understood as seeking to do justice between the competing claims of plaintiff and defendant: the only way to avoid (or evade) such tension would be to make it legally impossible to bring a tort case in which a finding for the plaintiff would imply the defendant's guilt on a criminal charge—which would have quite significant implications for the law of torts.[34]

I have talked so far about the implications of an acquittal for courts and for other officials of the legal system, but acquittals also have implications for all citizens. The law, after all, is supposed to be our law (if we aspire to live in a genuine democracy); its courts should act and speak in our name. When a court convicts the defendant, it does so in our name: it is we who convict and condemn him. Likewise, when a court acquits a defendant, finding that the PoI is undefeated, it is we who acquit him—we who say to him that he is still presumed innocent, "without reproach."[35] But this then requires us to treat him, outside the walls of the court, in a way consistent with that declaration—to treat him as innocent of the crime charged. It is important to be clear, however, regarding just what this does, and does not, require of us.

The PoI, as understood here, binds us as citizens, in our civic dealings with each other. In a polity such as our own, which values individual privacy and aims to leave its members as large as possible a "private" realm, in which they can make their own lives and pursue their own goods, our civic dealings are relatively limited and shallow: in engaging with our fellow citizens, simply as fellow citizens, we do not engage as friends or intimates who aim to share deeply in each other's lives; we engage as relative strangers, in the limited public realm that constitutes our civic life. Thus to be required to "presume" a fellow citizen to be innocent is not to be required to have or to reject any particular beliefs about her: I might still believe, or strongly suspect (in my heart) that she is guilty. It is not to be required to make her my friend (or to maintain the friendship that we had), or to be willing to engage with her in any of the many activities that citizens may privately pursue: for my fellow citizens need not be friends or intimates. All it requires is that I behave toward her, in our public interactions, as a fellow citizen in good standing; that I do not treat her as if she was guilty.[36]

IV. PRESUMING INNOCENCE IN THE PRETRIAL PROCESS

The previous section discussed some implications of the PoI that reach beyond the narrow confines of the criminal trial: implications both for those who have been convicted, who must at the sentencing stage be presumed to be innocent of anything of which they have not been proved to be guilty; and for those whose guilt has not been duly and properly proved, who must therefore be acquitted and be treated—by the court, by other officials, by fellow citizens—as innocent of the charges they faced. There are further questions, which we cannot pursue here, about what happens to those who have been convicted after they have completed their prescribed punishments. Can we say that they too should be again protected by a PoI—not by the PoI that operated at their trial, since they have been proved guilty of the offense for which they were convicted, but by a presumption that they can now be trusted again, in the way that citizens must generally be trusted, to refrain from crime? Or are they now legitimately subject to continuing suspicion, as "ex-offenders" who might well offend again?[37] However, I'll turn now to the role that a PoI might play at earlier, pretrial stages of the criminal process.

I suggested earlier that a version of the PoI is relevant to prosecutors deciding whether and with what to charge a suspect.[38] In a fuller discussion of the PoI as it might apply beyond the trial, we would also need to look at the activities of the police as they investigate crimes: Should we say that a PoI constrains how they may treat citizens—for instance, that it explains why certain kinds of intrusive police conduct, which treat those subjected to them as suspects, are legitimate only if the police have reasonable grounds to believe that the person is or might well be guilty of the offense under investigation?[39] But I'll focus here on the criminal process as it unfolds after a defendant has been charged and is awaiting trial.

There is typically some delay between becoming a defendant—being formally charged with an offense—and standing trial. Now courts could simply fix the trial date, and instruct the defendant to appear for trial on that date—on pain of being subject to arrest and sanctions if he fails to appear, or tries to subvert the trial process. But that is not what we do. Instead, the defendant must apply for bail if he wants to remain free pending his trial. He may then be freed "on his own recognizance," simply by promising to appear for trial, or he may have to post bail (provide guarantees for a sum of money that will be forfeit if he does not appear for trial); further conditions may be attached to bail, concerning where he may live or travel while awaiting trial or whom he may meet, or bail may be refused, in which case he is remanded in custody until his trial.[40] The grounds for denying bail are preventive: the court's concern is with the risk that the defendant will fail to appear for trial, or will commit offenses while on bail, or will obstruct the course of justice.[41]

The imposition of such restrictions on defendants awaiting trial, either by detaining them or by imposing restrictive conditions on the grant of bail, does not strictly contradict the PoI that operates in the criminal trial: it does not strictly presume the defendant to be guilty of the offense for which he is to be tried; even an innocent defendant might be tempted to flee or to interfere with the course of justice. But, first, it is in tension with that PoI, since the empirical likelihood that the defendant will flee, or interfere with the trial process, or commit offenses, is significantly affected by the likelihood that he is guilty of the offense charged: the court's judgment that restrictive bail conditions or a denial of bail are necessary must be affected by its judgment of how likely it is that the defendant is guilty.[42] Second, such restrictions seem inconsistent with the idea of civic trust, as a broader version or ground of the PoI: if we really trusted the defendant as a fellow citizen, we would have no reason to restrict or detain him.

However, matters are not that simple: the defendant is not simply a citizen who must be presumed, by the courts and his fellows, to be innocent of criminal wrongdoing. For he has acquired a new normative status, as someone against whom plausible evidence of criminal wrongdoing has been laid; that status, we can suggest, brings with it new burdens and duties, and qualifies the trust, the PoI, to which he is entitled. Those burdens include, as we noted in section 2, the burdens of being on trial, but they might also include burdens consequent upon being formally accused. We might argue, for instance, that, as a correlate of the civic trust that we should expect from our fellow citizens, we owe it to each other to reassure each other of our good behavior and our good intentions, in contexts in which there is good reason to doubt them.[43] One such context is the criminal trial: the evidence that the defendant committed an offense, which justifies bringing him to trial, can also give us good reason to suspect that he might abscond, or interfere with the trial process; the role of defendant brings with it not only the burdens involved in standing trial, but also the temptation to try to avoid those burdens by fleeing or interfering. We may therefore legitimately require him to reassure us that he will appear for trial, and will not interfere with the process; and since mere words are cheap, we may require that he back up his reassurance with something more material—by providing a financial bond, or accepting certain restrictions on his movements, to make his law-abiding intentions manifest. As a defendant, who has acquired a normative status that brings with it this justified suspicion of criminal wrongdoing, I show my respect for the law's authority and for my fellow citizens' legitimate anxieties by posting bail, or by accepting the (reasonable) conditions that the court attaches to my bail.

This line of argument shows that a system of bail, one that might attach conditions to the granting of bail, can be consistent with the PoI, once we understand the PoI in this context as a civic PoI that is qualified when a person is charged with a criminal offense. More precisely, it can justify a system of bail that treats all defendants, or all who are charged with the same kind of offense, equally. If decisions on the amount of bail, or the conditions to be imposed, are based on the court's judgment about how likely the individual defendant is to flee or to interfere (as they are now), they are liable to violate the civic PoI. The decision to set bail high, or to impose strict conditions, expresses suspicion directed at the particular defendant, as distinct from other defendants, but the justification of a bail system offered here attaches suspicion to the role of defendant, rather than to the particular individuals who fill that role. What the court should say to a defendant is "You must accept these requirements just because you are a defendant (facing a serious charge)." This makes clear that these burdens flow from the role that he must now play, and not from a particular suspicion of him as an individual. (We might add that if defendants are to be treated equally, the amount of bail required must be proportional to the individual defendant's means: a fair system of bail would be analogous to a system of "day fines" or "unit fines.")

This line of argument cannot, however, render a system of pretrial *detention* consistent with even a qualified version of the kind of civic trust that is, I have argued, expressed in the civic PoI. To detain a defendant is not just to require him to offer reassurances, to allay the suspicions that reasonably attach to his role: it is to treat him as someone who simply cannot be trusted—cannot be trusted even to fulfill the conditions that might be attached to bail—but that is to cease to treat him as a citizen who has not been proved guilty of the crime charged. If a defendant is granted bail, and even if conditions are attached to his bail, he is still trusted: he is subject to requirements and conditions to which non-accused citizens are not subject, but he is trusted to obey those requirements and conditions (in the sense in which we are all trusted to obey the law) and to present himself for trial. But if he is denied bail and detained pending his trial, he is denied even the qualified trust accorded to someone on bail; we treat him as someone who is entirely untrustworthy in relation to his pending trial. Thus, if we are to justify pretrial detention at all, we must justify it as an infringement of the PoI, which has significant implications concerning the conditions under which defendants can be detained, and the compensation that might be due to them for such an infringement of their rights.[44] I do not deny that we might be able to justify a trial system which allows such PoI-infringing detention, *in exceptional cases*, as a matter of crime-preventive necessity. Suppose a court has very strong evidence that the defendant is guilty of the crime charged, *and* that if granted bail (even with restrictive conditions) he is very likely to abscond, or to try to interfere with the course of justice, or to commit other crimes of the same kind as the one he is charged with committing: surely the law should allow (indeed require) the court to detain him pending his trial.[45] *Perhaps* it should—though further discussion is needed of how strong such evidence would need to be, and of the kinds of risk that we should expect ourselves and each other to accept as a consequence of maintaining the PoI.[46] But we must remember that if we allow this we are infringing the PoI, the defendant's right to be presumed innocent until proved guilty "according to law"; we therefore owe the defendant compensation, and also owe it to him to make sure that the conditions of his detention are as unrestrictive, and as distinct from penal imprisonment, as possible.[47]

CONCLUSION

This chapter has raised, but left unanswered, a number of questions about the scope, meaning and implications of the PoI: both about the meaning of the PoI, as traditionally understood, in the criminal trial, and about whether we can usefully talk, if not of the PoI, of presumptions of innocence in wider contexts than that. I have argued that, once we recognize the need to ground the in-trial PoI in deeper civic values, and ultimately in the idea of civic trust, we can see room for other presumptions of innocence to operate in other contexts related to criminal law. In a range of other contexts, in our dealings both with the state and its officials and with our fellow citizens, the question of whether we are guilty or innocent of a criminal offense is practically relevant; in such contexts, we can argue that those with whom we deal should, in the way they treat us, presume us to be innocent rather than guilty. Such presumptions have different implications and are defeasible in different ways (with different effects) in different contexts—which is why it is misleading to talk of "the PoI": but they can usefully be called "presumptions of innocence," grounded in a conception of democratic citizenship.

NOTES

1. Hence the oft-quoted dictum about the "golden thread" that runs "[t]hroughout the web" of criminal law, that the prosecution must prove the defendant's guilt. Woolmington v. DPP (1935) AC 462, at 481 (Viscount Sankey) (Eng.).

2. *See, e.g.*, Larry Laudan, *The Presumption of Innocence: Material or Probatory?* 11 Legal Theory 333, 336–37 (2005); Andrew Stumer, The Presumption of Innocence: Evidential and Human Rights Perspectives (2010); Bell v. Wolfish, 441 U.S. 520 (1979).

3. *See* Thomas Weigend, *There Is Only One Presumption of Innocence*, 42 Neth J. Legal Phil. 42, 193 (2013); Hock Lai Ho, *The Presumption of Innocence as a Human Right, in* Criminal Evidence and Human Rights 259 (Paul Roberts & Jill Hunter eds., 2012).

4. *See* Liz Campbell, *A Rights-Based Analysis of DNA Retention: Non-Conviction Databases and the Liberal State*, 12 Crim. L. Rev. 889 (2010).

5. *See* Patrick Tomlin, *Extending the Golden Thread? Criminalisation and the Presumption of Innocence*, 21 J. Pol. Phil. 44 (2013).

6. *See* Antony Duff, *Who Must Presume Whom to be Innocent of What?*, 42 Neth. J. Legal Phil. 170, 185–92 (2013).

7. *See generally* Paul Roberts & Adrian Zuckerman, Criminal Evidence, chap. 6 (2d ed., 2010); *see also* Stumer, *supra* note 2.

8. William Blackstone, 4 Commentaries on the Laws of England 352 (1765–69).

9. "When in doubt, for the accused." *See* Patrick Tomlin, *Could the Presumption of Innocence Protect the Guilty?* 8 Crim. L. & Phil. 431 (2014).

10. *See* Hamish Stewart, *The Right to be Presumed Innocent*, 8 Crim. L. & Phil. 407, 409 (2014) (on Kant's argument that the right to freedom that is fundamental to a liberal legal order includes "the quality of being . . . *without reproach*"); Immanuel Kant, The Metaphysics of Morals 238 (trans. Mary Gregor, 1996).

11. I talk throughout this chapter of "citizens," although many who appear in criminal courts as defendants are not citizens of the country in question: they are temporary visitors, or resident aliens, or refugees. For a justificatory explanation of this approach, see Antony Duff, *Relational Reasons and the Criminal Law*, 2 Oxford Stud. Phil. L. 175, 207–8 (2013).

12. *See* Dale Nance, *Civility and the Burden of Proof*, 17 Harv. J. L. & Pub. Pol'y 647 (1994); Jean Floud & Warren Young, Dangerousness and Criminal Justice 44 (1981) (citizen has "right to be presumed free of harmful intentions").

13. The first test that English prosecutors apply in deciding whether to take a case to court is whether "there is sufficient evidence to provide a realistic prospect of conviction." *Code for Crown Prosecutors*, para. 4.4 (2013), http://www.cps.gov.uk/publications/docs/ code_2013_accessible_english.pdf.

14. As in practices like that of "fiscal fines" in Scotland. *See* Peter Duff, *The Prosecutor Fine*, 14 Oxford J. Legal Stud. 565 (1994). On police cautions and other similar measures, see Andrew Ashworth & Mike Redmayne, The Criminal Process 166–9 (4th ed., 2010). Such disposals typically require an admission of guilt.

15. We cannot discuss the problematic issue of plea-bargaining here: see Richard Lippke, *Reforming Plea Bargaining, in* The New Philosophy of Criminal Law (Flanders & Hoskins eds., 2015); see Ashworth & Redmayne, The Criminal Process, *supra* note 14, at chap. 10.

16. *See, e.g.*, International Covenant on Civil and Political Rights, Art. 14(2).

17. *See Lambert* (2001) 3 WLR 206; P. Roberts, *The Presumption of Innocence Brought Home*, 118 Law Q. Rev. 41 (2002); Andrew Ashworth, *Four Threats to the Presumption of Innocence*, 10 Int'l J. Evidence & Proof 241, 252–56 (2006).

18. See *Lambert* (2001) 3 WLR 206, and *A-G's Reference No. 4 of 2002* (2004) UKHL 43; for a good example of such provisions, see Terrorism Act 2000, §§ 57, 118.

19. *See also* Antony Duff, *Presuming Innocence*, *in* PRINCIPLES & VALUES IN CRIMINAL LAW & CRIMINAL JUSTICE 52–38 (Lucia Zedner & Julian Roberts eds., 2012).

20. R. v. G. [2006] 1 WLR 2052, para. 36 (Lord Phillips CJ) (Eng.).

21. Victor Tadros & Stephen Tierney, *The Presumption of Innocence and the Human Rights Act*, 67 MOD. L. REV. 402 (2004); Victor Tadros, *Rethinking the Presumption of Innocence*, 1 CRIM. L. & PHIL. 193 (2007).

22. *See* Hansard HC vol 409, col. 248 (15 July 2003; Paul Goggins, a government minister).

23. *See* Ashworth, *supra* note 17, at 252–56; Duff, *supra* note 19, at 58–66.

24. *See* Blakely v. Washington, 124 S. Ct. 2531 (2004); United States v. Booker, 125 S. Ct. 738 (2005).

25. As was the case in *Blakely*.

26. *See* Peter Duff, *The Not Proven Verdict: Jury Mythology and "Moral Panics,"* 41 JURID. REV. 1 (1996).

27. Larry Laudan, *Need Verdicts Come in Pairs?*, 14 INT'L J. EVIDENCE & PROOF 1, 2 (2010).

28. *Id.* at 6. *See e.g.*, Criminal Procedure (Scotland) Act s. 210C(1) (alleged past criminal behavior can inform judgments of dangerousness even if the person was acquitted).

29. [2001] 1 Cr App R 115, at 145–46.

30. Hussain v. United Kingdom (2006) 43 EHRR 22 (Eng.), at paras. 7, 19. There are further issues, which we cannot discuss here, about the provisions that are sometimes made for criminal courts to order the confiscation of the proceeds of crimes from those who have been convicted of relevant offenses (*see, e.g.*, the English Drug Trafficking Act 1994 and Proceeds of Crime Act 2002): is it consistent with the PoI for a court to presume that a convicted defendant made confiscatable profits from crimes for which he was not actually convicted? *See, e.g.*, Briggs-Price (2009) 1 AC 1026 (Eng.); Victoria Ailes, *Proceeds of Crime and the European Convention on Human Rights*, 4 PROC. CRIME REV. 4 (2010).

31. On this and related issues, see Ho, *supra* note 3.

32. But not always: *see, e.g.*, Ashley v. Chief Constable of Sussex Police (2008) 1 AC 962 (Eng.).

33. As happened, notoriously, in the case of O. J. Simpson, who was controversially acquitted of murdering his wife, but then found civilly liable in a wrongful death suit brought by her family and ordered to pay an amount of damages that clearly implied that he was criminally guilty of murder.

34. The tension is highlighted in systems (such as those of Norway) in which the (alleged) victim of a crime can attach a civil case for damages to the criminal charge, and in which someone can thus be acquitted of a criminal charge, because his guilt is not proved beyond reasonable doubt, but be ordered by the same court, at the end of the same case, to pay civil damages: see Tom Hickman & Faisal Saifee, *Hammern v. Norway, O v. Norway, Ringvold v. Norway and Y v. Norway*, 5 EUR. HUM. RTS. L. REV. 539 (2003).

35. *See* Stewart, *supra* note 10.

36. Suppose I *know* that she is guilty, since I witnessed her crime? Depending on the crime, this will, of course, affect my personal dealings with her, but if she has been acquitted, it should not affect my civic dealings (such as they are).

37. *See* Duff, *supra* note 6, at 185–92; *see generally*, Zachary Hoskins, *Collateral Restrictions, in* THE NEW PHILOSOPHY OF CRIMINAL LAW (Flanders & Hoskins eds., 2015).

38. *See supra* note 13.

39. *See generally*, JOHN KLEINIG, ETHICS AND CRIMINAL JUSTICE, at chs. 3–2 (2008); ASHWORTH & REDMAYNE, *supra* note 14, at chs. 4–5.

40. *See* ASHWORTH & REDMAYNE, *supra* note 14, at chap. 8.

41. *See* Bail Act 1976, s. 4, and Schedule 1 (specifying the grounds on which bail may be denied).

42. *See* Bail Act 1976, s. 4, Schedule 1, Part I, para. 9.

43. *See* PETER RAMSAY, THE INSECURITY STATE: VULNERABLE AUTONOMY AND THE RIGHT TO SECURITY IN THE CRIMINAL LAW (2012).

44. The only conditions under which detention might be consistent with the PoI are, first, if the defendant tries to flee or to interfere with the trial process; and, second, if he has in the past fled or interfered with the trial: we could then argue that he has shown by his own conduct that

he cannot be trusted in these matters. *See also* Shima Baradaran, *Restoring the Presumption of Innocence*, 72 OHIO ST. L. J. 723 (2011); Lonneke Stevens, *Pre-Trial Detention: The Presumption of Innocence and Article 5 of the European Convention on Human Rights Cannot and Does Not Limit Its Increasing Use*, 17 EUR. J. CRIME, CRIM. L. & CRIM. JUSTICE 165 (2009).

45. Richard Lippke offered me the example of a defendant who has prior convictions for rape with a distinctive MO, who is now charged with a rape that (according to the evidence) involved the same MO, and perhaps also DNA evidence linking him to the crime: if there is strong evidence that he is indeed a serial rapist who is likely to rape again if released on bail, are we really to say that the court must nonetheless leave him at liberty pending his trial?

46. The issues here are similar to those raised by provisions for the preventive detention of offenders who are judged to be "dangerous." *See* Antony Duff, *Dangerousness and Citizenship*, *in* FUNDAMENTALS OF SENTENCING THEORY 141 (Andrew Ashworth & Martin Wasik eds., 1998).

47. For fuller development of the argument sketched here, see Antony Duff, *Pre-Trial Detention and the Presumption of Innocence*, *in* PREVENTION AND THE LIMITS OF THE CRIMINAL LAW 115 (Andrew Ashworth, Lucia Zedner, & Patrick Tomlin eds., 2012).

Part V

Sanctions

Chapter Eleven

Punishment as an Apology Ritual

Christopher Bennett

Normative theories of punishment are attempts to determine whether, or under what conditions, states or other agents would be doing the right thing in inflicting punishment. Modern Western criminal justice systems tend to recognize a range of purposes that are to be taken into consideration in sentencing, and which we might think of as providing the overall justifying and shaping aim for the criminal justice apparatus: deterrence, incapacitation, rehabilitation, retribution, and perhaps others. But it is not only the tidy-minded philosopher who might have a problem with this list. Two issues stand out. First, these different aims might conflict. Many situations might arise that will require one thing for deterrence, another for retribution. This problem might arise in all sorts of areas: deciding what to criminalize, what to prosecute, what standards of liability to employ, what sentence to impose, and so on. In this situation, it would be good to have guidance as to how these aims relate to one another and which should take priority when they conflict. Second, there is a question about the individual items on the list, and whether they should be there. Take deterrence: Is it acceptable to harm one person to deter others, or is that simply to use them as a means to an end? Take retribution: Is a desire for retribution an irrational emotional tendency that we should be containing or defusing rather than celebrating? It would be good to have a deeper grasp of why, or whether, these aims matter, and how they are most productively conceived.

In arguing for punishment as an Apology Ritual,[1] I try first and foremost to explain why retribution should be on the list. In the face of widespread skepticism about retribution, and the popularity of the view that retribution can at best provide limiting considerations rather than providing any positive reason for punishment, I argue that retribution, properly understood, is rooted in an attractive and plausible set of values. I provide some of the main details of this story next. But my view is that the fundamental attractiveness of retribution is that it is a response that treats agents as accountable for what they do (in a way that threatening them in order to deter them or locking them up to incapacitate them does not), and in doing so it includes them in the basic, central, and very everyday human activity of explaining and justifying our actions to one another. Yet the Apology Ritual is superior to other conceptions of retribution, as we will see, in that it does not rest on a brute assertion that it is good to inflict supposedly deserved suffering.

If this argument is successful, maybe we could proceed to build the case that retribution should be not just on the list, but taking priority as the overall aim of criminal justice. I do not need to commit myself to that more ambitious conclusion here, though some reasons in its favor will emerge next. Understanding what can be said in favor of retribution, and how it should best be understood, is essential if we are to give guidance about resolving conflicts among criminal justice aims, independently of whether, in the end, we think we can explain all that is important in criminal justice on the basis of a single overarching value such as retribution.

I explain the key features of my Apology Ritual account in section 1 of this chapter. I then consider how an account based on these key features can be refined in response to various initial questions that might be raised about it (section 2). In section 3 I locate the Apology Ritual in more detail in relation to some competing justifications of punishment. In section 4, I will seek to answer three of the major objections that have been made against it. I hope that by the end I will have convinced readers that we can see this form of retribution as a viable and attractive justification for punishment.

I. PUNISHMENT AS AN APOLOGY RITUAL

Bryson is not a bad man. He is the kind of person of whom it might be said that his heart is in the right place. However, he does have some flaws; and it will happen on occasion that these flaws lead him to act contrary to the basic forms of respect and care that (as he himself recognizes) are at the basis of a decent form of social life. He can be impetuous, quick to anger, weak in the face of temptation, childish, selfish . . . but in the aftermath he is self-critical enough—and, in the end, courageous enough—to know what he has to do. So if you are on the receiving end of (unjustified) bad treatment from Bryson one day, you can be fairly sure that the next he will come up to you, shamefaced but looking you in the eye, offering to take you for a drink or a coffee, or clutching some small gift as a token of his compunction, and apologize to you for his behavior. He will explain that he knows what he is like, that he is trying to change—he sincerely wants things to be different, and he is taking steps to make it that way—but that sometimes things get him that way. You might be moved to admit to having had a role in the altercation yourself—after all, it is rare that culpability in these matters is entirely one way—but he quickly moves on to the crucial point: he took it too far. Arguments and disputes, competition and conflict, the friction of social life: he can see that this is inevitably going to take place, but he feels bad because he went way beyond this, and he sees no justification for what he did. You part on better terms; your feelings about the original offense may still be raw, but you see that something a little strange and intimate has happened between you, that you have had someone expose themselves to you, emotionally speaking, and give you a glimpse into their soul. Bryson put himself into your hands for a moment and, although the offense will never go away, and you may indeed be wary of him in the future, the relationship between you is always now going to be strangely closer than before.

I begin with this example to introduce some ideas about the nature, familiarity and importance of apology—and its complexity. First of all, I am hoping that readers will recognize Bryson and find his example admirable—this is because we recognize that, while "sorry" is often indeed the hardest word, apology is the appropriate response to wrongdoing, and, if properly given (and sympathetically received), can have an important role in "putting things right" after wrongdoing. Putting things right clearly doesn't involve erasing the offense, or making it as though it had never been. But apology allows an offender to recognize himself as the agent of the wrong, recognize the authority of the behavioral standard violated, and yet nevertheless resume his place in a mode of social relations structured around those standards. Second, an apology can involve more than just words: although some verbal interaction is often important, other elements, such as doing something for, or giving something to, the victim (as restitution for what they lost, but also just in order to say sorry), and taking steps to make oneself the kind of person who doesn't do it again, are also essential to the apology being able to make things right—especially when the wrongdoing in question is an issue of some gravity. This last point is important—with apologies, the response has to fit the wrong, and there is some notion of proportionality such that one can see how serious someone thinks the wrong was from seeing what they feel it necessary to do in order to put it right. Third, apology works as an expression of some inner state of compunction or remorse in which the offender feels bad about what he has done, about himself as someone who would do such a thing, and about what he has made the victim go through—apology involves in part revealing that inner state to the recipients of the apology, and hence can involve a certain kind of intimacy that goes beyond the self-disclosure present in everyday polite relations.

The Apology Ritual account of punishment says that the key organizing principle of punishment should be making the offender engage in the sort of apologetic action that he would do willingly and spontaneously were he to be properly sorry for his wrongdoing.[2] Punishment, we might say—as long as we don't get distracted by the financial metaphor—should be about making the offender "pay his debts." We should understand "punishment," that is to say, to consist in whatever debts or obligations a person would have to fulfill as a result of his wrongdoing—obligations that can be identified by looking at what a properly sorry person would feel compelled to do to put things right.

Is the Apology Ritual a theory of *punishment*? Does requiring the offender to "pay his debts," or to do what he would do willingly if he were properly sorry, have to involve inflicting punishment or "hard treatment"? If all that an apology consisted in were saying sorry, the answer to this question might be no. But the crucial thing is that, when it comes to serious offenses, verbal apology is not the only, or even the most, important part of apologetic action. Equally, or even more, important are the actions one takes to back up what one is saying. How would one go about making up for the fact that one had stolen someone's car, or inflicting serious wounding with a knife? Not simply by saying sorry. One who is sincerely sorry would find mere utterance inadequate and would be moved to do more as a way of expressing their remorse.[3] Some of these remorseful actions might have to do straightforwardly with material repair. But some of them are done simply in order to express, or to give form to, one's feelings of remorse—and thereby to redeem oneself. We can call the latter type of action "penitential."[4] Thus in saying that the offender should be made to do what he would do anyway, I do not mean that he should be made to give a verbal apology: rather I mean he should be made to make the kinds of amends that he would deem necessary if properly sorry. To that extent the Apology Ritual is a theory of punishment (though this is not to say that it will endorse the conventional list of sentencing options).

Why should those invested with the authority to punish take as their guiding principle making the offender do what he would do if he were properly apologetic? For instance, one might think that this sounds like something punishing authorities would do if their aim were to reform offenders,[5] or if they thought that the victim had an enforceable right to an apology.[6] My view is not like either of those. Rather, I take the approach that the punishing authority's duty in the wake of wrongdoing is to express condemnation of the wrongdoing. The state, or the people—or whoever is properly invested with the authority to punish—does not (necessarily) have a duty to attempt to reform the offender, and does not (necessarily) have a duty to enforce the rights of individual victims to an apology—at any rate, not through the punishment system. As an authority, however, it should take some action to mark violations of those basic standards of behavior with which citizens can reasonably be expected to comply. The criminal law, on the view that interests me, consists in an authoritative, collective enactment of binding standards of acceptable behavior.[7] Without such action to mark violations as violations, the state would not be treating the avowed standards of criminal law as binding, and the action would hence be treated as permissible. It would be for the state to condone, or even to acquiesce in, or become complicit in, those violations.[8] Marking the wrongdoing as unacceptable is a necessary form of dissociation from those actions on the part of the authorities (or those in whose name the authorities act). On the Apology Ritual view, making the wrongdoer do what he should be doing if he were properly sorry therefore serves as a vehicle to express necessary condemnation of the action. It is an appropriate vehicle because of the familiarity and fittingness of the practice of apology, because making someone apologize is a way of saying that they have something to apologize *for* (and hence that they have done something wrongful), and because the proportionality between wrong and amends or penitential action means that the punishments envisaged by the Apology Ritual view can place different acts of criminal wrongdoing on a scale as regards their gravity.

On the Apology Ritual view, then, the reason the state has for making the offender apologize is compatible with seeing punishment as a response to a "public wrong." What the offender has done is not necessarily a public wrong in the sense of being an offense *against the state*. It is an offense against the victim; and it is wrong because of what is done to the victim, not because of what is done to the state. But the wrong is not only the business of the victim but also something that the state (or those in whose name the state acts) takes to fall within its remit, given that it has the remit of making authoritative collective decisions about which actions are acceptable and which are unacceptable for citizens to perform.[9] This leads on to an important point. Although I have said that the reason the state has a duty to express disapproval is that by expressing condemnation it will avoid condoning or acquiescing in the offense, this does not mean that every individual citizen also has a duty to express condemnation of every offender. The state has that duty only because it has a certain position (and claims a certain authority), which is that of having the right to decide upon and promulgate limits to the way citizens can act through the apparatus of the criminal law.

II. SOME INITIAL CONCERNS ABOUT THE APOLOGY RITUAL VIEW—AND RESPONSES

This talk of "symbols" or "vehicles" will be regarded by some as suspect. I have talked about punishment as condemnation; and perhaps it will be granted to me that condemnation must take place in *some* sort of language.[10] We can imagine someone asking why an act could not simply be marked as wrongful by an assertion to that effect—perhaps made to the offender in person in court. Why is it necessary that there should be a punishment? I think the answer to this is that punishment is necessary insofar as not punishing would undermine the seriousness of the condemnation. Central to the outlook of our practice of apology is the thought that it matters not just what you say but also what you do; sometimes recognizing the seriousness of what you have done requires that you indicate that you realize that the act was wrong, and that this realization should issue forth from your intellect and embody itself in your behavior in the form of a willingness to put things right. The same goes when we react to the wrongdoing of another: sometimes it requires not merely that we say or tell the agent that what she did was wrongful but also that we reflect that understanding of the situation in the way we treat her. Punishment carried out by a punishing authority is a distinctive case of condemnation, in that it is highly formal. After all, the behavior by which we indicate that we really mean our condemnation in ordinary nonlegal interpersonal life is not through making someone apologize.[11] But, as I have argued, this is the appropriate vehicle for serious and meaningful formal authoritative condemnation.

Isn't making someone publicly apologize—even if in some way a "fitting" symbol of disapproval—a degrading or humiliating thing to do?[12] The objection might be that this would be reminiscent of "forced confessions" of mediaeval times, or of Maoist compulsory repentance practices. The way to make this criticism stick, I think, is to concentrate on the way in which a morally effective apology requires that the person apologizing break down the normal distance of reserve, discretion and tact that polite relations maintain between people, and display their behind-the-scenes efforts to construct the moral self they present to the world. The state, or so the criticism goes, should not be in the business of requiring a person to engage in that kind of self-disclosure in the context of a coercive and public encounter such as trial and punishment. Nor should the state be putting its citizens in a position in which they might be penalized if they are not able publicly to perform the emotions they recognize to be appropriate. To sharpen the point, consider cases of controversial or mistaken condemnation (e.g., wrongful convictions): Should a person be required publicly to apologize for something she perhaps did not do, or perhaps has reasonable grounds for thinking is not wrong?

It is in response to concerns like these that my view is labeled the Apology *Ritual*.[13] I argue that, although punishment should be organized around the principle of apologetic action, the sentence has to be something that a person could just as well carry out despite rejecting its justice. Although insincerity normally defeats the moral effectiveness of an apology—a blatantly insincere apology can sometimes be worse than no apology at all—the ritual nature of the Apology Ritual is a virtue. By "ritual" I have in mind the criticisms sometimes made of ritual (particularly, it should be said, in the

Protestant tradition) that it is empty and formal external behavior. Even if one agrees that these features are vices in many cases of ritual, they are virtues in the Apology Ritual. The apologetic action needs to be ritualistic to the extent that it should avoid putting the offender in the humiliating position of being coerced to display emotional attitudes that he may not share. For this reason, when the Apology Ritual view says that the offender should be made to do what he would do if apologetic, this does not mean that he should be made to stand up and utter a public verbal apology. Apology Ritual punishment is designed in such a way that one can comply with the ritual perfectly and without humiliation as long as one's external behavior aligns with what is required—the inner state in which one does it is not of concern to the authorities in the sense that the offender has no legal duty to satisfy anyone of her sincerity, or to perform as if one were sincere. Lest I overstate the point, I should make it clear that the state need not refrain from encouraging or allowing sincere remorse from offenders; rather, the point is that there are good reasons to ensure that no offender feels compelled to display appropriate remorse.

If the Apology Ritual view were implemented, then, sentences would have to be activities that could be meaningfully experienced by the offender as a way of putting things right. In my mind, this largely rules out the use of imprisonment and fines, and it suggests the use of community service punishments in their place. I have also argued for the "Limited Devolution Model" of punishment whereby some questions regarding the exact nature of the sentence, or, for example, what the hours of community service will involve, might be devolved to a group consisting in various stakeholders, as in a restorative justice sentencing circle model.

Finally, if we ask who can justifiably be punished on the Apology Ritual view, then the answer is that we start with moral practices such as those involving apology and forgiveness and ask who can reasonably be included in those practices. Broadly speaking, the answer I have given is that an agent can be held responsible if she is capable of a kind of independent self-governance: that is, being able—in the main by herself and without external supervision—to identify basic moral standards and bring her behavior into line with them. Of course, much depends on what exactly "capable of" means in this context—this is why philosophers dispute about the precise sense of "could have done otherwise" that is relevant to moral responsibility. But that is not something we need to resolve here.

III. THE APOLOGY RITUAL AND THE PHILOSOPHY OF PUNISHMENT

Let us now expand on how the Apology Ritual view relates to other theories of punishment. Such theories might be categorized as falling into one of three rough groups. There are *forward-looking* theories that see punishment as justified only insofar as it brings some future benefit (a benefit outweighing the inherent unpleasantness of the punishment)—these are often thought of as instrumental or consequentialist theories. There are *backward-looking* theories that see punishment as called for by the nature and gravity of a wrongful action in the past, and regardless of whether it brings about any future benefit (other than the addressing of the past wrong)—often thought of as retributive theories. And there are *hybrid* views that seek in some way to combine the backward- and forward-looking options (although note that if hybrid views wish, in order to avoid a muddle of competing aims, to give priority to one or another element of which they are a hybrid, they can be seen as inclining one way or another).

A. Forward-Looking Views

The Apology Ritual view as I have put it forward so far can be seen as a fairly pure backward-looking view. Also, as I have said, it makes accountability central in a way that forward-looking views do not (since someone's being responsible seems irrelevant to whether a benefit can be produced by punishing them). However, the Apology Ritual view might also, without too much cutting and forcing, be combined into a hybrid theory, and hence could be seen as a theory of why there should be a backward-looking, retributive element to criminal justice, among others. Certainly, the theory is not entirely hostile to forward-looking considerations—one of the things I have stressed, for instance, is that basing a system of punishment on as familiar and resonant a practice as that of apology and forgiveness is a good way of making that system credible in the eyes of those who are affected by it. And it may be that other forward-looking considerations are compatible with it.

The Apology Ritual view has two main arguments against forward-looking views of punishment. First, as we have seen, it claims that a purely forward-looking view would ignore the identity of the offender as a responsible agent. Second, the Apology Ritual view is suspicious of hybrid theories of sentencing because the quantum of punishment in sentencing is the vehicle for the expression of condemnation, and so introducing elements into that quantum of punishment that are not derived from the seriousness of the act distorts the nature of the condemnation that is expressed in the sentence. However, it might be that both of these criticisms could be answered by distinguishing a retributive from a forward-looking element to the sentence:

in delivering the sentence, the sentencer could make it clear which elements were being imposed for which reason—how much as condemnation for the crime, how much for public safety, and so on. Perhaps, then, some forward-looking considerations could be grafted on to a system the basic shape of which conforms to the Apology Ritual's terms.

There might be a further argument against the use of forward-looking considerations, to the effect that treating offenders as independent and accountable means that public safety considerations should not enter into sentencing at all. This is an argument that has been put forward by R. A. Duff.[14] However, as I have put it forward so far, the Apology Ritual is neutral on this argument. It is not obvious that we should rule out the incorporation of the Apology Ritual into some sort of hybrid view.

B. Retributivism

The Apology Ritual is retributivist in the way that the practice of apology is retributivist; in other words, it is retributivist in seeing certain responses to wrongdoing as fitting, and not merely justified by their beneficial effects. However, it is not retributivist in the sense that it holds that it is intrinsically right that an offender should suffer as such as a result of the offense.[15] The Apology Ritual envisages various ways in which the process of punishment might be unpleasant for the offender—the shame of facing up to what has been done; the publicity of the process; the pains of remorse; the disruption caused by the punishment and its onerous nature[16]—but it sees these things as necessary constituents of a process whereby the moral effect of the wrongdoing as a transgression that cannot go unmarked can gradually be put right.

As I have recently argued,[17] retributivist theories could be seen as involving two elements. First, there is a claim that some sort of action is necessary to mark a wrongful act as intolerable and unacceptable—something to dissociate oneself from the wrong and avoid acquiescing in it. If a theory sees this element of dissociation as important independently of any future benefits that might be brought about—important, that is, simply in virtue of the offense and one's relation to the offender—it is a retributive theory. Second, a retributive theory will need to give an account of the kind of behavior that will successfully dissociate one from the offense. It is at this second step that the alleged centrality of suffering to retributivism usually enters; making the offender suffer is thought necessary to mark the act as wrong. However, it is this step that leaves many nonretributivists unimpressed, I believe rightly. What seems necessary is that one's dissociation from the offense be manifested in some sort of temporary and partial withdrawal from the offender (or, if one is the offender oneself, a kind of withdrawal from oneself, or treating oneself less well—that is the heart of the justification for penance, as I argue next). This will cause suffering—as a side effect. But the suffering is not good in itself. What is good is the adequate, proportionate recognition of the wrongdoing.

C. Hybrid Theories

In this section there are two main theories I would like to consider: first, H. L. A. Hart's two-level theory, which I will call the Fair Warning view; and second, the communicative theory associated with R. A. Duff.

On Hart's view,[18] the General Justifying Aim of punishment—that is, the reason we have to institute or maintain a system of punishment—is deterrence, but an unconstrained deterrent institution, Hart thinks, would impact excessively on people's liberty. The most effective deterrent institution would use strict liability, and this would mean that no one could predict or control whether they would be subject to the coercive power of the law. Given that, as he thinks, the job of a social institution like punishment is to balance effective protection by law with the maximal retention of individual freedom, constraints have to be introduced that limit the use of punishment to occasions on which liability is in some respect voluntarily incurred. Hence the promulgation of criminal law and the operation of a system of fault liability give citizens fair warning so that they can plan their activities so as to stay out of the way of the law's coercive grasp.

One question we might have about Hart's account is whether the effect of strict liability would really be as bad as Hart maintains, and hence whether he really does justify the hybrid institution over the deterrent one. The contrary justification for fault liability in criminal law—the one that Hart is at pains to reject—is the retributive view that says that fault liability aims to discriminate among the morally guilty and innocent because only the morally guilty should be subjected to the condemnatory power of punishment. This retributive view can explain why strict liability is so bad, because it opens the door to the moral smearing of the innocent. Hart's alternative explanation says rather that the need for fault liability stems from the disproportionate infringement of liberty. However, if one takes away the stigma of condemnatory punishment, as Hart does, and sees it merely as state coercion judged necessary for legitimate state goals, and if one also limits the state to using such coercion only when strictly necessary, the use of punishment might not be enough to trouble the friends of liberty too greatly. This is partly an empirical question—but it is worth noting that supporters of Hart tend often to accept his claims about this without too much scrutiny.

Our main question about Hart's theory, however, concerns what it misses. Hart rejects the retributive view, presumably on the grounds that it is either incoherent, morally objectionable, or simply insufficiently important to qualify as at least a contributor to the General Justifying Aim. If, on the contrary, one were to be convinced by something like the Apology Ritual view that expressing proportionate condemnation by making the offender do what they would do willingly if properly sorry is neither immoral, unimportant, or incoherent as an aim, and if one were also convinced that our moral independence, including our accountability to moral standards, is something that should be actively affirmed by our political institutions, then it might at least look as though Hart's view is seriously incomplete.

Duff's view is that punishment is a kind of secular penance that should be imposed on an offender in order to communicate condemnation of his wrongdoing, thus to elicit repentance and in the hope that the offender will come to actively will the imposed punishment as his own penance. Duff's view counts as a hybrid for my purposes because it has been his avowed aim to point out that, although he takes punishment to be retributive in the sense that it involves deserved condemnation, it is forward looking in that it aims to bring about the moral reform of the offender.

The Apology Ritual view shares important features of Duff's view, such as the commitment to condemnation as an important aim of punishment; the moral importance of penance, both as an aspect of interpersonal morality and as a justifiable part of punishment; and the importance of treating agents as capable of independent self-governance. Duff's theory, however, is subject to criticisms that the Apology Ritual view seeks to avoid. For instance, Duff's view seems to claim that the General Justifying Aim of punishment is the communication of condemnation to the offender and the hopeful search for their repentance and reform. This sounds to many like a disproportionate concentration on the moral reform of the individual offender by dubious means (for instance, is expressing condemnation really always the best way to elicit repentance?). Second, some have doubted that the state should really be in the business of the coercive moral reform of the offender—or even putting offenders into a position where they will feel compelled to express certain attitudes, whether they share them or not; what Andrew von Hirsch has termed "compulsory attitudinising."[19] Third, it looks as though the communicative view is in trouble when it is dealing with offenders who are already repentant and for whom punishment, by Duff's lights, has no point. Although it seems as though the answer to this should be that even the repentant (as they will recognize) need to do their penance, this suggests that the imposition of penance must be justified independently of its role in eliciting repentance—but Duff does not tell us what that independent justification is.[20] Indeed, he would have to go beyond the confines of a communicative theory of punishment to do so, since he would have to explain why the offender should be made to do penance even when doing so has no important communicative role.

By contrast, the Apology Ritual view gives an explanation of why, given that the state has a legitimate role in setting binding limits on acceptable behavior for citizens, it must then engage in meaningful dissociation from the offender's action in order not to treat it as acceptable: it is for this reason, as we have seen, that offenders should be made to do their penance. The Apology Ritual view avoids the other criticisms of Duff because it limits the state's aims in criminal justice to meaningful dissociation—aims that are part and parcel of the legitimate role of the state in setting binding limits to how we treat one another. It is not committed to the claim that the state should engage in coercive reform; rather, as I have said, punishment can be virtuously ritualistic.

IV. THREE FURTHER OBJECTIONS AND REPLIES

In this section, I consider and briefly respond to some further major lines of criticism that have been made of the Apology Ritual account.

A. Ritual and Reform

First, I would like to consider the concern that the "ritualistic" nature of the punishment envisaged by the theory effectively gives up an important benefit of introducing apology into criminal justice. Nick Smith has put the point this way:

> Bennett intentionally excludes just what seems most absent from and needed in current criminal processes: the genuine moral transformation of offenders towards compliance with just laws. We should hope that offenders will experience negative emotions—that they will feel guilty, remorseful and so forth—because this speaks to their moral transformation and their recognition of laws as just. An apology without experiencing the requisite negative emotions lacks central meanings.[21]

The criticism here is twofold: first, that my account is committed to using apology but in a way that empties it of meaning; and second, that in treating insincere or merely ritualistic apologies as sufficient, it foregoes an important opportunity for moral reform. Both of these criticisms miss the target, however. The use of apologetic action in the Apology Ritual account is modeled on the practice of apology, but the way in which it is modeled depends on a conception of the legitimate state aims that apologetic action is used to further. Moral reform is desirable, of course, but its desirability does not thereby show that it is something that states can legitimately pursue by coercive means. I agree that states should put resources into moral education and that some steps should be taken to confront persistent wrongdoers with the nature of their wrongdoing. However, that is a far cry from making the successful performance of a sincere apology (presumably as judged by state officials) an integral part of the punishment system and a condition of receiving more sympathetic treatment by that system. If we go down that line, we walk into the problems I outlined earlier and which motivate the ritualistic aspect of my view.[22]

It is quite compatible with the Apology Ritual that, as Smith says, we should "hope" that doing the kinds of amends that the Apology Ritual envisages will bring offenders to feel bad about what they have done. What my account insists, however, is that for the purposes of achieving the legal parallel of forgiveness and redemption—return of the rights lost as punishment—the process of atonement (or rather, again, its legal parallel) has to be conceived in such a way that it can be successfully carried out even by someone who feels no remorse. For this reason, although it sees moral reform as desirable, the Apology Ritual does not see such reform as an end that can be coercively carried out by the state. What can coercively be carried out, however, is proper dissociation from the wrongdoing through the expression of meaningful condemnation. Apology comes into this, but in a restricted and modified form—as the source of adequate symbols through which to express the condemnation and achieve dissociation. Hence the apology used by the Apology Ritual may, as Smith says, lack some of the meanings centrally associated with its use in interpersonal relations, but it has all of the meaning necessary for it to act as a vehicle for condemnation.

B. Penance

Second, I would like to address concerns about the notion of penance, which I follow Duff in putting at the heart of my account. In my understanding, the actual giving of a verbal apology can be relatively unimportant—at any rate this is not usually something that an offender should be required to do. More important is the action of making amends, where this includes compensation and restitution, but also penance. The penitential part of making amends I take to be action that is taken to be necessary to express how sorry one feels and not to repair some material harm one has caused—as in Bryson saying sorry with a gift in my earlier example. Some, however, have been unconvinced by my claim that one who is properly sorry would be motivated to do something penitential; Margaret Holmgren puts the point in this way:

> [A]n offender who has proper dignity and recognition self-respect will understand that he retains his capacity for moral agency and his basic status as a person in spite of what he has done. In this case he will use his capacities in a dignified, responsible manner, focusing on the positive contributions he can make to his victims and to others. He will not dwell in horror on his past record of moral performance and express self-contempt by undertaking an undignified, humiliating or masochistic penance.[23]

The criticism here is that penance is (a) unnecessary, (b) incompatible with genuine self-respect, and (c) inappropriately focused on oneself rather than what one can do for those one has harmed. Now it may be that these criticisms can justifiably be made of the notion of penance as understood by some people and perhaps some traditions. But Holmgren ignores a morally important notion of penance at work in our understanding of apology, and which is part of the logic of repentance. Although penance involves undertaking something onerous that one would not otherwise have been obliged to do, and the significance of which does not simply consist in repairing the harm caused by one's action, it can and usually is carried out by making some sort of "positive contribution to the victim and others." So penances do not need to be carried out simply by making oneself suffer. I find it hard, as Holmgren evidently does, to understand the view on which that could be a meaningful way of putting things right. Nevertheless, I think a fully repentant wrongdoer will usually feel compelled to do more than is necessary simply to bring about restitution and compensation; and it is this extra which—perhaps inadvisedly, given the baggage of the term that comes out in Holmgren's discussion—I have termed "penance." Why does the fully repentant wrongdoer feel compelled to do that extra?

My explanation of this goes back to my claims about dissociation. Moral error is not like theoretical error. When someone gets something wrong in philosophical discussion—even when it is something that, given their level of expertise, perhaps, they should have got right—it is enough that the error should be pointed out in the hope that it will be corrected next time. When someone gets something morally wrong, however—when it is serious and they were capable of getting it right—we treat it differently. Granted there can be excuses and justifications, but let us just assume a very clear case of wrongdoing for the sake of argument. It is not enough that we simply point out the problem. Rather, I claim, it is an important element of our practice that we feel it necessary to mark the wrongdoing as an unacceptable violation by altering our behavior toward the wrongdoer in a manner that is proportional to the gravity of the wrong. Moral wrongdoing alters relationships, calling for moral repair.[24] The way I interpret that is as a normative claim: moral wrongdoing *ought* to alter relationships, and moral repair is not merely smoothing over feelings but addressing moral demands that arise because of the fact that one has done something wrong. This is what I have called the "distancing" claim: that moral wrongdoing requires us in some way to alter our conduct toward the wrongdoer, distancing him partially and temporarily. We can see the need for penance when we think about the repentant wrongdoer sharing that view of himself, coming to have that attitude toward himself. The penitential attitude paradigmatically involves being less assertive of one's own wants and needs, of giving oneself and one's interests less of a central place in one's thought and plans, where this shift is motivated by the sense that what one has done requires one to distance oneself from oneself. The way this shift in attitude comes out in behavior is not as a desire to suffer—since, apart from anything else, that would involve not a decentring of attention to oneself, but rather a swallowing up of all other considerations by a self-indulgent concern for one's own moral purity. Rather applying the distancing attitude to oneself leads to a heightened awareness of those aspects of others' interests that might usually be displaced by legitimate pursuit of one's own concerns. That is the proper and justifiable basis of the penitential attitude.

C. Forfeiting Rights to Liberty

Finally, I would like to consider the criticism that the Apology Ritual account is fundamentally flawed, or at least seriously incomplete, because it doesn't address the fundamental question of how offenders lose their rights to liberty. The Apology Ritual might be able to explain why it would be *a good thing* for offenders to be punished. But the Apology Ritual has no answer to the question of why the state—or any other body—has the *right* to deprive an offender of the liberty to which they have a natural or pre-legal right. This question, so the criticism goes, would have to be addressed at the outset in any attempted justification of state punishment, meaning that the most successful type of theory of punishment would be a forfeiture theory that gives a convincing answer to how that pre-legal right to liberty can be foregone. Traditional justifications of punishment—of which, on this categorization, the Apology Ritual is one—fail because they do not deal with this question.

This criticism has been made in general terms by Christopher Heath Wellman:

> Because being punished appears to violate one's life, liberty and/or property rights, the permissibility of punishment seems to hinge on whether punishment is compatible with these rights. . . . Thus, contrary to the traditional strategy of citing the valuable aims which punishment can realize, the best approach for those who seek to explain the permissibility of punishment would seem to be to focus upon explaining how criminals have forfeited their rights against hard treatment.[25]

To apply this to the Apology Ritual account, the charge would be that even if we agree that it would be good for the state to dissociate itself from wrongdoing and express condemnation by making offenders engage in appropriate apologetic action, it would require a further step to show that the state had the right to carry this goal out in such a way as to impose it coercively on offenders. That further step would involve showing that offenders forfeit prelegal rights to liberty. The Apology Ritual fails, the charge would go, because it says nothing about such forfeiture.

Dealing with this charge fully would take more space than I have available at this stage, but let me begin by identifying an assumption that underpins this criticism. The assumption is that the notion of rights forfeiture has explanatory value independent of a "traditional" justification of punishment like the Apology Ritual account. It might help to make this clearer if I explain what would challenge this assumption. One response to Wellman's charge is to say that it is fine to talk about rights forfeiture, but to claim that we have no independent grasp of that notion except through the thought that it has now become permissible coercively to subject the offender to punishment. The explanation for that latter fact, on the Apology Ritual account, refers to the permissibility of some political entity deciding to set binding limits on acceptable action through the institution of the criminal law, and then marking violations of those limits with meaningful condemnation, where to be "meaningful" it has to be coercively imposed.

Now there may be elements of the Apology Ritual account that need to be filled out in more detail—in particular, perhaps, the initial step that talks about the permissibility and desirability of a state's setting up a criminal law in the first place to designate limits to behavior that will be binding in the relevant way. But the point at the moment is that, should that account be successful, it would *follow* from its success that, in effect, wrongdoers forfeit their right to liberty—they become justifiably liable to coercively imposed condemnation. But if we understand matters in this way, Wellman's criticism fails, for the forfeiture theory would not represent a genuine alternative to the traditional theories; rather it would merely be an implication of those theories. Thus we can see that Wellman's account assumes that forfeiture is explanatorily independent in thinking about the justifiability of punishment.

Once this assumption is brought into the light, though, we should at least note that some doubts that can be raised about it. The notion of forfeiture of rights has its natural home in certain specific contexts. For instance, in a situation where older pupils in a school are given exclusive use of a common room, but they abuse their position by using the room inappropriately or failing to keep it in order, they may be told that they have forfeited the right to the use of the room, and have the privilege withdrawn. (Though even here it is not clear that forfeiture is doing work entirely independently of, for example, considerations about the value of the room to the school, and the costs to others that the pupils' behavior creates.) Wellman's approach is to assume that the way in which bad behavior leads to the loss of rights in this case can be generalized to a whole range of other cases. However, this would require the explanation of a robust principle lying behind the forfeiture view that was genuinely independent of other justifications of punishment. The formulation of such a principle would have to be thick enough to yield determinate and morally plausible results, but thin enough to be explanatorily independent. It is far from clear that Wellman's attempt to spell out such a principle—that a person who violates the rights of others loses the same rights himself—is successful in overcoming the horns of that dilemma. And for that reason I am unconvinced that his claims to have discovered an alternative to the traditional justifications of punishment represent a genuine challenge to the Apology Ritual.

V. CONCLUSION

In this chapter I have tried to set out the main features of the Apology Ritual account of punishment. The key idea on this view is that punishment can be justified if it involves requiring the offender to engage in the kind of apologetic action that he would perform spontaneously and willingly if he were appropriately sorry for what he had done. The punishment is a ritual, however, because it can be successfully complied with in the absence of genuine remorse, and so the state is not attempting to coerce repentance. In putting forward this conception, I am articulating an ideal normative conception of punishment, not merely a description of how things actually work. However, one reason the Apology Ritual account is attractive is because it sees the operation of criminal justice as governed by a conception of wrongdoing and response that is continuous with the conception of wrongdoing and response that governs our interpersonal dealings; this makes criminal justice not simply the social engineering of the administrative state but also an operation with an interpersonal quality at its heart. Stressing the ultimately irenic aims of the practice of apology—which in the end seeks to reincorporate the wrongdoer into the moral community without compromising the authority of the norms violated by her action—also avoids the pitfalls of simple retributivism's emphasis on the inherent goodness of making the wrongdoer suffer. In addition to attempting to locate the Apology Ritual in relation to other theories of punishment, I have tried to spell out how it might be able to respond to criticisms that have been made of it. Readers will decide whether I have been successful.

NOTES

1. *See* Christopher Bennett, The Apology Ritual: A Philosophical Theory of Punishment (2008).
2. For purely stylistic reasons I term my imagined offenders "he."
3. See Richard Swinburne, Responsibility and Atonement, chap. 5 (1989); Nick Smith, *The Categorical Apology*, 36 J. Soc. Phil 473–96 (2005).
4. This part of the theory is a defense and elaboration of R. A. Duff's idea that criminal punishment should be seen as a kind of "secular penance." *See* R. A. Duff, Trials and Punishments (1986).
5. I take it that something like this is Duff's view—that the aim of punishment is to evoke repentance. *See also* R. A. Duff, Punishment, Communication and Community (2001).
6. For this view, *see* Nick Smith, Justice Through Apologies: Remorse, Reform and Punishment (2014).

7. For an exploration of some of these claims about political authority, see Christopher Bennett, *Expressive Punishment and Political Authority*, 8 OHIO ST. J. CRIM. L. 285. (2011).

8. Christopher Bennett, *State Denunciation of Crime*, 3 J. MORAL PHIL. 288, 288–304 (2006).

9. For this interpretation of the idea of crime as "public wrong," *see* DUFF, *supra* note 5, at 61–63.

10. Igor Primoratz, *Punishment as Language*, 64 PHIL. 187 (1989).

11. As I have argued, the way in which we typically express condemnation in interpersonal contexts is through some form of distancing. *See* Christopher Bennett, *The Varieties of Retributive Experience*, 52 PHIL. Q. 145 (2002).

12. For this criticism of my view, see SMITH, *supra* note 6, at 64.

13. For a further development of this point, see Christopher Bennett, *Taking the Sincerity Out of Saying Sorry: Restorative Justice as Ritual*, 23 J. APPLIED PHIL. 127 (2006).

14. *See* sources cited *supra* notes 3–4.

15. The philosophical defense of this claim is most prominently associated with Michael Moore. For a good articulation of his view, see Michael S. Moore, *The Moral Worth of Retribution*, *in* RESPONSIBILITY, CHARACTER AND THE EMOTIONS (Ferdinand Schoeman ed., 1989).

16. *See* Bennett, *supra* note 11.

17. Christopher Bennett, *Penal Disenfranchisement*, CRIM. L. & PHIL. (forthcoming), http://www.academia.edu/5877411/Penal_Disenfranchisement.

18. I am taking Hart's view to be most clearly set out in the key passages of the section called "The Rationale of Excuses" in the chapter titled *Prolegomenon to the Principles of Punishment* and the chapter titled *Legal Responsibility and Excuses*. H.L.A. HART, PUNISHMENT AND RESPONSIBILITY: ESSAYS IN THE PHILOSOPHY OF LAW 17–53 (1968).

19. ANDREW VON HIRSCH, CENSURE AND SANCTIONS (1995).

20. Duff himself recognizes and responds to this criticism. DUFF, *supra* note 5, at 118–20. See also the different justification offered for the need to express condemnation. *Id.* at 28. The latter statement of Duff's position invites the interpretation that the point of condemnation is—as I believe—dissociation before it is communication. Duff does not develop this line of thought, however, and it is not clear how he thinks it sits with the idea of punishment as communication; I believe that he overlooks the idea of dissociation because it sounds "expressive" rather than communicative—and he is suspicious that expression need not deal with the offender as a rational agent. *Id.* at 79–80. I believe that there is a richness to the notion of expression that Duff overlooks. *See, e.g.*, Christopher Bennett, *The Expressive Function of Blame*, *in* BLAME: ITS NATURE AND NORMS (D. Justin Coates & Neal A. Tognazzini eds., 2013).

21. SMITH, *supra* note 6, at 64. For a similar line of criticism, see José Luis Martí, *The Limits of Apology in a Democratic Criminal Justice: Some Remarks on Bennett's* The Apology Ritual, 31 TEOREMA 119 (2012), http://philpapers.org/archive/BENSTA-5; *see also* Antony Duff, *Penal Coercion and the Apology Ritual*, 31 TEOREMA 109 (2012).

22. For the development of a related set of concerns, focusing on the social construction of emotion and emotion behavior, *see* RICHARD WEISMAN, SHOWING REMORSE: LAW AND THE SOCIAL CONTROL OF EMOTION (2014).

23. MARGARET HOLMGREN, FORGIVENESS AND RETRIBUTION: RESPONDING TO WRONGDOING 226 (2012).

24. For this apt term, *see* MARGARET U. WALKER, MORAL REPAIR: RECONSTRUCTING MORAL RELATIONS AFTER WRONGDOING (2006).

25. Christopher H. Wellman, *The Rights Forfeiture Theory of Punishment*, 122 ETHICS 371 (2012).

Chapter Twelve

Equity, Not Mercy

Mary Sigler

It's hard to argue with mercy. Throughout history, mercy has figured prominently in our religious, cultural, and literary traditions, nearly always reflecting well on the character of those who dispense it. Associated in the first instance with divine benevolence, mercy is "twice blest," exalting giver and recipient alike.[1] In ancient Rome, Seneca counseled mercy (*clementia*) in an environment of extreme violence and cruelty under color of law.[2] In the eighteenth century, William Blackstone and Alexander Hamilton favored a political mechanism for the exercise of mercy in their respective societies "to soften the rigor of the general law"[3] that might otherwise be "too sanguinary and cruel."[4] In the modern criminal justice setting, calls for mercy are similarly cast as a means of mitigating the extreme harshness of criminal punishment.

The appeal of mercy as a moral ideal is obvious. The virtue of mercy reflects a settled disposition to regard others with benevolence and compassion and to act from those motivations on appropriate occasions. More modestly, one may act mercifully on a particular occasion out of kindness or concern for another. At a minimum, acts of mercy involve relief from hardship or suffering by one who holds the power to inflict something more. Who could deny the value of benevolence, compassion, and the relief of suffering?

Proponents of mercy in the criminal justice context draw considerable rhetorical force from these positive associations. As a general matter, no person or institution wishes to be "merciless." Indeed, to lack mercy is to be cruel, heartless, begrudging, inhumane—to reject not only God's example but also *Shakespeare's*. In the current climate, the scholarly and popular literature on criminal justice is dominated by voices insisting that punishment in the United States is excessive and unreasonably harsh. Mercy is promoted as a tool to counter this punitive excess.

In many of these accounts, the term "mercy" is used broadly to refer to almost any instance of (or basis for) remitting the harshness of punishment. Although unobjectionable as a colloquial matter, this indiscriminate usage is conceptually problematic. The problem is not that "mercy" has a fixed meaning that precludes application to some subset of these cases—the discredited "definitional stop."[5] Rather, mercy understood in this broad sense distorts at least two concepts that are essential to our legal, moral, and political life. The broad use of the term mercy denies us the conceptual resources to assess the distinctive operation of traditional mercy—an act of grace that cancels or mitigates what is due out of compassion or concern for the recipient. Even more important, broad mercy effectively diminishes the concept of justice, alleviating the pressure it would otherwise exert to redress claims of right.

In place of mercy as an institutional mechanism, I make a case for equity. Itself an ancient and venerable concept, equity is often associated (sometimes conflated) with mercy. But unlike mercy, a freestanding virtue, equity is an instrument of justice. Indeed, according to Aristotle, "It is a kind of justice, and not a distinct state of character."[6] Against the backdrop of a legal code that is necessarily general in its orientation—providing universal rules to order human affairs—equity focuses on the particulars, fine-tuning the law's application to the messy reality of individual cases. In this way, "the law takes account of the majority of cases," but equity promotes true justice "in so far as law is defective on account of its generality."[7] Reflecting this complexity, the modern criminal law includes opportunities for the exercise of discretion to allow decision makers to do justice within the parameters of the rule of law.

To make the case for equity, and against mercy, I begin by exploring the concept of mercy in both its traditional and broad senses. Drawing on the work of various mercy skeptics, this analysis suggests that traditional mercy, despite its importance as a moral virtue, is problematic in a system of criminal justice. Among other problems, extending mercy means failing to give some offenders the punishment they deserve; it also undermines our commitment to equal justice under law. I then focus on recent calls for one or another form of "prudential mercy" to serve as a kind of "counter-ratchet" in the domain of criminal justice.[8] This discussion highlights the perils of unfettered discretion in the context of criminal justice and the costs of conceptualizing all instances of leniency as mercy. For if punishment is excessive, it is unjust, and the mechanism for relief is to assert one's (or another's) rights, not to beg for mercy.

I then turn to equity as an alternative. Equity, like mercy, operates in the realm of discretion, but, unlike mercy, equity aims at justice, for "[e]quity involves weighing all justice-visible properties"[9] in order to reach a fully just decision. In the legal context, equitable judgment represents a form of guided discretion in which decision making is both searchingly particular and constrained by authoritative standards of justice. A careful analysis of the concept of discretion underscores both the promise and pitfalls of the discretion with which we empower actors in the criminal justice process. Equity, not mercy, should structure their deliberations.

I conclude with some observations about the undeniable affinity between equity and the virtue of mercy. Rooted in the concept of *epieikeia*, equity and mercy countered the indifference and cruelty of justice in the ancient world. In that setting, the particularity of equity facilitated the leniency of mercy, becoming "so closely linked as to be aspects of the same concept."[10] For "a merciful stance will allow a disposition for equitable treatment to be realized."[11] In the modern world, however, the insights of *epieikeia* are built into the structure of criminal justice—in the grading of offenses, the opportunities for discretion, and the prohibition on cruelty. As a result, the case for mercy in criminal justice—from Seneca to Hamilton and beyond—loses much of its force. But while the justice constraints of equity circumscribe the inclination to leniency in modern criminal justice, a merciful disposition, then and now, enables the particularized scrutiny of equitable—and just—decision making.

I. MERCY

In general terms, "mercy" may refer broadly to a variety of situations in which someone has the power to impose suffering on another and refrains from doing so. As Andrew Brien has observed, the term "mercy" may be used to describe any act of forbearance in the context of a power relationship—an "act of mercy"—that need not involve any particular motivation, state of character, or exercise of legitimate power.[12] Instead, the merciful actor is simply one who "had reasons to pursue events that would cause suffering, but instead set those reasons aside and performed merciful acts."[13] In this very broad sense, an act of mercy may be undertaken by a duly authorized public official or a common street thug, either of whom may refrain from exercising his capacity to inflict suffering for any reason or no reason at all.

More conventionally, especially in the context of the criminal law, talk of mercy implies a benevolent motivation—that the merciful actor was moved by compassion or concern for the well-being of another subject to his legitimate authority. Although an official may have occasion to remit an offender's suffering for any number of reasons—to induce cooperation, for example, or to reward a political ally—we generally reserve the concept of mercy for cases that involve benevolence toward the recipient. Thus, leniency, in the domain of criminal justice, "counts as mercy only when it is motivated by concern for the good of the person to whom it is shown."[14] Moreover, in this context, the specific kind of suffering that mercy relieves is punishment, "deliberately inflicted hard treatment meant as censure for wrongdoing, which the person authorized to punish typically has an obligation to impose."[15] Finally, what I will call "traditional mercy," owing to its origins in the prerogative of divine and earthly sovereigns, presupposes that mercy is an act of grace or charity subject to a decision maker's discretion. On this account, mercy may be sought, even begged for, but it cannot be claimed as a matter of right.

A. Traditional Mercy

The act of grace that constitutes traditional mercy may be personal or institutional.[16] In the realm of interpersonal relationships—family and friends, colleagues and business associates—we routinely benefit from one another's mercy for the small and large transgressions of daily life. We show mercy in this sense by forgiving a debt that is owed or otherwise refraining from demanding what is due (an apology or other form of amends) out of compassion or concern for the debtor. In more extreme cases of interpersonal conflict, the private law model provides a mechanism for resolving disputes between individuals. As Jeffrie Murphy notes, Shakespeare's celebrated paean to mercy in *The Merchant of Venice* arises in the private law setting, as Portia implores Shylock to remit Antonio's debt when he defaults on their contract.[17] In this case, there is "room for mercy" because Shylock has a right, but not an obligation, to demand satisfaction.[18]

In the public law setting, particularly in the context of criminal justice, the role of mercy is more complicated. As an initial matter, because retributive justice dominates the criminal justice paradigm, the law operates with the general expectation that those guilty of a criminal offense deserve to be punished and that the state has an obligation to impose it.[19] Where justice consists (essentially) in punishing according to desert, mercy is distinguished by its divergence from justice. Traditional mercy thus requires the state to withhold the full measure of what is due or deserved—inflicting punishment that stops "short of what might have been deservedly imposed"[20]—based on sympathetic concern for the offender.

The challenges of traditional mercy in the institutional setting are well established. In his influential analysis of traditional mercy in the modern criminal law, Murphy highlights the paradox of mercy's relationship to justice:

> [I]f we simply use the term mercy to refer to certain of the demands of justice (e.g., the demand of individuation), then "mercy" ceases to be an autonomous virtue and instead becomes a part of . . . justice. It thus becomes obligatory, and all the talk about gifts, acts of grace, supererogation, and compassion becomes quite beside the point. If, on the other hand, mercy is totally different from justice and actually requires (or permits) that justice sometimes be set

> aside, it then counsels injustice. In short, mercy is either a vice (injustice) or redundant (a part of justice).[21]

Across a range of retributive perspectives, this inherent tension between mercy and justice gives rise to skepticism about a formal role for traditional mercy in the criminal justice process.[22] According to a communicative conception of retributive punishment, the process of trial and sentencing is meant to communicate censure for acts of criminal wrongdoing—"the more serious the crime, the more severe the deserved censure."[23] On this view, as Antony Duff notes, "[m]ercy seems to flout the demands of penal justice" because it entails disproportionately lenient treatment. Duff thus conceptualizes mercy as an "intrusion" of values from outside the domain and logic of criminal justice, an intrusion that may be justified only in rare cases.[24] Because the purpose of punishment is "to bring the offender to face up to, focus on, the wrong he has done,"[25] an offender experiencing a grievous loss (e.g., the death of a child or spouse) at the time of sentencing will be understandably, even appropriately, distracted. In that event, the remission of punishment may be merciful—and justified—based on compassionate considerations extraneous to criminal justice.

In a similar vein, even a classic retributivist can acknowledge the potential for mercy to find its way, however indirectly, into the criminal justice process. Despite her categorical rejection of a role for mercy as a legitimate feature of criminal justice,[26] Heidi Hurd observes that the (socially desirable) cultivation of character traits suited to loving relationships in one's private life may be in tension with the (morally responsible) rejection of merciful considerations as a criminal justice official. Thus, "while retributivists are right that mercy has no philosophical place in a system devoted to retributive justice, they are wrong to think that it has no psychological place."[27] We can thus expect private mercy to have "spill-over effects" in the domain of criminal justice.[28] In these cases, mercy is not justified—as an aspect of criminal justice or as an intrusion from a broader domain of value; it instead reflects an inevitable limitation of a distinctly human institution.

In addition to the problem of disproportionality, a second source of concern about mercy's role in criminal justice is the threat it poses to equality. Central to our conception of justice is the principle that like cases should be treated alike. That is, in a polity committed to equal justice under law, state institutions must treat individuals equally absent morally relevant differences that might justify a departure.[29] In the context of criminal justice, an official moved to show traditional mercy to a particular offender—because of some compassion-inspiring feature of the offender or his offense—thereby establishes a basis for showing mercy to all others who share that feature. But as Murphy notes, the identification of grounds for mercy that apply in principle to all similar cases seems at odds with the idea of mercy as an act of grace or charity. For "[i]f there are good reasons for mercy—relevant features that ought to incline the mind—they will be and remain good reasons whether they are acted on or not."[30] Under these circumstances, an official deciding to extend mercy in some cases but not (relevantly similar) others creates a situation of inequality—and injustice. Either mercy is due to all who are similarly situated as a matter of equal justice or it is arbitrarily extended only to some.

B. Prudential Mercy

At this point, I hope to have said enough to raise doubts about the role of traditional mercy in criminal justice. I now turn to alternative conceptions of mercy designed specifically to mitigate the harshness of modern criminal punishment. In particular I will focus on what Carol Steiker calls "prudential mercy," though I will also consider other generally compatible alternatives under that heading. These accounts are united by a high degree of despair about the current system of criminal justice and a shared faith in the redemptive power of discretion. But despite the searing indictments of American-style criminal justice on which they are predicated, these mercy alternatives threaten to hinder, rather than advance, the cause of justice.

Steiker advocates prudential mercy as a "counter-ratchet" to punitive excess in the United States and other western democracies.[31] After first offering an account of the pathological nature of philosophy, politics, and law (at least in relation to criminal justice), she urges actors in the criminal justice process to take an expansive approach to their powers of (generally unreviewable) discretion. Prosecutors making charging decisions, juries reviewing criminal cases, and judges sentencing offenders—all "should broaden their conceptions of their discretionary powers so as to open themselves to a wider range of considerations that might move them to exercise a veto power over the imposition of punishment in particular cases."[32] In this way, "prudential mercy" reflects both a pragmatic and a more philosophical dimension: "rooted in the predictable failures of our discourses of justice,"[33] but also capturing the essence of traditional mercy, "a conscious setting aside of whatever prevailing accounts of 'justice' would otherwise govern the punishment calculus."[34] These "exercises of 'merciful' discretion [should] involve leniency based on compassionate concern for the offender."[35]

Advocates of merciful discretion (in the prudential sense) recognize the familiar hazards of discretionary judgment. Indeed, as Rachel Barkow notes, "our legal culture has come to view unreviewable discretion to decide individual cases as the very definition of lawlessness."[36] In particular, unreviewable discretion sits uneasily with the rule of law, which holds that all are equally subject to reasonable public legal standards and processes in the administration of justice. Because discretionary actors hold the power to make final decisions without reference to, or regard for, consistency or fairness—and without articulating (or even having) reasons for their judgments—it is practically impossible to determine the basis for or validity of their decisions. Moreover, the various mechanisms for discretion in the criminal justice process, including jury nullification and executive clemency, not only present opportunities for mercy but also open the door for discriminatory decision making. From this perspective, "the exercise of mercy has a different face and a far more problematic one, for it is likely that the institutional opportunities for the exercise of mercy in the criminal justice system are also sources of a substantial part of the system's disparate impact along the lines of race, ethnicity, and class."[37]

Despite these concerns, advocates maintain that the potential of merciful discretion is worth the risk. "At some point—and part of the argument [here] is that we have reached it—punitive policies are so disabling to minority communities that reducing the impact of such policies might trump other considerations (i.e., reducing discrimination and disparity) that have long been thought to be paramount."[38] Indeed, the mechanisms of merciful discretion are more important than ever "in today's political climate, in which legislators succumb to get-tough politics, write harsh laws, and tie the hands of judges."[39] Advocates also hold out hope for systemic reform, the idea that discrete acts of merciful discretion "will shape the incentives of prosecutors and legislators and ultimately alter public discourse regarding penal policy."[40]

Beyond the practical calculation—about whether prudential mercy will, on balance, do more good than harm—is the question of justice. As Steiker notes, avoiding the injustice of a disproportionate sentence is "something which individual defendants have a right to demand, whereas mercy is generally conceived of as something for which one begs or pleads and that is bestowed as a matter of grace rather than as a matter of duty."[41] Despite this recognition, she distrusts the political process that establishes criminal justice policy as well as the sentencing authorities who impose punishment in individual cases. "Premising the exercise of prudential mercy on distrust of our capacity for justice and on fear that we might impose too much punishment works against the smugness and self-righteousness that can attend the imposition of punishment."[42]

We should not underestimate the potential for smugness and self-righteousness—common vices not generally confined to one side of a debate—but neither should we succumb to false modesty. It would be disingenuous to recast the confident assurance that we punish too many too much as an exercise in self-doubt. Prudential mercy, predicated on the conviction that we punish too harshly, does not seem to doubt. A commitment to moral humility in the domain of criminal justice requires that we proceed "with caution, regret, humility, and with the vivid realization that we are involved in a fallible and finite institution."[43] It does not require, or countenance, that we abandon the principles and processes of justice.[44]

II. EQUITY

The close association between equity and mercy reflects their common origins in ancient legal systems characterized by profound injustice. As Nussbaum reminds us, the crude "justice" of the ancients did not accommodate the particularities of individual circumstances, indifferent as they were to considerations of motive, intention, and blameworthiness.[45] Thus, Oedipus, innocently unaware of his parentage, is condemned for parricide and incest, despite the obvious grounds for exculpation. In this environment, equity's attention to particularity—fitting the law to the details of the individual case—aligns with mercy's mitigation of "deserved" punishment. Both incline toward leniency.

In the eighteenth century, Blackstone links equity and mercy in defending the pardon power, insisting that the monarch must be able "to extend mercy, wherever he thinks it is deserved: holding a court of equity in his own breast, to soften the rigor of the general law, in such criminal cases as merit an exemption from punishment."[46] He thus rejects "what no man will seriously avow, that the situation and circumstances of the offender (though they alter not the essence of the crime) ought to make no distinction in the punishment."[47] Reflecting a similar concern for the inflexible harshness of the legal code, Hamilton defends the executive pardon: "The criminal code of every country partakes so much of necessary severity, that without an easy access to exceptions in favor of unfortunate guilt, justice would wear a countenance too sanguinary and cruel."[48]

A. Distinguishing Equity and Mercy

Since the time of Blackstone and Hamilton—and Oedipus—the rigid law that condemned (at least) all felons to death has been relaxed in various ways to permit, even require, more particularized judgments about criminal liability. In the ancient world, the infliction of brutal punishment did not require a culpable mental state or even the commission of an offense. Closer to home, the common law did not initially recognize various defenses to criminal liability, such as insanity, self-defense, infancy, or provocation. In these circumstances, mercy effectively provided the only outlet for taking account of individual variations in offenders and offenses.

The advent of the modern criminal code, however, attenuates the connection between equity and mercy. Our commitment to particularization and proportionality is reflected in the elaborate grading of offenses and punishment according to culpability, the recognition of excuses and justifications that diminish or defeat blameworthiness, and the elimination of the death penalty for all but the most serious murders. In addition, the availability of various discretionary mechanisms allows for further individuation. In this context, equity and mercy no longer share a common purpose, for the leniency that mercy favors is at odds with the justice that equity serves. In the interest of justice, discretionary actors—prosecutors, jurors, executives, and sentencing authorities—should be guided by equity, not mercy.

Despite the improvements of modern criminal justice, the system remains far from perfect. In addition to the inevitable imperfections of any human institution, Aristotle highlighted the inherent limitations of a general legal code designed for the "majority of cases." Then as now, a mechanical application of law is bound to result in serious injustice absent a means for adjusting the law to the particularities of individual cases. Discretion, duly constrained, serves that function.

B. Discretion

Mercy, as Shakespeare instructs, is not "strain'd," but equity *is* constrained—by justice.[49] This analytic distinction between equity and mercy is usefully illuminated by Ronald Dworkin's account of discretion in legal decision making.[50] Dworkin notes that in ordinary usage, discretion implies a standard of judgment:

> The concept of discretion is at home in only one sort of context; when someone is in general charged with making decisions subject to standards set by a particular authority. . . . Discretion, like the hole in a doughnut, does not exist except as an area left open by a surrounding belt of restriction.[51]

Dworkin further distinguishes between "weak" and "strong" discretion. Discretion in the (first) weak sense obtains when the standards one must apply require the use of judgment rather than mechanical application.[52] This sort of discretion is at work, for example, when a sergeant is ordered by his lieutenant to choose the "five most experienced men" for a particular mission.[53] The sense in which the sergeant's choice is discretionary is that the decision of which five are the "most experienced" may require a difficult judgment about what constitutes relevant experience.[54]

Strong discretion, by contrast, applies in cases where a decision maker is "simply not bound by standards set by the authority in question."[55] Thus, rather than telling the lieutenant that he must choose the five most experienced men, the lieutenant tells him that he may choose any five men for patrol. Dworkin notes that even strong discretion is not immune from criticism. "An official's discretion means not that he is free to decide without recourse to standards of sense and fairness, but only that his decision is not controlled by a standard furnished by the particular authority."[56] An official who exercises discretion in this sense "can be said to have made a mistake, but not to have deprived a participant of a decision to which he was entitled."[57]

The distinction between equity and mercy maps more or less neatly on to the distinction between weak and strong discretion. Equity accords with weak discretion insofar as it is circumscribed by the authoritative standards of justice. Equitable discretion in the criminal justice context involves difficult judgments about the complex details of individual cases and their relevance, if any, to a just outcome. The decision maker is not free to render any decision for any reason; he is bound to take account of justice-relevant particulars amid the "raw material of human behavior."[58] This requires "insight, perception, clear thinking, determination, and [a] sympathetic stance towards" the offender.[59] For Aristotle, it means adopting a "ruling such as the legislator himself would have given if he had been present there, and as he would have enacted if he had been aware of the circumstances."[60] In this way, equitable discretion is constrained by the standards of justice.

Mercy, at least in the traditional sense,[61] corresponds to strong discretion. According to Seneca, it is distinguished by "freedom in decision; it sentences not by the letter of the law, but in accordance with what is fair and good; it may acquit and it may assess the damages at any value it pleases."[62] Merciful discretion thus involves more than sensitive attention to individual particularities; it requires an "inclination of the mind to leniency in exacting punishment."[63] It means "going outside considerations of moral justice or equity, and treating a person more leniently than is generally thought warranted by her overall deserts."[64] Like strong discretion, an exercise of mercy may be judged unwise or unfair, but it cannot be said to have deprived another of a decision to which he was entitled. As an instance of grace or charity, it may be exercised (or not) for any reason (or no reason) at all.

In the criminal justice system, we empower various actors with unreviewable discretion. A jury decision to acquit, for example, or an executive decision to pardon are practically impervious to challenge or review. Under these circumstances, we might wonder what difference it makes whether discretion is equitable or merciful—especially if we are happy with the result.

The case for equitable rather than merciful discretion is normative, affirming a commitment to the rule-of-law values that structure our legal and political institutions, including the system of criminal justice. From this perspective, the grounds for decision, even those involving unreviewable discretion, should conform to authoritative standards of justice. In the criminal law context, this means that decision making should reflect considerations of desert and proportionality, and the related value of equality. Merciful discretion consciously neglects these values that equitable discretion makes central to just decision making.

Consider the power of jury nullification. In making the case for prudential mercy, Steiker suggests that we instruct juries that they *may*, rather than *must*, decide a criminal case according to the authoritative definition of the relevant legal standards as provided by the judge.[65] She notes in this connection that the jury's power is after all unreviewable.[66] In fact, as a practical matter, we are unlikely to know in any case whether a decision to acquit reflects a judgment that the state failed to prove its case beyond a reasonable doubt or whether the jury collectively decided that it did not agree with the decision to criminalize, prosecute, or punish this offense or this offender.

The fact of the jury's power to "operate outside the law"[67] does not establish that it has the legitimate authority to do so. As a normative matter, the jury's discretion is weak only, constrained by authoritative standards of law that purport to control its judgment.[68] Although the jury can, as a practical matter, disregard the law with impunity, its defiance should not generally be encouraged or celebrated.[69]

The role of discretion in executive pardons is somewhat different. A president or governor effectively enjoys unreviewable power to grant or deny relief for any reason or no reason at all. But unlike juries, the executive (depending on the jurisdiction) may not be bound by authoritative standards that apply to his deliberations. In that case, he has discretion in the strong sense, though his decision is still subject to judgment according to standards of sense and fairness. Thus, an executive who decides "stupidly, maliciously, or carelessly"[70] may be appropriately faulted for flouting public values, such as impartiality or fairness, or if he fails to provide a satisfactory account of his decision making.

Historically, executives have been reluctant to explain their decisions to pardon. In at least some cases, however, their stated reasons raise serious concerns about the grounds of their decisions. In 1999, for example, Governor Mel Carnahan of Missouri, a lifetime supporter of capital punishment, commuted the death sentence of a triple murderer "as a tribute to the Pope," who happened to be in town.[71] Although no one doubted the governor's power to make the commutation decision, its apparent arbitrariness represents a striking abuse of that power. Armed with strong discretion, Carnahan seems to have acted without a reasonable public justification. Indeed, precisely because it represents a form of strong discretion, the legitimacy of the executive pardon power is highly questionable in a liberal democratic polity committed to public reason and the rule of law.

Finally, we might conceptualize an act of discretionary decision making as a form of civil disobedience. A jury instructed according to the standards of the law may find that as a matter of conscience it cannot impose criminal liability and punishment, or a governor may declare that he cannot sign a death warrant.[72] Notably, because acts of civil disobedience are distinguished by the willful and public refusal to conform to a legal standard perceived to be unjust, they presuppose that authoritative standards exist and apply.[73] As a normative matter, such open defiance at least marks the decision as self-consciously lawless. Moreover, as Hurd points out, such cases are compelling, when they are, not because they involve "the exercise of mercy, but rather the achievement of justice."[74]

For advocates of merciful discretion, however, equity does not go far enough. Although it has the potential to tailor criminal liability and punishment to better approximate justice, it necessarily stops short of mercy. Because equity aims at justice, it will not stop "short of what might have been deservedly imposed."[75] Because it disciplines discretion according to authoritative standards of justice, it will not systematically produce sentencing outcomes less harsh than those currently imposed. In short, equity will not satisfy those who believe that, at least in the current environment, leniency is more urgent than equal justice under law.

CONCLUSION

Equitable discretion is not a panacea for all that ails the criminal justice system. Although it can refine and tailor the law's application, equity is ultimately only as good as the conception of justice it serves. But the case for equity does not depend on the view that our system of criminal justice, vastly improved since the time of Seneca, is at last free from all defects. It is precisely the persistent limitations of the institutions of criminal justice that require the mechanisms of discretion and good judgment, as well as the possibility of reform. Where justice itself is fundamentally misconceived, the fitting response is not a plea for charity, but the full-throated roar of moral indignation.

Merciful discretion is not a tenable strategy in a polity committed to the values of justice, equality, and the rule of law. The resort to mercy in the criminal justice process not only undermines these values through discrete acts of unconstrained discretion; more destructive from the standpoint of justice is the posture of mercy that casts offenders as supplicants, denying them the firm footing and dignity of a claim of right. We need not begrudge the beggar, but neither, in a decent society, should that be his best hope for relief.

The advocates of broad mercy counter that the "one-way ratchet" of criminal justice policy that produces ever-harsher punishment is a "durable feature of the criminal justice landscape for the foreseeable future."[76] Recent (and historical) trends in criminal justice suggest that the concern, while valid, is almost certainly overstated.[77] But mercy *is* a one-way ratchet, operating only as a mechanism of mitigation and leniency. The call for prudential mercy assumes that we know—that discretionary decision makers can be confident—that our criminal justice policies are wrong and excessively harsh. Because such confidence is rarely warranted, we might better place our faith in equity, committing not to leniency but to justice.

In fact, at least some of what is sought in the name of mercy actually sounds in equity, "the 'particularized justice' that is necessary because '[t]he drafters of legal rules cannot anticipate and take account of every case where a defendant's conduct is "unlawful" but not blameworthy.'"[78] Given the close historical connection between equity and mercy, this convergence is unsurprising. The virtue of mercy is a trait of character, a certain stance that allows "a disposition for equitable treatment to be realized."[79] Rooted in the concept of *epieikeia*, both equity and mercy require sensitive attention to the particulars of individual cases. Equity's distinctive virtue is fidelity to justice and the rule of law.

NOTES

1. Portia defends the exercise of mercy:

The quality of mercy is not strain'd,
It droppeth as the gentle rain from heaven
Upon the place beneath: it is twice blest;
It blesseth him that gives and him that takes:
'Tis mightiest in the mightiest: it becomes
The throned monarch better than his crown;
His sceptre shows the force of temporal power,
The attribute to awe and majesty,
Wherein doth sit the dread and fear of kings;
But mercy is above this scepter'd sway;
It is enthroned in the hearts of kings,
It is an attribute to God himself;
And earthly power doth then show likest God's
When mercy seasons justice.

WILLIAM SHAKESPEARE, THE MERCHANT OF VENICE, act 4, sc.1.

2. LUCIUS ANNAEUS SENECA, *De Ira (On Anger)*, *in* 1 SENECA: MORAL ESSAYS 301 (John W. Basmore trans., Jeffrey Henderson ed., 1928) ("Marcus Maruius . . . had his ankles broken, his eyes gouged out, his tongue and hands cut off, and little by little and limb by limb [Roman dictator] Sulla tore him to pieces").

3. WILLIAM BLACKSTONE, 4 COMMENTARIES ON THE LAWS OF ENGLAND: A FACSIMILE OF THE FIRST EDITION OF 1765–1769, at 397–402 (University of Chicago Press, 1979), http://press-pubs.uchicago.edu/founders/documents/a2_2_1s17.html.

4. THE FEDERALIST NO. 74 (Alexander Hamilton).

5. H.L.A. HART, PUNISHMENT AND RESPONSIBILITY: ESSAYS IN THE PHILOSOPHY OF LAW 5 (1968).

6. ARISTOTLE, THE NICHOMACHEAN ETHICS 200 (J.A.K. Thomson trans., Penguin Classics, 1955).

7. *Id.* at 199–200.

8. Carol S. Steiker, *Criminalization and the Criminal Process: Prudential Mercy as a Limit on Penal Sanctions in an Era of Mass Incarceration*, *in* THE BOUNDARIES OF THE CRIMINAL LAW 27, 49–52 (R.A. Duff et al. eds., 2010).

9. Andrew Brien, *Mercy Within Legal Justice*, 24 SOC. THEORY & PRAC. 83, 106–7 n. 1 (1998).

10. Martha C. Nussbaum, *Equity and Mercy*, *in* Punishment and Rehabilitation 212, 214 (Jeffrie G. Murphy ed., 3d ed. 1995).
11. Brien, *supra* note 9, at 95.
12. *Id.* at 85.
13. *Id.*
14. R.A. Duff, *Mercy*, *in* The Oxford Handbook of Philosophy of Criminal Law 470 (John Deigh & David Dolinko eds., 2011).
15. John Tasioulas, *Mercy*, 103 Proc. Aristotelian Soc'y 101, 104 (2003).
16. Indeed, traditional mercy is paradigmatically at once both personal and institutional, reflecting the "king's two bodies." Ernst H. Kantorowicz, The King's Two Bodies (1957). According to the European conception of monarchy in the Middle Ages—derived from the model of Christ's earthly and divine forms—the king was understood simultaneously as a flesh-and-blood person and an embodiment of the polity. *Id.* at 198.
17. Jeffrie G. Murphy, *Mercy and Legal Justice*, *in* Jeffrie G. Murphy & Jean Hampton, Forgiveness and Mercy 162, 175 (1988).
18. *Id.* In fact, despite Portia's eloquence, Shylock is unmoved by her plea for mercy and remits the debt only when he is threatened with dire legal sanctions.
19. My limited claim for this purpose is that punishment is widely acknowledged to be a retributive practice, not that retribution is accepted as the *justification* for punishment. *See* Hugo Adam Bedau, *Punishment*, *in* Stanford Encyclopedia of Philosophy (Edward N. Zalta ed., 2010), http://plato.stanford.edu/entries/punishment/.
20. Seneca, *supra* note 2, at 435.
21. Murphy, *supra* note 17, at 169.
22. As Duff observes, mercy also poses challenges for consequentialist accounts of punishment. Duff, *supra* note 14, at 471.
23. R.A. Duff, Punishment, Communication, and Community 132 (2001). *E.g.*, Tasioulas, *supra* note 15, at 115; Jean Hampton, *The Retributive Idea*, *in* Forgiveness and Mercy, *supra* note 17, at 134.
24. R.A. Duff, *The Intrusion of Mercy*, 4 Ohio St. J. Crim. L. 362 (2007). Duff elsewhere notes that such cases "must be unusual, if the criminal law is to be possible." Duff, *supra* note 14, at 480.
25. Duff, *The Intrusion of Mercy*, *supra* note 24, at 368.
26. "I take it to be clear . . . that institutional acts of mercy—at the prosecutorial, judicial, or gubernatorial level—are morally (and therefore legally) indefensible, at least on grounds consistent with a retributive theory of punishment." Heidi M. Hurd, *The Morality of Mercy*, 4 Ohio St. J. Crim. L. 398 (2007).
27. *Id.* at 421.
28. *Id.* at 420.
29. Stefan Gosepath, *Equality*, *in* Stanford Encyclopedia of Philosophy (Edward N. Zalta ed., 2007) ("[W]hat is here at stake is a moral principle of justice, basically corresponding with acknowledgment of the impartial and universalizable nature of moral judgments"), http://plato.stanford.edu/archives/spr2011/entries/equality/.
30. Murphy, *supra* note 17, at 181. *See also* Duff, *The Intrusion of Mercy*, *supra* note 24, at 365 ("[M]ercy discriminates between offenders whose penal desert is relevantly similar"); Dan Markel, *Against Mercy*, 88 Minn. L. Rev. 1421, 1455–56 (2004) ("If everyone is entitled to the same package of liberties safeguarded by political and legal institutions, it is hard to see how granting mercy to some offenders but not to others effectuates this ideal"), http://papers.ssrn.com/sol3/Delivery.cfm/SSRN_ID553641_code342089.pdf?abstractid=392880&mirid=1.
31. Steiker, *supra* note 8, at 49. For similar claims, see Nussbaum, *supra* note 10, at 228–29, 248; Tasioulas, *supra* note 15, at 115, 119.
32. Steiker, *supra* note 8, at 50.
33. *Id.* at 51.
34. *Id.* at 52.
35. *Id.* Barkow, in contrast, is agnostic about the grounds for discretionary actors to exercise mercy. Rachel E. Barkow, *The Ascent of the Administrative State and the Demise of Mercy*, 121

HARV. L. REV. 1332, 1333 n. 5 (2008), http://harvardlawreview.org/2008/03/the-ascent-of-the-administrative-state-and-the-demise-of-mercy/.

36. Barkow, *supra* note 35, at 1335.

37. Carol S. Steiker, *Tempering or Tampering? Mercy and the Administration of Criminal Justice*, *in* FORGIVENESS, MERCY, AND CLEMENCY 19 (Austin Sarat & Nasser Hussain eds., 2007). Barkow makes a similar observation. Barkow, *supra* note 35, at 1335.

38. Steiker, *supra* note 8, at 56.

39. Barkow, *supra* note 35, at 1365. Elsewhere Barkow suggests that mercy is needed now even more than in the eighteenth century when Alexander Hamilton defended the importance of the pardon power. This is an odd claim since in Hamilton's day, virtually every felony was punishable by death. James R. Acker & Charles S. Lanier, *May God—or the Governor—Have Mercy: Executive Clemency and Executions in Modern Death Penalty Systems*, 38 CRIM. L. BULL. 200, 206 (2000), http://www.deathpenaltyinfo.org/documents/AckerClemency.pdf.

40. Steiker, *supra* note 8, at 57. Barkow expresses a similar hope. Barkow, *supra* note 35, at 1360.

41. Steiker, *supra* note 8, at 51.

42. *Id.* at 52.

43. JEFFRIE G. MURPHY, PUNISHMENT AND THE MORAL EMOTIONS: ESSAYS IN LAW, MORALITY, AND RELIGION 42 (2012).

44. Barkow praises executive clemency and jury nullification because they operate "outside the law." Barkow, *supra* note 35, at 1363–64. Similarly, Steiker celebrates discretionary mercy as a way to "subvert" the regime of criminal justice. Steiker, *supra* note 8, at 51. Finally, Austin Sarat links mercy with clemency, which he deems an "essentially lawless process." Austin Sarat, *Mercy, Clemency, and Capital Punishment: Two Accounts*, 3 OHIO ST. J. CRIM. L. 273, 275 (2005), http://moritzlaw.osu.edu/osjcl/Articles/Volume3_1/Commentary/Sarat_3-1.pdf.

45. Nussbaum, *supra* note 10, at 218. Nussbaum also highlights the indifference to individual culpability in the ancient world. In cases where the original offender is dead, "a substitute target must be found, usually some member of the offender's family." *Id.*

46. BLACKSTONE, *supra* note 3.

47. *Id.*

48. THE FEDERALIST NO. 74 (Alexander Hamilton). Note that Hamilton and Blackstone emphasized, above all other considerations, the political advantages of a "well-timed offer of pardon." *Id.* According to Blackstone, regular pardons from the king, "coming immediately from his own hand, endear the sovereign to his subjects, and contribute more than any thing to root in their hearts that filial affection, and personal loyalty, which are the sure establishment of a prince." BLACKSTONE, *supra* note 3.

49. "What identifies an action as 'equitable' is its compliance with some comprehensive standard of justice. . . ." Brien, *supra* note 9, at 95.

50. This account is adapted from a discussion of Dworkin in a previous work. Mary Sigler, *Contradiction, Coherence, and Guided Discretion in the Supreme Court's Capital Sentencing Jurisprudence*," 40 AM. CRIM. L. REV. 1151, 1172–75 (2003).

51. RONALD DWORKIN, TAKING RIGHTS SERIOUSLY 31 (1978). Dworkin's insight echoes an opinion by Justice William Brennan. McGautha v. California, 402 U.S. 103, 285 (1971) (Brennan, J., dissenting) ("[D]iscretion, to be worthy of the name, is not unchanneled judgment; it is judgment guided by reason and kept within bounds").

52. Weak discretion in Dworkin's second sense refers to a decision maker with final, unreviewable authority. DWORKIN, *supra* note 51, at 32. This accurately describes the circumstances of decision for most discretionary actors in the criminal justice system—including jurors with the power to nullify and executives with the power to pardon—but it does not inform a normative account of how that power should be exercised.

53. *Id.*

54. *Id.*

55. *Id.*

56. *Id.*

57. *Id.*

58. ARISTOTLE, *supra* note 6, at 199.

59. Brien, *supra* note 9, at 91. Note that a sympathetic stance means an openness to particularity, not (necessarily) an inclination to leniency. Aristotle: "Sympathetic judgement is a correct judgement that decides what is equitable; a correct judgement being one that arrives at the truth." ARISTOTLE, *supra* note 6, at 219.

60. ARISTOTLE, *supra* note 6, at 199.

61. Prudential mercy, a sort of hybrid, is harder to categorize. To the extent that it is intended to achieve justice, it is better conceptualized as a form of equity. To the extent that it is committed to leniency as such, it is more akin to traditional mercy. Steiker seems to embrace both. *See* Steiker, *supra* note 8, at 51: "Under such a prudential account, mercy neither competes with justice, nor tempers it . . . rather, it prevents us from doing *injustice* in the name of justice." *See also id.* at 50 ("[E]xercises of 'merciful' discretion involve leniency based on compassionate concern for the offender").

62. SENECA, *supra* note 2, at 445.

63. *Id.* at 435.

64. Brien, *supra* note 9, at 94.

65. Steiker, *supra* note 8, at 54.

66. *Id.* at 50.

67. Barkow, *supra* note 35, at 1363.

68. Of course the jury's discretion is also weak in Dworkin's second sense—practically unreviewable.

69. Sparf v. United States, 156 U.S. 51 (1895). In *Sparf*, the Supreme Court declined to require that jurors be informed of their power to nullify, emphasizing that nullification threatens the rule of law: "Public and private safety alike would be in peril if the principle be established that juries in criminal cases may, of right, disregard the law as expounded to them by the court, and become a law unto themselves. *Id.* at 101. *See also* United States v. Thomas, 116 F. 3d. 606, 614 (2d Cir. 1997) ("Nullification is, by definition, a violation of a juror's oath to apply the law as instructed by the court—in the words of the standard oath administered to jurors in the federal courts, to 'render a true verdict according to the law and the evidence.'" (quoting FEDERAL JUDICIAL CENTER, BENCHBOOK FOR U.S. DISTRICT COURT JUDGES 225 [4th ed. 1996]).

70. DWORKIN, *supra* note 51, at 33.

71. Gustav Neibuhr, *Governor Grants Pope's Plea for Life of a Missouri Man*, N.Y. TIMES, Jan. 9, 1999, at A1 (quoting Carnahan), http://www.nytimes.com/1999/01/29/us/governor-grants-pope-s-plea-for-life-of-a-missouri-inmate.html.

72. The Fugitive Slave Act of 1850 generated some of the most high-profile instances of jury nullification in the United States, as many Northern juries refused to convict individuals charged with aiding the escape of Southern slaves. An example of a "conscientious" governor is Tony Anaya of New Mexico, who commuted the sentences of everyone on death row during his final year in office because he believed capital punishment to be "inhumane, immoral, and anti-God." Robert Reinhold, *Outgoing Governor in New Mexico Bars the Execution of 5*, N.Y. TIMES, Nov. 27, 1986, at A1, http://www.nytimes.com/1986/11/27/us/outgoing-governor-in-new-mexico-bars-the-execution-of-5.html. Of course, Anaya's action defied a campaign promise he had made to stay, rather than commute, all death sentences. James Coates, *A Governor's Fit of Conscience over an Unconscionable Crime*, CHI. TRIB., Dec. 7, 1986, at 3, http://articles.chicagotribune.com/1986-12-07/news/8604010437_1_noel-johnson-toney-anaya-garrey-carruthers.

73. KIMBERLEY BROWNLEE, CONSCIENCE AND CONVICTION: THE CASE FOR CIVIL DISOBEDIENCE 1 (2012).

74. Hurd, *supra* note 26, at 400.

75. SENECA, *supra* note 2, at 435.

76. Steiker, *supra* note 8, at 30, 35. *See also* Barkow, *supra* note 35, at 1359.

77. Erik Eckholm, *In a Safer Age, U.S. Rethinks Its "Tough on Crime" System*," N.Y. TIMES, Jan. 13, 2015, at A1 (describing bipartisan efforts to achieve cuts in federal sentencing), http://www.nytimes.com/2015/01/14/us/with-crime-down-us-faces-legacy-of-a-violent-age-.html?_r=0; Editorial, *Strong Steps on Sentencing Reform*, N.Y. TIMES, July. 21, 2014, at A20 ("In 2013 alone, 35 states passed at least 85 reform-minded bills that created community-based

alternatives to prison, helped inmates re-enter society, and increased the use of data to help judge a person's risk of re-offending, according to the Vera Institute of Justice"), http://www.nytimes.com/2014/07/22/opinion/Strong-Steps-on-Sentencing-Reform.html; E. J. Hurst, II, *Federal Sentencing and Prison Reform now Bipartisan Issues*, THE HILL, Aug. 13, 2014 (noting that younger Republicans "are working with Capitol Hill Democrats to shorten federal sentences, reduce populations in overcrowded prisons and even to count (and reconsider) the thousands of federal crimes on the books"), http://thehill.com/blogs/pundits-blog/crime/214998-federal-sentencing-and-prison-reform-now-bipartisan-issues.

78. Barkow, *supra* note 35, at 1360. Barkow also notes that "[j]urors and the executive . . . bring valuable perspective and individualization that are otherwise lacking from application of the criminal law." *Id.* at 1363. Similarly, according to Steiker, prudential "mercy neither competes with justice nor tempers it . . . rather it prevents us from doing injustice in the name of justice." Steiker, *supra* note 8, at 51.

79. Brien, *supra* note 9, at 95.

Chapter Thirteen

Collateral Restrictions

Zachary Hoskins

When a person is convicted of a criminal offense, what follows from this? Most obviously, the person is subject to some formal sanction: incarceration, probation, community service, a fine, etc. But a formal sentence is not the only burdensome legal consequence of a criminal conviction. Convicted offenders are subject to a host of other legal burdens, as well. Many U.S. states as well as many other countries make criminal records widely accessible to potential employers, landlords, or the public generally.[1] In the United States, various states restrict certain offenders' access to a range of jobs, including teacher, chiropractor, accountant, police officer, architect, and beautician; other jurisdictions, such as England and Wales, have similar (albeit generally less extensive) employment bans.[2] Federal U.S. law permits, and in some cases requires, public housing authorities to deny housing to certain classes of offenders.[3] Sex offenders, in particular, are often denied housing near parks, schools, or other areas where children are frequently present.[4] Federal U.S. law imposes a lifetime ban on welfare benefits for people with felony drug convictions (some states have opted out of the law; many others have not).[5] And many countries, as well as many U.S. states, impose voting bans of varying lengths on people with criminal convictions.[6] There are also restrictions on drivers' licenses, adoption of children, travel, and many other goods.

There are other, informal consequences of a legal conviction: social stigma, family tensions, and so on. My focus in this chapter, however, is on the formal legal restrictions imposed by the state. As these examples suggest, although such measures can be found in various legal systems, they are more prevalent and typically more severe in the United States. The measures constitute significant burdens for those subject to them; indeed, they are in many cases more burdensome than the formal sentence itself. And although they are typically consequences of a conviction, some follow even from arrests that did not lead to conviction.[7]

What should we make of these restrictions? Traditional legal practice typically treats them as civil measures, and thus as distinct from the criminal sanction, the punishment, itself. On this view, punishment is handed down by a sentencing judge for a particular defendant, whereas these other measures are created by legislative or regulatory bodies and imposed on entire classes of individuals. They often are referred to as *collateral* legal consequences of conviction, to distinguish them from conviction's *direct* consequences (the punishment).

A number of legal scholars and practitioners have challenged this view, however. Whatever we choose to call these restrictions, say the critics, they actually constitute additional forms of punishment. Jeremy Travis termed them "invisible punishment" to underscore that although they are not part of the formal sentencing process and have not traditionally figured prominently in debates about sentencing policies, they are punishment nonetheless.[8] U.S. Supreme Court Justice John Paul Stevens echoed this sentiment, writing, "In my opinion, a sanction that (1) is imposed on everyone who commits a criminal offense, (2) is not imposed on anyone else, and (3) severely impairs a person's liberty is punishment."[9] Many scholars and activists, perhaps motivated to make visible what they believe has for too long been invisible, refer to the various measures straightforwardly as "collateral punishment."[10]

This chapter examines whether so-called collateral restrictions should be treated as civil measures or as forms of punishment. The point is not to provide a taxonomy of existing restrictions as falling into one category or the other, but rather to examine which sorts of considerations are appropriate to making such determinations. In what follows, I first say a bit about what's at stake in whether we treat the restrictions as forms of punishment or civil measures. I then flesh out and critically assess two general approaches to thinking about the question: an approach that appeals to the practical implications of treating them one way or another, and an approach that looks to the functions of punishment and asks whether the various restrictions are punitive in their function. I argue that we should opt for the second approach. If we do, we'll find that traditional legal practice's blanket treatment of these restrictions as civil measures is untenable, but we should equally find problematic the view that all burdensome legal consequences of a criminal conviction constitute punishment. Instead, if we focus on the distinctive features of criminal punishment itself, then we should expect that whether restrictive legal measures constitute punishment will depend on the particular measure, its purpose(s) and social meaning. In the final section, I address various implications of this conclusion for legal practice and the philosophy of criminal law.

I. WHAT'S AT STAKE

How we think of collateral restrictions—as civil measures or as forms of criminal punishment—matters in at least two senses. First, if collateral restrictions are best understood as forms of punishment, then we should treat them as such: we should make these forms of "invisible punishment" visible by bringing them into the formal criminal process. If we did so, then this would mean that certain legal protections would attach to collateral restrictions that do not currently apply.[11] Because punishment has traditionally been regarded as such a serious exercise of state coercion, a number of legal safeguards exist to help protect the rights of those facing criminal prosecution and punishment: protection against double jeopardy, the right to be informed of the punishment that may follow from a guilty plea, and protection against ex post facto laws, among others. If we treat collateral restrictions as forms of punishment, then these safeguards would constrain their imposition as they now constrain the imposition of traditional forms of punishment.

One general implication, then, of treating collateral restrictions as forms of punishment is that they should be subject to the same sorts of legal protections that govern other impositions of punishment. This would also mean that current restrictions, insofar as they are not governed by these safeguards, would be unjustified.

But there is a second, normatively more fundamental sense in which it matters whether we treat these restrictions as punishment. Suppose that we did incorporate the various collateral restrictions formally into the criminal process, recognizing them as forms of punishment and attaching the same legal safeguards that govern the imposition of punishment generally. There would still be a question of whether restrictions on employment, housing, and so on, are justified as forms of punishment. Thus we would need to ask whether such restrictions are consistent with whatever aims are appropriate to punishment, and also consistent with whatever considerations we believe should constrain the pursuit of these aims. If these restrictions are forms of punishment, in other words, then the questions relevant to their justification will be the same as the questions we must ask about incarceration, community service, capital punishment, or other forms of punishment: Are these kinds of response to crime appropriate?

If, however, restrictions on employment, voting, housing, and so on are best treated not as forms of punishment but rather as civil measures, then we must instead ask what would justify these additional, nonpunitive exercises of coercive state power. Theorists of punishment have long debated whether and why punishment is justified. Despite persistent disagreement about the answers to these questions, most theorists have at least agreed that to justify punishing someone is to justify subjecting her to burdensome treatment (involuntary imprisonment, for example) that would typically be impermissible. Collateral restrictions are also burdensome (again, sometimes more burdensome than the formal sentence itself), but if they are not forms of punishment, then they cannot draw justification from whatever considerations ostensibly justify punishment. We would need to ask, then, what would justify the state in imposing these additional burdensome measures beyond the scope of punishment itself.

Given the distinct functions of the criminal and civil law, it should not be surprising if different normative considerations govern whether various collateral restrictions would be justified as forms of punishment or as civil measures. If this is so, then some sorts of restrictions might be justifiable as civil measures but not as forms of punishment, or vice versa. Also, some policies might be justifiable both as punishment and as civil measures, but for different reasons or in different circumstances.

Whether we treat collateral restrictions as forms of punishment or as civil measures thus has implications both for whether and why the restrictions are justified and for what sorts of legal protections attach to these measures. On what basis, then, should we determine how these restrictions are to be treated in practice? In what follows, I consider two candidate approaches.

II. PRACTICAL IMPLICATIONS

One way to think about whether to treat collateral restrictions as forms of punishment would be in terms of the practical implications of one approach or the other. In the United States, courts have pointed to the practical difficulties that would arise in attempting to inform defendants of the full range of restrictions to which they might be subject as the result of a guilty plea. As Michael Pinard explains:

> Some have asserted that it is simply too impractical for trial courts to first gather the relevant consequences attendant to each individual conviction, and then inform defendants of the consequences. The task is particularly burdensome given the expansive dockets that stifle criminal courts. It is made even more complicated by the fact that collateral consequences are not centralized, but rather are scattered throughout federal and state statutes, state and local regulatory codes, local rules, and local policies.[12]

We might see such practical considerations as constituting sufficient reasons to maintain the distinction between collateral restrictions and punishment—and thus reasons to maintain that defendants are entitled to be notified about the range of punishments to which they may be subject but not about collateral restrictions they may face. Other courts have contended that treating collateral restrictions as among the direct consequences of conviction (i.e., as punishment) could lead scores of defendants to appeal their convictions on grounds that they pleaded guilty without being sufficiently informed of the consequences of the plea.[13] Each of these arguments points to certain supposedly undesirable consequences that would be promoted by treating collateral restrictions as forms of punishment; thus distinguishing collateral restrictions from punishment is instrumentally justified insofar as it allows us to avoid these bad consequences.

There is something troubling about this sort of approach. It seems to get things the wrong way around. That is, it begins with the prospect that treating collateral restrictions as punishment will create certain practical difficulties and takes this as a reason not to treat them as such. But if collateral restrictions do share the essential features of punishment, if they function as additional punitive measures, then the fact that treating them as punishment would create practical difficulties does not by itself constitute a compelling reason to treat them as something else. The potential difficulties in informing defendants considering guilty pleas might instead give society reason to impose fewer collateral restrictions, or make them easier to identify, so that defense attorneys would have a reasonable chance of advising their clients. Similarly, the prospect that people who previously pleaded guilty might challenge their convictions if we began to treat collateral restrictions as punishment is less worrisome if we believe that these restrictions do function as additional punishment. If so, then rather than being troubled by the prospect of numerous appeals, we might think this is precisely what should happen: These defendants offered guilty pleas without being properly informed about the full range of punishment they might face, and so they are justified in appealing their convictions.

Attempting to settle whether collateral restrictions should be treated as forms of punishment by appealing solely or primarily to certain practical consequences is thus unsatisfying; it appeals to the wrong sort of reasons. (It would be like making decisions about the moral or legal status of nonhuman animals on the basis of what implications this would have for our diets.) What we need to ask, instead, is whether restrictions on employment, voting, and so on do function as additional forms of punishment. What implications there are for legal practice will then depend on how we answer this question, not the other way around. In the next sections, I consider whether collateral restrictions in fact constitute forms of punishment.

Before moving to the next section, though, it's worth noting that those who endorse treating collateral restrictions as punishment might also be motivated by practical considerations. For them, the motivating consideration might be that if the various measures were brought under the umbrella of criminal law as forms of punishment, then individuals potentially subject to these measures would be afforded the sorts of protections we discussed before: rights to make an informed plea, against double jeopardy, against ex post facto laws. Here again, the thought is that treating collateral restrictions as punishment is justified insofar as doing so has desirable practical effects: namely, that those subject to collateral restrictions enjoy the various protections. As before, this approach seems to get things the wrong way around. It elides a host of more fundamental questions: What are the distinctive features of punishment in virtue of which we believe special protections are warranted? Do collateral restrictions share these features? In my view, we do better to begin with these sorts of questions; once we sort out whether collateral restrictions actually constitute forms of punishment, then we can address the various implications for legal practice.

III. DO COLLATERAL RESTRICTIONS FUNCTION AS PUNISHMENT?

Suppose, then, that we focus on the question of whether collateral restrictions in fact function as forms of punishment. To sort out the answer, we need an understanding of punishment itself: What are its distinctive features? And do collateral restrictions share these features?

Legal and moral theorists are not univocal in their definitions of punishment. As a starting point, however, we can consider the well-known account offered by H. L. A. Hart. Building on the work of Antony Flew and Stanley Benn, Hart writes that the central case of punishment consists of five conditions:

a. It must involve pain or other consequences normally considered unpleasant.
b. It must be for an offense against legal rules.
c. It must be of an actual or supposed offender for his offense.
d. It must be intentionally administered by human beings other than the offender.
e. It must be imposed and administered by an authority constituted by a legal system against which the offense is committed.[14]

Some theorists have objected to one or more of the conditions set out in the Flew-Benn-Hart account of punishment. For instance, some have argued that (b) and (e) are too limiting. Punishment can happen outside of legal contexts: Parents punish children, friends may punish friends, vigilantes might even be said to punish those who escape legal punishment. Considering these extra-legal instances of punishment might help to shed light on the justification of punishment in the legal context.[15] Our central question, however, is whether collateral restrictions are forms of legal punishment. Those on both sides of this debate presumably agree that these measures are imposed by legal authorities as a consequence of legal violations.

Collateral restrictions appear to meet the other conditions, as well: They are undeniably unpleasant, or burdensome. They are imposed on actual or supposed offenders. And they are intentionally administered by people other than the offenders. Thus the Flew-Benn-Hart account appears to lend some support to the view that collateral restrictions are in fact forms of punishment.

Notice, though, that conditions (b) and (c) both tell us that punishment is *for* an offense. We sentence a man to prison *for* murdering his brother, or to a term of probation *for* shoplifting. The punishment is a response to the offense. Some collateral restrictions, although we may say they are triggered by an offense or are a consequence of an offense, may not seem to be for the offense. In particular, for measures intended as purely preventive—laws that prohibit child sex offenders from living near schools or parks, for example—the prior offense might be argued to function only as evidence that the offender is dangerous; the offense itself may not be seen as the reason for the restriction. So there may be some collateral restrictions that do not meet all of the Flew-Benn-Hart conditions for punishment.

In addition to this, the Flew-Hart-Benn account appears incomplete in two key respects: First, punishment is not merely a burdensome response to a supposed offense—it is characteristic of punishment that it is *intended* to be burdensome. Other state policies may inflict burdens on people. Paying taxes is, by many accounts, a burden. Taxation isn't intended to be burdensome, however; the point of taxation is to generate revenue to pay for public goods. Although it is a foreseeable consequence of maintaining a taxation scheme that many citizens will regard it as a burden, the scheme is not intended to be burdensome. Rather, burdensomeness is a side effect; it is incidental to the goal of taxation. In other words, a tax scheme could still do its job even if no one subject to it regarded it as a burden.

Punishment is different. If people subject (or potentially subject) to punishment did not regard it as a burden, then punishment would not be doing its job: For those who contend that the aim of punishment is to deter potential offenders, the burdensomeness of punishment is an essential feature of the practice—if it weren't burdensome, it would be ineffective as a deterrent. Similarly, on the retributivist view that punishment inflicts deserved suffering on wrongdoers, it is obviously essential that punishment be burdensome. Other accounts characterize punishment as a deserved expression of societal condemnation, an attempt to morally educate offenders, a means of removing an offender's unfair advantage, or something else. On any of these accounts, the burdensomeness of punishment is not merely incidental to the goal to be achieved; it is not a mere side effect. Punishment is intended to be burdensome.

Note that punishment's burdens aren't *merely* intended; they are intended in the service of some supposedly justifiable end. Prison terms, fines, community service, or other forms of punishment are intended to be unpleasant because they thereby help to maintain a credible deterrent threat, or inflict the suffering offenders deserve, or express society's condemnation of the wrongdoing, etc. If the state imposed intentionally harsh measures on offenders simply for the sake of imposing harsh measures—that is, with no reference to their being deserved, or useful to some valuable end—then such measures would not constitute punishment. Rather, they would merely be gratuitous state inflictions of suffering.[16]

In addition, at least since the publication of Joel Feinberg's seminal article "The Expressive Function of Punishment," it has widely been held to be a distinctive feature of punishment that it serves to express society's *condemnation* of a criminal for her wrongdoing.[17] Some accounts take this condemnatory element to play a crucial role in the justification of punishment;[18] others disagree, but it is generally accepted that one of punishment's distinctive features is that it expresses condemnation. This condemnatory element is not central, for example, to compensation in tort law. Thus, if a defendant in a civil suit is required to pay compensatory damages, the aim of the decision, at least in principle, is not to censure the defendant but to see that those harmed by the defendant's actions, negligence, etc., are compensated.[19]

Not everyone accepts that burdens, to count as punishment, must be intended to be burdensome and must express societal condemnation. Michael Cholbi, for example, defends something closer to the Flew-Benn-Hart account. For Cholbi, punishment is "*any deprivation, suffering, or constraint of liberty imposed on criminal offenders by the state or judicial authority as a direct legal consequence of those offenders' unlawful behavior*."[20] Two things are worth noting about this definition: First, it is in one sense even friendlier than the Flew-Benn-Hart account to those who would classify all collateral restrictions as punishment, as instead of stating that punishment is *for* an offense—and thus possibly excluding purely preventive measures where the offense is taken merely as evidence of dangerousness—Cholbi's definition states only that punishment is "a direct legal consequence" of the offense. Second, and more important for present purposes, Cholbi's definition (like the Flew-Benn-Hart account) omits any requirement that punishment be condemnatory or intended as burdensome.

Cholbi counts it as one of the virtues of this definition that various collateral restrictions would constitute punishment: "On this definition, revocation of driver's licenses . . . removal of children from the custody of criminally negligent parents, and the disenfranchisement of felons all count as punishments."[21] Given that our central question is whether collateral restrictions constitute punishment, however, it would be question-begging to count as a point in favor of Cholbi's preferred definition of punishment the fact that it implies that various collateral restrictions are forms of punishment.[22] Instead, we should ask whether his definition seems to get the right answer in other cases, or whether it is susceptible to counterexamples.

As Cholbi points out, his definition captures uncontroversial examples of punishment, such as incarceration, fines, and execution.[23] Of course, an account of punishment as a condemnatory and intentionally burdensome response to an offense also captures these cases, so this is not a point in favor of his definition. He also points out that his definition can account for why legal fees or the loss of a job due to incarceration are not punishment: they are not direct legal consequences of unlawful behavior.[24] But again, a condemnatory, intended burdens account can also explain these cases: neither legal fees nor the loss of a job when one is imprisoned are condemnatory, intended burdens imposed by a legal authority in response to a crime.

Cholbi's definition doesn't fare as well in other cases. Consider this example: Peg steals a car. She is later apprehended, and the legal authorities take the car away from her and return it to the rightful owner. If this is as far as things go, it seems we'd be hard pressed to say that Peg was punished for her crime. Notice, though, that the legal authorities have imposed a deprivation on Peg as a direct legal consequence of her unlawful behavior. We may agree that the authorities are depriving Peg of something to which she is not entitled, but this is irrelevant to Cholbi's definition, as it counts as punishment *any* deprivation, suffering, or constraint of liberty imposed on offenders by legal authorities as a direct legal consequence of their crime. Thus on Cholbi's definition, it appears that Peg is thereby punished when authorities take the car.

In my view, however, confiscating the car would not count as punishment insofar as, although it may be burdensome to Peg to lose the car, the confiscation is not an intentionally burdensome, condemnatory response to her offense. Rather, the intent is simply to return the car to its rightful owner; whether this is burdensome to Peg is irrelevant. Similarly, that being required to return the car expresses no condemnation is evident when we consider that Peg would be required to return it even if she acquired it with no knowledge that it was stolen, and so was not blameworthy. Thus in the case where she has intentionally stolen the car, if legal authorities simply return it to the owner without imposing some further burden (incarceration, fines, probation), then we could object that society had not conveyed its condemnation of Peg's wrongdoing.

Consider another case: Steve suffers from a sexually transmitted disease. He is found guilty of intentionally trying to infect numerous sexual partners with the disease. Suppose that as a consequence of being found guilty, Steve is required by legal authorities to contact his previous sexual partners to inform them that they have been exposed to the disease. If we assume (plausibly) that Steve finds being required to contact his past partners extremely unpleasant, then, on Cholbi's definition, it appears that this constitutes punishing Steve.

But here again, this seems to be the wrong answer. If this were the only legal response to Steve's wrongdoing, then we could reasonably object that he was not punished for his offense. This is because, although being made to contact his past sexual partners might be burdensome for Steve, it is not intended to be burdensome; the intention is simply to ensure that people possibly infected with a disease are informed of this fact. Steve's behavior creates a public health risk, and thus he might be legally required to inform his previous partners even if he had been unaware at the time (and had no reason to believe) that he was infected—that is, even if his previous behavior did not merit condemnation. So, in the case where Steve did intentionally infect his partners, it seems that merely requiring him to inform them does not constitute punishment. Again, Cholbi's preferred definition apparently gets the wrong answer.

Cases such as Peg's and Steve's indicate that not every burdensome measure imposed by legal authorities on a convicted offender as a direct legal consequence of her offense thereby constitutes punishment. To count as punishment, the measure must be a condemnatory, intentionally burdensome response to the offense.

IV. ASSESSING COLLATERAL RESTRICTIONS

Returning, then, to our central question, do collateral restrictions constitute forms of punishment? This typically will depend on whether they are intended to be burdensome and whether they function to express societal condemnation of the offender's wrongdoing. (Notice that if a measure expresses condemnation of an offense, this implies that the measure is a response to the crime, not merely a consequence of it.) Determining whether some restriction is intended to be burdensome and whether it expresses condemnation is no small task. How should we begin to assess whether various restrictions meet these conditions?

First consider the intentionality requirement: Punishment is intended to be burdensome—and not just intended as a gratuitous infliction of a burden, but intended as burdensome in the service of some supposedly justifiable end. One question to ask, then, in considering some given legal restriction, is what function, if any, its burdensomeness serves. Put differently, could the restriction do its job even if it weren't generally regarded as burdensome, or is its burdensomeness the means by which it serves its purpose? If the burdensomeness of the measure is the means by which it serves its intended purpose, then this is an indication that the burdensomeness is intended, too. Conversely, if the burdensomeness of some restriction is not the means by which it does its job—if it could, in principle, do its job even if it weren't burdensome—then this is an indication that the measure is either (a) foreseeably but not intentionally burdensome, as when Steve is required to inform his past partners about his sexually transmitted disease, or (b) intended to be burdensome, but not in the service of any ostensibly justifiable end (thus, an infliction of gratuitous suffering by the state).

To sort out whether a given restriction could do its job even if it weren't burdensome, we need to have an idea of what purpose it serves. As we've seen, if the point of some measure is to help reduce crime by deterring potential offenders, or to inflict deserved suffering, or effectively to express societal condemnation, then burdensomeness is arguably an essential feature.[25] Other purposes, however, might be served by measures that are merely foreseeably burdensome, rather than intentionally so. For example, the state might impose policies requiring offenders to compensate their victims for the harms they caused.[26] Although it is likely that such policies often would be burdensome to offenders, the burdensomeness would not be essential to the policy. Rather, the point would be (as in tort law) to repair the harms done to the victim. Thus even if compensating victims typically did not constitute a burden for offenders, this would not undermine whether the compulsory compensation policies effectively did their job. This indicates that although such policies would be foreseeably burdensome to those subject to them, they would not be intentionally so.

As another example, state-mandated employment restrictions for certain classes of offenders are often defended (albeit controversially) on grounds that these policies help to ensure public safety by keeping offenders out of jobs where they might constitute a threat to their colleagues, patrons, or others. Such restrictions are undoubtedly burdensome for most individuals subject to them, but arguably they are not intentionally burdensome. If, counterfactually, offenders did not regard such restrictions as burdensome, this would not in itself undermine whatever effectiveness they have as community protection measures.

Not all measures aimed at reducing crime can be regarded as merely foreseeably rather than intentionally burdensome. In particular, deterrent measures also aim to reduce crime, but they do so by providing a compelling disincentive to potential offenders. Here, the burdensomeness is intended; deterrent measures cannot deter if potential offenders don't regard them as unpleasant. But restrictions that aim to keep potentially dangerous offenders away from vulnerable populations attempt to reduce crime not by deterrence but by incapacitation. Such restrictions are incapacitative in that they bar offenders from being in certain situations in which they might harm others. The effectiveness of such measures in reducing crime is not dependent on their being a burden to those subject to them. In this respect, then, collateral restrictions that aim to reduce crime through deterrence look more like punishment than do those that aim to reduce crime through incapacitation.

One might object that this analysis implies that incapacitation, one of the most widely cited aims of punishment, is not in fact a punitive aim. I accept this implication. In my view, locking people in prison with the sole aim of incapacitating them (rather than to deter, exact retribution, communicate censure, etc.) does not constitute punishing them. If this seems implausible, consider that the state could, in theory, incapacitate people effectively even if the conditions of confinement were so luxurious that neither offenders nor members of the public generally viewed being locked up as burdensome. Such confinement would not constitute punishment (as we've seen, punishment is burdensome), which indicates that incapacitation is not itself a punitive aim. In practice, however, central rationales for incarcerating offenders typically include not only considerations of incapacitation but also deterrence, retribution, censure, reform, and so on, for which the effectiveness of incarceration depends on its being burdensome. Thus incarceration, at least in its standard cases, is properly regarded as punishment even if one of its frequently cited aims is nonpunitive.

Similarly, particular collateral restrictions may have more than one purpose. They may aim, for example, both to incapacitate supposedly dangerous individuals and also to deter potential offenders. In cases such as this, where one purpose of a restriction requires that it be burdensome but the other purpose does not, should we regard the whole policy itself as intentionally burdensome? In my view, as long as at least one of the purposes of a restriction requires that it be burdensome, then we have good reason to count the restriction as meeting the "intentionally burdensome" condition.

What about the condemnatory aspect of punishment? How should we sort out whether the various collateral restrictions express condemnation? Here, I think, things get especially difficult. We might ask whether lawmakers who create the various restrictions intend them to express condemnation. But, of course, what one intends to express and what one actually expresses are not always the same thing. Alternatively, we might ask whether those subject to the restrictions take them to express condemnation. The message received by offenders may not be the same as the message intended by lawmakers—and, indeed, different offenders may interpret the restrictions differently.

Alternatively, maybe we should ask about the more general social meaning of the various restrictions. Legislators who create these restrictions, after all, are supposedly our representatives, acting in our name, and punishment, at least in principle, is typically thought to convey the condemnation of the political community generally. Thus, perhaps, in considering whether particular restrictions express condemnation, we should focus not on the intentions of the particular legislators who created them, or even on the interpretations of particular individuals subject to them, but rather to the restrictions' broader social meaning.

We might make some headway with the question of whether some restriction expresses condemnation by asking, of a given measure, what noncondemnatory purpose it might serve. Think again of Peg, the car thief. Peg is blameworthy for what she did. But even if, counterfactually, Peg were blameless—perhaps because she came into the possession of the car without knowing (and having no reason to believe) that it was stolen—the state would still have a plausible rationale for confiscating the car: namely, to return it to its rightful owner. Thus there is a clear noncondemnatory basis for the confiscation policy. The state would not, by contrast, have any plausible rationale for locking counterfactually blameless Peg in prison. Indeed, if after the state confiscated the car, it sentenced counterfactually blameless Peg to a prison term, she might complain that she had been wrongly condemned. If the state's purpose in confiscating the car is independent of Peg's blameworthiness, then this is at least some (albeit not decisive) indication that the policy is not condemnatory. In this respect, restrictions for which the purpose is tied to the subject's blameworthiness look like somewhat better candidates to be considered punishment. Restrictions for which the purpose is independent of the subject's blameworthiness look somewhat less likely to constitute punishment.

This analysis is admittedly too brief, and it raises many difficult questions: In particular, I acknowledge that the analysis hasn't provided anything like definitive guidance as to how we should determine in actual cases what purpose(s) some measure serves, whether it is intended to be burdensome, or what social meaning it carries. I don't have definitive answers to these questions. In the next section, though, I say a bit about why I don't believe this is a problem for my account.

V. PRINCIPLE AND PRACTICE

I have tried to defend a principled distinction between punishment and civil measures according to which punishment is intentionally burdensome and condemnatory. Other theorists have offered similar accounts. Some critics have argued, however, that attempts to carve out and maintain a distinction between criminal and civil measures, while perhaps laudable in principle, are doomed to fail in practice. Attempting to distinguish these neatly into categories of criminal and civil is not tenable. Many policies are both punitive and regulatory in their function and cannot be neatly separated. Furthermore, asking judges or other legal officials to determine, in practice, whether some hybrid policy is *primarily* criminal or civil will lead to unpredictable, inconsistent results.[27] Perhaps, then, in the interests of consistency, simplicity, and fairness, we should stop trying to sort burdensome legal measures into categories of criminal or civil and simply treat all of these measures as punishment.

I confess I don't find this line of objection particularly compelling. The law employs any number of in-principle distinctions that are often challenging to maintain in practice. For example, theorists develop accounts of what capacities defendants must have if they are to be held responsible for their crimes. In practice, however, determining who falls on which side of the relevant lines will typically be a difficult endeavor and may not generate entirely consistent results. As another example, it is widely accepted, among both punishment theorists and members of the public generally, that punishment should not be more severe than an offender deserves given the seriousness of the crime. Desert doesn't lend itself, however, to clear, definitive prescriptions in particular cases. We shouldn't conclude from either of these cases, however, that the principled lines (between those who may and may not be held responsible, or between deserved and excessive punishment), because they are difficult to maintain in practice, should be abandoned.

Similarly, it would be a mistake to conclude, because of the practical difficulty of differentiating between legal burdens that are condemnatory and intentionally burdensome and those that are not, that we should give up trying to make such determinations. The alternative, a sort of blanket classification strategy of all burdensome legal measures as one or the other, admittedly has some appeal, not least because it allows us to avoid thorny questions about intentions, purposes, social meaning, and so on. But this strategy buys simplicity at the cost of ignoring part of what is truly distinctive, and distinctively challenging to justify, about punishment as a social practice. As we have seen, it is not just that the state imposes burdens on certain individuals (although this is undoubtedly significant)—it is also that the state intends punishment to be burdensome, and that in punishing it thereby expresses society's condemnation of these individuals. These features are relevant to consideration of how to classify collateral restrictions, even if they do not in practice lend themselves to simple, precise determinations. Sometimes messiness is warranted.

VI. IMPLICATIONS

To conclude, I want to highlight some implications of the account developed here for legal practice as well as for the philosophy of criminal law. First, given that considerations of intentions, purposes, and social meanings are relevant to sorting out whether or not some restriction constitutes punishment, we shouldn't be surprised if some restrictive policies, in some contexts, do qualify as forms of punishment and others do not. This indicates that the traditional legal practice of treating essentially any measure that is not part of an offender's formal sentence as a civil measure is unjustified. Courts faced with making determinations in particular cases would do well to avoid facile reliance on legislative claims that the measures are intended as regulatory rather than punitive. Legislatures have clear interests in keeping collateral restrictions on the civil side of the divide, as this allows them to exercise more control over individuals' lives without having to worry about the range of due-process safeguards in place to protect criminal defendants.

By the same token, it would oversimplify things to conclude that collateral restrictions generally, insofar as they are legally imposed burdensome consequences of a conviction, are forms of punishment. Rather, what is needed from the courts in these cases is an exercise in practical reason. In judges' best estimation, are particular collateral restrictions burdensome to those subject to them? Are they intended to be burdensome? Is their burdensomeness essential to their purpose? Do they express societal condemnation of those subject to them? These are the sorts of questions that should ground the categorization of collateral restrictions as civil or criminal measures.

The prospect that not all collateral restrictions can plausibly be regarded as forms of punishment has implications for the philosophy of criminal law, as well. Philosophical discussions of criminal law traditionally have been dominated by the justification of punishment. Echoing the standard narrative, David Boonin describes "the problem of punishment" this way:

> Legal punishment involves treating those who break the law in ways that it would be wrong to treat those who do not. . . . How can the line between those who break such laws and those who do not be morally relevant in the way that the practice of punishment requires it to be?[28]

In recent decades, criminal law theorists have increasingly engaged with a broader range of philosophical questions: questions about what sorts of behaviors are properly criminalized, about criminal procedure, about criminal responsibility, about the authority and legitimacy of the state, and more. Still, the importance of these questions has often been characterized in terms of their relationship to punishment. We should worry about overcriminalization primarily because it produces too much punishment;[29] our conception of responsibility matters because we need to know whether offenders can be held responsible for their crimes through punishment; the sort of state authority with which we are primarily concerned in this context is the authority to impose punishment.[30]

The centrality of punishment in these inquiries is understandable. Punishment is, after all, the paradigmatic example of the exercise of coercive state power over citizens. But as we have seen, it is not the only exercise of such power. Given the proliferation of collateral restrictions in recent decades, and the likelihood that not all of these can plausibly be characterized as forms of punishment, criminal law theory's preoccupation with punishment appears too limited. Boonin's question—regarding what justifies the state in treating people with criminal convictions in ways that it would be wrong to treat those who haven't been convicted—is not merely a problem of punishment. It is a problem of state responses to a criminal conviction more generally. Indeed, given that in current legal practice collateral restrictions may attach even to arrests, we should really be asking what (if anything) justifies the state in treating people with *criminal records* in ways that would be wrong to treat those without such records. Given the enormous number of people who have criminal records (an estimated sixty-five million U.S. adults, for example, and roughly ten million people in the United Kingdom[31]), theorists concerned with the justification of state-sanctioned harsh treatment would do well to broaden their concern to consider the full range of legal restrictions that may accompany a criminal record, not just punishment itself.

NOTES

1. For U.S. criminal record policies, *see After Prison: Roadblocks to Reentry* (2009), 8, in Legal Action Center report (2009), http://www.lac.org/roadblocks-to-reentry/upload/lacreport/Roadblocks-to-Reentry--2009.pdf. For England and Wales, *see* Jessica Abrahams, *What Can't You Do with a Criminal Record?* PROSPECT (May 22, 2013), http://www.prospectmagazine.co.uk/features/criminal-record-chris-huhne-vicky-pryce-ched-evans.

2. For U.S. laws, see *National Inventory of the Collateral Consequences of Conviction* (NICCC), a project of the American Bar Association, http://www.abacollateralconsequences.org/. For a list of barring offenses in England and Wales, see *Factsheet 5A: Relevant Offenses England and Wales*, DISCLOSURE AND BARRING SERVICE, https://www.gov.uk/government/uploads/system/uploads/attachment_data/file/208203/dbs-factsheet-05a.pdf.

3. *See* 42 U.S.C. § 1437d (q)(1); 24 C.F.R. § 982.553(a)(2); and 42 U.S.C. § 13661 (c).

4. *See* Corey Rayburn Yung, *Banishment by a Thousand Laws: Residency Restrictions on Sex Offenders*, 85 WASH. U. L. REV. 101 (2007).

5. 21 U.S.C. § 862a (a).

6. For U.S. states' laws, see *State Felon Voting Laws*, PROCON.ORG, http://felonvoting.procon.org/view.resource.php?resourceID=000286; for other countries' laws, see, for example, Isobel White, *Prisoners' Voting Rights*, Standard Note SN/PC/01764, House of Commons Library (July 4, 2013), 47–57; Sauvé v. Canada (Chief Electoral Officer), (2002) 3 S.C.R. 519 (Can.); Roach v. Electoral Commissioner (2007), 233 C.L.R. 162.

7. As of 2009, thirty-eight U.S. states allowed employers and occupational licensing authorities to deny jobs or licenses to people with arrests that never led to a conviction. Similarly, public housing authorities in the United States are legally permitted to deny housing to applicants based on arrests. *See After Prison: Roadblocks to Reentry*, *supra* note 1.

8. Jeremy Travis, *Invisible Punishment: An Instrument of Social Exclusion*, *in* INVISIBLE PUNISHMENT: THE COLLATERAL CONSEQUENCES OF MASS IMPRISONMENT 15 (Marc Mauer & Meda Chesney-Lind eds., 2003).

9. Smith v. Doe, 538 U.S. 84, 113 (2003) (Stevens, J., dissenting).

10. *See, e.g.*, Jill S. Levenson, Ryan T. Shields, & David A. Singleton, *Collateral Punishments and Sentencing Policy Perceptions of Residence Restrictions for Sex Offenders and Drunk Drivers*, 25 CRIM. JUST. POL'Y REV. 135 (2014); Brian K. Pinaire, Milton J. Heumann, & Jennifer Lerman, *Barred from the Bar: The Process, Politics, and Policy Implications of Discipline for Attorney Felony Offenders*, 13 VA. J. SOC. POL'Y & L. 290, 294 (2005–2006).

11. *See* Jenny Roberts, *The Mythical Divide between Collateral and Direct Consequences of Criminal Convictions: Involuntary Commitment of "Sexually Violent Predators,"* 93 MINN. L. REV. 670 (2008); Michael Pinard, *An Integrated Perspective on the Collateral Consequences of Criminal Convictions and Reentry Issues Faced by Formerly Incarcerated Individuals*, 86 BOSTON U. L. REV. 623 (2006); Gabriel J. Chin, *The New Civil Death: Rethinking Punishment in the Era of Mass Conviction*, 160 U. PENN. L. REV. 1789 (2012).

12. Pinard, *supra* note 11, at 646; *see also* Gabriel J. Chin, *Race, the War on Drugs, and the Collateral Consequences of Criminal Conviction*, 6 J. GENDER, RACE, & JUSTICE 253, 254 (2002).

13. Pinard, *supra* note 11, at 647.

14. H. L. A. HART, PUNISHMENT AND RESPONSIBILITY 4–5 (1968); *see also* Antony Flew, *The Justification of Punishment*, 29 PHILOSOPHY 291 (1954); S. I. Benn, *An Approach to the Problems of Punishment*, 33 PHILOSOPHY 325 (1958).

15. *See* LEO ZAIBERT, PUNISHMENT AND RETRIBUTION (2006); Douglas Husak, *Does the State Have a Monopoly to Punish Crime? in* THE NEW PHILOSOPHY OF CRIMINAL LAW (Flanders & Hoskins eds., 2015).

16. As David Boonin puts it, "That would reduce punishment to sadism." DAVID BOONIN, THE PROBLEM OF PUNISHMENT 14 (2008).

17. Joel Feinberg, *The Expressive Function of Punishment*, 49 THE MONIST 397 (1965).

18. For two seminal examples, see Jean Hampton, *The Moral Education Theory of Punishment*, 13 PHIL. & PUB. AFFAIRS 208 (1984), and R. A. DUFF, PUNISHMENT, COMMUNICATION, AND COMMUNITY (2001).

19. *See* R. A. Duff, *Repairing Harms and Answering for Wrongs*, *in* PHILOSOPHICAL FOUNDATIONS IN THE LAW OF TORTS 212 (John Oberdiek ed., 2014). We need not deny, of course, that in practice defendants may often feel a required compensatory payment as a condemnatory burden, but this is not, in principle, the purpose of civil damages.

20. Michael Cholbi, *Compulsory Victim Restitution is Punishment: A Reply to Boonin*, 2 PUBLIC REASON 85, 87 (2010) (emphasis in original).

21. *Id.*

22. This is not to say that Cholbi begs any questions in his article. His central question is not whether collateral restrictions are punishment, so it begs no questions for him to count in favor of his definition of punishment that, according to it, collateral restrictions would count as punishment.

23. *Id.*

24. *Id. at* 88.

25. There has been a fair amount of debate about whether an expression of societal condemnation must be burdensome. *See, e.g.*, Nathan Hanna, *Say What? A Critique of Expressive Retributivism*, 27 LAW & PHIL. 123 (2008). *But see* M. Margaret Falls, *Retribution, Reciprocity, and Respect for Persons*, 7 LAW & PHIL. 25 (1987).

26. *See, e.g.*, BOONIN, *supra* note 16, chap. 5.

27. Susan R. Klein raises these sorts of worries about Carol Steiker's attempt at a similar sort of conceptual and normative analysis to the one I've engaged in in this chapter. *See* Susan R. Klein, *Redrawing the Civil-Criminal Boundary*, 2 BUFF. CRIM. L. REV. 681 (1999); *see also* Carol S. Steiker, *Punishment & Procedure: Punishment Theory & the Criminal-Civil Procedure Divide*, 85 GEO. L. REV. 4 (1997).

28. BOONIN, *supra* note 16, at 1.

29. *See, e.g.*, DOUGLAS HUSAK, OVERCRIMINALIZATION 14 (2008).

30. *See* Christopher Heath Wellman, *Rights and State Punishment*, 106 J. PHIL. 8 (2009); Husak, *supra* note 5.

31. *See* Michelle Natividad Rodriguez & Maurice Emsellem, *65 Million "Need Not Apply": The Case for Reforming Criminal Background Checks for Employment*, THE NATIONAL EMPLOYMENT LAW PROJECT 3, 27 n. 2 (March 2011), http://www.nelp.org/content/uploads/2015/03/65_Million_Need_Not_Apply.pdf. The UK figure comes from the Police National Computer in 2014.

Selected Bibliography

Alexander, Larry (2013). "You Got What You Deserved." *Criminal Law and Philosophy* 7, no. 2: 309–19.

Altman, Andrew, and Christopher Heath Wellman (2004). "A Defense of International Criminal Law." *Ethics* 115, no. 1: 35–67.

Ashworth, Andrew, Lucia Zedner, and Patrick Tomlin, eds. (2012). *Prevention and the Limits of the Criminal Law*. Oxford: Oxford University Press.

Baradaran, Shima (2011). "Restoring the Presumption of Innocence." *Ohio State Law Journal* 72: 723–76.

Bennett, Christopher (2008). *The Apology Ritual: A Philosophical Theory of Punishment*. Cambridge: Cambridge University Press.

Besson, Samantha, and John Tasioulas, eds. (2010). *Philosophy of International Law*. Oxford: Oxford University Press.

Brettschneider, Corey (2007). "The Rights of the Guilty: Punishment and Political Legitimacy," *Pol. Theory* 35: 175–99.

Brownlee, Kimberley (2010). "Responsibilities of Criminal Justice Officials." *Journal of Applied Philosophy* 27, no. 2: 123–39.

Burns, Robert (1999). *A Theory of the Trial*. Princeton, NJ: Princeton University Press.

Campbell, Liz (2010). "A Rights-Based Analysis of DNA Retention: Non-Conviction Databases and the Liberal State." *Criminal Law Review*: 889–905.

Chiao, Vincent (2013). "Punishment and Permissibility in the Criminal Law." Law and Philosophy 32: 729–65.

Davidovic, Jovana (2012). "The International Rule-of-Law and Killing in War." *Social Theory and Practice* 38, no. 3: 531–52.

Dolovich, Sharon (2004). "Legitimate Punishment in a Liberal Democracy." *Buffalo Criminal Law Review* 7: 307–442.

Dubber, Marcus D. (2002). *Victims in the War on Crime*. New York: New York University Press.

Duff, Antony, Lindsay Farmer, Sandra E. Marshall, Massimo Renzo, and Victor Tadros, eds. (2014). *Criminalisation: The Political Morality of the Criminal Law*. Oxford: Oxford University Press.

Duff, Antony, Lindsay Farmer, Sandra E. Marshall, Massimo Renzo, and Victor Tadros, eds. (2011). *The Constitution of Criminal Law*. Oxford: Oxford University Press.

Duff, R. A. (2001). *Punishment, Communication, and Community*. Oxford: Oxford University Press.

Duff, R. A. (1986). *Trials and Punishments*. Cambridge: Cambridge University Press.

Duff, R. A., and Stuart Green, eds. (2011). *Philosophical Foundations of Criminal Law*. Oxford: Oxford University Press.
Durkheim, Emile (1893). *The Division of Labor in Society*. W. D. Halls, trans. Macmillan, 1984.
Dzur, Albert W. (2012). *Punishment, Participatory Democracy, and the Jury*. Oxford: Oxford University Press.
Feinberg, Joel (1965). "The Expressive Function of Punishment." *The Monist* 49, no. 3: 397–423.
Flanders, Chad (2013). "Pardons and the Theory of the 'Second Best'." *Florida Law Review* 65, no. 5: 1559–95.
Garland, David (2001). *The Culture of Control*. Oxford: Oxford University Press.
Goldberg, John C. P., and Benjamin C. Zipursky (2010). "Torts as Wrongs." *Texas Law Review* 88: 917–86.
Green, Stuart (2013). "Vice Crimes and Preventive Justice." *Criminal Law and Philosophy* 8.
Hampton, Jean (1984). "The Moral Education Theory of Punishment." *Philosophy and Public Affairs* 13: 208–38.
Harel, Alon (2008). "Why Only the State May Inflict Criminal Sanctions: The Case against Privately Inflicted Sanctions." *Legal Theory* 14: 113–33.
Hart, H. L. A. (1968). *Punishment and Responsibility*. Oxford: Oxford University Press.
Hoskins, Zachary (2014). "Ex-Offender Restrictions." *Journal of Applied Philosophy* 31, no. 1: 33–48.
Husak, Douglas (2008). *Overcriminalization: The Limits of the Criminal Law*. Oxford: Oxford University Press.
Kleinfeld, Joshua (2013). "A Theory of Criminal Victimization." *Stanford Law Review* 65: 1087–152.
Kleinig, John (2008). *Ethics and Criminal Justice*. Cambridge: Cambridge University Press.
Lacey, Nicola (2001). "Responsibility and Modernity in Criminal Law." *Journal of Political Philosophy* 9, no. 3: 249–76.
Laudan, Larry (2006). *Truth, Error, and the Criminal Law*. Cambridge: Cambridge University Press.
Lippke, Richard (2011). *The Ethics of Plea Bargaining*. Oxford: Oxford University Press.
Loughnan, Arlie (2012). *Manifest Madness: Mental Incapacity in Criminal Law*. Oxford: Oxford University Press.
Markel, Dan, Chad Flanders, and David Gray (2011). "Beyond Experience: Getting Retributive Justice Right." *California Law Review* 99: 605–28.
Mauer, Marc, and Meda Chesney-Lind, eds. (2003). *Invisible Punishment: The Collateral Consequences of Mass Imprisonment*. New York: New Press.
May, Larry (2004). *Crimes against Humanity: A Normative Account*. Cambridge: Cambridge University Press.
May, Larry, and Zachary Hoskins, eds. (2010). *International Criminal Law and Philosophy*. New York: Cambridge University Press.
Moore, Michael (1989). "The Moral Worth of Retribution." In F. Schoeman, ed., *Responsibility, Character and the Emotions*. Cambridge: Cambridge University Press.
Ristroph, Alice (2014). "Just Violence," *Arizona Law Review* 56: 1017–63.
Roberts, Paul, and Jill Hunter, eds. (2012). *Criminal Evidence and Human Rights*. Oxford: Hart Publishing.
Scott, Robert E., and William J. Stuntz (1992). "Plea Bargaining as Contract." *Yale Law Journal* 101: 1909–68.
Sigler, Mary (2011). "The Methodology of Desert." *Arizona State Law Journal* 42: 1173–86.
Simmons, A. John (1999). "Justification and Legitimacy." *Ethics* 109: 739–71.
Smith, Nick (2014). *Justice through Apologies: Remorse, Reform and Punishment*. Oxford: Oxford University Press.
Steiker, Carol S. (2007). "Tempering or Tampering? Mercy and the Administration of Criminal Justice." In Austin Sarat and Nasser Hussain, eds., *Forgiveness, Mercy, and Clemency*. Stanford, CA: Stanford University Press.

Stewart, Hamish (2014). "The Right to Be Presumed Innocent." *Criminal Law and Philosophy* 8: 407–20.

Tadros, Victor (2011). *The Ends of Harm*. Oxford: Oxford University Press.

Tomlin, Patrick (2013). "Extending the Golden Thread? Criminalisation and the Presumption of Innocence." *Journal of Political Philosophy* 21: 44–66.

von Hirsch, Andrew (1995). *Censure and Sanctions*. Oxford: Oxford University Press.

Zedner, Lucia, and Julian Roberts, eds. (2012). *Principles and Values in Criminal Law and Criminal Justice*. Oxford: Oxford University Press.

Index

List of Contributors

Christopher Bennett is a reader at the University of Sheffield Department of Philosophy.

Vincent Chiao is assistant professor at the University of Toronto Faculty of Law.

Jovana Davidovic is assistant professor at the University of Iowa Department of Philosophy.

R. A. Duff is professor at the University of Minnesota Law School, and professor emeritus at the University of Stirling Department of Philosophy.

Chad Flanders is associate professor at the Saint Louis University School of Law.

Stuart P. Green is distinguished professor of law at Rutgers Law School.

Zachary Hoskins is assistant professor at the University of Nottingham Department of Philosophy.

Douglas Husak is distinguished professor at the Rutgers Department of Philosophy.

Joshua Kleinfeld is associate professor at the Northwestern University School of Law and an affiliated faculty member at the Northwestern Department of Philosophy.

Richard L. Lippke is professor at the Indiana University Department of Criminal Justice.

Arlie Loughnan is associate professor and ARC Research Fellow at the University of Sydney Law School.

Sandra Marshall is professor emeritus at the University of Stirling Department of Philosophy.

Alice Ristroph is professor of law and Eileen Denner Research Scholar at Seton Hall University School of Law.

Mary Sigler is associate dean and professor at Arizona State University's Sandra Day O'Connor College of Law.

www.ingramcontent.com/pod-product-compliance
Ingram Content Group UK Ltd.
Pitfield, Milton Keynes, MK11 3LW, UK
UKHW012036150926
475560UK00001B/44

9 781783 484133